# Content Area Reading

# Content Area Reading

**FOURTH EDITION**

## Richard T. Vacca
## Jo Anne L. Vacca
*Kent State University*

HarperCollins*College*Publishers

Acquisitions Editor: Christopher Jennison
Development Editor: Anita Portugal
Project Coordination and Text Design: PC&F, Inc.
Cover Design: Kay Petronio
Photo Researcher: Leslie Coopersmith
Production Manufacturing: Michael Weinstein/Paula Keller
Compositor: PC&F, Inc.
Printer and Binder: R.R. Donnelley & Sons Company
Cover Printer: The Lehigh Press, Inc.

For permission to use copyrighted material, grateful acknowledgment is made to the copyright holders on pp. 407–408, which are hereby made part of this copyright page.

Content Area Reading, Fourth Edition

**Library of Congress Cataloging-in-Publication Data**

Vacca, Richard T.
 Content area reading / Richard T. Vacca, Jo Anne L. Vacca.—4th ed.
  p.  cm.
 Includes bibliographical references and index.
 ISBN  0-673-52215-6
 1.  Content area reading.  I. Vacca, Jo Anne L.  II. Title.
LB1050.455.V33  1993
428.4'3— dc20                                    92-39115
                                                    CIP

93  94  95  96  9  8  7  6  5  4  3  2

Our real journey . . . is interior; it is a matter of growth, deepening, and an even greater surrender to the creative action of love and grace in our hearts.

—*Thomas Merton*

## To Verna Tilton

Who showed us that the road less traveled does indeed make all the difference.

# Contents

## PART II:   INSTRUCTIONAL ALTERNATIVES

## CHAPTER 4   Developing Vocabulary Knowledge and Concepts

## CHAPTER 5   Activating Prior Knowledge and Interest

Twelve years—that's how long it has been since we first published *Content Area Reading*. Much to our surprise and delight, what began as a modest attempt to show how reading can become a workable and sensible part of content area teaching has expanded into an ambitious exploration of *content literacy*—the ability to use reading and writing to learn subject matter across the curriculum. *Workable* and *sensible* remain the key words of this edition. Our goal remains as true now as it was 12 years ago: to inspire teachers, whether novice or veteran, to examine instructional alternatives that bridge the gap between learners and texts within the framework of existing teaching practice. How can you build upon, refine, and extend what you do already in light of what is known about the powerful bonds that exist among language, literacy, and learning?

Two shifts in direction occur in this edition of *Content Area Reading*. The first places reading within the broader context of using language and literacy to learn. Language (and its many uses) is the predominant vehicle by which teachers, students, and authors communicate with one another. Yet it's easy to lose sight of, or underestimate, the roles that language and literacy play in teaching and learning. In this edition, we are more explicit about the interrelatedness of reading, writing, speaking, and listening and the impact of integrated language activity on learning.

It's hard to imagine teaching without meaningful talk and purposeful listening. Who would deny the powerful role that spoken language plays in teaching and learning? The uses of language in content areas, however, involve more than talking and listening. Verbal interactions between teachers and students and students and other students serve learning well, but other modes of language—written language, for example—are also crucial to learning. A text, by its very nature, might represent a single written word, a paragraph, several pages, a chapter, or an entire book. Texts, whether written by scholars who are strangers to students or by students themselves, are pivotal tools in the development of independent learners. Yet texts often remain silent and neglected in content area classrooms. In this book, we explore how to create active learning environments in which students—individually and in collaboration with one another—know how to use reading, writing, speaking, and listening to think and learn *about* texts, *with* texts, and *through* texts.

The reality of literacy use in content areas is that many students, for reasons that are explored in this book, have become passive nonparticipants in the process of thinking and learning with texts. Yet caring and knowledgeable teachers can make a dramatic difference in the way students use texts to learn.

A second shift in direction is a subtle but dramatic one. In previous editions we have used the term "learning from text" to reflect the process students engage in as they interact with written language in content areas. The expression "learning *from* text" has been widely used, as Rob Tierney and Dave Pearson (1992) suggest, as if a text is a welter of information to be mastered by readers rather than a tool by which readers construct meaning. The use of the preposition *from* suggests a one-way act in which meaning flows from the text to the reader. In this edition of *Content Area Reading*, the prepositional shift from *from* to *with* places the act of reading squarely in the context of a human transaction between two parties rather than the transmission of information from one party to another. Learning with texts suggests that readers have much to contribute to their own learning as they interact with texts to make meaning and construct knowledge. Active learners search for meaning in everything they discuss and listen to and read and write about.

This edition retains all the features of the highly popular third edition while making improvements in its organization and overall coverage of teaching and learning strategies. *Content Area Reading* remains readable, practical, theory based, and strategy oriented. New chapters explore what it means to teach with texts, think and learn with texts, and learn with literature. In addition, this edition includes up-to-date, expanded discussions related to portfolio assessment, collaborative learning, metacognition, vocabulary and concept development, comprehension and study strategies, reader-text interactions, writing-reading relationships, and environments for learning in content areas.

The fourth edition of *Content Area Reading* is divided into three parts. Part One, "Learners and Texts," examines the relationship between language and learning, the concept of literacy as it applies to the study and acquisition of subject matter, the cognitive and metacognitive influences on thinking and learning with texts, and the roles that planning, discussion, and cooperative learning play in bringing learners and texts together in the content area classroom. Part Two, "Instructional Alternatives," offers a multitude of theory-based, practical teaching activities and strategies for content area instruction. Part Three, "Assessment," focuses on ways in which teachers can make authentic assessments of students' use of reading and writing strategies to learn subject matter.

Each chapter begins with a quotation to help you reflect on the theme of the chapter; a chapter overview, in which the relationships among important ideas are visually depicted; a set of questions that serve as a frame of reference; and an organizing principle. At a glance, these organizing principles capture the major themes of the fourth edition:

1. Teachers play a critical role in helping students to realize a potentially powerful use of language, which is to engage the mind in thinking and learning with texts.

2. Thinking with texts reflects the processes by which authors and readers can link minds and engage in learning conversations with one another.

3. Bringing learners and texts together involves putting to work plans and practices that result in active student involvement and collaboration.

4. To teach words well means giving students multiple opportunities to build vocabulary knowledge, by learning not only how words are conceptually related to one another but also how they are defined contextually in the material that the students are studying.

5. Piquing interest and raising expectations about the meaning of texts create a context in which students will read with purpose and anticipation.

6. There's a critical difference between asking questions that evaluate a product (what students learn and remember as a result of their interactions with texts) and questions that guide a process (engaging and sustaining students in their efforts to think and learn as they interact with texts and with one another).

7. Reading guides scaffold learning by providing the kind of instructional support that allows students to interact with and respond to difficult texts in meaningful ways.

8. Writing facilitates learning with texts by helping students to explore, clarify, and to think deeply about ideas and concepts encountered in reading.

9. A content area teacher is in a strategic position to show students how to use study strategies independently as they interact and learn with texts.

10. When content area teachers combine the use of textbooks with literature, they extend and enrich the curriculum.

11. Instructional assessment is a continuous process that makes use of multiple methods of gathering relevant data for instructional purposes.

A special thanks to Sue Misheff of Malone College for her draft of Chapter 10, "Learning with Literature," which resulted in a very important addition to our book. We would be remiss if we didn't acknowledge James Rycik for helping us to rethink the chapter on studying texts. Our heartfelt appreciation is also extended to Linda Burkey and Nancy Prosenjak for their support and contributions, especially to the revision of the Instructor's Manual. We wish to also thank Chris Jennison, our editor at HarperCollins, and our reviewers: Once again, you pushed us to think harder and write better.

R. T. V.
J. L. V.

## Reviewers:

Brother Leonard Courtney, University of St. Thomas
Christine C. Draper, Gardon College
Mary Ann Gray, Millersville University of Pennsylvania
Kathy Jongsma, Supervisor of Reading, Northside School District, San Antonio TX
Judy C. Lambert, University of Wisconsin, Oshkosh
Theodore Lasko, Elmira College
Betty McEady-Gillead, California State University, Sacramento
Pamela Michel, SUNY Osmego
Reed R. Mottley, University of Southern Mississippi
Gary Rice, University of Texas, El Paso
Catherine C. Richard, Newberry College
Robert J. Rickelman, University of North Carolina-Charlotte
Christine C. Schaefer, Whitman College
Nancy R. Stone, University of Wisconsin, Oshkosh
Joan A. Suedmeyer, Boise State University
James E. Walker, Clarion University of Pennsylvania
Beverly Walmsley, Lewis-Clark State College
Dan A. White, Abilene Christian University
Jim Worthington, Seattle Pacific University

# PART I

# Learners and Texts

# 1

# Teaching with Texts

I was desperate to keep my brain alive.

—*Terry Anderson, the last of 13 American hostages to be set free in Lebanon*

## ORGANIZING PRINCIPLE

Throughout his 2455 days in captivity, Terry Anderson waged an inner struggle with his worst fear: that he "would lapse into some kind of mental rot." As horrendous as his experience was, Anderson kept his brain alive through the sustaining power of language. His ordeal did not prevent him from communicating with fellow hostages—first by teaching them a sign language that he half-invented, and then by developing a system of taps against the wall. And throughout his captivity, he fought to keep his brain alive by badgering his captors for books, and more books, until they were eventually delivered by the boxload. Terry Anderson knew all too well that the mind matters.

His experiences as a hostage dramatize that the real value of language lies in its uses. It is not an exaggeration to suggest that texts helped to keep Anderson's mind and spirit alive, let alone that they kept his brain from mental and physical decay. *Brain* and *mind*, two terms often used interchangeably, explain what humans do best—thinking. Whereas the brain is a physical organ with its own intricate chemistry and physiology, the mind has a life of its own. To read is to engage the mind in thinking. And language is an important vehicle that makes thinking possible; that makes thinking uniquely human. Reading is a powerful means of putting language to use purposefully—whether it is to learn, to imagine, or to enjoy. Using language to think and learn with texts—this is what content area reading is all about.

Teaching with texts is no easy matter. Although texts are routinely assigned in content area classrooms, showing students how to think and learn with texts infrequently enters into the plans of teachers. When students become too dependent on teachers, not their own minds, as their primary source of thinking and learning, they are rarely in a strategic position to learn how to learn, or to keep their minds alive. This need not be the case. How students interact with texts, other students, and the teacher is reflected in the organizing principle of this chapter: *Teachers play a critical role in helping students to realize a potentially powerful use of language, which is to engage the mind in thinking and learning with texts.*

Study the Chapter Overview. It's your map to the major ideas that you will encounter in the chapter. The Overview shows the relationships that exist among the concepts you will study. Use it as an organizer. What is the chapter about? What do you know already about the content to be presented in the chapter? What do you need to learn more about?

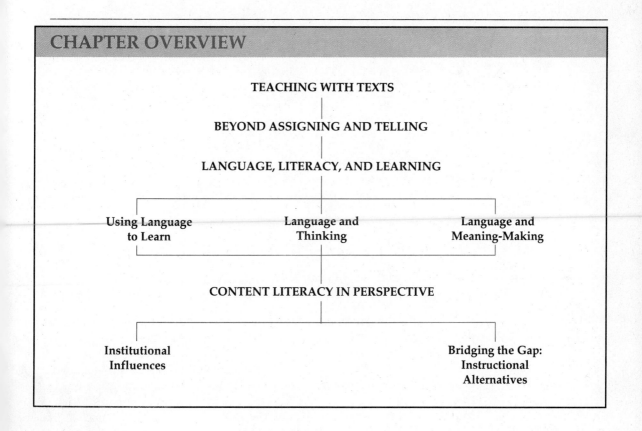

## CHAPTER OVERVIEW

**TEACHING WITH TEXTS**

**BEYOND ASSIGNING AND TELLING**

**LANGUAGE, LITERACY, AND LEARNING**

| Using Language to Learn | Language and Thinking | Language and Meaning-Making |

**CONTENT LITERACY IN PERSPECTIVE**

| Institutional Influences | | Bridging the Gap: Instructional Alternatives |

In conjunction with the Chapter Overview, take a moment or two to study the Frame of Mind. The Frame of Mind uses key questions to help you think about the ideas that you will read about. Our intent is to create a mental disposition for learning, "a critical frame of mind," if you will, to better interact with ideas that we, as authors, have organized and developed in the chapter. When you finish reading, you should be able to respond fully to the questions posed in the Frame of Mind.

## FRAME OF MIND

1. How does the practice of assigning and telling stifle active learning with texts and deny students' responsibility for learning on their own?

2. How are language, literacy, and learning interrelated?

3. What does it mean to use language to learn?

4. What is content literacy?

5. How does the institutional structure of elementary and secondary schools influence content literacy practices?

6. Why do instructional alternatives for content literacy require reflective inquiry and self-examination?

Teachers know when they're on a roll. They are fully tuned in to everything that is going on around them. Their teaching is inspired. Their students' minds are alive.

The classroom is a crucible, a place where the special mix of *teacher, student, and text* come together to create wonderfully complex human interactions that stir the minds and spirits of learners. Some days, of course, are better than others. When you're on a roll, the things that you thought about doing, and the classroom surprises that you didn't expect, click into place. A creative energy imbues teaching and learning.

Sometimes, however, lessons limp along. Others just bomb—so you cut them short. The four or so remaining minutes before the bell rings are a kind of self-inflicted wound. Nothing is more unnerving than waiting for the bell to ring when students don't have anything meaningful to do.

Consider a science teacher's reflection on the way things went in one of her classes. "Something was missing," she explained. "The students aren't usually as quiet and passive as they were today. Excuse the pun, but the chemistry wasn't there. Maybe the text assignment was too hard. Maybe I could have done something differently. Any suggestions?" The teacher, like most good teachers, cares about what she does. She wants to know how to improve her craft. She knows that when the chemistry is there, teaching is its own reward.

And then there was a student teacher apprenticing in an English classroom in a middle school. Two weeks on the job, and he had discovered the unexpected joy of teaching the same lesson for the third time in a row. "By seventh period, I had finally gotten it [the lesson] right! I couldn't get any of the students in my third-period class to talk about the story they had read. So I decided to make some changes. The discussion in fifth period was better. By seventh period, the class discussion turned out just as I hoped it would." Learning to teach, as the novice discovered, involves thoughtful trial and error and a willingness to make changes when something doesn't work for you in the classroom.

Both the veteran and the novice bring a sensitivity and a spirit of reflective inquiry to their teaching. They care about what they do and how they do it. As Eliot Eisner (1985) so aptly put it:

> Teaching can be done as badly as anything else. It can be wooden, mechanical, mindless, and wholly unimaginative. But when it is sensitive, intelligent, and creative—those qualities that confer upon it the status of an art—it should, in my view, not be regarded, as it so often is by some, as an expression of unfathomable talent or luck but as an example of humans exercising the highest levels of their intelligence. (p. 77)

To be a teacher in the 1990s means exercising the highest levels of intelligence in coping with difficult issues: the curriculum, content delivery, school climate, classroom control, dropout rates, accountability, children and youth at risk of failure, and racial, social, and cultural diversity to name a few. There is unrelenting pressure on teachers to respond to problems of all types. What is abundantly clear is that as important as academic content is, there's more to being an artful teacher than having a rich and deep understanding of a subject.

Academic content, nevertheless, is the *raison d'être* for most teachers who are wedded to a discipline. Yet, it is much more difficult to teach somebody something than merely to know that something: "The teacher of the American Revolution has to know both a great deal about the American Revolution and a variety of ways of communicating the essence of the American Revolution to a wide variety of students, in a pedagogically interesting way . . ." (Shulman, 1987). What to teach and how to teach it are nagging problems for classroom teachers. For some, using texts to teach content contributes to the problem. For others, showing students how to learn with texts is part of the solution.

Why bring learners and texts together in the classroom? Texts, after all, are but one medium for learning academic content. What is the value of texts in the content areas?

While we're not suggesting that texts are the only source for learning, or that they should be, they will continue to be indispensable tools for constructing knowledge, sharing the experiences, ideas, and feelings of others, and developing new insights and perspectives. Learning how to teach with texts contributes significantly to the way you think about teaching, learning, and curriculum. Throughout this book, we invite you to examine content area teaching practices, and the assumptions underlying those practices, in light of promising strategies for text learning and active student involvement.

Although books come with the territory, using texts to help students acquire content doesn't work well for many teachers. Teaching with texts is more complex than it appears on the surface. Whether you're a novice or a veteran teacher, using texts effectively requires the willingness to explore instructional alternatives and to move beyond assigning and telling.

## BEYOND ASSIGNING AND TELLING

Your own personal history as a student, we wager, has etched into memory an instructional blueprint that teachers in your past probably followed: *Assign* a text to read (usually with questions to be answered) for homework; then in subsequent lessons, *tell* students through question-and-answer routines what the material they read was about—explaining the ideas and information that the students encountered in print. As Alvermann and Moore (1991) put it, the dominant interactional pattern between teacher and students during class presentation of the assigned material "consists of the following moves: the teacher solicits a student to answer a question; the teacher listens to the student's response; and the teacher evaluates or modifies the student's response" (p. 969). Such is the ebb and flow of assign-and-tell instructional routines in content area classrooms.

There's more to teaching with texts than assigning and telling. Assigning and telling are common but uninspired teaching practices that bog students down in the mire of passive learning. Assign and tell, more often than not, dampens active involvement in learning and denies students ownership and responsibility for the acquisition of content. Teachers place themselves, either by design or by circumstance, in the unenviable position of being the most active participant during classroom interactions with students.

No wonder John Goodlad (1984) portrayed textbook assignment, lecture, and recitation (a form of oral questioning in which teachers already know the answers to the questions they ask) as the dominant activities in the core instructional repertoire of many content area teachers. Goodlad and his research associates concluded from a monumental study of schools that: "The data from our observations in more than 1000 classrooms support the popular image of a teacher standing in front of a class imparting knowledge to a group of students" (p. 105). His team of researchers found that the prevalence of assign-and-tell practices increases steadily from the primary to the senior high school years.

At both the elementary and the secondary school level, for example, "teacher talk" dominates the classroom. According to Sirotnik (1983), teachers "outtalk" students by a three-to-one ratio. Try to recall what it was like when you were in school. Well-intentioned teachers, more likely than not, assigned texts to be read as homework, only to find that for one reason or another many of the students didn't quite grasp what they were assigned to read. Some didn't read at all. Others read narrowly and mindlessly to answers questions assigned for homework. Still others may have gotten tangled in text, stuck in the underbrush of facts and details. So class time was spent filling students' heads with information that they didn't learn well from texts in the first place.

Imparting knowledge in this fashion reminds Brozo and Simpson (1991) of a poster hanging on a colleague's door. The poster "satirically depicts teaching as a teacher with a spigot for a mouth opening into a funnel attached to the top of a child's head. The idea is that knowledge flows from teachers and fills students' heads much like water into a bucket" (p. 6). While the poster exaggerates the idea to comic proportions, it contains more than a kernel of truth.

When teachers impart knowledge with little attention to how a learner acquires that knowledge, students soon become nonparticipants in the academic life of the classroom. Assign-and-tell practices not only result in passive reading, they also influence the way students view themselves in relation to texts. The following Calvin and Hobbes cartoon has Calvin thinking of himself as "informationally impaired." He avoids doing homework (and, no doubt, using texts to learn) to feel good about himself. His inimitable alter ego, Hobbes, captures the irony of Calvin's dilemma by asking, "Your self-esteem is enhanced by remaining an ignoramus?"

Shifting the burden of learning from teachers' shoulders to students' is in large measure what this book is about. What does it mean to teach with texts? Why teach with texts? How does text-related teaching prepare students to learn how to learn in content area disciplines? The answers to these questions lie in understanding the relationships that exist among language, literacy, and learning. Throughout the book we invite you to explore the role that language and literacy play in learning and acquiring content knowledge.

# Calvin and Hobbes
### by Bill Watterson

**Source:** Calvin and Hobbes copyright 1992 Watterson. Reprinted with permission of Universal Press Syndicate. All rights reserved.

Content area classrooms are filled with the potential of human activity, interaction, and transactions. Language, and its many uses, is the vehicle by which teachers, students, and authors communicate with one another. Human beings think *with* language. Yet it's easy to lose sight of, or take for granted, the role that language and literacy play in teaching and learning.

## LANGUAGE, LITERACY, AND LEARNING

Imagine what classrooms would be like without talk. Try getting through a class period or an entire school day in silence. Not impossible, but difficult, isn't it?

The uses of language in content area classrooms, however, involve more than talk. Although verbal interactions between students and teachers serve learning well in various instructional contexts, other modes of language are also crucial to learning. Imagine, for example, what learning would be like without texts. Texts? Our hunch is that it's far easier for you to envision teaching and learning without texts than without talk.

Yet a *text*, by its very nature, is language—written language. It may consist of a single word, sentence, paragraph, page, chapter, or book. Writers of texts communicate with readers in the same way that speakers use language to communicate with listeners. Language is language, whether it's spoken, written, or signed.

In content area classrooms, the *textbook* is the prevalent form of text used by teachers to help students explore subject matter. Class sets of single required textbooks predominate in elementary and secondary classrooms (Alvermann and Moore 1991). Today, however, many teachers, especially in the elementary and middle grades, are exploring alternatives to *the* textbook. They are using a variety of authentic "real world" texts to engage students in subject matter learning. Learning with literature is a topic we explore in depth in Chapter 10. One of the more important instructional decisions that a teacher must grapple with is the role that text—written language—plays in teaching and learning.

Teaching with texts requires its fair share of strategy. But it involves more than assigning pages to be read, lecturing, or using questions to check whether students have read the material the night before. To use texts strategically, you must first be aware of the powerful bonds that link language to literacy and learning.

### Using Language to Learn

Language is inextricably tied to human development and learning. Language and thought are interdependent. Without language, it would be difficult to grow intellectually, let alone socially and emotionally. The ability to use language as a functional tool to serve personal, social, intellectual, and academic needs is what separates human beings from other species in the animal kingdom. For humans who are born without impairment, physical or otherwise, language learning is as natural as learning to walk. As we grow and interact with significant others in our environment, we learn language by using language to satisfy needs. And throughout our lives, we use language to learn, to imagine, and to expand our knowledge of the world in the context of speaking, listening, reading, and writing.

To be literate in content area classrooms, students must learn how to use reading and writing to explore and construct meaning in the company of authors, other learners, and teachers. Using reading and writing in the classroom to help students to think and learn with texts doesn't require specialized training on the part of content teachers. Much of what we have to offer in this book is common sense, supported by research and experience, applied to teaching and learning. Nor does the pursuit of content literacy diminish the teacher's role as a subject matter specialist. To help students to become literate in a given discipline does not mean to teach students *how to read or write*. Instead, reading and writing are tools that they use to construct knowledge—to discover, clarify, and extend meaning—in a given discipline. Using language to learn underscores students' meaning-making, thought-producing capabilities. To this end, every teacher has a role to play.

## Language and Meaning-Making

Language helps a learner to make sense of the world, to understand and to be understood. As a result, language and meaning cannot be severed from one another. Language isn't language unless meaning-making is involved. Oral language, without meaning, is mere prattle—a string of senseless, meaningless speech sounds. Written language, without meaning, is a cipher of mysterious markings on paper. Try reading the text from the Russian newspaper *Moskovsky Komsomoletz* in Box 1.1.

Do you know what the news report is about? Can you read it aloud? Why doesn't it make sense? Study the photograph that accompanies the article. Did you ask yourself, "Who are the people posing in the picture? Where are they from? Why are they gathered together?" Try constructing a scenario based on the photograph: *What do you think* the news story is about?

An English translation of the news article is located in Box 1.2 on page 12. Compare your predictions of what the story's about with it.

What is the point of this demonstration? The Russian language, of course, is based on an alphabetic system that differs from ours. For most English speakers, it's difficult, perhaps impossible, to read the news article aloud unless you are already familiar with Russian. But meaning-making involves more than cracking an alphabetic code. Language, whether oral, written, or signed, is a complex system of symbols and the rules for using

BOX 1.1    A News Story from *Moskovsky Komsomoletz*

# РЕЦЕПТ ВЫЖИВАНИЯ

— Каждый из нас должен быть экологом, только тогда мы выживем — так считают американские учителя, преподаватели из группы «Международное наследие». Их главная задача — разработка универсальных школьных программ по экологическому воспитанию. В Советский Союз они приехали по приглашению экологического центра ЦК ВЛКСМ и проведут у нас целый месяц. А свой первый визит эти милые, раскованные, улыбчивые американцы нанесли в редакцию «МК». И остались очень довольны.

those symbols. Within this complex system, linguists, those who study language, have identified *subsystems* which are associated with the symbols and rules of language. When a person uses language, these subsystems are always interactive and operate in concert with one another.

For example, in spoken language, one of the subsystems of language involves its *phonology*—its speech sounds. According to the noted linguist Alvin Liberman of Yale University, language revolves around phonology, which he describes as a small number of meaningless sounds that can convey an infinite number of meaningful messages in many languages (Bower 1992). The *phonological subsystem* allows people to use their knowledge of the rules which govern the structure, distribution, and sequencing of speech sounds to communicate in their native tongues. Written language, on the other hand, involves knowledge of the rules and conventions of the *graphophonic subsystem* governing letter-sound relationships. The reason it is difficult to translate the text written in Russian from print to Russian speech sounds is that most English-speaking people are not knowledgeable or experienced with the rules and conventions underlying the graphophonic subsystem of the Russian language.

Nevertheless, you are able to read a text such as Lewis Carroll's "Jabberwocky" with little trouble, even though Carroll invents or "coins" words such as *chortled* and *toves* throughout the poem. Try reading "Jabberwocky" aloud:

### Jabberwocky

'Twas brillig, and the slithy toves
    Did gyre and gimble in the wabe;
All mimsy were the borogoves,
    And the mome raths outgrabe.

"Beware the Jabberwock, my son!
    The jaws that bite, the claws that catch!
Beware the Jubjub bird and shun
    The frumious Bandersnatch!"

He took his vorpal sword in hand:
    Long time the manxome foe he sought—
So rested he by the Tumtum tree,
    And stood awhile in thought.

And, as in uffish though he stood,
    The Jabberwock, with eyes of flame,
Came whiffling through the tulgey wood,
    And burbled as it came!

One, two! One, two! And through and through
    The vorpal blade went snicker-snack!
He left it dead, and with its head
    He went galumphing back.

"And hast thou slain the Jabberwock?
　　Come to my arms, my beamish boy!
O frabjous day! Callooh! Callay!"
　　He chortled in his joy.

'Twas brillig and the slithy toves
　　Did gyre and gimble in the wabe:
All mimsy were the borogoves,
　　And the mome raths outgrabe.

What is quickly apparent from your reading of the poem is that going from print to speech is a hollow act unless meaning-making is involved in the transaction. This is where the other subsystems of language come into play.

The *syntactic subsystem* governs the rules of syntax. That is to say, in oral and written language, knowledge of syntax—grammatical relationships and the structure of sentences—allows speakers and writers to determine the order of words used in producing language. Readers and listeners, likewise, use syntactic knowledge to interpret language—to make sense and to anticipate meaning. Readers, for example, use their knowledge of the meaningful arrangement of words in sentences. The order of words provides important information during reading.

Suppose you were reading about the process of osmosis in a biology text and came to the sentence:

Osmosis is the process by which form in a the dissolved of substance or gas a liquid through to passes a from another medium one membrane.

Although you may have been able to read the words, you probably made little sense out of what you read. The sentence makes more sense when the words are arranged like so: "Osmosis is the process by which *a dissolved substance in the form of a liquid or gas passes through a membrane from one medium to another.*" Even though syntax is important in meaning-making, some readers may still have difficulty understanding the sentence because they do not bring enough *semantic knowledge* to key concepts such as *dissolved*, *substance, membrane,* and *medium*.

---

**BOX 1.2    An English Translation of the News Story from *Moskovsky Komsomoletz***

**A Way for Survival**

"Each of us is to be an ecologist, this is the only way for us to survive,"—this is what American educators representing Legacy International Organization think. Their major concern is developing "universal curriculum on ecological education." They have arrived in the USSR on the invitation of the Ecological Center of the Central Committee of the "Young Communist League" and are to stay here for a month. Their first official visit was to the *Moskovsky Komsomoletz* editorial board. And these charming, smiling, relaxed people were pleased.

To better understand the role semantic knowledge plays in meaning-making, return to the poem "Jabberwocky." You probably made sense of what the poem is about. First of all, Lewis Carroll didn't alter syntax. Syntactic knowledge is a strength that you and most readers bring to the reading act. But syntactic knowledge alone is not sufficient to explore and construct meaning with texts. To use reading to learn, you must actively bring what you already know to the text to make meaning.

Your reading of "Jabberwocky" is meaningful because you used *prior knowledge* to construct meaning for Carroll's text. Try rewriting the poem using your own words. If you and a colleague or two were to compare your rewrites, you undoubtedly would find similarities in meaning, but also important differences—important because the differences reflect the knowledge of the world that you as a reader bring to the text.

The *semantic subsystem* reflects a language user's world knowledge: the prior knowledge, concepts, experiences, perspectives, attitudes, values, and skills that you bring to reading, writing, talking, and listening. **The single most important variable in learning with texts is a reader's prior knowledge.** The more you already know and bring to a particular text during reading, the more such knowledge facilitates the acquisition of content. In Chapter 2, we elaborate on this elemental but powerful notion and the implications it holds for thinking and learning with texts.

## Language and Thinking

Language is the vehicle that allows human beings to think and to be thoughtful. Terry Anderson demanded books of his captors to keep his mind from decaying. He fought for the right to engage in dialogue and thought, not only with other hostages, but also with authors. Helping learners to be thoughtful with texts means engaging them in *cognitive* and *metacognitive* thinking activities—topics of discussion in Chapter 2. From a cognitive perspective, students need to know how to produce and interact with texts in order to discover, organize, retrieve, and elaborate upon content. From a metacognitive perspective, students who are literate in a given discipline are more likely to think with texts if they are aware of and use strategies.

We are fond of a story that Bill Bernhardt (1977) tells in the book *Just Writing*. The story is from the diary of an African slave named Olaudah Equiano whose master was a ship's captain. Equiano was mystified by the relationship that his master had with books:

> I had often seen my master employed in reading and I had a great curiosity to talk to the books as I thought [he] did . . . for that purpose I have often taken up a book and have talked to it and then put my ears to it, when alone, in hope it would answer me; and I have been very much concerned when I found it remained silent. (From *Interesting Narrative of Olaudah Equiano, 1789*.)

Equiano was on the right track. He intuitively recognized that reading is a language process—that it involves a dialogue between reader and author—but his strategies for engaging the mind in that dialogue were inappropriate. For many students today, reading for meaning is as mysterious a process as it was for Equiano more than two hundred years ago. And texts remain as silent.

Thinking with texts is a strategic act. To put into perspective how language works to facilitate thinking and learning, utilize what you learned about language subsystems from the previous section as you read the text, "How to Ruin an Association," in Box 1.3.

Reflect on your reading of "How to Ruin An Association." Did the progressive substitution of letters disrupt your efforts to comprehend the passage? Probably not, at least not until the final paragraph. Perhaps your fluency, the ability to read at a conversational pace, slowed down with each succeeding paragraph, but chances are you were still able to engage in a meaningful dialogue with the author of the text.

From a strategic point of view, a reader's main goal is to make sense out of what is read. To do this, readers interact with text by making use of prior knowledge as well as knowledge of and expectations for written language. Students who struggle with the reading process often are unaware of *the role the reader plays* in comprehending and learning with texts. A strategic reader's mind is alive with questions, *cognitive questions* as Frank Smith (1988)

---

**BOX 1.3     How to Ruin an Association**

Once upon a time, the Midtown Chapter was one of the most active Chapters in the association. It was a smooth-running, efficient organization that enjoyed great prestige in the community.

Then one day, things began to change. One of the members said to himself, "No one will miss me. I have so many other things to do, I think I'll drop out of the Chapter's activities."

So hx bxgan to avoid Chaptxr functions. Hx rxfusxd to accxpt his rxsponsibilitixs, and thx Chaptxr had to limp along with onx lxss mxmbxr. Of coursx, thx Chaptxr could gxt along without him, but it mxant that onx of thx rxmaining mxmbxrs had to doublx up and do twicx as much work as bxforx.

Thxn, onx morx mxmbxr dxcidxd to givx up his sharx of Chaptxr activitixs. This mxant thzt two mxmbxrs hzd to do doublx duty.

Thxn z third mxmbxr droppxd jut, znd thrxx jf thx jthxrs hzd tj wjrk hzrdxr thzn xvxr.

Thxn z fjurth drjppxd jut, znd mjrx jf qhx rxmzining zctivx mxmbxrs sqzrqxd wjrking hzdxr thzn xvxr.

Zs qimx wxnq jn, mzny mjrx jf qhx Chzptxr mxmbxrs ljsq inqxrxsq, znd prxqqy sjjn qhx Chzptxr wzs bxing run by jnly z fxw mxmbxrs, znd iq ljjkxd lilx qhis: Qkj kzqxx kzjxqk jxk jzkxqk kqjz xjq kzjx xjz. Zkxq kqx zkkxq, kjz zkzxjqk zkk xkkq x xkziq kzjxq.

called them. Although cognitive questions will vary from reader to reader, they allow the strategic reader to interact with the content of the communication: What is this text about? What is the author trying to say? What is going to happen next? What does the author mean? So what? Such questions help the reader to anticipate meaning, search for information, reject, modify, or confirm educated guesses, infer and elaborate upon the content of the author's text.

The last paragraph of "How to Ruin an Association" is challenging. As a reader, you are acutely aware that you are in trouble—that the text no longer is making sense as you struggle to make meaning.

What strategies do you use to get out of trouble? Do you reread? Do you make use of the way the author organizes his ideas in the text by asking yourself, "What is the thesis or main point of the passage and how does the author develop it?" Do you try to figure out the author's system for making letter substitutions? Do you attempt to use syntactic and semantic knowledge to make sense out of the last lines of text? Do you ask somebody for help?

The last paragraph of "How to Ruin an Association" is difficult for several reasons. The sheer number of letter substitutions within words significantly affects most readers' ability to use letter/sound information. So you're left to other resources. You may have reread the first sentence of the concluding paragraph more than once, utilizing a system of letter substitution, the syntax, and the semantic knowledge you bring to the text to translate the sentence from print to speech as follows:

> As time went on, many more of the Chapter members lost interest, and pretty soon the Chapter was being run by only a few members, and it looked like this:

Your reading of the lines that follow the colon, however, may be analogous to hitting the wall in a marathon run. The text poses what seems to be an insurmountable task. The author takes away the reader's ability to use the rules and conventions of the graphophonic and syntactic subsystems. No longer can you rely on the mechanics and form of written language to make sense. But as a strategic reader, you recognize that you do have the semantic system—your prior knowledge—to construct a meaningful ending.

As a result, you may have inferred from the last paragraph that "it" and "this" in the phrase "and it looked like this" refer respectively to the Chapter and the chaotic, disorganized string of markings that follow the colon. Hence, you may have drawn an analogy between the Chapter and the disorganized, chaotic string of letters. Some of you may also have reasoned: Since the text starts out in a story-like manner, "Once upon a time . . .," the ending must signal the moral of the story. In your own words, then, what is the moral of the story? Any reasonable response provides an ending to the text.

Reading, as you might surmise, is a constructive process in which readers need not be word-perfect to comprehend a text effectively. Immature readers tend to approach reading as if it were a word-perfect, "roll-your-eyes-over-the-print" act. What they must recognize, however, is that reading is an active process which takes place behind the eyes. The meaning of a text does not reside in the print itself, but in the interactions and transactions that take place between the reader and the author. A content-literate student knows how to construct meaning with texts.

## CONTENT LITERACY IN PERSPECTIVE

Content literacy—the ability to use reading and writing to learn subject matter in a given discipline—is a relatively new term that holds much potential for students' acquisition of content (McKenna and Robinson 1990). To better understand what it means to be content literate in a discipline, examine the general construct of the term *literacy* and how it is used in today's society.

Literacy is a strong cultural expectation in the United States and other technologically advanced countries. Society places a heavy premium on literate behavior and demands that its citizens acquire literacy for personal, social, academic, and economic success. But what does it mean to be literate?

Literacy is a term whose meaning fluctuates from one context to another. Literacy, on one hand, may be used to describe how knowledgeable a person is in a particular subject. What do you know about computers and how to use them? Are you, for example, *computer literate*? In the same vein, the term *cultural literacy* describes what an educated person should know about the arts, literature, and other determinants of culture.

The most common use of the term *literacy* has been to denote one's ability to read and write a language. In the past century, the term has undergone variations in meaning. It has been used to depict the level of competence in reading and writing—*functional literacy*—that one needs to survive in society; one's lack of education—*illiteracy*—manifested in an inability to read and write a language; and one's lack of a reading habit—*aliteracy*—especially among those who have the ability to read and write, but choose not to.

The more researchers inquire into literacy and what it means to be literate, the more complex and multidimensional the concept becomes. Literacy is situational. In other words, a person may be able to handle the literacy demands of a task in one situation or context, but not in another. Hence, *workplace literacy* refers to the situational demands placed on workers to read and write effectively (Mikulecky 1990). These demands vary from job to job. *Family literacy* is used to describe how family interactions influence the language competence of young children (Taylor 1983). Because the environments for learning literacy vary from family to family, some young children enter school more literate than others.

The term *content literacy* underscores the situational demands placed on students to use reading and writing to learn subject matter. How a student uses literacy to learn in social studies may differ from that student's use of literacy in science or mathematics. Suppose you were to accompany Darryl, a sophomore at Warren Harding High, through a typical school day.

Toward the end of his first period American history class, where the students have been studying the events leading up to the Bay of Pigs invasion during John F. Kennedy's presidency, the teacher calls on Darryl to read out loud to the class a textbook section describing Fidel Castro's overthrow of the Cuban dictator, Fulgencio Batista:

> Even more dangerous than the continuing crisis over Berlin was that of the Soviet arms build-up in Cuba. On this rich island, just ninety miles from Florida, a flamboyant young revolutionist, Fidel Castro, had overthrown the reactionary dictatorship of Fulgencio Batista in 1959. At first Castro's government appeared to promise democracy and progress, but it became more and more dictatorial and leftist. Thousands of Cubans fled to the United States as Castro abolished civil liberties and nationalized much property, including that owned by citizens of the United States. American leaders began to take drastic economic action against Castro's Cuba by cutting off loans and restricting trade. More and more Castro turned to the Soviet Union and China, while he and his followers shouted against "Yankee Imperialism."*

Darryl reads lifelessly, in a monotone, completing the reading just as the bell rings. He grabs his stuff from the desk and hurries off to biology, where the class has been involved in a study of microorganisms. Five minutes into the lesson, the teacher reinforces a point she is making during her lecture by asking Darryl to read about euglenas and their method of locomotion:

> Since euglanas possess some characteristics of plants and some of animals, they have been claimed by both botanists and zoologists. Because of one of their methods of locomotion, they are often placed in the protist phylum Mastogophora (mass-ti-GAH-fuh-ruh), although some biologists put them in a phylum of their own. The organism swims by means of flagellum attached to the anterior end. The flagellum—nearly as long as the one-celled body—rotates, thus pulling the organism rapidly through the water. †

Darryl navigates his way through the euglena passage, occasionally faltering as he reads. When asked to tell the class what the passage is about, he gropes for a word or two. "I dunno. Eugenas [sic] or something." His teacher manages a smile, praises him for his effort, corrects the pronunciation of euglenas, and proceeds to explain what Darryl read to the class.

Mercifully, the period ends for Darryl. So he heads for Algebra I, where the class has been working on word problems. He is asked by his teacher to read one of the problems. "Why me?" he murmurs under his breath, but then proceeds to read out loud:

> An airmail parcel may weigh from 8 ounces up to 70 pounds, but the sum of the length and girth may be no more than 100 inches. What are the dimensions (length, width, height) of the longest acceptable airmail parcel, in the shape of a rectangular solid, that is twice as long as it is wide and that is two inches higher than it is wide?‡

*Shafer, et al., *United States History for High School*
†Otto and Towle, *Modern Biology*
‡Dolciani, et al., *Modern School Mathematics, Algebra I*

The next period is Darryl's English class, where the students are in the midst of a unit on war poetry. The teacher asks for a volunteer to read a poem. Darryl raises his hand! He likes this class. And he read the poem, "Refugee in New England," the night before. He handles the task with more purpose and confidence than he exhibited with the reading tasks from the previous classes. Here are the opening stanzas of the poem:

> Across the snow the water-color blue shadows of woods ran out to meet the wall crannied with whiteness; and the thin boy, new to alien winters, watched his shadow fall beside a pine's, and saw himself grow tall in the wide sunlight where the rime-frost flew.

> In this American woods there was no sound save when a green bough slipped its load to earth.

> Strange peace was here. Even the dog's bark, bound hillward from the farmhouse, held a dearth of urgency. The bright air flung its worth upward: "Oh, there you are!"—a friendly sound. The young boy wept, his cheek against cold ground.*

The scenario above illustrates how demanding a task it is to switch gears from content area text to content area text. What demands do the various texts place on Darryl's ability to read? What demands does the task—reading aloud to the class—place on Darryl? What other factors besides the nature of the text and task are likely to affect his content literacy?

As you might surmise, a variety of classroom-related factors influence one's content literacy in a given discipline—the reader's prior knowledge of, attitude toward, and interest in the subject; the reader's purpose; the language and conceptual difficulty of the material; the assumptions the author makes about his or her audience of readers; the way the author organizes ideas; the teacher's beliefs about and attitude toward the use of texts.

Although texts add an important dimension to learning in content classrooms, text authors are the invisible, often neglected participants in classroom interactions. As O'Brien and Stewart (1992) observe, a disparity often exists between how content area teachers *value* reading and how they *attend* to it.

One of the most compelling reasons for resistance to content literacy is tied to the strong cultural and institutional forces which influence teaching at elementary and secondary school levels. As we explain in the next section, dramatic changes are occurring in the way elementary teachers are viewing literacy and learning, but at the secondary school level change has been slow. Teachers at this level often resist active reading and writing practices for a variety of complex reasons, some of which are related to strongly rooted beliefs about their roles and responsibilities as content specialists. For example, reading and writing are often perceived by content area teachers as additional instructional burdens rather than as tools for learning. Confusion arises when teachers mistake learning to read and write with reading and writing to learn. One of the misconceptions held by subject matter teachers is that they will be saddled with the responsibility of

*Frost, Francis in Clarke (ed.), *The New Treasury of War Poetry*

basic skills instruction and remedial teaching, both of which require special-ized preparation outside of their areas of content expertise. The star-crossed cliché, "every teacher is a teacher of reading," contributes to the misconcep-tion and conveys little meaning to content teachers.

## Institutional Influences on Content Literacy

Entry into the teaching profession constitutes membership into a culture with deeply rooted beliefs, values, institutional goals, and organizational patterns (O'Brien and Stewart 1992). As institutions, schools are difficult to change. Forces within the culture and organization of schools work against change and exert enormous influence on the way teachers view their roles, think about instruction, and enact curriculum.

Cultural and institutional forces affect content literacy at both the ele-mentary and the secondary school level. Elementary and secondary schools are fundamentally different in their goals and the ways they are organized. Some of these differences are obvious: Elementary schools emphasize the teaching of basic skills in self-contained classrooms, whereas secondary schools are comprised of subject matter specialties within departments. While an elementary school teacher may work with 25 to 30 students a day, a secondary school teacher routinely works with 125 to 150 students, five or six instructional periods a day.

Another difference between elementary and secondary schools lies in their institutional mission. Whereas the secondary school is subject-matter centered, a prevailing institutional goal of elementary schools has been to teach children the basic skills of literacy and numeracy. Within the tradi-tions of a basic skills mission, elementary school teachers have perceived their roles as skills deliverers and have spent much of their time, especially in the primary grades, on "the three Rs." Subject matter areas such as sci-ence, health, and social studies often have received short shrift in relation to the teaching of basic skills. By fourth grade, there has been greater emphasis on the content areas of the curriculum, but reading and writing, more often than not, continue to be taught as separate subjects rather than being woven into the fabric of subject matter learning.

As a result, a false dichotomy usually is created in the elementary school and extends into the secondary school: that children *learn to read* in the primary grades and *read to learn* in the intermediate grades and beyond. A "learn to read/read to learn" mentality leads to *assumptive teaching* (Herber 1978). That is to say, teachers assume that students will be able to handle the demands inherent in subject matter reading and learning; yet lit-tle preparation if any is provided by teachers on how to apply literacy to content area learning tasks. Throughout the grades, teachers operate under the faulty assumption that reading skills learned in the elementary schools suffice for a lifetime of reading. No wonder a secondary school teacher often forms the inaccurate opinion that students will transfer the ability to read to subject matter learning.

Nevertheless, the winds of change are evident in elementary schools. The *whole language* movement has rocked the status quo and holds much promise for the reform of literacy practices (Vacca and Rasinski 1992). From an instructional perspective, whole language teaching is based on the principles of an integrated curriculum and authentic literacy experiences within meaningful contexts for learning.

Content area literacy practices are as essential to the instructional repertoire of elementary school teachers as they are to secondary school teachers. As Dorothy Watson (1989) has argued, *"The content areas are grist for the literacy mill* in the elementary grades. Students listen, speak, write, and read about science, art, music, math, social studies, games and sports, cooking, sewing, nutrition—anything that is important in their lives" (p. 137). What elementary school teachers are rallying around is the recognition that children use language to learn *something*. That something is content. A rich and meaningful content, conveyed through literature and information texts, provides the foundation for learning to read and write as children use reading and writing to learn.

While whole language is making significant inroads in changing the curriculum of elementary schooling, secondary schools remain seemingly impervious to change. A remarkable sameness and uniformity, characterized by teacher-centered practices, have existed in secondary schools throughout the twentieth century (Goodlad 1984; Sizer 1985).

Larry Cuban, a noted educational historian, demonstrates a relationship between a durable, persistent core of teaching practices and the organizational structure of secondary schools. He traces the constancy of a "core repertoire" of instructional practices to earlier educational reform and to an institutional structure that makes it difficult for teachers to change their practices:

> Large graded schools, self-contained classrooms, 50-minute periods, multiple curricula . . . and standardized tests were structural innovations designed by earlier generations of reformers to make teaching both efficient and productive. These structural reforms became the organizational DNA to which subsequent generations of teachers adapted by inventing teacher-centered classroom tactics: lecturing, large-group instruction, reliance on a textbook . . . recitation. This particular pedagogy, forged from daily experience in the classroom, worked. Teacher-centered classroom tactics enabled teachers to maintain order with large groups of children and, at the same time, to convey content that the community deemed appropriate. (Cuban 1986, p. 8.)

There has been, in short, a "terribly thin" margin for change in secondary schools.

We are more optimistic about the prospect of change *within* individual teachers than within the organizational structure of secondary schools. By change, we are not suggesting radically different teaching behavior, but rather a transition from teacher-centered to student-centered practices. If transitions are to occur, then teachers, whether at the preservice or inservice level, must think critically and reflectively about what they do (or plan to do) as they consider instructional alternatives.

## Bridging the Gap with Instructional Alternatives

When texts are the vehicles for learning, content teachers have a significant role to play. That role can be thought of in a metaphorical way as "bridge building." Your task is to span the gap between students' prior knowledge and experience, attitudes, interests, and reading abilities on one river bank and the ideas, concepts, and relationships of your subject area that lie on the other side. Like bridge builders, you need to know the terrain on each side of the river and the breadth of the gap to be spanned. You also need to have a variety of strategies and techniques for construction. Then, and only then, can a structure be built that will provide access to the content that you so earnestly want students to reach.

"Bridging the gap" reflects the *functional* nature of reading and writing to learn. It suggests that you are in a better position than a reading teacher to show students how to use strategies that they actually need to acquire content knowledge. Strategies aren't taught or applied in isolated lessons apart from the mainstream of content area teaching. More and more students will learn how to use texts effectively as you build healthy concepts of reading and writing to learn, reflect upon what you believe about teaching, and examine instructional alternatives in light of current practices.

Making a transition from teacher-centered to student-centered practice involves incorporating new strategies into an existing instructional framework. At the preservice level, O'Brien and Stewart (1992) contend that prospective teachers must learn to question what practicing teachers do and to confront the issues of resistance related to institutional practices. To this end, you must examine issues related to the organizational structure of schools and the constraints the typical work day places on what is taught and how it is taught. What effect, for example, does tracking students by ability have on compromising teaching practices? How does the implicit or hidden curriculum influence what you do and how you do it?

Teachers who engage in reflective inquiry are in a better position to consider changes in the way they use reading and writing to learn than teachers who do not. Alvermann (1992) recommends that you inquire into current and alternative teaching strategies by exploring "practical arguments." This approach allows you to assess the underlying premises and assumptions for maintaining a particular practice. Study the dialogue between a social studies teacher and a colleague in Box 1.4. The teacher assesses his teaching practices and the assumptions underlying those practices. The colleague uses the teacher's "practical arguments" to introduce him to a promising instructional alternative, one of many that we will present in the remainder of this book.

Throughout this and ensuing chapters, we are encouraging you to engage in practical arguments as a way of thinking critically about content literacy in your classrooms. The challenge lies in meshing promising alternatives into existing classroom practices. From an instructional perspective,

---

**BOX 1.4    Examining Practical Arguments: A Dialogue Between Two Teachers**

The dialogue that takes place in Peter Townsend's homeroom at Central High School (all names are fictitious) is between himself and Marlene Kincaid, another social studies teacher on special assignment at Central High School. Marlene, who has been a participant in a three-year staff development project in content area reading, is in her second year of working with teachers in the district. She is experienced in assisting colleagues to analyze their own practical arguments for maintaining the status quo or for making changes in their instructional routines.

**Peter:** I guess the principal is pretty determined to get us to change our teaching . . . to make our classrooms more student centered, right?

**Marlene:** Yes, I guess that's a fair conclusion to draw. Still, as you know, it wasn't her decision alone. The results of the faculty's self-study report showed a majority of the teachers favoring a move away from so much teacher-centered textbook instruction here at Central High.

**Peter:** True . . . but you forget, I'm a firm believer in helping my kids with the content of their history textbook. It's just that the book is too hard for them. There's no way they can read it on their own and make any sense of it. I tell them pretty much everything they need to know about the content . . . I suppose I spoon-feed them, but they do well on my exams as a result of my telling them what's in the text. It's a real dilemma . . . I'd like to think I was helping them learn how to deal with their textbook on their own, but it's impossible.

**Marlene:** Let's try something. Are you willing to examine some of the assumptions underlying your belief that your students can't learn unless you're here to spoon-feed them the information from their textbook?

**Peter:** Sure, why not . . . It sounds like an interesting process.

**Marlene:** Okay, here is what I need you to do. During the coming week, jot down the things you do in your lectures that you think make it easy for your students to understand the content of their textbooks. Then list the assumptions that cause you to do these things. When we meet next week, we'll talk about the observations you have made about your current practice.

**One Week Later . . .**

**Marlene:** [looking at a sheet of notebook paper Peter has given her] I see that you have listed three things that make your lectures over the textbook easy to understand. You mention that you use the structure of your discipline (history) as a framework for your lecture notes. You also mention that when the author's structure, or frame, isn't made clear in the textbook, you impose your own. Finally, you say that you always walk around the room as you lecture so that you can monitor whether your students' notes reflect the same structure as your own. Good! Now we're ready for the next step in the process. I'd like to hear your reasons for doing these three things.

**Peter:** Well . . . I know that a good many historical texts are structured around a problem/solution frame. For example, authors might use this frame when they want to write on the topic of opening up China to the West . . . The problem would be the difficulty European traders experienced as they tried to reach Asia by an all-land route; the solution would be the discovery of safer water routes and better sailing vessels. There are several other frames that historians use in their writing . . . but I guess you have the idea. I just organize my lecture notes according to the text structure that I see best fitting the content I'm trying to teach. It helps my students. If they don't get the information from their texts, at least they get it from my notes.

**Marlene:** Yes, what you are doing with text structure makes sense to me. In fact, it reminds me of an article that I read in one of the recent issues of the Kappan. It described how students can be taught to construct their own graphic representations of the different organizational schemes authors use when they write textbooks. As I recall, there were even some key questions . . . that would help students anticipate how a history text, . . . for example, might be organized.

**Peter**: Students can draw diagrams of how information in their textbooks is structured.

**Marlene:** Yes, if they're shown how to do this. Would you like me to make you a copy of the article?

**Peter**: Sure, I'd like to see how this might be done. Being able to graphically show how important ideas are organized in a textbook sounds like a good idea . . . .

**Source:** From *Reading in the content area: Improving classroom practice* by Dishner, Readence and Moore. Copyright 1992. Reprinted with permission of Kendall/Hunt Publishing Company.

teaching with texts in the ways that we will suggest throughout this book means continually reflecting on several questions: What do you currently do with texts (or plan on doing)? Why do you do what you do? How can you adjust and build on what you do?

## LOOKING BACK, LOOKING FORWARD

In this chapter we invited you to begin an examination of content area teaching practices, and the assumptions underlying those practices, in light of promising instructional alternatives for text learning and active student involvement. Teachers play a critical role in helping students to realize a potentially powerful use of language—to learn with texts. Learning with texts is an active process. Yet assigning and telling are still common teaching practices that often have the unfortunate consequence of dampening students' active involvement in learning. To shift the burden of learning from teacher to student requires an understanding of the importance of the relationships that exist among language, literacy, and learning. As a result, we explored the role that language and literacy play in the acquisition of content knowledge. Using language to learn with texts is what content area reading is all about. Instead of teaching students how to read or write, we use reading and writing as tools to construct knowledge—to discover, to clarify, and to extend meaning—in a given discipline.

Content literacy underscores the situational demands placed on students to use reading and writing to learn subject matter. Content teachers are in a strategic position to show students how to use reading and writing strategies that are actually needed to acquire content knowledge. Furthermore, teachers who engage in reflective inquiry are more likely to consider changes in the way they use reading and writing to learn than teachers who do not.

In the next chapter, we explore the role that cognition and metacognition play in thinking and learning with texts. You will examine some of the influences and processes underlying reading to learn in content classrooms. It is essential that students actively participate in conversations to promote thinking and learning. What you must do to create active learning environments now shifts to what you need to know about thinking and learning with texts.

## SUGGESTED READINGS

Alvermann, D. E. & Moore, D. W. (1991). Secondary school reading. In P.D. Pearson, R. Barr, M. L. Kamil, & P. Mosenthal (eds.), *Handbook of reading research*, Vol. II. New York: Longman.

Cambourne, B. (1984). Language, learning, and literacy. In Butler, A. & Turbill, J. *Towards a reading/writing classroom.* Portsmouth, NH: Heinemann.

Edelsky, C., Altwerger, B., & Flores, B. (1991). *Whole language: What's the difference?* Portsmouth, NH: Heinemann.

Goodlad, J. (1984). *A place called school.*New York: McGraw-Hill.

Goodman, K. (1986). *What's whole in whole language.* Portsmouth, NH: Heinemann.

Gee, T. C. & Forester, N. (1988). Moving reading instruction beyond the reading classroom. *Journal of Reading, 31,* 505–511.

Herber, H. (1978). *Reading in the content areas* (2nd ed.). Englewood Cliffs, NJ: Prentice-Hall.

Ratekin, N., Simpson, M. L., Alvermann, D. E., & Dishner, E. K. (1985). Why teachers resist content reading instruction. *Journal of Reading, 28,* 432–437.

Schallert, D. L. & Roser, N. L. (1989). The role of reading in content area instruction. In Lapp, D., Flood, J., & Farnon, N. (eds.), *Content area reading and learning.* Englewood Cliffs, NJ: Prentice-Hall.

Stewart, R. A. & O'Brien, D. G. (1989). Resistance to content-area reading: A focus on preservice teachers. *Journal of Reading, 32,* 396–401.

Tierney, R. J. & Pearson, P. D. (1992). Learning to learn from text: A framework for improving classroom practice. In Dishner, E. K., Bean, T. W., Readence, J. E., & Moore, D. W. (eds.), *Reading in the Content Areas: Improving classroom instruction.* Dubuque, IA: Kendall-Hunt.

Vacca. R. T. & Rasinski, T. V. (1992). *Case studies in whole language.* Fort Worth, TX: Harcourt Brace Jovanovich.

# 2

# Thinking and Learning with Texts

Reading transcends the mere transmission of information: It fosters an imaginative dialogue between the text and the reader's mind that actually helps people to think.

—*Stratford P. Sherman*

## ORGANIZING PRINCIPLE

Behind every academic text is a writer or a writing team such as the two of us—real people doing real work. Writers work at their craft because they believe that they have something worthwhile to say and reasons for saying it. Some write to entertain, others to inform. Authors like us do the latter. When writers talk directly to readers as we're doing now, text linguists have labeled the process *metadiscourse,* a mouthful of a word that describes what the writer does to engage the reader in conversation. Most readers don't think about what a writer does to draw them into conversation. They don't need to know. But writers do. An effective author knows that when readers actively engage in a dialogue with the author, they think about the author's content—connecting the old (what they know) to the new (what they don't know)—as they read to learn. Thinking with texts suggest that readers have much to contribute to the learning process as they interact with authors to make meaning and construct knowledge.

Content area reading underscores the dialogue, the learning conversation if you will, that occurs between the reader and the writer. An imaginative dialogue takes place in the reader's mind, and therein lies the wonder and mystery of reading. The organizing principle of this chapter spotlights the dynamics involved in the conversation: ***Thinking with texts reflects the processes by which authors and readers can link minds and engage in learning conversations with one another.***

Study the Chapter Overview. Link what you know to the concepts in the Overview. Take a moment or two to reflect on what you know about the psychological dimensions of thinking and learning. What do you think we will say about the relationships between cognitive and metacognitive processes? Also, examine the questions in the Frame of Mind. These key questions help us to frame the ideas that we present in conversation with you. Use the questions to guide your reading.

## CHAPTER OVERVIEW

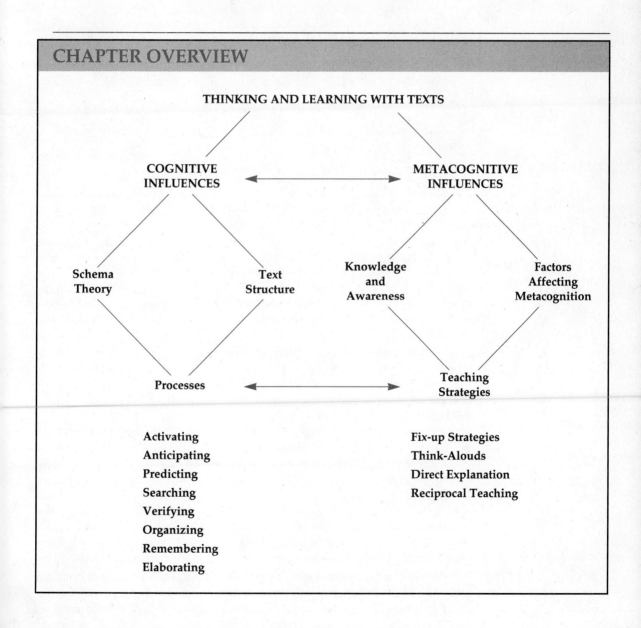

**THINKING AND LEARNING WITH TEXTS**

**COGNITIVE INFLUENCES**  ⟷  **METACOGNITIVE INFLUENCES**

Schema Theory     Text Structure     Knowledge and Awareness     Factors Affecting Metacognition

Processes  ⟷  Teaching Strategies

Activating               Fix-up Strategies
Anticipating             Think-Alouds
Predicting               Direct Explanation
Searching                Reciprocal Teaching
Verifying
Organizing
Remembering
Elaborating

## FRAME OF MIND

1. Why is thinking with texts a conversation between reader and author?

2. What are some of the cognitive processes involved in reading?

3. How does schema influence comprehension and learning?

4. How does text structure influence comprehension and learning?

5. What is metacognition?

6. Which metacognitive factors influence comprehension and learning?

7. What are fix-up strategies?

8. What role do think-alouds and direct explanations play in modeling learning strategies?

9. How would you use reciprocal teaching in a content area?

Although metaphors come and go, one that has been around since the ancient Greeks is as powerful today as it was centuries ago: Thinking is a conversation. It is a dialogue you have with yourself in the recesses of your mind. When a reader engages in an imaginative dialogue with an author, the conversation metaphor takes an incredibly complex process—reading—and provides a familiar context for describing what happens inside the reader's head.

The conversations that take place between readers and authors transcend time and space. Texts make it possible to bring readers and authors together, even dead authors, in content area classrooms. There is a catch, however. Thinking and learning with texts require students to actively participate in the conversation.

A conversation works only when its participants are mutually involved in sharing and negotiating meaning. In everyday conversations, there is always an exchange of ideas between two or more parties—a give-and-take dialogue—around topics of mutual interest and relevance. Similar characteristics hold true whenever learning conversations occur in content classrooms, unless they break down or never get started. Dialogues easily turn into monologues when the transmission of information in a content area classroom becomes more important than the transaction of ideas among students, teachers, and authors.

All too often, academic texts are viewed as sacred canons, authoritative sources of knowledge by which the information in a field is transmitted from generation to generation of learners. The expression "learning *from* text" has been used widely in content area reading, as if a text were indeed a canon to be mastered rather than a tool to learn and construct meaning. The preposition *from* suggests a one-way act in which meaning flows from party A (the text author) to party B (the reader).

The prepositional shift from *from* to *with* is subtle but dramatic (Tierney and Pearson 1992). It places the act of reading to learn squarely in the context of a human transaction between two parties rather than a transmission of information from one party to another. Thinking with texts suggests that readers have much to contribute to the learning process as they interact with authors to make meaning and construct knowledge.

In the previous chapter, we suggested that texts remain silent for too many students. So we explored, by way of an introduction to content area reading, what it means to teach with texts in active learning environments. In this chapter our intent shifts from what you must do to create active learning environments to what you need to know about thinking and learning with texts. As a result, we examine some of the psychological influences and processes underlying reading to learn in content area classrooms. Cognitive and metacognitive processes underscore the psychological nature of reading to learn.

## COGNITIVE INFLUENCES ON READING TO LEARN

How people acquire and construct knowledge is the subject of cognition. Coming to know has been a source of study, mainly within the tradition of philosophical inquiry, for centuries. More than 2300 years ago, for example, Socrates engaged Theaetetus in a dialogue on the subject of knowledge. In response to the question, "What is the thinking process?" Socrates explains: "I have a notion that, when the mind is thinking, it is simply talking to itself, asking questions and answering them. . . . So I should describe thinking as discourse, and judgment as a statement pronounced, not aloud to someone else, but silently to oneself" (Plato 1966).

Thinking with texts invites a covert discourse, one that takes place inside the head, between the reader and author. What Socrates had to say about thinking raises issues that are as relevant today as they were more than 2300 years ago. Today, however, thinking and knowing are the subject of inquiry from multidisciplinary perspectives, including psychology, hermeneutics, semiotics, artificial intelligence, and literary analysis. Throughout the twentieth century in particular, cognition has been explored within the context of psychological inquiry: How does the mind work when people use language to facilitate comprehension and learning?

In this century alone, literally tens of thousands of research studies have been conducted to shed light on the cognitive processes associated with comprehension and learning. Yet a popular writer like Robert Fulghum puts the mysteries of cognition in terms a layman can understand as he reflects on a teaching incident in his life.

Fulghum, the author of *All I Really Need to Know I Learned in Kindergarten* and other books, has a knack of discovering elemental truths in ordinary, everyday events and experiences. One such discovery came when he was teaching a beginning drawing class and had prepared a presentation on the impact of brain research on the process of art. To make his points as illustrative as possible he used pictures and anatomy charts of the brain, and even brought a cantaloupe to class, tossing it around from student to student, so that they would get some sense of the size of the brain.

The brain, however, remained abstract to his students until one class member, whose father was a research neurosurgeon at a medical school, volunteered to bring a human brain to class. So she did. When the brain arrived, the students asked Fulghum for his thoughts on the matter.

What did Fulghum think? He responded to the class's query by noting that the brain is made up of raw meat; that he had some understanding of how it works from a mechanical standpoint, likening it to a motor; that the brain is all chemistry and electricity. Fulghum then shifted his response from the brain as a physical organ—"a lump of meat"—to its wondrous workings:

> This three-pound raw-meat motor . . . contains all the limericks I know, a recipe for how to cook a turkey, the remembered smell of my junior-high locker room, all my sorrows, the ability to double-clutch a pickup truck, the face of my wife when she was young, formulas like $E = MC^2$, and $A^2 + B^2 = C^2$, the Prologue to Chaucer's *Canterbury Tales*, the sound of the first cry of my first-born son, the cure for hiccups, the words to the fight song of St. Olaf's College, fifty years' worth of dreams, how to tie my shoes, the taste of cod-liver oil, an image of Van Gogh's "Sunflowers," and a working understanding of the Dewey Decimal System. It's all there in the MEAT. . . . (Fulghum 1989, p. 41)

The classroom experience serves as a springboard for reflection as Fulghum celebrates the uniqueness of the brain as a meaning-making organ:

> Look around and see the infinite variety of human heads. . . . And know that on the inside such differences are even greater—what we know, how we learn, how we process information, what we remember and forget, our strategies for functioning and coping. . . .
>
> From a practical point of view, day by day, this kind of information makes me a little more patient with the people I live with. I am less inclined to protest, "Why don't you see it the way I do?" and more inclined to say, "You see it *that* way? Holy cow! How amazing!" (pp. 42–43)

Robert Fulghum captures the constructive nature of the brain and suggests that people negotiate meaning in life based on their store of memories: everything that they have ever sensed, experienced, and learned. From a cognitive perspective, psychologists have used constructs such as *long-term memory, cognitive structure,* and *schema* to characterize how people store and organize knowledge in memory. The brain actively seeks, selects, organizes, stores, and when necessary, retrieves and utilizes information about the world (Smith 1988). The prior knowledge that students bring to learning has important implications for content area reading. These implications are supported by a *schema theoretic view* of reading and language comprehension.

## Schema, Comprehension, and Learning

Students are in a strategic position to learn with texts whenever they utilize prior knowledge to construct meaning for new material that they are studying. To this extent, the *schema* reflects the experiences, conceptual understandings, attitudes, values, skills, and strategies a reader brings to a text situation. Schema is the technical term used by cognitive scientists to describe how people organize and store information in their heads. Given Fulghum's anecdote, a cognitive psychologist would say that Fulghum accessed various *schemata* (the plural of schema) in fondly recalling information-laden events, skills, and experiences in his life.

*Schema activation* is the mechanism by which people access what they know and match it to the information in a text. In doing so, they build on the meaning they already bring to the reading situation. Indeed, schemata have been called "the building blocks of cognition" (Rumelhart 1982) because they represent elaborate networks of information that people use to make sense out of new stimuli, events, and situations.

Read, for example, the text in Box 2.1, and when you finish reading, use the space provided in the box to interpret what you think the passage is about.

If you have the opportunity to share your interpretation of the passage with others, you will probably find wide variance in the meaning that you have constructed for the text. What contributes to the differences in interpretation and comprehension? First, you probably had difficulty making sense, because you didn't have enough contextual background provided to

---

**BOX 2.1    "Stone Foxes" Passage\***

I was looking over this audience and I say nothing but stone foxes. I thought to myself, as soon as the eagle flies, I'm going to go out and rent me a hog, or maybe a deuce-and-a-quarter. I'm not sure. Then I want to find the honcho of this organization to let him know that I'm going to lay dead because I'm going with my hog and stone fox to the killing floor.

What is the passage about?

**Source:** *Author unknown

understand the passage. You don't know who the "I" is in the passage or what his or her goal is. So let us give you some context: the "I" in the passage is a young adult, an African-American male, looking for a date at his place of employment. Now that you have this additional information, the passage may be less of a problem to comprehend. Try reading it again.

Based on your study of Chapter 1, you probably recognize that you have to know the language of the text to comprehend it with any sense of satisfaction. The more unfamiliar you are with the language of a text, the more difficult it is to comprehend. Given the context, you undoubtedly recognize that the passage is written in a vernacular that some of you might describe as "street talk." More precisely, the passage reflects an African-American dialect, sometimes referred to as black English or black dialect.

Words and phrases such as *stone fox, deuce-and-a-quarter, lay dead, eagle flies, hog,* and *killing floor* must be interpreted within the context of the passage. If you are familiar with black dialect, you should have little trouble accessing what you know to construct meaning. For instance, if you know that *stone foxes* represent extremely good-looking women, you should have little trouble engaging a schema for what constitutes a good-looking woman. Each person's schema for a good looking woman will undoubtedly include different images, features, and examples. But we imagine this is what Fulghum is getting at when he exclaims, "You see it *that* way. Holy cow! How amazing!"

In the same vein, many of you initially may have interpreted *hog* to be a vehicle, perhaps a Harley-Davidson motorcycle. Within the context of the passage, however, it makes sense to assume that hog may be an abbreviated term for *gashog* or *roadhog,* in which case you probably interpreted hog to mean a big car, perhaps a Cadillac or a Lincoln. Then what is a deuce-and-a-quarter? A Buick Electra 225.

In ordinary conversation, the language by which people communicate often doesn't pose problems for comprehension. In academic content areas, however, the reader needs to be familiar with the language of a discipline, lest the text begins to create trouble for the reader the way the "stone fox" passage caused you a problem on your first attempt to comprehend it. Bransford and Stein (1984, p. 53) make this clear with the passage in Box 2.2.

According to Bransford and Stein, the passage in Box 2.2 poses a comprehension problem because readers do not know enough about Pete or his goal. Pete, it turns out, is an astronomer and his goal is to call into question current theories about the formation of the solar system based on data collected from a NASA spaceship's voyage to Venus. Does this information help to better comprehend the letter? Maybe. Yet Bransford and Stein (1984) point out: "Most people feel that it [information about Pete's goal] helps comprehension to some extent. However, unless they are knowledgeable about astronomy, they are unable to make many inferences about the letter" (p. 54). For example, what is the relationship, if any, between high levels of the isotopes of argon and theories of the formation of the solar system? To answer the question requires readers to make an inferential leap by utilizing what they know to fill in gaps in the information presented in the letter.

| BOX 2.2 | Letter to Jim |
|---------|---------------|

Dear Jim,

Remember Pete, the guy in my last letter? You'll never guess what he did last week. First, he talked about the importance of mass spectrometers. He then discussed the isotopes of argon 36 and argon 38 and noted that they were of higher density than expected. He also cited the high values of neon found in the atmosphere. He has a paper that is already written, but he is aware of the need for further investigation as well.

Love,

Sandra

**Source:** Reprinted with permission from Bransford, J. D., & Stein, B. S. (1984). *The ideal problem solver: A guide to improving thinking, learning, and creativity.* New York: W. H. Freeman and Co.

**How Schema Influences Comprehension.** Schemata, as you might surmise, greatly influence reading comprehension and learning. When a match occurs between students' prior knowledge and text material, a schema functions in at least three ways.

First, a schema provides a framework for learning that allows readers to *seek and select* information that is relevant to their purposes for reading. In the process of searching and selecting, readers are more likely to *make inferences* about text. Inferences occur in situations where you *anticipate* content and *make predictions* about upcoming material or, as we just suggested, *fill in gaps* in the material during reading.

Second, a schema helps readers to *organize* text information. The process by which you organize and integrate new information into old facilitates the ability to *retain* and *remember* what you read. A poorly organized text makes it difficult for readers to comprehend. We'll illustrate this point in more detail when we discuss the influences of text structure on comprehension and retention in the next section of this chapter.

And third, a schema helps readers to *elaborate* information. When you elaborate what you have read, you engage in a cognitive process that involves deeper levels of insight, judgment, and evaluation. You are inclined to ask, "So what?" as you engage in conversation with an author.

**A Schema-Based Demonstration.** To illustrate these cognitive processes in action, we will use a workshop activity.

In workshops for content teachers we occasionally read the short story "Ordeal by Cheque" by Wuther Grue (first published in *Vanity Fair* magazine in 1932). The story is extraordinary in that it is told entirely through the bank checks of the Exeter family over a 28-year span. The workshop participants interact in small groups, with each group assigned the task of constructing the meaning of the story. At first glance the groups don't know what to make of their task. "You must be kidding!" is a typical response. At this point, we engage the groups in a prereading activity to activate prior knowledge, declare purposes for reading, and arouse interest in the story. We assign them the activity in Box 2.3, which depicts in chart form the essential bits of information contained on the first eight checks of the story. Group members collaborate as they respond to the task of answering the three questions that accompany the chart: What is the story about? Who are the main characters and what do you know about them? What do you predict will happen in the remainder of the story?

We invite you to analyze the information on the chart.

Are you able to construct what has taken place thus far in the story? What inferences did you make about the characters?

Here are some typical responses to these questions:

"A baby boy was born. He's named after his father."

"The Exeters must be 'fat cats.' The old man's loaded."

"He spends $83 for toys in 1903! He probably bought out the toy store."

"Lawrence Jr. must be a spoiled brat!"

"Yeah, how can any kid born with the proverbial silver spoon in his mouth not turn out spoiled?"

"Let's not jump to conclusions. Why is he spoiled?"

"Look, the family sent him to a military academy after he screwed up at the private school."

---

**BOX 2.3      Prereading Activity for "Ordeal by Cheque"**

Here are the essential bits of information contained in the first few checks of the story:

| ENTRY DATE: | PAID TO: | AMOUNT: | SIGNED BY: |
| --- | --- | --- | --- |
| 8/30/03 | a baby shop | $148.00 | Lawrence Exeter |
| 9/2/03 | a hospital | $100.00 | Lawrence Exeter |
| 10/3/03 | a physician | $475.00 | Lawrence Exeter Sr. |
| 12/10/03 | a toy company | $83.20 | Lawrence Exeter Sr. |
| 10/6/09 | a private school for boys | $1250.00 | Lawrence Exeter Sr. |
| 8/6/15 | a military academy | $2150.00 | Lawrence Exeter Sr. |
| 9/3/21 | a Cadillac dealer | $3885.00 | Lawrence Exeter Sr. |
| 9/7/21 | an auto repair shop | $228.75 | Lawrence Exeter Sr. |

What is the story about? How would you describe the main characters? What do you think will happen in the remainder of the story?

"No, no. It was fashionable in those days to first send your child to a private school until he was old enough for military school. The super-rich send their children to exclusive schools—it's as simple as that."

"Maybe so, but the kid is still a spoiled brat. His father buys him a Cadillac, probably for graduation from the academy, and four days later, it's in the body shop for repair."

"The father overindulges his son. I wonder what will happen to 'Junior' when he has to make it on his own?"

This demonstration illustrates that readers not only read the lines to determine what an author says, but also read between the lines to infer meaning and beyond the lines to elaborate the message. Now read "Ordeal by Cheque" in its entirety on pages 36–39. As you read you will undoubtedly find yourself raising questions, predicting, searching for relationships among the pieces of information contained in each check, inferring, judging, and elaborating.

**What the Demonstration Tells Us.** The statements made about Lawrence Exeter and his son are the result of schema activation. We often ask workshop participants to examine the basis for their initial suppositions about the father and the son in the story. Some speak with authority, citing knowledge and beliefs about how the rich live. Others couch their inferences about the Exeters as hunches which need to be pursued as more information is revealed in the story.

The activity also activates the workshop participants' prior knowledge of stories. Some use their story schema to establish a setting and identify a problem around which the remainder of the story will revolve. Based on the information from the chart in Box 2.3, what appears to be the problem in the story? And how do you predict it will be resolved?

The 15 or so minutes that it takes to complete the prereading activity is time well spent. Not only do participants have a framework in which to construct meaning for the story, but also expectations have been raised for the content of the checks they have yet to read. The predictions they make for the remainder of the story, while general, often suggest that they have surmised the author's intent.

The insights into comprehension presented here will be developed in succeeding chapters within the framework of instructional alternatives related to content area reading. What these insights tell the classroom teacher is this: Readers must "work" with print in an effort to explore and build meaning. Reading is first and foremost a conversation, a give and take exchange, between the reader and the author of the text. However, the burden for learning is always on the reader. As a result, content area reading instruction should center around a search for meaning. The teacher guides comprehension and helps students develop ideas through varied forms of instructional activity—some of which are to be presented in the remainder of this book.

# ORDEAL BY CHEQUE

## BY WUTHER CRUE

LOS ANGELES, CALIF. Apr. 18th 19 10    No. ____

**HOLLYWOOD STATE BANK** 90-984
6801 SANTA MONICA BOULEVARD

PAY TO THE ORDER OF *City Bicycle Co.*    $52.50

*Fifty two* ———————— 50/ DOLLARS

*Lawrence Exeter Sr.*

---

LOS ANGELES, CALIF. Aug. 30th 19 03    No. ____

**HOLLYWOOD STATE BANK** 90-984
6801 SANTA MONICA BOULEVARD

PAY TO THE ORDER OF *Goosie Gander Baby Shoppe*    $148.50

*One hundred & forty eight* ——— 50/ DOLLARS

*Lawrence Exeter*

---

LOS ANGELES, CALIF. Aug. 26th 19 15    No. ____

**HOLLYWOOD STATE BANK** 90-984
6801 SANTA MONICA BOULEVARD

PAY TO THE ORDER OF *Columbia Military Acad.*    $2,150.00

*Twenty-one hundred & fifty* ——— XX DOLLARS

*Lawrence Exeter Sr.*

---

LOS ANGELES, CALIF. Sept. 2nd 19 03    No. ____

**HOLLYWOOD STATE BANK** 90-984
6801 SANTA MONICA BOULEVARD

PAY TO THE ORDER OF *Hollywood Hospital*    $100.00

*One hundred* ——————— XX DOLLARS

*Lawrence Exeter*

---

LOS ANGELES, CALIF. Sept. 3rd 19 21    No. ____

**HOLLYWOOD STATE BANK** 90-984
6801 SANTA MONICA BOULEVARD

PAY TO THE ORDER OF *Hollywood Cadillac Co.*    $3,885.00

*Thirty eight hundred & eighty five* XX DOLLARS

*Lawrence Exeter Sr.*

---

LOS ANGELES, CALIF. Oct. 3rd 19 03    No. ____

**HOLLYWOOD STATE BANK** 90-984
6801 SANTA MONICA BOULEVARD

PAY TO THE ORDER OF *Dr. David M. McCoy*    $475.00

*Four hundred & seventy five* ——— XX DOLLARS

*Lawrence Exeter Sr.*

---

LOS ANGELES, CALIF. Sept. 7th 19 21    No. ____

**HOLLYWOOD STATE BANK** 90-984
6801 SANTA MONICA BOULEVARD

PAY TO THE ORDER OF *Wilshire Auto Repair Service*    $288.76

*Two hundred & eighty-eight* ——— 76/ DOLLARS

*Lawrence Exeter Sr.*

---

LOS ANGELES, CALIF. Dec. 19th 19 03    No. ____

**HOLLYWOOD STATE BANK** 90-984
6801 SANTA MONICA BOULEVARD

PAY TO THE ORDER OF *California Toyland Co.*    $83.20

*Eighty three* ——————— 20/ DOLLARS

*Lawrence Exeter, Sr.*

---

LOS ANGELES, CALIF. Oct. 15th 19 21    No. ____

**HOLLYWOOD STATE BANK** 90-984
6801 SANTA MONICA BOULEVARD

PAY TO THE ORDER OF *Stanford University*    $339.00

*Three hundred & thirty-nine* ——— XX DOLLARS

*Lawrence Exeter Sr.*

---

LOS ANGELES, CALIF. Oct. 6th 19 09    No. ____

**HOLLYWOOD STATE BANK** 90-984
6801 SANTA MONICA BOULEVARD

PAY TO THE ORDER OF *Palisades School for Boys*    $1,250.00

*Twelve hundred & fifty* ——— XX DOLLARS

*Lawrence Exeter, Sr.*

---

LOS ANGELES, CALIF. June 1st 19 23    No. ____

**HOLLYWOOD STATE BANK** 90-984
6801 SANTA MONICA BOULEVARD

PAY TO THE ORDER OF *Miss Daisy Windsor*    $25,000.00

*Twenty-five thousand* ——— XX DOLLARS

*Lawrence Exeter Sr.*

**Check 1**

LOS ANGELES, CALIF. June 9th 19 23 No. _____

HOLLYWOOD STATE BANK 90-984
6801 SANTA MONICA BOULEVARD

PAY TO THE ORDER OF French Line, Ile de France $585.00

Five hundred & eighty-five ———— xx DOLLARS

Lawrence Exeter Sr.

**Check 2**

LOS ANGELES, CALIF. Aug. 23rd 19 23 No. _____

HOLLYWOOD STATE BANK 90-984
6801 SANTA MONICA BOULEVARD

PAY TO THE ORDER OF Banque de France $5,000.00

Five thousand ———— xx DOLLARS

Lawrence Exeter Sr.

**Check 3**

LOS ANGELES, CALIF. Feb. 13th 19 26 No. _____

HOLLYWOOD STATE BANK 90-984
6801 SANTA MONICA BOULEVARD

PAY TO THE ORDER OF University Club Florists $76.50

Seventy-six ———— 50/ DOLLARS

Lawrence Exeter Sr.

**Check 4**

LOS ANGELES, CALIF. June 22nd 19 26 No. _____

HOLLYWOOD STATE BANK 90-984
6801 SANTA MONICA BOULEVARD

PAY TO THE ORDER OF University Club Florists $312.75

Three hundred & twelve ———— 75/ DOLLARS

Lawrence Exeter Sr.

**Check 5**

LOS ANGELES, CALIF. Aug. 11th 19 26 No. _____

HOLLYWOOD STATE BANK 90-984
6801 SANTA MONICA BOULEVARD

PAY TO THE ORDER OF Riviera Heights Land Co. $56,000.00

Fifty-six Thousand ———— xx DOLLARS

Lawrence Exeter Sr.

**Check 6**

LOS ANGELES, CALIF. Oct. 30th 19 26 No. _____

HOLLYWOOD STATE BANK 90-984
6801 SANTA MONICA BOULEVARD

PAY TO THE ORDER OF Renaissance Interior Decorators $22,000.00

Twenty-two thousand ———— xx DOLLARS

Lawrence Exeter Sr.

**Check 7**

LOS ANGELES, CALIF. Nov. 18th 19 26 No. _____

HOLLYWOOD STATE BANK 90-984
6801 SANTA MONICA BOULEVARD

PAY TO THE ORDER OF Beverly Diamond & Gift Shoppe $678.45

Six hundred & seventy-eight ———— 45/ DOLLARS

Lawrence Exeter Sr.

**Check 8**

LOS ANGELES, CALIF. Nov. 16th 19 26 No. _____

HOLLYWOOD STATE BANK 90-984
6801 SANTA MONICA BOULEVARD

PAY TO THE ORDER OF Hawaii Steamship Co. $560.00

Five hundred & sixty ———— xx DOLLARS

Lawrence Exeter Sr.

**Check 9**

LOS ANGELES, CALIF. Nov. 21st 19 26 No. _____

HOLLYWOOD STATE BANK 90-984
6801 SANTA MONICA BOULEVARD

PAY TO THE ORDER OF Lawrence Exeter, Junior $200,000.00

Two hundred thousand ———— xx DOLLARS

Lawrence Exeter Sr.

**Check 10**

LOS ANGELES, CALIF. Nov. 22nd 19 26 No. _____

HOLLYWOOD STATE BANK 90-984
6801 SANTA MONICA BOULEVARD

PAY TO THE ORDER OF Ambassador Hotel $2,250.00

Twenty-two hundred & fifty ———— xx DOLLARS

Lawrence Exeter Sr.

**Check 11**

LOS ANGELES, CALIF. Dec. 1st 19 26 No. _____

HOLLYWOOD STATE BANK 90-984
6801 SANTA MONICA BOULEVARD

PAY TO THE ORDER OF University Club Florists $183.50

One hundred & eighty-three ———— 50/ DOLLARS

Lawrence Exeter Sr.

**Check 12**

LOS ANGELES, CALIF. Feb. 18 19 27 No. _____

HOLLYWOOD STATE BANK 90-984
6801 SANTA MONICA BOULEVARD

PAY TO THE ORDER OF Cocoanut Grove Sweet Shoppe $27.00

Twenty-seven ———— DOLLARS

Lawrence Exeter Jr.

LOS ANGELES, CALIF. *July 16* 19 *27* No. _____

## HOLLYWOOD STATE BANK 90-984
### 6801 SANTA MONICA BOULEVARD

PAY TO THE ORDER OF *Parisian Gown Shoppe*   *$25 00*

*Nine hundred, twenty five* ~~~~ DOLLARS

*Lawrence Exeter, Jr.*

---

LOS ANGELES, CALIF. *Dec. 1* 19 *27* No. _____

## HOLLYWOOD STATE BANK 90-984
### 6801 SANTA MONICA BOULEVARD

PAY TO THE ORDER OF *Anita Lingerie Salon*   *$750 00*

*Seven hundred, fifty* ~~~~ DOLLARS

*Lawrence Exeter Jr.*

---

LOS ANGELES, CALIF. *April 1* 19 *28* No. _____

## HOLLYWOOD STATE BANK 90-984
### 6801 SANTA MONICA BOULEVARD

PAY TO THE ORDER OF *Parisian Gown Shoppe*   *$150 00*

*Eleven hundred, fifty* ~~~~ DOLLARS

*Lawrence Exeter, Jr.*

---

LOS ANGELES, CALIF. *Nov. 1* 19 *28* No. _____

## HOLLYWOOD STATE BANK 90-984
### 6801 SANTA MONICA BOULEVARD

PAY TO THE ORDER OF *Moderne Sportte Shoppe*   *$562 00*

*Five hundred, sixty two* ~~~~ DOLLARS

*Lawrence Exeter, Jr.*

---

LOS ANGELES, CALIF. *July 1* 19 *29* No. _____

## HOLLYWOOD STATE BANK 90-984
### 6801 SANTA MONICA BOULEVARD

PAY TO THE ORDER OF *The Bootery*   *$45 25*

*One hundred, forty-five* ~ *25/* DOLLARS

*Lawrence Exeter, Jr.*

---

LOS ANGELES, CALIF. *Aug 23* 19 *29* No. _____

## HOLLYWOOD STATE BANK 90-984
### 6801 SANTA MONICA BOULEVARD

PAY TO THE ORDER OF *Tony Spagoni*   *$26 00*

*One hundred, twenty six* ~ DOLLARS

*Lawrence Exeter Jr.*

---

LOS ANGELES, CALIF. *Aug 30* 19 *29* No. _____

## HOLLYWOOD STATE BANK 90-984
### 6801 SANTA MONICA BOULEVARD

PAY TO THE ORDER OF *Tony Spagoni*   *$26 00*

*One hundred, twenty six* ~~~~ DOLLARS

*Lawrence Exeter, Jr.*

---

LOS ANGELES, CALIF. *May 25* 19 *30* No. _____

## HOLLYWOOD STATE BANK 90-984
### 6801 SANTA MONICA BOULEVARD

PAY TO THE ORDER OF *University Club Florists*   *$87 00*

*Eighty seven* ~~~~ DOLLARS

*Lawrence Exeter, Jr.*

---

LOS ANGELES, CALIF. *May 28* 19 *30* No. _____

## HOLLYWOOD STATE BANK 90-984
### 6801 SANTA MONICA BOULEVARD

PAY TO THE ORDER OF *Broadway Diamond Co.*   *$575 00*

*Five hundred, seventy five* ~ DOLLARS

*Lawrence Exeter Jr.*

---

LOS ANGELES, CALIF. *Nov. 13* 19 *30* No. _____

## HOLLYWOOD STATE BANK 90-984
### 6801 SANTA MONICA BOULEVARD

PAY TO THE ORDER OF *Miss Flossie Wentworth*   *$50,000 00*

*Fifty thousand* ~~~~ DOLLARS

*Lawrence Exeter, Jr.*

---

LOS ANGELES, CALIF. *Nov. 14* 19 *30* No. _____

## HOLLYWOOD STATE BANK 90-984
### 6801 SANTA MONICA BOULEVARD

PAY TO THE ORDER OF *Wall & Smith, attys. at Law*   *$525 00*

*Five hundred twenty five* ~ DOLLARS

*Lawrence Exeter, Jr.*

---

LOS ANGELES, CALIF. *Nov. 15* 19 *30* No. _____

## HOLLYWOOD STATE BANK 90-984
### 6801 SANTA MONICA BOULEVARD

PAY TO THE ORDER OF *Mrs. Lawrence Exeter, Jr.*   *$5000 00*

*Five thousand* ~~~~ DOLLARS

*Lawrence Exeter, Jr.*

LOS ANGELES, CALIF. *June 20* 19 *31*   No. _____

**HOLLYWOOD STATE BANK** 90-984
6801 SANTA MONICA BOULEVARD

PAY TO THE ORDER OF *Clerk, Reno Municipal Court* $52 00

*Fifty-two* ——————————— DOLLARS

*Lawrence Exeter, Jr.*

---

LOS ANGELES, CALIF. *June 20* 19 *31*   No. _____

**HOLLYWOOD STATE BANK** 90-984
6801 SANTA MONICA BOULEVARD

PAY TO THE ORDER OF *Marie Wharton Exeter*   $75,000

*One hundred seventy five thousand* ——— DOLLARS

*Lawrence Exeter, Jr.*

---

LOS ANGELES, CALIF. *June 20* 19 *31*   No. _____

**HOLLYWOOD STATE BANK** 90-984
6801 SANTA MONICA BOULEVARD

PAY TO THE ORDER OF *Walker & Walker*   $700 00

*Seven hundred* ——————————— DOLLARS

*Lawrence Exeter, Jr.*

---

LOS ANGELES, CALIF. *June 20* 19 *31*   No. _____

**HOLLYWOOD STATE BANK** 90-984
6801 SANTA MONICA BOULEVARD

PAY TO THE ORDER OF *Wall & Smith*   $450 00

*Four hundred fifty* ——————— DOLLARS

*Lawrence Exeter Jr.*

---

LOS ANGELES, CALIF. *July 1* 19 *31*   No. _____

**HOLLYWOOD STATE BANK** 90-984
6801 SANTA MONICA BOULEVARD

PAY TO THE ORDER OF *Tony Spagoni*   $100 00

*One hundred* ——————————— DOLLARS

*Lawrence Exeter, Jr.*

---

LOS ANGELES, CALIF. *July 2* 19 *31*   No. _____

**HOLLYWOOD STATE BANK** 90-984
6801 SANTA MONICA BOULEVARD

PAY TO THE ORDER OF *Tony Spagoni*   $100 00

*One hundred* ——————————— DOLLARS

*Lawrence Exeter, Jr.*

---

LOS ANGELES, CALIF. *July 3* 19 *31*   No. _____

**HOLLYWOOD STATE BANK** 90-984
6801 SANTA MONICA BOULEVARD

PAY TO THE ORDER OF *Peter Ventizzi*   $25 00

*Twenty-five* ——————————— DOLLARS

*Lawrence Exeter Jr.*

---

LOS ANGELES, CALIF. *July 5th* 19 *31*   No. _____

**HOLLYWOOD STATE BANK** 90-984
6801 SANTA MONICA BOULEVARD

PAY TO THE ORDER OF *Hollywood Hospital*   $100 00

*One hundred* —————————— xx DOLLARS

*Lawrence Exeter, Jr.*

---

LOS ANGELES, CALIF. *July 15th* 19 *31*   No. _____

**HOLLYWOOD STATE BANK** 90-984
6801 SANTA MONICA BOULEVARD

PAY TO THE ORDER OF *Dr. David M. McCoy*   $175 00

*One hundred & seventy-five* —— xx DOLLARS

*Lawrence Exeter Jr.*

---

LOS ANGELES, CALIF. *July 16th* 19 *31*   No. _____

**HOLLYWOOD STATE BANK** 90-984
6801 SANTA MONICA BOULEVARD

PAY TO THE ORDER OF *Hollywood Mortuary*   $1,280 00

*Twelve hundred & eighty* ——— xx DOLLARS

*Lawrence Exeter*

---

**Source:** Courtesy Vanity Fair. Copyright © 1932 (renewed 1960) by The Condé Nast Publications Inc.

## Text Structure, Comprehension, and Learning

Another important aspect of cognition merits consideration. Participation in the "Ordeal by Cheque" activity not only reinforces the powerful role that prior knowledge plays in interpreting text but also illustrates the importance of the text itself. The conceptual and structural demands in a text selection influence comprehension. Readers must search for and find relationships among pieces of information (often called propositions) and concepts.

Pearson and Johnson (1978) bemusedly note that the readers of their book *Teaching Reading Comprehension* had encountered "the word *relation* so often that you are near the point of hoping you never see it again. We have used it often, because that is what we think comprehension is about—seeing relations among concepts and propositions" (p. 228). Most authors do not write carelessly or aimlessly. They impose structure—an organization among ideas—on their writings. Perceiving structure in text material improves learning and retention. When students are shown how to see relationships among concepts and propositions, they are in a better position to respond to meaning and to distinguish important from less important ideas.

Educational psychologists from Thorndike (1917) to Kintsch (1977) and Meyer and Rice (1984) have shown that organization is a crucial variable in learning and memory. Likewise, for more than 50 years, reading educators have underscored the recognition and use of text organization as essential processes underlying comprehension and retention (Salisbury 1934; Smith 1964; Niles 1965 and Herber 1978).

**Identifying Text Patterns.** Content area texts are written to inform. This is why exposition is the primary mode of discourse found in texts. This is not to say that some authors won't at times attempt to persuade or entertain their readers. They may. However, their primary business is to *tell, show, describe,* or *explain.* It stands to reason that the more logically connected one idea is to another, dependent on the author's informative purpose, the more coherent is the description or the explanation.

*Text patterns* represent the different types of logical connections among the important and less important ideas in expository material. A case can be made for five text patterns that seem to predominate in expository writing: *description, sequence, comparison-contrast, cause-effect,* and *problem-solution.*

Here are descriptions and examples for these top-level structures.

1. *Description.* Listing information about a topic, event, object, person, idea, etc. (facts, characteristics, traits, features), usually qualifying the listing by criteria such as size or importance. This pattern connects ideas through description by listing the important characteristics or attributes of the topic under consideration. Niles (1965) and Bartlett (1978) find the description pattern to be the most common textbook organization. An example follows:

There were several points in the fight for freedom of religion. One point was that religion and government should be kept apart. Americans did not want any form of a national church as was the case in England. Americans made sure that no person would be denied his or her religious beliefs.

2. *Sequence.* Putting facts, events, or concepts into a sequence. An author will trace the development of the topic or give the steps in the process. Time reference may be explicit or implicit, but a sequence is evident in the pattern. The following paragraph illustrates the pattern:

John F. Kennedy was the Democratic candidate for President when in October 1960 he first suggested there should be a Peace Corps. After he was elected, Kennedy asked his brother-in-law, Sargent Shriver, to help set up a Peace Corps. In March 1961 Kennedy gave an order to create the organization. It wasn't until September that Congress approved the Peace Corps and appropriated the money to run it for one year.

3. *Comparison-contrast.* Pointing out likenesses (comparison) and/or differences (contrast) among facts, people, events, concepts, etc. Study the example below:

Castles were built for defense, not comfort. In spite of some books and movies that have made them attractive, castles were cold, dark, gloomy places to live. Rooms were small and not the least bit charming. Except for the great central hall or the kitchen, there were no fires to keep the rooms heated. Not only was there a lack of furniture, but what there was was uncomfortable.

4. *Cause-effect.* Showing how facts, events, or concepts (effects) happen or come into being because of other facts, events, or concepts (causes). Examine the paragraph below for cause and effects:

The fire was started by sparks from a campfire left by a careless camper. Thousands of acres of important watershed burned before the fire was brought under control. As a result of the fire, trees and the grasslands on the slopes of the valley were gone. Smoking black stumps were all that remained of tall pine trees.

5. *Problem-solution.* Showing the development of a problem and the solution(s) to the problem. Consider the following example:

The skyrocketing price of oil in the 1970s created a serious problem for many Americans. The oil companies responded to the high cost of purchasing oil by searching for new oil supplies. This resulted in new deposits being found in some third world nations, such as Nigeria. Oil companies also began drilling for oil on the ocean floor, and scientists discovered ways to extract oil from a rock known as oil shale.

Authors often showcase text patterns by giving readers clues or signals that will help them figure out the structure they are using. Readers usually become aware of the pattern if they are looking for the signals. A signal may be a word or a phrase that helps the reader follow the writer's thoughts. Linguists call these words *connectives,* or *ties,* because they connect one idea to another (Halliday and Hasan 1976).

Study Figure 2.1 for connectives that authors use to call attention to the organizational patterns just defined.

Awareness of the pattern of *long stretches* of text is especially helpful in planning reading assignments. In selecting a text passage of several paragraphs or several pages from the textbook, teachers first need to determine whether a predominant text pattern is contained in the material. This is no easy task.

**Analyzing Text Patterns.** Expository writing is complex. Authors do not write texts in neat, perfectly identifiable patterns. Within individual paragraphs of a text assignment, several kinds of thought relationships often may exist. Suppose an author begins a passage by stating a problem. In telling about the development of the problem, the author *describes* a set of events that contributed to the problem. Or perhaps the author *compares* or *contrasts* the problem under consideration to another situation. In subsequent paragraphs, the solution(s) or attempts at solution(s) to the problem are stated. In presenting the solution(s), the author uses heavy description and explanation. These descriptions and explanations are logically organized in a *sequence.*

**Figure 2.1    READING SIGNALS**

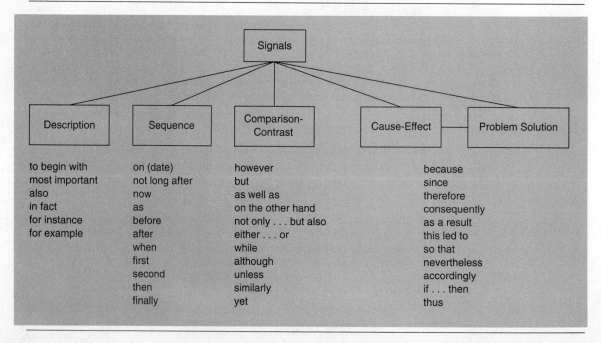

The difficulty that teachers face is one of analyzing the overall text pattern, even though several types of thought relationships are probably embedded within the material. Analyzing a text for a predominant pattern depends in part on how clearly an author represents the relationships in the text.

Several guidelines follow for analyzing text patterns. First, look for the most important idea in the text selection. Are there any explicit signal words that indicate a pattern that will tie together the ideas throughout the passage? Second, study the content of the text for additional important ideas. Are these ideas logically connected to the most important idea? Is a pattern evident? Third, outline or diagram the relationships among the superordinate and subordinate ideas in the text selection. Use the diagram to specify the major relationships contained in the text structure and to sort out the important from less important ideas.

Excerpts from five pages of text in a chapter on "Northern North America" are presented next. The chapter is from a junior high level textbook by Drummond (1978) called *The Western Hemisphere.* The excerpts provide a flavor of the predominant text pattern contained in the selection. Read the excerpts. Then study the diagram in Figure 2.2. It outlines the structure and the subordination of ideas in the material.

> The people of the United States and Canada are alike in many ways. They are similar in their language and religion. Most of the people in the United States and Canada speak English. In the Canadian province of Quebec, however, most of the people are French-speaking. In the American Southwest, many U.S. citizens speak Spanish. . . . Minor differences in pronunciation and speech habits exist from one place to another in the two countries. . . .
>
> Many different religions are found in the United States and Canada. There are more Protestants than Catholics in both countries. . . . Many Jewish people also live in the United States and Canada. Religious freedom is provided every person in both countries.
>
> Economic life is similar throughout Northern North America. Most city dwellers work in manufacturing plants or in service or sales occupations. Most people living in rural areas use power-driven tools and machines. . . .
>
> Both the United States and Canada use a *monetary,* or money system based on dollars and cents. In recent years a dollar. . . .
>
> . . . both the United States and Canada enjoy political stability. The governments of both countries are federal systems—with national governments and state or provincial governments. . . .
>
> Both countries have a Supreme Court. . . .
>
> Both the United States and Canada have developed a high standard of living by making efficient use of available natural resources. There are two main reasons for this efficiency. . . . (pp. 268–274)

Whereas text patterns specify the logical connections among ideas in expository text, *story structure* defines the basic elements of well-developed narrative material. Recently, various story grammars have been proposed by researchers to analyze a story's structure—the way it is put together.

**Figure 2.2     DIAGRAM OF TEXT PATTERN (COMPARISON-CONTRAST)**

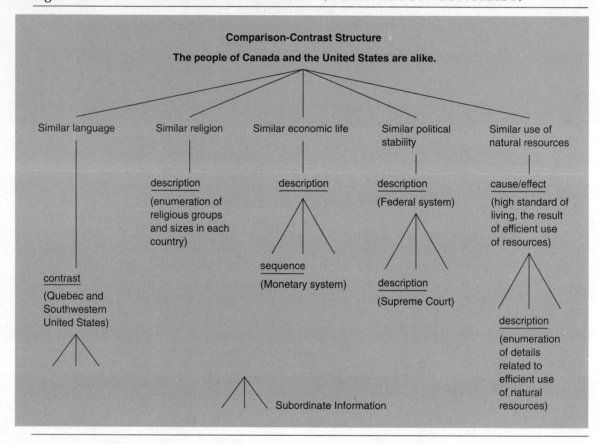

**Analyzing Story Structure.**  Most simple stories in Western culture actually aren't as simple as they might appear on the surface. During the past decade, cognitive psychologists have demonstrated how complex the underlying structure of a story can be. These psychologists have attempted to identify the basic elements that make up a well-developed story (Mandler and Johnson 1977; Thorndyke 1977; Stein and Glenn 1979). Their efforts have led to the development of several variations of *story grammar*. Just as sentence grammar provides a way of describing how sentences are constructed, story grammar helps to specify the basic parts of a story and how those parts tie together to form a well-constructed story.

What do most well-developed stories have in common? While individual story grammars may differ in their level of specificity, most researchers would agree that a narrative centers around a *setting, plot,* and *theme.* The setting introduces the main character(s) [protagonist(s)] and situates the character(s) in a time and place. The plot of a story is made up of one or more *episodes.* The intricacies of a story are often manifested in its episodic structure. A simple story has a single episode. More complex stories may have two, several, or many episodes as well as different settings. However, even a single-episode story is defined by an intricate causal chain of elements. These basic elements or events include:

- **An initiating event:** either an idea or an action that sets further events into motion.
- **An internal response:** the protagonist's inner reaction to the initiating event, in which the protagonist sets a *goal* or attempts to solve a *problem.*
- **An attempt:** the protagonist's efforts to achieve the goal or alleviate the problem. Several attempts, some failed, may be evident in an episode.
- **An outcome:** the success or failure of the protagonist's attempts.
- **A resolution:** an action or state of affairs that evolves from the protagonist's success or failure to achieve the goal or alleviate the problem.
- **A reaction:** an idea, an emotion, or a further event that expresses the protagonist's feelings about success or failure of goal attainment/problem resolution or that relates the events in the story to some broader set of concerns.

Box 2.5 contains an analysis of a popular short story often taught in a sophomore-level English course, "The Sniper," by Liam O'Flaherty.

---

**BOX 2.4    Story Analysis**

*Story:* **"The Sniper"**

*Author: Liam O'Flaherty*

| **PLOT** | **THEME** |
|---|---|
| *Episode* | |
| *Setting:* The story takes place on a June night 50 years ago in Dublin, Ireland, on a rooftop near O'Connell Bridge. | The moral dilemma inherent in war |
| *Character(s):* Two snipers opposing one another | |

*Chain of Events*

*Initiating event:* A Republican sniper is spotted and shot by an enemy sniper. The sniper is hit in the arm, so consequently he is unable to fire his rifle.

*Internal response:* The Republican sniper swears to himself in anger and resolves to shoot the enemy (Free Stater) sniper. He must eliminate the sniper in order to escape before morning's light.

*Attempt/Outcome:* The Republican sniper crawls to a new position, where he replaces his cap on his rifle muzzle, raises it, and consequently draws fire from the enemy sniper. He pretends to be dead.

*Resolution:* The enemy sniper falls for the trick and stands up, and the Republican sniper is able to kill him with his revolver. (The enemy's body falls to the street below.) He has survived.

*Reaction:* After taking a drink, the sniper's nerves are steadied, and he decides to look at the enemy sniper to see if he had known him before the army split. He also admires him for being such a good shot. Turning over the dead body, the sniper looks into his brother's face.

The episodic events in the story form a causal chain. Each event leads to the next one as the main character moves toward goal attainment or problem resolution. Determining the theme of a story involves moral, psychological, or philosophical judgment on the part of the reader. When readers evaluate the theme, they are making meaning or constructing knowledge. Involving students in the thematic content of stories is a personal process. Students' awareness of how profound the theme is will vary, depending on the background knowledge and experiences they bring to the story. However, a reader must learn to deal with theme in relation to the story's plot: What does the story *mean* to you in addition to what it tells? What is the author *trying to say* to you through the protagonist's actions? What do you see in the story regardless of what the author may have meant?

Teachers who analyze a story's structure for setting, plot, and theme are in a better position to make decisions about instruction. According to Gillet and Temple (1982), teachers can make good use of story structure depending on whether (1) there is access to reading materials that are written around perceivable story structures, (2) students have developed a sense of story structure (i.e., they have developed a schema for how stories are put together), and (3) students use their schema for stories to predict what is coming next in a new story. However, before teaching a story, Beck and her associates (1979) recommend analyzing a story for its underlying structure.

A story analysis helps you examine the story so that the questions asked during discussion will create a coherent framework for understanding and remembering the text. Therefore, a story analysis defines what most stories have in common—its key structural elements.

Most students lack the sophistication needed to engage in conversations with authors because they are still in the process of maturing as readers. The conceptual and structural demands of text are often greater than the levels of reading maturity that students bring to the task. Yet by the time they reach the middle grades, students have a need and a capacity to be self-directing and independent. To read independently, students need to know what to do when they run into trouble. They must become aware of *what* the demands of various reading tasks are and *how* to handle them. In the process of doing so, students must learn to recognize *when* or *why* they are not comprehending. Independent learning requires knowledge and awareness of cognitive processes. The psychological term for such knowledge is *metacognition.*

## METACOGNITIVE INFLUENCES ON READING TO LEARN

Students develop strategies for thinking and learning with texts. Although these strategies vary from learner to learner, they can be put to effective use when needed for specific reading tasks. The difference between skilled and less skilled readers rests in knowledge of the strategies: how to use them, when to use them, and why to use them. Good readers know how to approach text and make plans for reading. They also  know how to locate and summarize important points, organize information, and even get out of jams when they run into trouble with a difficult text. Less skilled readers often flounder with tasks that require reading content area texts because they lack knowledge of and control over the strategies necessary for effective textbook learning.

Teaching students how to become strategic readers capable of monitoring their learning is an important element of comprehension and content area instruction. As Paris, Lipson, and Wixson (1983) so aptly put it, "... thinking about one's thinking is at the core of strategic behavior" (p. 295). Teaching therefore has to go beyond the "you should" stage or a litany of imperatives. A learner needs not only exhortations, but also a good model or two.

Metacognition involves awareness of, knowledge about, regulation of, and ability to control one's own cognitive processes (Brown, Bransford, Ferrara, & Campione 1983; Flavel 1976, 1981). Simply, it is your ability to think about and control your own learning.

Metacognition, as it applies to reading, has two components. The first component is metacognitive *knowledge;* the second is *regulation.* Metacognitive knowledge includes self-knowledge and task knowledge. Self-knowledge is the knowledge students have about themselves as learners. Task knowledge is the knowledge they have about skills, strategies, and resources necessary for the performance of cognitive tasks. The second component, *self-regulation,* involves the ability to monitor and regulate comprehension through behaviors and attitudes that capitalize upon metacognitive knowledge (Baker & Brown 1984). Self- and task knowledge, and self-regulation are tandem concepts. The former are prerequisites for the latter. Together self-knowledge, task knowledge, and self-regulation help to explain how maturing readers can begin to assume the lion's share of responsibility for their own learning.

Teachers have metacognition for their particular subject areas. Translating your metacognition into lessons that students understand is the crux of content area teaching. Science teachers, for example, have metacognition for science. They have knowledge about themselves as scientists, they have knowledge of the tasks of science, and they have the ability to monitor and regulate themselves when conducting experiments, writing results, or reading technical material. Science teachers can monitor and regulate themselves because they know how to perform a set of core process strategies. They know how to observe, classify, compare, measure, describe, organize information, predict, infer, formulate hypotheses, interpret data, communicate, experiment, and draw conclusions. These are the same strategies a student taking a science course is expected to learn. A science teacher's job is to get students to think like scientists. The best way for students to learn to think like scientists is to learn to read, experiment, and write like scientists (Baker 1991).

Showing students how to think like scientists, historians, literary critics, mathematicians, health care professionals, artists, or auto mechanics puts them on the road to independent learning. To be an independent learner, students need to know the whats, whys, hows, and whens of strategic reading and thinking. They should know enough about knowing to recognize the importance of (1) using a variety of strategies to facilitate comprehension and learning, (2) analyzing the reading task that confronts them, (3) reflecting upon what they know or don't know about the material to be read, and (4) devising plans for successfully completing the reading, and evaluating and checking their progress in accomplishing the task (Brown 1978).

To accomplish this goal, teachers need to know if students know enough about their own reading and learning strategies to approach content area text assignments flexibly and adaptively. How students approach reading is the key. Different text assignments may pose different problems for the reader to solve. This is why students must be aware of the nature of a particular reading task and how to handle it when assigned text material. Is the student sophisticated enough to ask questions about the reading task? make plans for reading? use and adapt strategies to meet the demands inherent in the particular text assignment? Or does a student approach every text assignment in the same manner—plowing through or slugging along, whichever the case may be—with little notion of why, when, or how to read the text material? Plowing through cumbersome text material just once is more than most students can cope with. The prospect of rereading or reviewing seems downright dreadful. However, teachers are in a position to show students that working with the material doesn't necessarily mean twice inflicting upon oneself the agony of slow, tedious reading.

To be in command of their own reading, students must know what to do when they run into trouble. This is what the comprehension monitoring and comprehension regulation of self-regulation are all about. Do students have a repertoire of strategies within reach to get out of trouble if they stumble into a state of confusion and misunderstanding? Are they aware of how, when, and why to apply these strategies?

The experienced reader responds to situations in text in much the same manner that the experienced driver responds to situations on the road. Reading and driving become fairly automatic processes until something happens. As Milton (1982) notes, "Everything is fine for experienced drivers as long as they are in familiar territory, the car operates smoothly, they encounter no threat from other drivers, weather, road conditions, or traffic . . . . But, let even one factor become problematic, and drivers shift more attention to the process of driving" (p. 23).

And so it goes for the reader, experimenter, or problem solver who suddenly gets into trouble with a text assignment. Attention shifts from automatic processing to strategies that will help work the learner out of the jam that has arisen. The problem encountered may parallel the driver's—unfamiliar territory or getting temporarily lost. Only in the learner's case it is the text, procedure, or problem that is unfamiliar and difficult. It doesn't take much to get lost in the author's line of reasoning, the text organization, the scientific process, or mathematical formulas.

Other problems that may disrupt smooth reading might involve a concept too difficult to grasp, word identification, or the inability to identify the important ideas in the text. These problems represent major roadblocks which, if left unattended, could hamper the reader's attempts to get the gist of the text passage or construct knowledge and build meaning. It is in problem situations such as these that metacognitive processes play an important role in learning from text. The goals for students using metacognitive problem-solving processes therefore include: (1) recognizing **when** problem situations occur, (2) identifying **what** is wrong, (3) recognizing **why** the problem situation is occurring, (4) identifying **what** strategies might be used to deal with the problem, (5) selecting a strategy that gets at **what** is wrong, (6) knowing **how** to apply the strategy, and (7) **deciding** whether or not using the strategy has solved the problem and if the problem-solving process should continue.

## Factors Influencing Reading and Learning Strategies

Metacognitive knowledge and the ability to use reading and learning strategies are closely linked together. Perhaps the linkage helps to explain why many students have difficulty learning effectively. As Armbruster, Echols, and Brown (1982) explain: "Before the learner can use effective . . . [reading and learning] . . . strategies, he/she must be aware of text, task and self, and how they interact to effect learning" (p. 22). Students in content area learning situations need to consider four factors that undergrid effective learning: (1) affect and learner characteristics, (2) the nature of the reading materials, (3) the strategies to be used, and (4) the reading task that is the purpose of learning.

**Learner Characteristics and the Affective Domain.** Students need to take into account and deal with their perceptions of themselves as readers and learners. Do they have an image of themselves as competent comprehenders? Do they lack confidence? How do they deal with negative feelings toward reading and learning? Do they procrastinate? Do they lack interest in the subject? What is their motivation when approaching a text assignment? Do they do assignments just to meet minimal requirements or to get high grades? Do they have a sense of purpose? Do they pause to consider what they know or don't know about the material to be read? Have they settled into a state of learned helplessness in which they perceive themselves as unable to overcome failure? Questions such as these can be posed in brief self-awareness sessions that teachers conduct for students.

Why take the time to create teacher awareness and self-awareness of learner characteristics? According to Johnston and Winograd (1985), when poor readers don't use reading strategy, it might be because of both cognitive problems and affective factors or metacognitive self-knowledge. A learner's concept of his or her own reading ability may affect how much risk the learner decides to take in attempting to read difficult material.

Kletzien (1991) studied strategy use by high school students who were good and poor comprehenders. She found that both use the same reading strategies. The differences between the two groups relate to their willingness to try a variety of strategies and their persistence in using strategy when faced with frustration-level material. Kletzien concludes that the difference between the groups is in the regulation of comprehension strategies.

The instructional activities presented throughout this book and particularly in this chapter are powerful tools that give students a sense of accomplishment, self-confidence, and control as readers and learners. In addition, the results of the assessment procedures in Chapter 11 provide an avenue for teachers to share with students what they will need to do to be successful with print. A collaborative assessment of reading and learning strategy use is an initial step toward effective reading and learning.

**Nature of the Reading Materials.** As students prepare to read, they must consider the text material that has been assigned. How well is it organized? Is a predominant text pattern recognizable? Do the headings and subheadings signal the main and subordinate ideas in the material? Do the chapter's introduction and summary help the reader predict the author's main points? Is the text poorly written?

Older students (junior high through college) become increasingly better able to make use of extended study time than children below seventh grade (Brown and Smiley 1977). Moreover, high school students who are good comprehenders are more aware of text patterns (Kletzien 1991). The key to both of these findings lies in the older and/or better students' greater sensitivity to the way texts are organized and how the organization affects readings. These students are able to predict in advance the important elements of a text and then read effectively to identify the author's main ideas and supporting information. In short, older students and good comprehenders are able to capitalize on their knowledge of textual important and its role in comprehending.

**Reading and Learning Strategies.** Sharon Smith (1982) suggests several major categories of text activities in which mature readers engage. These categories are especially applicable to students in middle and senior high content area classrooms: cursory text activities, constructive text activities, and monitoring activities.

Cursory text activities help students to analyze the reading task at hand and devise plans for reading. These strategies involve inspectional reading. Do students know how to preview an assignment? Do they skim for main points, predict, and anticipate content? Cursory text strategies enable readers to focus on decisions: What is important? What is especially difficult? What are the key terms and concepts? What should be skipped? How should one begin?

Constructive text activities help students build meaning and process information in depth. Strategies for summarizing text, outlining, and note taking discussed in Chapter 9 help students to discriminate the essential from the inessential as well as to synthesize and organize information. What is the text about? What does it mean? What is the significance of the material? How can the meanings be used? The instructional strategies in Chapters 4, 5, 6, 7, and 8 demonstrate for students how to engage in constructive meaning-building activities.

The monitoring strategies students should consider are directly related to metacognitive awareness and experiences with text. Do students recognize reading obstacles and make conscious decisions to do something about them? Do they, for example, ignore certain problems and read on because the problem is not critical to understanding? Do students change the rate of reading—slowing down or speeding up—depending upon the purpose for reading and the difficulty of the material? Do they reread selectively? Do they monitor comprehension by checking with other students or the teacher to see if they are on the right track?

**The Reading Task.** The fourth factor that students must take into consideration is the reading task itself. Do they understand the assignment? Are the teacher's expectations clear? Are they aware that different tasks require different strategies?

Invariably a teacher will complain that students read text assignments superficially—just enough to parrot back answers to questions that accompany the text. Superficial reading occurs because students search for the portions of the text that satisfy the questions and skip everything else. Alternatives to this scenario lie in the critical tasks that teachers ascribe to reading and students' reasons for reading. If, for example, students view the purpose of reading as getting a passing grade on an assignment that consists of answering a set of assigned questions, then superficial involvement is probably justifiable. However, students must recognize and understand that reading text means more than finding answers to questions at the end of a chapter. And that's where teachers can help.

## Fix-Up Strategies

When readers find that they cannot summarize or answer questions, comprehension problems are occurring. Common comprehension problems occur when the reader does not understand:

1. a key word or words,

2. a phrase or sentence,

3. how sentences relate to one another,

4. the meaning or purpose of a paragraph,

5. how paragraphs, sections, or chapters relate to one another,

6. the meaning or purpose of extended text.

Common comprehension problems also occur because of confusion when:

1. text information doesn't agree with what the reader already knows,

2. ideas don't fit together because one can't tell who or what is being referred to,

3. ideas don't fit together because they seem contradictory,

4. information is missing or not clearly explained.

Good readers recognize when these problems occur and try to **fix up** or improve their comprehension.

Cicchetti (1990) identifies six common fix-up strategies to improve comprehension:

1. Ignore the word or phrase and read on.

2. Think of an example.

3. Think of a visual image.

4. Read ahead and connect information.

5. Reread and connect information.

6. Use text patterns, signal words, and pronouns to make connections (pp. 20–21).

Let's use the following explanation of rational numbers from an eighth-grade mathematics text to illustrate some fix-up strategies:

> **Rational numbers** are those numbers that can be written as a ratio $a/b$, where both $a$ and $b$ are integers and $b \neq 0$.*

**Ignore the Word or Phrase and Read on.** If readers get stuck on the term "rational numbers," they can *ignore the term and read on.* By doing this, they come to the definition of the term.

**Think of an Example.** If the definition of the term doesn't help, the reader can *think of an example* (like $1/3$) that fits into the ratio $a/b$, where both $a$ and $b$ are integers and $b \neq 0$.

**Think of a Visual Image.** If an example is not enough, the reader can *think of a visual image* (like a number line) on which all positive and negative integers and fractions can be located.

**Read Ahead and Connect Information.** If the reader *reads ahead* he or she will see:

positive rational numbers: $\frac{3}{4}$  0.6, or $\frac{6}{10}$  3, or $\frac{3}{1}$  0.3, or $\frac{1}{3}$

negative rational numbers: $^-\frac{5}{8}$  $^-3.7$, or $^-\frac{37}{10}$  $^-12$, or $^-\frac{12}{1}$  $^-0.16$, or $^-\frac{1}{6}$

*Houghton Mifflin Mathematics Level 8, 1987, p. 320

Rational numbers can be graphed on a number line. Positive rational numbers are to the right of zero. Negative rational numbers are to the left of zero.

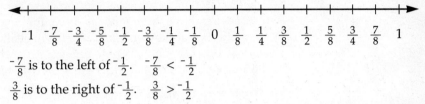

$$-\frac{7}{8} \text{ is to the left of } -\frac{1}{2}. \quad -\frac{7}{8} < -\frac{1}{2}$$

$$\frac{3}{8} \text{ is to the right of } -\frac{1}{2}. \quad \frac{3}{8} > -\frac{1}{2}$$

Now that the reader has read ahead, he or she can *connect information* like the "ratio $a/b$, where both $a$ and $b$ are integers and $b \neq 0$" correspond to the numbers shown on the number line.

**Reread and Connect Information.** If the reader has not made the connections between the definitions and the examples given in the text at this point, he or she could fix up comprehension by *rereading and connecting information*. This might only require returning to the top of the page and rereading the definition, or it might require turning back to previous lessons in which positive and negative integers were explained.

Now let's use an earth science text to further illustrate fix-up strategies:

> **Cleavage and Fracture** The way a mineral breaks also helps identify it. . . . **Cleavage** (KLEE.vij) is the tendency of a mineral to break along smooth surfaces. These surfaces follow weaknesses in the mineral's structure. Some minerals do not break along smooth surfaces. They **fracture** (FRAK.chuhr), or break unevenly.
>
> **Special Properties** Some minerals can be identified by a special property they have. For example, jade gives off a bell-like sound when you tap it. . . .
>
> **How Minerals Are Used**
>
> Minerals are useful because of their properties. They are used to make products ranging from electric light bulbs to steel.[*]

**Use Text Patterns, Signal Words, and Pronouns to Make Connections.** If readers do not initially understand cleavage and fracture but know how to use *text patterns*, they might recognize the compare-contrast pattern of the text. In comparing "cleavage and fracture," they see that all the sentences talk about "breaking." "Cleavage," however, is breaking along smooth surfaces, which contrasts with "fracture," or breaking unevenly.

If readers do not understand the connection between sentences and see *signal words* like "for example" in the second sentence of the second paragraph, this signal will help to clarify the relationships among the sentences. A bell-like sound therefore refers to a special property of jade.

If readers don't see how ideas fit together because the who or what being discussed is unknown, they can look for *pronouns* that link and connect

[*]Macmillan Earth Science, 1989, pp. 213–214

sentences. For example, the reader must understand that "they" in the last sentence of the third paragraph refers to "minerals" in the previous sentence to understand what products are made of.

Baker (1991) recommends six questions for students to ask themselves when they read to help monitor their comprehension. The six questions correspond to six standards of comprehension evaluation (lexical, external consistency, propositional cohesiveness, structural cohesiveness, internal consistency, informational completeness). The six questions are:

1.  Are there any words I don't understand?

2.  Is there any information that doesn't agree with what I already know?

3.  Are there any ideas that don't fit together because I can't tell who or what is being talked about?

4.  Are there any ideas that don't fit together because I can't tell how the ideas are related?

5.  Are there any ideas that don't fit together because I think the ideas are contradictory?

6.  Is there any information missing or not clearly explained? (adapted from Baker 1991, p. 10)

Teachers, however, cannot just tell students about fix-up strategies or just put up posters with questions for students to ask themselves as they read and expect fix-up strategies to be used. *Think-aloud* is a strategy that goes beyond telling by modeling comprehension fix-up strategies.

## Think-Alouds

In think-alouds, teachers make their thinking explicit by verbalizing their thoughts while reading orally. Davey (1983) explains that this helps readers clarify their understanding of reading and their understanding of how to use strategies. Students will more clearly understand the strategies after a teacher uses think-alouds because they can see how a mind actively responds to thinking through trouble spots and constructing meaning from text.

Davey (1983) suggests five basic steps when using think-alouds. First, select passages to read aloud that contain points of difficulty, ambiguities, contradictions, or unknown words. Second, have students follow silently and listen to how trouble spots are thought through while orally reading and modeling thinking aloud. Third, have students work with partners to practice think-alouds by taking turns reading short, carefully prepared passages and sharing thoughts. Fourth, have students practice independently, using a checklist as shown in Figure 2.3 to involve all students while verifying use of the procedures. Finally, integrate practice with other lessons and provide occasional demonstrations of how, why, and when to use the strategies to provide for transfer and maintenance.

**Figure 2.3    CHECKLIST FOR SELF-EVALUATION OF THINK-ALOUDS**

While I was reading how did I do?    (Put an X in the appropriate column.)

|  | Not very much | A little bit | Much of the time | All of the time |
|---|---|---|---|---|
| Made predictions |  |  |  |  |
| Formed pictures |  |  |  |  |
| Used "like-a" |  |  |  |  |
| Found problems |  |  |  |  |
| Used fix-ups |  |  |  |  |

**Source:** From Think Aloud—Modeling the Cognititve Processes of Reading Comprehension by Beth Davey. *Journal of Reading*, October 1983. Reprinted with permission of Beth Davey and the International Reading Association.

Five points that can be made during think-alouds are showing how:

1. to develop hypotheses by making predictions,

2. to develop images by describing pictures forming in one's head from the information being read,

3. to link new information with prior knowledge by sharing analogies,

4. to monitor comprehension by verbalizing a confusing point,

5. to regulate comprehension by demonstrating fix-up strategies.

Let's look at how each of these points can be modeled in a middle school earth science class.

**Develop Hypotheses by Making Predictions.** Looking back to the earth science text on page 53, you could model how to develop hypotheses by making predictions from the title. You might say, "From the title, 'How Minerals Are Used,' I predict that this section will tell about things that are made out of different minerals." The text continues:

> Some of the most valuable minerals are found in ores. An **ore** is a mineral resource mined for profit. For example, bauxite (BAWK.sight) is an ore from which aluminum is taken. Iron is obtained from the ore called hematite (HEE.muh.tight). Bauxite and hematite are metallic minerals.
>
> Metallic minerals are metals or ores of metals. Gold, iron, and aluminum are examples of metals. Metals are important because of their many useful properties.
>
> One useful property of many metals is malleability (mal.ee.uh.BIL.uh tee). **Malleability** is the ability to be hammered without breaking. Malleability allows a metal to be hammered into thin sheets.

**Develop Images.** To model how to develop imaging at this point you might stop and say, "I have a picture from a scene I saw in a movie about the Old West. I see a blacksmith pumping bellows in a forge to heat up an iron horseshoe. When the iron turns a reddish orange, he picks it up with his tongs and hammers. The sparks fly but slowly the horseshoe changes shape to fit the horse's hoof."

The text continues:

> Another property of many metals is ductility (duk.TIL.uh.tee). **Ductility** is the ability to be pulled and stretched without breaking. This property allows a metal to be pulled into thin wires.

**Share Analogies.** To model how to link new information with prior knowledge, you might share the following analogies. "This is like a time when I tried to eat a piece of pizza with extra cheese. Every time I took a bite, the cheese kept stretching and stretching into these long strings. It is also like a time when I went to the county fair and watched people make taffy. They got this glob of candy and put it on a machine that just kept pulling and stretching the taffy, but it never broke."

The text continues:

> Metals share other properties as well. All metals conduct heat and electricity. Electrical appliances and machines need metals to conduct electricity. In addition, all metals have a shiny, metallic luster.

**Monitor Comprehension.** To model how to monitor comprehension, you can verbalize a confusing point. "This is telling me that metals have a metallic luster. I don't know that that is. I'm also confused because I thought this section was going to be about things that are made out of different minerals. This is different than what I expected."

**Regulate Comprehension.** To model how to correct lagging comprehension, you can demonstrate a fix-up strategy. "I'm confused about what metallic luster means and I don't know why the authors are talking about this when I expected them to talk about stuff made out of minerals. Maybe if I ignore the term 'metallic luster' and keep on reading I'll be able to make some connections to what I expected and figure it all out." The text continues:

> Very shiny metals, like chromium, are often used for decorative purposes. Many metals are also strong. Titanium (tigh.TAY.nee.uhm), magnesium (mag.NEE.zee.uhm), and aluminum are metals that are both strong and lightweight. These properties make them ideal building materials for jet planes and spacecraft.

"Oh, they're talking about properties of metals that make them especially good for making certain things, like aluminum for jets because it is strong and lightweight. Now I understand why they're talking about properties. I'll bet chrome and chromium are just about the same because I know chrome is the shiny stuff on cars. I think metallic luster must mean something like shiny because chromium reminds me of chrome."

Knowledge of fix-up strategies and how to think like the teacher can be useful to students, but this knowledge is not enough. Think-alouds can provide some practice, but students need *guided* practice with feedback to become familiar with the **hows, whens,** and **whys** of self-regulation.

## Direct Explanation

Herrmann (1988) suggests using *direct explanation* for helping students understand how the reading process works. When using direct explanation, the teacher verbally models mental reasoning processes on how to monitor comprehension and how to fix a comprehension breakdown when it occurs. As the lesson progresses, the teacher shapes students' understanding of reasoning processes by having them explain how they are making sense of the text. As students explain, the teacher monitors what they say and provides additional explanation to help them reason like experts.

The following eight-step decision-making process facilitates the planning of a direct explanation lesson:

1. *Decide which reasoning processes to teach,* like how to figure out hard words and complicated terms or how to figure out what is important when reading a content area text. Then consider, "Why is it important?" and "When will the students need to use it?"

2. *Decide how the reasoning process works.* For example, when trying to figure out complicated vocabulary terms students use semantic (meaning), syntactic (structure), and graphophonic (letter/sound) information. When trying to figure out what is important, a student will find that a content text usually gives organizational and typographic aids.

3. *Collect several samples of text,* some that can be used for modeling the reasoning process and some that cannot.

4. *Look at the way the text tries to help students understand, organize, and study the content* (review questions, vocabulary activities, outlines, etc.) and decide what is helpful in explaining the reasoning process.

5. *Decide what to say when introducing the lesson* so students understand what reasoning process is being taught, why it is important, and when it should be used.

6. *Decide what to say and do* while modeling how and when to use the reasoning process.

7. *Go through the text* and look for opportunities to use the reasoning process, also noting passages that do not facilitate the targeted reasoning process.

8. *Try to anticipate problems students will have* while they are learning when and how to use the reasoning process. Select passages that can be used to clear up misunderstanding.

Direct explanation is best used at the beginning of lessons to help students learn the whats and hows of constructing meaning with text. The next teaching strategy, *reciprocal teaching,* is an excellent follow-up to direct explanation. Reciprocal teaching helps students learn how to apply the strategy learned during direct explanation so that they can understand the author's message.

## Reciprocal Teaching

Herrmann (1988) suggests reciprocal teaching for helping students figure out how to read, study, and learn with texts. When using reciprocal teaching, you model how to use four comprehension activities (generating questions, summarizing, predicting, and clarifying) while leading a dialogue. Then students take turns assuming the teacher's role. A key to the effectiveness of this strategy is adjusting the task demand to support the students when difficulty occurs. As the process goes on, you slowly withdraw support so that students continue learning. When students experience difficulty, you provide assistance by lowering the demands of the task.

When planning a reciprocal teaching lesson, there are two phases. In the first phase, there are five steps:

1. Find text selections to demonstrate the four comprehension activities.

2. Generate appropriate questions.

3. Generate predictions about each selection.

4. Locate summarizing sentences and develop summaries for each selection.

5. Note difficult vocabulary and concepts.

In the second phase, decisions are made about which comprehension activities to teach based on the students needs. It also helps to determine students' present facility with the activities so that one is prepared to give needed support during the process. After students are familiar with more than one strategy, reciprocal teaching can be used to model the decision-making process about which strategy to use. Reciprocal teaching can also be used to check whether or not the comprehension breakdown has been repaired and if not, why not.

A middle school social studies teacher decided that his students were having difficulty understanding important terms in their text that were central to understanding the author's message. He developed a lesson that combined direct explanation for construction of meaning and reciprocal teaching for understanding the author's message. The first part of his lesson used direct explanation for focusing on vocabulary when lack of understanding of key words caused comprehension breakdown. He then used reciprocal teaching to be certain that the reasoning process he had modeled during the direct explanation portion of his lesson was practiced under his guidance. He concluded by creating a mental set for application and transfer. His first step was to activate prior knowledge, have students make predictions about the selection, tell what reasoning process was going to be taught, tell why the reasoning process was important, and discuss when it would be used.

T: Today we're going to read about the U. S. Constitution. How many of you have heard of the Constitution? [Students respond.] Look at the picture at the bottom of page 119. The caption says "The people who came together at the Constitutional Convention knew they had an important job to do" [Silver Burdett Social Studies Level 5, 1986, *The United States and its Neighbors* pp. 118–119]. What are they doing in the picture?

S: There are a whole bunch of guys standing around looking at one guy writing.

T: Right, now look at page 118. What is the title of this selection?

S: "The Constitution of the United States" [Silver Burdett Social Studies Level 5, 1986. *The United States and its Neighbors* pp. 118–119].

T: Good. Now there's something I want you to know about this selection: There are some new terms that are important for you to figure out so that you can understand the author's message. Before we read the selection, I'm going to teach you how to figure them out so that when you come to them you'll be able to figure them out and understand the author's message on your own.

His second step was to think out loud to model WHEN the reasoning process should be used.

T: I'm going to pretend that I don't know a term in this story. Watch what happens. "Articles of Confederation." Hmmm. [Teacher pretends he doesn't understand a hard term.] I don't know that word, but I know it is important because it is part of a subheading. I'll skip it for now because this paragraph should tell me what it is. "With independence came many problems. The United States were joined together under one government by the Articles of Confederation" [Silver Burdett Social Studies Level 5, 1986. *The United States and its Neighbors* pp. 118–119]. Hmmm. Now I know the United States were joined or glued together by this thing. "The articles listed the powers of the central government and the powers of the states." Uh oh, this doesn't make sense to me. I'd better go back and figure this out because I've stopped understanding.

His third step was to think out loud HOW to use the reasoning process to repair the comprehension breakdown.

T: I'll sound it out, the back end looks like nation, so con-fed-er-ation. Articles of Confederation. That still doesn't tell me what it means.

Let's see, the articles listed—articles like in the newspaper—stuff written down. This stuff written down was joining the states together under one government. When I joined a club, we stuck together because we wrote down a list of rules for the members. The rules told who got to do what. [Teacher reads sentences over again.] It sounds like the Articles of Confederation is a list of rules that tells what the central government gets to do and what the states get to do. That makes sense now.

His fourth step was to check how students interpreted the information by asking them to tell or show when and how to use the reasoning process.

**T:** Now, how would you figure out the hard word in this sentence?

**S:** At first I'd keep on reading because it might tell you later on.

**T:** That's good, sometimes when you read a little further you are given a definition. What else did I think about when that didn't work?

**S:** Sounding out the word.

**T:** Sometimes that helps too, but there is something else to try. Watch and listen again. [Repeat procedure with another term.]

His fifth step was to review the title and pictures and ask for predictions before reading.

**T:** Now we're going to read the selection about the U.S. Constitution. Look at the pictures on pages 119 and 120, then read the title again. In your own words, predict what you think this selection is about. What do you expect to learn?

[Students make predictions.]

[Teacher gives positive reinforcement for making predictions, jots them on the chalkboard, then summarizes predictions.]

**T:** Now remember, there are difficult terms in this selection and when you come to one, try to figure it out like I showed you.

His sixth step was to read aloud a small portion of the text.

His seventh step was to ask a question about the content, invite students to answer, then ask individuals to share questions they had generated.

**T:** My question is: Why was the United States in danger of failing?

**S:** Because they wouldn't cooperate.

**T:** Who wouldn't cooperate?

**S:** The states wouldn't cooperate with the central government.

**T:** Correct. Does anyone else have a question?

His eighth step was to summarize what had been read by identifying the gist of that paragraph and how he arrived at that summary.

> **T:** My summary is that the Articles of Confederation didn't give the central government enough power so the United States was in danger of failing. I thought of that summary because Articles of Confederation was the subheading of this paragraph. After the paragraph told what they were, it mainly told about the problems they caused because the central government didn't have enough power, which lead up to the last line that said the United States was in danger of failing. Do you have anything that should be added to my summary?

His ninth step was to check on the reasoning process to see if it was working, helping him to figure out difficult terms.

> **T:** Is there an unclear meaning in this paragraph?
>
> **S:** Yes. It says the states were quarreling with each other.
>
> **T:** Can big pieces of land argue with each other?
>
> **S:** No.
>
> **T:** That's right. What is the author doing here?
>
> **S:** He's making the states act like people.
>
> **T:** Yes, so what does he mean?
>
> **S:** He's saying that the people living in the states were arguing, because we know two pieces of land couldn't be arguing.
>
> **T:** Good reasoning. Are there any other parts of this paragraph that are unclear? [No student response.]

His tenth step was to ask for predictions about the next segment using the new subheading and what they had already learned. He then selected a student to be the next "teacher."

After students took turns playing the role of teacher, his final step was to close the lesson by inviting students to summarize the content of the entire selection as well as when, why, and how to use the reasoning process. He also initiated transfer by creating a mental set for using the reasoning process in future reading by explaining how the same reasoning could be applied to science or any subject area. He developed and maintained use of the reasoning process through scaffolded instruction in other subjects through modeling, guided practice, and prompting in all content area reading.

# LOOKING BACK, LOOKING FORWARD

Content area reading is exemplified by the concept of learning *with* texts. Cognitive processes involved in reading are the means by which authors and readers link minds and engage in learning conversations. In this chapter, we explored some of the influences and processes underlying reading to learn in content classrooms. In particular, we emphasized the role that schema plays in comprehension. Schema or prior knowledge allows readers to (1) seek and select, (2) organize text information, and (3) elaborate information encountered in texts.

The way authors organize their ideas is another powerful factor in learning with texts. Because authors write to communicate, they organize ideas to make them accessible to readers. A well-organized text is a considerate one. The text patterns that authors use to organize their ideas revolve around sequence, description, comparison-contrast, cause-effect, and problem-solution. The more students perceive text patterns the more likely they are to remember and interpret ideas encountered in reading.

The components of metacognition were also explained because of their importance in teaching students how to become strategic readers capable of monitoring their own learning. Students need to be aware of how they interact with texts in content area learning situations. Also, we explored in this chapter how to teach for metacognition, with the goal of making students more aware, confident, and competent in using strategies for comprehension and learning. Fix-up strategies, think-alouds, direct explanation, and reciprocal teaching were explained with examples from actual classroom situations.

How do content area teachers bring students and texts together within the context of active learning environments? The key lies in how you plan for content literacy. In the next chapter, you will explore an instructional framework for single-text lessons as well as thematic unit planning that allows you to coordinate a variety of texts with a wide range of instructional alternatives. As part of planning, you will also consider the role of discussion and collaborative, cooperative learning experiences in bringing students and texts together.

## SUGGESTED READINGS

Anderson, R. C. (1984). Role of reader's schema in comprehension, learning, and memory. In Anderson, R., Osborn, J., & Tierney, R. (eds.), *Learning to read in American schools: Basal readers and content tests.* Hillsdale, NJ: Erlbaum.

Brown, A., Armbruster, B., & Baker, L. (1986). The role of metacognition in reading and studying. In Orasanu, J. (ed.), *Reading Comprehension: From research to practice.* Hillsdale, NJ: Erlbaum.

Flavell, J. (1979). Metacognition and cognitive monitoring. *American Psychologist. 24,* 906–911.

Herrmann, B. A. (1988). Two approaches from helping poor readers become more strategic. *The Reading Teacher, 43,* 24–28.

McGee, L. M. (1982). Awareness of text structure: Effects on children's recall of expository text. *Reading Research Quarterly, 17*, 581–590.

Muth, K. D. (ed.). (1990). *Children's comprehension of text: Research into practice.* Newark, DE: International Reading Association.

Paris, S. G., Wasik, B. A., & Turner, J. C. (1991). The development of strategic readers. In Pearson, P. D., Barr, R., Kamil, M. L., & Mosenthal, P. (eds.), *Handbook of reading research, Vol. II.* New York: Longman.

Pearson, P. D. (1985), Changing the face of reading comprehension instruction. *The Reading Teacher, 38*, 724–738.

Rosenblatt, L. (1978). *The reader, the text, the poem.* Carbondale, IL: Southern Illinois University Press.

# 3

# Bringing Learners and Texts Together

To win without risk is to triumph without glory.

—*Pierre Corneille*

## ORGANIZING PRINCIPLE

Bringing learners and texts together is not without its risks or its rewards. Without risks, teaching often lacks adventure and innovation. Adventuresome teachers have enough confidence in themselves to experiment with instructional alternatives, even if they are uncertain of the outcomes. They are willing to go out on a creative limb and then reflect upon what they do and why. If there is such a thing as glory in teaching, it often accompanies the teacher who dares to depart from the norm.

When students use reading and writing to learn, there's little room for assign-and-tell practices, passive learning, or students sitting in straight rows with little opportunity for interaction. Teachers who create active learning environments in their classrooms know that something not worth doing isn't worth doing well. This is especially true of passive text learning. Showing students how to use literacy to learn academic content is worth doing—and worth doing well. The time it takes to plan for reading will get the results you want: active and purposeful learning of text materials. What planning does is give the teacher a blueprint for making decisions. The blueprint may be for a single text assignment or for multiple reading experiences involving a variety of texts. The organizing principle underscores the importance of active text learning in content area classrooms: *Bringing learners and texts together involves putting plans and practices to work that result in active student involvement and collaboration.*

How teachers plan lessons and units of study are cornerstones in content area reading. As you prepare to read this chapter, ask yourself why "the classroom context"—the physical, psychological, and social environments that evolve from the interactions among teachers, students, and texts—is positioned at the center of the Chapter Overview.

## CHAPTER OVERVIEW

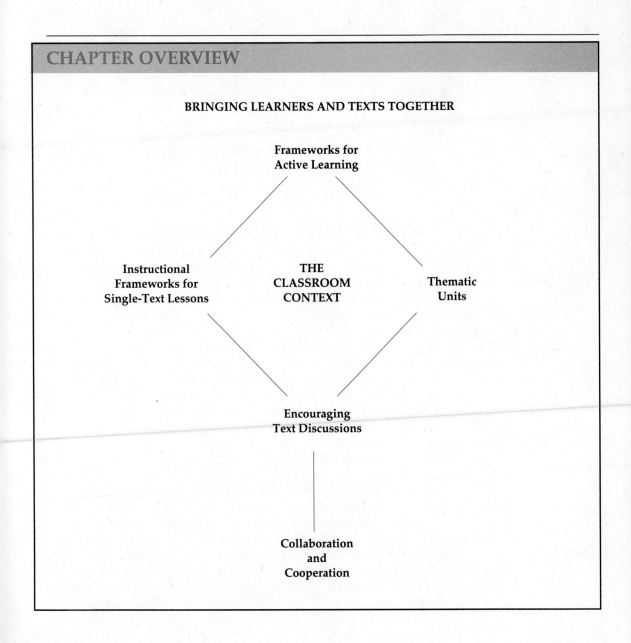

**BRINGING LEARNERS AND TEXTS TOGETHER**

Frameworks for
Active Learning

Instructional
Frameworks for
Single-Text Lessons

THE
CLASSROOM
CONTEXT

Thematic
Units

Encouraging
Text Discussions

Collaboration
and
Cooperation

## FRAME OF MIND

1. How can content teachers organize instruction so that students will become actively involved in reading? Why do readers need structure?

2. What is involved in designing an instructional framework for a single text assignment?

3. How does planning a thematic unit help the teacher to coordinate instructional activities and a multitude of texts?

4. What kinds of discussion can students engage in as they interact with texts and one another? How can teachers create an environment for text-related discussions?

5. Why are cooperative groups and team learning useful for text-related discussions?

The faculty room is a gathering place. Observe, some time, the pockets of human activity that form. When they are not talking shop with one another, it's not surprising to see a group of teachers staking out territory along speciality lines. During any given free period English teachers might be heard discussing a current best-seller, social studies teachers hotly debating the latest world crisis, or science teachers questioning the validity of the greenhouse effect on global warming.

Good teachers know their subject matter. Professional competence is often judged according to how well informed and up to date a colleague is in a particular field. Good teachers also know that an intimate knowledge of a subject in itself isn't a sure ticket to success in the classroom. Another aspect of professional competence lies in getting content across to students.

Getting content across is always a challenging task. The challenge is more pronounced than ever when texts become a vehicle for learning. To be able to bring learners and texts together isn't a small feat, but neither is it an impossible one.

Assign-and-tell practices are deeply rooted in the culture of American schools. The sight of a teacher shouting a reading assignment to students as they hustle out the door at the end of the period probably continues to happen more than we would like to admit. Under these conditions the reading assignment is purposeless. Why read it? The answer students give too frequently is "because it was assigned." The only real purpose for such reading is to get through the material. Getting through is the prime motivation when the assignment lacks any sense of where students are going and how they will get there.

Answering questions at the end of the selection is an important part of the getting-through syndrome. A favorite ploy of some students is to give the teacher a three-liner—an answer to a question that fills up three lines on a sheet of paper. Whether or not the response is thought out or fully developed, three lines suffice.

The class discussion that follows such an assignment usually slips quickly away from students to the teacher. If students can't or won't learn the material through reading, they'll get it through lecture or other means.

Mark Twain wrote in *Life on the Mississippi*, "I'll learn him or I'll kill him!" The same principle applies in spirit to assign-and-tell practices in classrooms. If students learn anything, they learn that they don't have to read course material because there are alternative routes to acquiring the information. The end result is passive reading or no reading at all.

By now, our bias as authors is evident: Texts should be an important part of the *classroom context* in which teaching and learning occur. The interactions and transactions among teachers, students, and texts form the very basis for classroom communication, comprehension, and learning. To bring students and texts together requires an appreciation of the *classroom context*.

## THE CLASSROOM CONTEXT

What happens in a particular class on a particular day depends on the interactions that occur among the teacher, the students, and the material being studied. The classroom context, generally speaking, refers to all those factors that influence what happens during teaching. These factors operate on different levels.

On one level, for example, the *physical context* influences what happens in the classroom. Space may constrain or restrict participation depending on how a teacher interprets the situation. You see, the decision is still the teacher's to make. A math teacher explained why she didn't decide on small-group work in one class but permitted it in another. "I didn't go with group problem solving in my second-period class . . . too many unruly students and not enough room to spread them apart." Some teachers use their surroundings to promote learning. Bulletin boards reflect themes or topics being studied; a display area prominently arrays students' written work for others to read. Of course, some teachers remain oblivious to the physical environment that they and students inhabit together. A room, after all, is just a room. It's the interaction that counts. Interactions are first and foremost social. And because they are social, interactions involve language, both verbal and nonverbal.

The *social context* for learning has a tremendous effect on what happens in the classroom. The social environment depends on what teachers and students do together. Classroom learning is as much collaborative as it is individual. It often involves on-the-spot decision making: Who gets to do what? with whom? when? where? Because most learning situations in the classroom are face-to-face encounters, they necessarily entail language. Most instructional routines, therefore, build upon a series of conversational acts between teacher and students, and students and students. These acts are governed by rules (Green and Harker 1982). Students quickly learn the rules and interact with the teacher or other students accordingly.

In content area classrooms, communication between teacher and students, students and other students, and students and authors always occurs within a *language context,* that is to say, the *pragmatic* or practical situation in which reading, writing, talking, and listening take place.

A math teacher assigns a chapter section on the topic "Angles," as well as several problems to be solved using information from the text. The context includes the students' purposes, the reading task, the set of relationships established over time between the math teacher and the students, the relationship of the students to the author(s) of the textbook, and all the conditions surrounding the learning situation. The context affects the way students will interact with the text and the quality of that interaction. The students' purposes, for example, will influence how they read the material. The task—reading to solve problems—also affects the way students will approach the text and tackle the assignment.

The classroom context is a source of study and fascination for teachers who search for meaning in what they do. Teaching is tough, complicated, and demanding work that doesn't get easier with time, just better. It gets better because teachers are learners. And one of the ways a teacher learns best is through on-the-job experience. The more experienced you become at what you do, the more you develop "craft knowledge" or wisdom of practice (Leinhardt 1990).

*Pathima, mathima* is an old Greek expression. Loosely translated, it means, "You learn from the things that happen to you." And teachers do. The problem, of course, is that it is difficult to learn about teaching from experience if you're not tuned in to the context in which teaching and learning occur.

The development of craft knowledge about content literacy practices begins with the awareness that reading to learn involves a departure from assign-and-tell routines. Tuning in to the classroom context leads a teacher to ask, "How can I create active learning environments where students not only act upon ideas encountered in texts, but also interact with one another?" Bringing students and texts together requires you to tune in to those classroom factors and conditions that support active learning and then plan frameworks for instruction that will get you the results you seek.

Someone in the world of business once said that 90 percent of your results come from activities that consume 10 percent of your time. Applied to education, the time teachers take to plan and organize active learning environments is time well spent. Planning appropriate frameworks for instruction may include the design of lessons revolving around single text assignments or thematic units revolving around student-centered inquiry and self-selection from an array of text possibilities.

What's the first thing that comes to mind when you think of lesson planning?

"That's as old as the ancient mariner."

"Restrictive!"

"Something I did way back when—during student teaching, not since."

We don't think any of these things, but neither do we suggest that a lesson plan must have a certain format, that objectives must be written a certain way, and so on and so forth. Instead, we contend that lesson organization is a blueprint for action, that having a plan in advance of actual classroom teaching is just good common sense.

The ability to organize a single lesson or a unit (a series of lessons) is a thread that runs throughout content area reading. A game plan is essential. Students respond well to structure. They need to sense where they are going and how they will get there when reading content materials. Classroom experiences without rhyme or reason won't provide the direction or stability that students need to enable them to grow as readers.

Lessons should be general enough to include all students and flexible enough to allow the teacher to react intuitively and spontaneously when a particular plan is put to work in actual practice. In other words, lessons shouldn't restrict decisions about instruction that is in progress, but instead should encourage flexibility and change.

Some teachers, no doubt, will still argue that a lesson plan is an outdated educational artifact, that it's too restrictive for today's learners. Yet we're convinced that "to say that lesson planning is not appropriate is to say that thinking in advance of acting is inappropriate" (Mallan and Hersh 1972, p. 41). A good lesson plan provides a framework for making decisions—nothing more, nothing less.

## DESIGNING INSTRUCTIONAL FRAMEWORKS

Teachers tend to do their planning by focusing on activities they will do with students rather than proceeding from a list of objectives to instructional activities. Time preparing single-text lessons should focus on what will be happening in the classroom; for example, what the teacher will be doing and what the students will be doing. The value of imagining should not be underestimated as a planning tool. Teachers think about instruction by envisioning in their minds how classroom activities are likely to unfold for a particular group of students in a particular instructional context. Thinking through a lesson in this manner is like playing an imaginary videotape of a lesson in which the teacher plans the questions to be asked, the sequence of instructional activity, and the adjustments to be made should something not work.

Throughout this book, we encourage you to imagine how a alternative instructional strategies and activities will work and what adjustments you might have to make in order to meet your own particular needs and fit the classroom context operating in your classroom. If you have yet to teach, we invite you to imagine how you might use strategies and activities in thoughtfully planned lessons.

There's no one way to plan an effective single-text lesson. The Instructional Framework (IF) offers the content teacher a fairly representative approach for lesson organization (Herber 1978). In Chapter 6, variations on the IF are explained. Regardless of which type of plan is used, certain provisions must be made for any reading lesson to be effective. What the teacher does *before reading, during reading,* and *after reading* is crucial to active and purposeful reading.

The IF can help teachers envision a single lesson involving reading. A single lesson doesn't necessarily take place in a single class session; several class meetings may be needed to achieve the objectives of the lesson. Nor does each component of an IF necessarily receive the same emphasis for any given reading assignment; the difficulty of the material, students' familiarity with the topic, and teacher judgment all play a part in deciding upon the sequence of activities you will organize. What the IF tells you is that readers need varying degrees of guidance. As we show throughout this book, there are prereading, reading, and postreading activities which will support students' efforts to make meaning and construct knowledge through integrated language use. Components of an IF can be examined in Figure 3.1.

## Before, During, and After Reading

An IF that includes activity and discussion before reading reduces the uncertainty students bring to an assignment. Prereading activities get students ready to read, to approach text material in a critical frame of mind, and to seek answers to questions they have raised about the material.

During the prereading phase of instruction, a teacher often places emphasis on one or more of the following: (1) motivating readers, (2) building and activating prior knowledge, (3) introducing key vocabulary and concepts, and (4) developing metacognitive awareness of the task demands of the assignment and the strategies necessary for effective learning.

A key factor related to motivation involves activating students' interest in the text reading. However, before taking into consideration how to motivate students, a fundamental question first needs to be raised: "Why should students be interested in this lesson?" Upon reflection, a teacher may even wish to consider whether he or she is interested in the material! If teachers are going to be models of enthusiasm for students, then the first step is to find something in the material to really get excited about. Enthusiasm—it is almost too obvious to suggest—is contagious.

**Figure 3.1**   **THE INSTRUCTIONAL FRAMEWORK (IF) IN CONTENT AREAS**

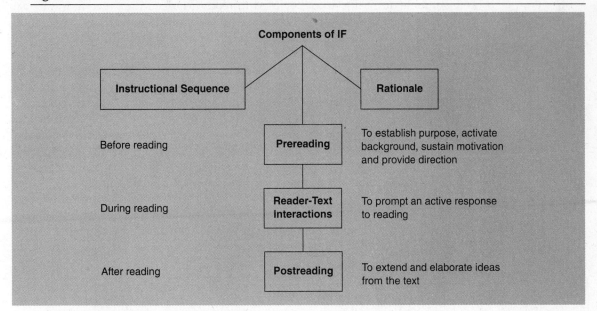

Building and activating prior knowledge for a lesson and presenting key vocabulary and concepts are also essential to prereading preparation. In making decisions related to prior knowledge, it's important to review previous lessons in light of present material. What does yesterday's lesson have to do with today's? Will students make the connection to previously studied material? Sometimes several minutes of review prior to forging ahead into uncharted realms of learning can make all the difference in linking new information to old. Furthermore, when deciding which vocabulary terms to single out for prereading instruction, we emphasize three questions that should be considered: What key words will students need to understand? Are all the terms equally important? Which new words carry heavy concept loads?

Prereading might also include discussions that develop awareness of the reading task at hand and the strategies needed to handle the task effectively. These are metacognitive discussions. Providing direction is another way of saying that students will develop task knowledge and self-knowledge about their own learning strategies. Helping students to analyze the reading task ahead of them or modeling a learning strategy that students will need during reading are two metacognitive activities that quickly come to mind. Several general questions to ask in planning for a metacognitive discussion are: What are the most important ideas in the lesson? What strategies will students need to learn these ideas? Are the students *aware* of these strategies?

An IF should also include provisions for guiding the search for information during reading. In other words, students need to be shown how to think with texts as they read.

Teachers easily recognize the important parts of a text assignment. Most students don't. Instead, they tend to read (if indeed they read at all) every passage in every chapter in the same monotonous manner. Each word, each sentence, each paragraph is treated with equal reverence. No wonder a gap often exists between the text material and the student.

Guidance during reading bridges the gap between students and text so that students can learn how to read selectively, to distinguish important from less important ideas, to perceive relationships, and to respond actively to meaning.

Ideas encountered before and during reading may need clarification and elaboration after reading. Postreading activities create the structure needed to refine emerging concepts. For example, a social studies teacher was nearing completion of a unit on Southeast Asia. She asked students to reflect upon their reading by using the activity in Box 3.1 as a springboard to discussion and writing. The writing and follow-up discussion refined and extended thinking about the ideas under study. The questions "Who is best qualified?" and "Who is the specialist in the field?" prompted students

---

**BOX 3.1     Postreading Activity for Southeast Asia Lesson**

I.  *Directions:* A rice farmer, a Buddhist monk, a government official, and a geographer all feel competent to speak on any of the topics listed below. Who really is best qualified? Who is the specialist in each field? On the blank line preceding each topic place the letter of the correct specialist.

(a) rice farmer
(b) Buddhist monk
(c) government official
(d) geographer

_____ 1. forested regions of Thailand
_____ 2. the life of Siddhartha Guatama
_____ 3. amount of rice exported each year
_____ 4. monsoon rains in Southeast Asia
_____ 5. harvesting rice
_____ 6. causes of suffering
_____ 7. the art of meditation
_____ 8. the Menam river basin
_____ 9. amount of rice produced per acre
_____ 10. pagodas in Thailand
_____ 11. number of Buddhists living in Bangkok
_____ 12. virtues of a simple life
_____ 13. the rice festival in Bangkok
_____ 14. the Temple of the Emerald Buddha
_____ 15. attainment of nirvana—perfect peace

II. *Directions:* Pretend you are the rice farmer, the Buddhist monk, the government official, or the geographer. Write a paragraph in which you reveal your professional attitude toward and opinion about the approaching monsoon season.

to sort out what they had learned. The teacher provided just enough structure by listing topics from various facets of Southeast Asian culture for students to focus thinking and make distinctions.

Activities such as the one in Box 3.1 reinforce and extend ideas. Writing activities, study guides, and other postreading activities are springboards to thinking and form the basis for discussing and articulating ideas developed through reading.

## Two Examples of Single-Text Lessons

At the Cleveland School of Science, sixth graders were assigned a text selection on how bees communicate. The text told the story of Professor Karl von Frisch, an entomologist who had studied bees for years. The story focused on his experimental observations leading to the discovery of communication behavior among bees. The teacher's objectives were to (1) involve students in an active reading and discussion of the text assignment and (2) have them experience some of the steps scientists go through when performing laboratory or field experiments.

Here's how she planned her instructional activities:

I. Prereading
    A. Before introducing the text, determine what students presently know about bees:

        Who has observed bees in a close-up situation?
        What do you notice about bees that seems unique to them?
        When you see a bee, is it by itself, or usually in a group?
        Why do you think bees swarm in groups?

    B. Connect students' responses to the questions to the text assignment. Introduce the story and its premise.
    C. Form small groups of four students each and direct each group to participate in the following situation:

        Professor Karl von Frisch worked with bees for many years. He was puzzled by something he had observed again and again.

        When he set up a table on which he placed little dishes of scented honey, he attracted bees. Usually he had to wait for hours or days until a bee discovered the feeding place. But as soon as one bee discovered it, many more came to it in a short time. Evidently, the one bee was able to communicate the news of food to other bees in its hive.

        Pretend you are a scientist helping Professor von Frisch. How could you find out how the bees communicate? How do they tell each other where the food is located? List ten things you could do to find out the answers to these questions.

    D. Have the students share their group's top five ideas with the class. Write these on the chalkboard.

II.  Reader-Text Interactions
   A.  Assign the selection to be read in class.
   B.  During reading, direct students to note the similarities and differences between their ideas on the board and Professor von Frisch's experimental procedures.

III.  Postreading (Day Two)
   A.  Discuss the previous day's reading activity. How many of the students' ideas were similar to von Frisch's procedures? Different?
   B.  Extend students' understanding of the inquiry process that scientists, like von Frisch, follow. Divide the class into groups of four students to work on the following exercise:

All scientists follow a pattern of research in order to form answers for the questions they have about different subjects. For example, von Frisch wanted to know about how bees communicated. He (1) formed a question, (2) formulated an experiment in order to answer the question, (3) observed his subjects in the experiment, and (4) answered the question based on the observations he made.

Now it's your turn! Tomorrow we are going on a field trip to the park to experiment with ants and food. Your first job as a scientist is to devise a question and experiment to fit your question. After we return, you will write your observations and the answer to your question. You will be keeping notes on your experiment while we are in the park.

Question:

Experiment:

Observations:

Answer:

   C.  Conduct the experiment the next day at the park. Each group will be given a small amount of food to place near an existing anthill. They will record their notes and take them back to the classroom. Each group's discoveries will be discussed in class.

By way of contrast, study how a high school French teacher taught Guy de Maupassant's short story "L'Infirme" to an advanced class of language students. The story is about two men riding in a train car. Henry Bonclair is sitting alone in a train car when another passenger, Revalière, enters the car. This fellow traveler is handicapped, having lost his leg because of a bullet during the war. Bonclair wonders about the type of life he must lead. As he looks upon the handicapped man, Bonclair senses that he has made his acquaintance a few years earlier. He asks the man if he is not the person he assumes him to be. Revalière is that man. Now Bonclair remembers that

Revalière was to be married. He wonders if he had gotten married before the accident or after the accident or if at all. Bonclair inquires. No, Revalière had not married, refusing to ask the girl to put up with a deformed man. However, he is on his way to see her, her husband, and her children. They are all very good friends.

The French teacher formulated five objectives for the lesson:

1. to teach vocabulary dealing with the concept of *infirmity*;

2. to foster students' ability to make inferences about the reading material in the context of their own knowledge;

3. to foster students' ability to make predictions of what will happen in a story in light of the background they bring to the story;

4. to foster students' ability to evaluate their predictions in light of the story;

5. to use the story as a basis for writing a dialogue in French.

Two of the activities, the *graphic organizer* and the *inferential strategy,* used in the French teacher's plan will be explained in depth in Part Two of this book. The steps in the plan are outlined here:

I. Prereading
  A. Begin the lesson by placing the title of the story on the board: "L'Infirme." Ask students to look at the title and compare it to a similar English word (or words). Determine in a very general way what the story is probably about. (A handicapped person.)
  B. On the overhead, introduce key words used in the story by displaying a *graphic organizer:*

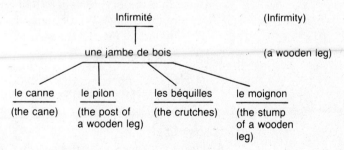

  C. Use the *inferential strategy.* Ask and discuss with the class the following three sets of questions. Have the students write down their responses.
    (1a) Vous avez tous vu quelqu'un qui est très estropié à cause de la perte d'une jambe ou d'un bras. Qu'est-ce qui traverse votre esprit? (De quoi est-ce que vous vous demandez?)

(You probably have all seen someone who is very crippled due to the loss of a leg or arm. When you see such a person, what crosses your mind? What do you wonder about?)

**(1b)** Dans l'histoire Bonclair voit cet jeune infirme qui n'a pas de jambe. Qu'est-ce que vous pensez traverse son esprit?

(In the story Bonclair sees a young cripple who has no leg. What do you think crosses his mind? What does he wonder about concerning this person?)

**(2a)** Quand vous voyez quelqu'un qui a l'air familier mais vague, qu'est-ce que vous voulez faire? Qu'est-ce que vous faites? Quels sont souvent les résultats?

(When you see someone who looks vaguely familiar, what do you want to do? What do you do? What are often the results?)

**(2b)** Dans cette histoire Bonclair se souvient vaguement qu'il a fait la connaissance de cet infirme. Prédites qu'il fait et prédites les résultats.

(In this story, Bonclair remembers vaguely having met this man Revalière. Predict what he does and the results.)

**(3a)** Imaginez que vous êtes fiancé(e) à un jeune homme ou à une jeune femme. Puis vous avez un accident et vous êtes estropié(e). Qu'est-ce que vous feriez? Voudriez-vous vous marier? Pourriez-vous compter sur l'autre de vous aimer encore?

(Imagine that you are engaged to a young man or woman. Then you have a serious accident and are badly crippled. What would you do? Would you still want to marry? Could you still expect the other to love you?)

**(3b)** Dans notre histoire Revalière a eu un accident juste avant son marriage. Prédites ce qu'il a fait et ce qu'il a compté de la jeune fille. Prédites les résultats.

(In our story, Revalière had an accident just before his upcoming marriage. Predict what he did and what he expected of his intended. Predict the results.)

II. Reader-Text Interactions
   A. Assign the reading, instructing students to keep in mind their prior knowledge and predictions, noting possible changes in their predictions.

III. Postreading
   A. Upon completion of the reading, conduct a follow-up discussion with the class. Relate their predictions to what actually happened, noting how our background knowledge and experience of the world lead us to think along certain lines.
   B. Through the discussion, note changes and refinements of student predictions and when they occurred.
   C. Vocabulary exercise. Distribute a ditto on which is reproduced a *vocabulary-context reinforcement exercise*. All vocabulary items

studied in the prereading section would be listed along with sentences taken from the story with blanks to be filled in with the appropriate word. There are fewer sentences than word choices listed. Allow seven or eight minutes for this exercise, then call for responses with students reading (in clear French) the complete sentence.

**D**. Have the class form groups of four with at least one male and female in each group. Establish the following situation:

Une jeune fille vient d'être estropiée dans un accident de natage. Son fiancé lui a téléphoné. Il veut lui parler. Qu'est-ce qu'il veut lui dire? On frappe à la porte. C'est lui.
(A young lady has been crippled for life in a swimming accident. Her fiancé has just called. He wants to come over and talk. What does he want to talk about? There is a knock at the door. It is he.)

Think together, drawing on your past knowledge and/or experiences of situations like this. Write a group dialogue in French between the girl and her fiancé of 15 to 20 lines. What might he have to tell her? How then might she react?

Select a boy and a girl to present the group's dialogue to the class.

The two IFs have the same underlying structure. Each plan provides a set of experiences designed to move students from preparation to read, to interaction with text, to extension and elaboration of concepts integral to the material under study. The plans are developed by teachers for real instructional purposes. Neither IF should be thought of as perfect. However, they represent products that show how teachers translated knowledge about content area reading into plans for active learning. As such, the IFs reflect working models.

How teachers imagine instructional activities in single-text assignments will vary by grade level and the sophistication of the students. The same is true of developing plans for a thematic unit. In the next section, we go beyond considerations for planning single-text lessons to decisions related to a series of lessons and multiple reading experiences.

## DEVELOPING THEMATIC UNITS

While the IF lends itself to a single-text lesson, a thematic unit organizes instruction around activities, texts, and learning experiences. The thematic unit is a planning tool that includes (1) a title reflecting the thematic or topical nature of the unit, (2) the major concepts to be learned, (3) the texts and information sources to be studied by students, (4) the unit's instructional activities, and (5) provisions for evaluating what students have learned as a result of participating in the unit.

Although a thematic unit may include multiple text opportunities, this doesn't mean that a predominant source of information such as the textbook will be excluded from the unit. Thematic unit planning simply provides more options to coordinate a variety of information sources. Prereading, reading, and postreading activities become an integral part of unit teaching. When the teacher plans a thematic unit, the mesh of activities designed to achieve content-related objectives will give students a sense of continuity, and they won't get a mishmash of unrelated experiences.

Listing texts and resources is an important part of preparation in planning the unit. One reason why a unit is so attractive a means of organization is that the teacher can go beyond the textbook—or, for that matter, bypass it. Students often welcome the respite from continuous single-text instruction. A wide array of literature, both imaginative and informational, will give students opportunities for an intense involvement in the theme under study. Trade books, pamphlets, periodicals, reference books, newspapers, magazines, and audiovisual materials are all potential alternative routes to acquiring information. When a teacher organizes a unit topically or thematically with a variety of texts, students begin to assume the lion's share of responsibility for learning.

A *content analysis* is a major part of teacher preparation in the development of a unit of study. The content analysis results in the *what* of learning. It elicits the major concepts and understandings that students should learn from reading the unit materials. Through content analysis, the major concepts become the objectives for the unit. It doesn't matter whether these content objectives are stated in behavioral terms or not. What really matters is that you know which concepts students will interact with and develop. Therefore, it's important to decide upon a manageable number of the most important understandings to be gained form the unit. This means setting priorities; it's impossible to cover every aspect of the material that students will read or be exposed to.

A middle school science teacher's content analysis for a unit on the respiratory system yielded these major concepts to be taught:

1. Living things require oxygen.

2. Living things give off carbon dioxide.

3. Living things exchange oxygen and carbon dioxide during respiration.

4. When living things oxidize organic substances, carbon dioxide is given off.

5. When living things oxidize organic substances, energy is given off.

6. Sugars and starches are foods that store energy.

7. The respiratory system of living things is responsible for the exchange of gases.

8. Breathing is a mechanical process of living things, and respiration is a chemical process that happens in the cells of living things.

**9.** The body uses only a certain part of the air that we take in during breathing.

Stating these content objectives permits the science teacher to select texts and plan the *how* of the unit: the instructional activities.

The actual framework of a thematic unit will vary. For example, you might organize a unit entirely on a sequence of lessons from assignments from a single textbook. This type of organization is highly structured, and even restrictive in the sense that it often precludes the use of various kinds of literature rich in content and substance. However, a thematic unit can be planned so that the teacher will (1) use a single textbook to begin the unit and then branch out into multiple-text study and differentiated activities, (2) organize the unit entirely on individual or group inquiry and research, or (3) combine single-text instruction with multiple-text activities and inquiry.

Branching out provides the latitude to move from single-text lessons to independent learning activities. The movement from single to multiple information sources exposes students to a variety of texts that may be better suited to their needs and interests.

A thematic unit on spatial relationships for a high school art class provides an example of how a teacher planned concept objectives, activities, and materials. First she listed the major concepts to be taught in the unit:

**1.** Humans are aware of space about them as functional, decorative, and communicative.

**2.** Space organized intuitively produces an aesthetic result, but a reasoned organization of space can also lead to a pleasing outcome if design is considered.

**3.** Occupied and unoccupied space have positive and negative effects on mood and depth perception.

**4.** The illusion of depth can be created on a two-dimensional surface.

**5.** The direction and balance of lines and/or forms create feelings of tension, force, and equilibrium in the space that contains them.

**6.** Seldom in nature is the order of objects so perfect as to involve no focal point or force or tension.

Then she developed the activities and identified texts to be used in the unit. See Table 3.1. As you study the table, again keep in mind that some of the text-related activities suggested will be explored in Part II of this book.

For additional examples of thematic units, with descriptions of activities and literature sources, refer to Chapter 10, *"Learning with Literature."*

Instructional activities within the unit may be initiated through flexible grouping patterns. Whole class, small group, and individual learning are all important vehicles for classroom interaction. Interaction is another way of saying that students learn with texts in social collaboration—through cooperative effort. Students' interactions with one another permit them to pool

**Table 3.1     ACTIVITIES AND TEXTS**

| Text-related Activities | Texts |
|---|---|
| 1. Graphic organizer | Graham Collier, *Form, Space, and Vision* |
| 2. Vocabulary and concept bulletin board | |
| 3. Prereading exercise | Chapter 3, Collier |
| 4. Prereading exercise | Chapters 6 and 7 |
| 5. Reading guide | Chapters 6 and 7 |
| 6. Reading guide | Chapter 11 |
| 7. Vocabulary exercise | Chapter 3 |
| 8. Vocabulary exercise | Chapters 6 and 7 |
| 9. Vocabulary exercise | Chapter 11 |
| 10. Student's choice (list of projects for research study) | H. Botten, *Do You See What I See?* |
| | H. Helfman, *Creating Things That Move* |
| | D. McAgy, *Going for a Walk with a Line* |
| | L. Kampmann, *Creating with Space and Construction* |
| | G. Le Frevre, *Junk Sculpture* |
| | J. Lynch, *Mobile Design* |
| 11. Hands-On: | Assortment of construction materials needed for activities |
| Ink dabs | |
| Straw painting | |
| Dry seed arrangement | |
| Cardboard sculpture | |
| Positive/negative cutouts | |
| Perspective drawing | |
| Large-scale class sculpture | |
| Mobiles | |
| Space frames | |
| 12. Filmstrip | *Calder's Universe* |
| 13. Field trip to studio of a sculptress | |
| 14. Field trip to museum | |
| 15. Learning corner | Displays of artists' works with questionnaires to be filled out about them |

knowledge, to compare understandings, and to share and negotiate meanings. A classroom context that encourages discussion brings learners and texts together to explore and construct meaning.

## ENCOURAGING TEXT DISCUSSIONS

If you were to observe in a content area classroom over several days, you would be apt to notice text selections assigned along with several questions for "discussion" the next day. However, the next day's discussion may never surface. In its place you might witness quizzing, interrogating, or other forms of recitation.

Discussion can best be described as conversational interactions between teacher and students as well as between students and other students. The teacher doesn't ask questions over long stretches of time, although questions are used judiciously throughout most discussions. As a result, discussion signifies an exchange of ideas and active participation among all parties involved.

Asking questions, even those designed to get students to open up and share their understanding of text, doesn't always result in a good discussion or, for that matter, a bad discussion; just nondiscussion. It is important to recognize that many students have become used to tuning out. Because of the preponderance of noise in their daily lives, school included, they have grown accustomed to turning a deaf ear. The equivalent of noise in a classroom instructional situation occurs whenever students do not make sense out of what they are doing or what is happening (Smith 1988). Students stand a better chance of participating attentively in discussion when they have a clear sense of purpose, understand the discussion task, and are given explicit directions and clear explanations.

Different types of discussion have different purposes. Let's explore some of these purposes and the types of discussion activity that are likely to unfold when students converse about what they have read.

## Purposes and Types of Discussion

Many of the instructional activities in this book are inextricably tied to discussion of one kind or another. Discussion allows students to respond to text, build concepts, clarify meaning, explore issues, share perspectives, and refine thinking. But effective discussions don't run by themselves. For a discussion to be successful, a teacher essentially has to be willing to take a risk or two.

Whenever you initiate a discussion, its outcome is bound to be uncertain, especially if its purpose is to help students think critically and creatively about what they have read. Often a teacher may abandon discussion for the safety of recitation, where the outcome is far more predictable. A text discussion, however, should be neither a quiz show nor, at the opposite end of the continuum, a bull session (Roby 1987). Yet when discussions aren't carefully planned, students often will feel a sense of aimlessness or become easily threatened by the teacher's questions. Being quizzed about text material or just shooting the bull are apt to close doors on active text learning.

Different purposes for text discussion lead to different types of discussion being used by content area teachers. *Guided discussions* and *reflective discussions* provide varying degrees of structure for students to interact with one another in text learning situations.

**Guided Discussion.**  If your aim is to develop concepts, clarify meaning, and promote understanding, the most appropriate discussion my be *informational*. The main objective of an informational discussion is to help students grapple with issues and understand important concepts. When the discussion task is information centered, Kindsvatter, Wilen, and Ishler (1991) suggest that teachers use a guided discussion.

In a guided discussion, the teacher provides a moderate amount of structure as he or she directs students to think about what they have read through the use of questions and/or teacher-developed guide material. Because the emphasis is on content understanding and clarification, it is important to recognize the central role of the teacher in a guided discussion. This role is primarily that of *instructor*. That is to say, your responsibilities lie in asking questions, in probing student responses because clarifications are needed to extend thinking, in encouraging student questions, and in providing information to keep the discussion on course.

The instructor role is one to which most teachers are accustomed. The potential problems, however, with this role lie in teacher domination of the discussion. As Alvermann, Dillon, and O'Brien (1988) cautioned: When overused, the instructor role "can result in a discussion that more nearly resembles a lecture and frequently may confuse students, especially if they have been encouraged to assume more active roles in discussion" (p. 31).

Sometimes a guided discussion may resemble a recitation, but it differs markedly in purpose from recitation. Although there are frequent teacher-student exchanges in a guided discussion, its purpose is to help students make interpretations and share with one another what the text means to them.

A guided discussion can easily take a *reflective turn*. When teachers consciously shift gears from guided discussion to reflective discussion, so shifts their role in the discussion.

**Reflective Discussion.** A reflective discussion is different from a guided discussion in several respects. The purpose of a reflective discussion is to require students to engage in critical and creative thinking as they solve problems, clarify values, explore controversial issues, and form and defend positions. A reflective discussion, then, presumes that students have a solid understanding of the important concepts they are studying. Without basic knowledge and understanding of the ideas or issues under discussion, it would be difficult for students to support opinions, make judgments, or justify and defend positions.

The teacher's role during a reflective discussion shifts from that of instructor to that of participant. The participant role allows you to assume group membership status so that you can contribute to the discussion by sharing ideas and expressing your own opinions: "Teachers can guide students to greater independence in learning by modelling different ways of responding and reacting to issues, commenting on others' points of view, and applying critical reading strategies to difficult concepts in the textbooks" (Alvermann, et al. 1988, p. 31).

## Creating an Environment for Discussion

Discussion is one of the major process strategies in the content area classroom. Since many of the strategies in this text revolve around discussion of some sort, we offer several suggestions for creating an environment in which discussion takes place, whether in small-group or whole-class situations.

First, arrange the room in such a way that students can see each other and huddle in conversational groupings when they need to share ideas. A good way to judge how functional a classroom is for discussion purposes is to select a discussion strategy which does not require continuous question asking. For example, in the next chapter we will see how brainstorming involves a good mixture of whole class and small-group discussion. Students need to alternate their attention from the chalkboard (where the teacher or another student is writing down all the ideas offered within a specified time) to their small groups (where they might categorize the ideas) back to the front of the room (for comparison of group categories and summarization). If students are able to participate in the various stages of brainstorming with a minimum of chair moving or other time-consuming movements, to see the board and to converse with other students without undue disruption then the room arrangements are adequate or conducive to discussion.

Second, encourage a climate in which everyone is expected to be a good listener, including the teacher. Let each student speaker know that you are listening. As the teacher begins to talk less, students will talk more. Intervene to determine why some students might not be listening to each other or to praise those who are unusually good role models for others. Accept all responses of students in a positive way.

Try starting out with very small groups of no more than two or three students. Again, rather than use questions, have students react to a teacher-read statement ("Political primaries are a waste of time and money"). In the beginning, students may feel constrained to produce answers to questions to satisfy the teacher. A statement, however, serves as a possible answer and invites reaction and justification. Once a statement is given, set a timer or call time by your watch at two-minute intervals. During each interval one student in the group may agree or disagree *without interruption*. After each group member has an opportunity to respond, the group summarizes all dialogue, and one person presents this to the class (Gold and Yellin 1982, pp. 550–552).

Third, establish the meaning of the topic and the goal of discussion: "Why are we talking about railroad routes and how do they relate to our unit on the Civil War?" Also, explain directions explicitly and don't assume that students will know what to do. Many of the content area reading strategies in this book involve some group discussion. Frequently, strategies progress from independent, written responses to sharing, comparing those responses in small groups, then to pooling small-group reactions in a whole-class discussion. Without the guidance of a teacher who is aware of this process, group discussion tends to disintegrate.

Fourth, keep the focus of the discussion on the central topic or core question or problem to be solved. One way to begin discussion is by asking a question about a perplexing situation or establishing a problem to be solved. From time to time, it may be necessary to refocus attention on the topic by piggybacking on comments made by particular students. "Terry brought out an excellent point about the underground railroad in northern

Ohio. Does anyone else want to talk about this?" During small-group discussions, a tactic that keeps groups on task is to remind them of time remaining in the discussion.

Keeping the focus is one time when teachers may legitimately question to clarify the question. They may also want to make sure that they understood a particular student's comment, "Excuse me, would you repeat that?" Often, keeping the discussion focused will prevent the class from straying away from the task.

And finally, avoid ineffective behavior that is bound to squelch discussion. Try, for example, not to repeat questions, whether they are your own or the students'. Give students enough think time to reflect on possible answers before calling on someone or rephrasing your question. Moreover, try to avoid repeating answers or answering your own question. (One way to prevent yourself from doing the latter is to resist having a preset or "correct" answer in your own mind when you ask a question beyond a literal level of comprehension.) Do not interrupt students' responses or permit others to interrupt students' responses. Do, however, take a minute or two to summarize and bring closure to a group discussion just as you would with any instructional strategy.

Both guided and reflective discussions may be conducted within the context of the whole class or in small groups. A small-group discussion, whether guided or reflective, places the responsibility for learning squarely on students' shoulders. Because of the potential value of collaborative learning, we underscore the invaluable contribution of cooperative team learning.

## EMPHASIZING COLLABORATION AND COOPERATION

Active learning environments integrate whole-class, small-group, and individual learning activities. Whole-class presentation is an economical means of giving information to students when the classroom context lends itself to information sharing. A whole-class activity, for example, may be used to set the stage for a new thematic unit. The unit introduction, discussion of objectives, and background building can all take place within whole-class structure. However, the chief drawback of whole-class presentation is that it limits active participation among students. While whole-class interaction provokes discussion to an extent, it cannot produce the volume of participation necessary to read and learn actively from content materials. The teacher often reverts to showmanship to enlist the active participation of the majority of students in a whole-class discussion. We often used to wonder why many teachers ended each working day totally exhausted. Although a little showmanship never hurt a lesson, no burden seems more difficult to carry or mentally fatiguing than to feel the need to perform in order to get students involved in learning. A viable alternative lies in the use of cooperative learning groups.

Cooperative learning, simply defined, is an organizational structure in which groups of students pursue academic goals through collaboration (Hilke 1990). The goals of cooperative learning, therefore, are to foster collaboration in an academic context, to develop students' self-esteem in the process of learning, to encourage the development of positive group relationships, and to enhance academic achievement (Johnson, Johnson, and Holubee 1990).

Cooperative groups facilitate active participation and should be a primary form of classroom organization when bringing learners and texts together. Students produce more ideas, participate more, and take greater intellectual risks in small-group or team learning situations. A cooperative group, with its limited audience, provides more opportunity for students to contribute ideas to a discussion and take chances in the process. They can try out ideas without worrying about being wrong or sounding dumb—a fear that often accompanies risk taking in a whole-class situation.

## Variations on Cooperative Groups That Bring Learners and Texts Together

Bringing learners and texts together in social collaboration to engage in discussions may be achieved through the use of cooperative teams. Many variations on cooperative team learning are possible. Several cooperative grouping patterns, in particular, work well within the context of content literacy practices and text-related discussions. The cooperative groups described below give you a feel for how students might collaborate in their interactions with texts and with one another as they explore meaning and make sense out of what they are reading.

**Jigsaw Groups.**   Interdependent team learning with texts may be achieved through jigsaw groups (Aronson 1978). Jigsaw teaching requires students to specialize in a content literacy task that contributes to an overall group objective. Jigsaw groups are composed of students divided heterogeneously into three to six member teams. Each student on a team becomes an expert on a subtopic of a theme or topic that the class is reading about. Not only is the student accountable for teaching the other members of the group about his or her subtopic, but he or she is also responsible for learning the information other group members provide during their jigsaw discussions.

For example, a life-science teacher in a middle school engages students in a thematic unit on the topic of birds. As part of the unit of study, he divides the class into five six-member jigsaw groups. Each member of a group is expected to become an expert on one of the following concepts in the unit: the relationship between birds and reptiles, the adaptation of various species of birds to their environments, the migration patterns of birds, the adaptation of birds for flight, the economic importance of birds, and the identification of various families and species.

As part of the jigsaw strategy, members of the different teams who share the same subtopic meet in temporary "expert groups" to discuss what they are reading and learning. Each of the expert groups has a variety of resource materials and texts made available by the teacher to help them explore and clarify their subtopics. When the members in each of the expert groups complete their tasks, they return to their jigsaw teams to teach and share what they have learned. As a jigsaw member presents his or her findings, the other members listen and take notes in preparation for a unit exam the teacher will give on the overall topic.

**Student Teams Achievement Divisions (STAD).** Student teams lend themselves well to content area learning situations that combine whole-class discussion with follow-up small-group activity. The originator of STAD groups, Robert Slavin (1988), emphasizes the importance of achieving team learning goals, but also recognizes that individual performance is important in cooperative groups.

STAD groups work this way: The teacher introduces a topic of study to the whole class, presents new information, and then divides the class into heterogeneous four-member groups of high-, average-, and low-achieving students to engage in follow-up team study. The goal of team study is to master the content presented within the framework of the whole-class discussion. As a result, team members help each other by discussing the material problem solving, comparing answers to guide material, and quizzing one another to ensure that each member knows the material. The students take periodic quizzes, prepared by the teacher, following team study. A team score is determined by the extent to which each member of the team improves over past performance. A system of team awards based on how well students individually perform ensures that team members will be interdependent on one another for learning.

**Circles of Learning.** Johnson, Johnson, and Holubee (1990) underscore the importance of positive interdependence through a cooperative learning model. Similar to STAD, learning circles mesh whole-group study with small-group interactions and discussion. Learning circles may be comprised of two to six members of varying abilities who come together to share text resources and help each other learn. All of the content literacy activities that we present in this book can be adapted to the type of interdependent learning teams that are suggested by Johnson and Johnson. However, cooperative groups don't run by themselves. You have to plan for the success of positive interdependence by teaching students how to use collaboration skills to work interdependently in teams, and then facilitating group process as students engage in discussion and interaction.

The Johnsons suggest 18 steps for structuring circles of learning, some of which include the following: specifying content objectives, deciding the size of the group, assigning students to groups, arranging the room, planning instructional activities and guide material to promote interdependent learning, explaining the academic task, explaining criteria for success, structuring the division of labor within groups, structuring individual accountability and intergroup cooperation, monitoring students' behavior, teaching the skills of collaboration, providing task assistance as needed, evaluating student learning, and assessing how well the teams functioned.

Group brainstorming, prediction, problem solving, discussion, mapping, and writing strategies, all of which are to be discussed in Part Two, are easily woven into the fabric of cooperative learning circles. Coming to group consensus on a variety of discussion tasks is an important outcome in cooperative learning groups. Students need to be shown how to engage in a cooperative process of consensus building as they come to terms with what they can or cannot support as a result of their interactions with texts and one another.

**Group Investigation.** In this grouping pattern, students in teams of two to six collaborate on inquiry topics of interest to them within the context of a thematic unit and the major concepts of study. Each group selects a topic to investigate and cooperatively plans the inquiry in consultation with the teacher. Each research team, for example, decides how to investigate the topic, which tasks each member will be responsible for, and how the topic will be reported. The groups then conduct the investigation, synthesize their findings into a group presentation, and make their presentations to the entire class. The teacher's evaluation includes individual performance and the overall quality of the group presentation. In Chapter 9, we explore in more detail how to help students conduct and report research.

**Learning in Dyads.** Cooperative learning may also occur in dyads in which students work in pairs to help each other to read and study texts (Larson and Dansereau 1986). The pairs begin by reading two pages of text silently. After both have completed the reading, one student, the *recaller*, orally summarizes what has been read. The other partner, the *listener*, corrects any misunderstandings the recaller may have as well as clarifies or elaborates on what was read. The partners then switch roles for the next two pages. The process repeats and continues until the text assignment has been read.

Although it would be appropriate to pair two students of similar ability, it would also be beneficial to pair students of differing ability. You will achieve positive interdependence in each dyad according to the evaluation scheme that you employ. For example, you might decide to assign two performance grades: an individual grade to each partner based on a quiz of the material and a group grade based on the average of the two quiz scores. Or each dyad could receive the same grade for the assignment—an average of the two scores.

**Group Retellings.** Group retellings underscore the importance of *conceptually related readings* in which each member of a cooperative group reads a different text on the same topic. For example, Wood (1987) illustrates the use of group retellings in a health class. Students of differing ability work in groups of three or more, reading timely articles or brochures on the topic of safety in the home. A magazine article might describe an eyewitness account of a home fire resulting from an electrical overload. A brochure from the local fire department might outline the precautions to take to avoid such a mishap, perhaps emphasizing the hazards associated with an overloaded circuit. A newspaper editorial might warn parents against leaving their children unattended and unfamiliar with safety hazards in the home.

After reading, each member of the group shares what he or she has read while the other members of the team listen, and at any point share additional information and insights into the topic based on their readings. According to Wood, group retellings of this nature capitalize on the pleasure derived from sharing newly learned information with a friend.

## Structuring Cooperative Groups

Organizing learners and texts around cooperative groups shifts the burden of learning from teacher to student. However, team learning is complex. Cooperative groups don't run by themselves. Students must know how to work together and how to use techniques they have been taught. The teacher in turn must know about small-group processes. The practical question is "How will individual students turn into cooperative groups?" Anyone who has ever attempted small-group instruction in the classroom knows the dilemma associated with the question. Many conditions can confound team learning if plans are not made in advance—in particular, teachers must decide on such matters as the size, composition, goals, performance criteria of small groups, and division of labor within a group.

**Group Size.** The principle of "least group size" operates whenever you form learning teams. A group should be just large enough to include all the skills necessary to solve a problem or complete a task. A group that's larger than necessary provides less chance for individual participation and greater opportunity for conflict. If too many students are grouped together, there's bound to be a point of diminishing returns. Group size for content area reading should range from two to six members (depending, of course, on the type of reading task). Since most small-group activities will involve discussion, three- or four-member groups are probably best.

**Group Composition.** Homogeneous grouping is often not necessary for discussion tasks. Both intellectual and nonintellectual factors will influence a small group's performance, and the relationship between intelligence and small-group performance is often surprisingly low. Experiential and social background, interests, attitudes, and personality contribute greatly to the success of a cooperative group. Grouping solely by reading or intellectual ability short-changes all students and robs discussion of diversity.

Readers who struggle with the process shouldn't be relegated to tasks that require minimal thinking or low-level responses to content material. What quicker way to unintentionally initiate misbehavior than to group together students who are experiencing difficulty in reading? People learn from one another. A student whose background is less extensive than other students' can learn from them. The student who finds reading difficult needs good readers as models. Furthermore, the student who has trouble reading may in fact be a good listener and thinker who will contribute significantly to small-group discussion.

As you plan team learning situations, you should take into consideration the following critical variables: the *goal(s)* of the cooperative group, the *task(s)* in which the group is to engage, the *interdependence* of group members as they pursue goals and engage in tasks, and the *roles* and division of labor within groups.

**Group Goals and Tasks.** Team learning is goal-oriented. The manner in which goals and paths to task completion are perceived affects the volume and quality of involvement by students in the group. If group goals are unclear, members' interest quickly wanes. Goals must also be directly related to the task. The conditions of the task must be clearly defined and understood by individual members of the group.

Therefore, you should explain the criteria for task performance. For example, when students work with reading guides such as those that are suggested in this book, they should attempt to adhere to such criteria as the following:

1. Read the selection silently and complete each item on the guide individually or with others in the group, depending on the teacher's specific directions.

2. Each item should be discussed by the group.

3. If there is disagreement on any item, a group member must defend his or her position and show why there is a disagreement. This means going back into the selection to support one's position.

4. No one student dominates a discussion or bosses other members around.

5. Each member contributes something to each group discussion.

As students work on literacy activities in their groups, the teacher can facilitate performance by reinforcing the criteria that have been established.

**Positive Interdependence.** Groups lack cohesiveness when learning isn't cooperative but competitive, when students aren't interdependent on each other for learning but work independently. However, social scientists and instructional researchers have made great strides since the 1970s at understanding the problems of the competitive classroom. Researchers at Johns Hopkins University in particular (Slavin 1988; Johnson and Johnson 1987) have studied the practical classroom applications of cooperative principles of learning. The bulk of their research suggests that cooperative small-group learning has positive effects on academic achievement and social relationships. Positive interdependence can be achieved through a variety of schemes in which you award and reward students for collaborative effort (Johnson and Johnson 1990). For example, a social studies teacher attempted to have students adhere to desired discussion behaviors during their interactions in small groups (these discussion behaviors were basically the same as those discussed in the previous subsection under performance criteria). Each small group earned a performance grade for discussing text assignments in a six-week thematic unit. Here's how the group members earned their grades.

1. Each member in the group was observed by the teacher to see how well the desired discussion behaviors were exhibited.

2. On Friday of a week, each group earned a color reward with so many points: green = 1 point, blue = 2 points, black = 3 points, red = 4 points. The color that a group earned was based on how well it had performed according to the criteria for discussion.

3. Each member of the group received the color (and the points that went with it) that the total group earned. This meant that if one or two members of the group did not carry out the appropriate discussion behaviors, the entire group was penalized with a lower point award.

4. The color for each student in the class was charted on a learning incentive chart.

5. Each week the small groups changed composition by random assignment.

6. The points attached to each color added up over the weeks. When the unit was completed, so many points resulted in a performance grade of A, B, C, or D.

A curious thing happened as a result of the reward system. On the Monday of each week that students were randomly assigned to new groups, they immediately went to the learning incentive chart to check the color received the previous week by each of the other members in their new group. Motivation was high. Group pressure was such that individual students who did not receive high points the previous week were intent on improving their performance in the new group.

**Group Roles and Division of Labor.** If cooperative groups are to be successful, members must divide the work of the group among one another and understand their differentiated roles within the group. Therefore, consider assigning complementary and interconnected roles that specify responsibilities that the group needs to perform in order to accomplish a joint task. Johnson and Johnson (1990) define several roles, which may vary according to the nature of the task, some of which follow:

*Leader:* The group leader facilitates the work of the group. Leadership skills may include *giving directions* (reviewing instruction, restating the goals of the group, calling attention to time limits, or offering procedures on how to complete the task most effectively;) *summarizing* aloud what has been read and/or discussed, and *generating* responses by going beyond the first answer or conclusion and producing a number of plausible answers to choose from.

*Reader:* The reader in the group is responsible for reading the group's material aloud so that the group members can understand and remember it.

*Writer/Recorder:* The writer/recorder records the responses of the group on paper, edits what the group has written, and makes sure the group members check for content accuracy and completeness.

*Checker:* The checker makes sure the group is on target by checking on what is being learned by the members. The checker, therefore, may ask individuals within the group to explain or summarize material being discussed.

*Encourager:* The encourager watches to make sure that all the members in the group are participating and invites reluctant or silent members to contribute (Johnson and Johnson 1990).

In order for students to understand the roles and the responsibilities of each role, you will need to develop knowledge and awareness for each through a variety of metacognitive activities. Discuss each role, model and demonstrate appropriate behavior and responses, role-play with students, coach, and provide feedback during actual group discussions.

We believe the main reason for the infrequent use of small groups is the frustration that teachers experience when teams lack cohesion and interdependence. Uncooperative groups are a nightmare. No wonder a teacher abandons or is hesitant to use small groups in favor of whole-class instruction, which is easier to control. Small-group instruction requires risk taking on the part of the teacher as much as it encourages risk taking among students.

## LOOKING BACK, LOOKING FORWARD

Content area teachers can plan instruction that will lead to active text learning. Students must act upon ideas in print but also interact with one another when learning with texts. The Instructional Framework and the thematic unit provide the structure for bringing learners and texts together in content areas.

The Instructional Framework makes provisions for prereading, reading, and postreading instruction for single text lessons. This particular lesson structure helps teachers to imagine the kinds of activity to use before, during, and after reading. A unit, on the other hand, helps the teacher to organize instructional activities around multiple texts. Unit planning gives you much more latitude to coordinate resource materials and activities. Unit activities can be organized around the whole class, small groups, or individuals. The emphasis, however, should be on individual and team learning. An effective content classroom thrives on small-group interactions, team learning situations, and text discussion.

In Part II of this book numerous instructional activities, which are alternatives to assign-and-tell practices and passive learning routines, are suggested. We begin an exploration of instructional alternatives in Chapter 4 by examining the relationships between the vocabulary of a content area—its special and technical terms—and concepts. How can a teacher help students to interact with the language of a content area, and in the process of doing so, show them how to define, clarify, and extend their conceptual knowledge?

## SUGGESTED READINGS

Aronson, E. (1978). *The jigsaw classroom.* Beverly Hills, CA: Sage.

Clark, C., & Yinger, R. (1980). *The hidden world of teaching: Implications of research on teacher planning.* Research Series No. 77 East Lansing, MI: Institute for Research on Teaching.

Cooper, J. (1982). The teacher as decision maker, in J. Cooper (ed.), *Classroom teaching skills.* Lexington, MA: Heath.

Johnson, D. W. & Johnson, R. T. (1987). *Learning together and alone: Cooperation, competition, and individualistic learning.* Englewood Cliffs, NJ: Prentice-Hall.

Joyce, B., & Weil, M. (1986). *Models of teaching* (3rd ed.). Englewood Cliffs, NJ: Prentice-Hall.

Peterson, P., Marx, R., & Clark, C. (1978). Teacher planning, teacher behavior and student achievement. *American Education Research Journal, 15,* 413–432.

Sharon, S. (1980). Cooperative learning in small groups: Recent methods and effects on achievement, attitudes and ethnic relations. *Review of Educational Research 50,* 241–271.

Slavin, R. (1986). *Using student team learning.* Baltimore, MD: Johns Hopkins University Press.

Webb, N., & Kenderski, C. (1984). Student interaction and learning in small-group and whole-class settings. In P. Peterson, L. Wilkinson, and M. Hallinan (eds.). *The social context of instruction.* New York: Academic Press.

Wood, K. (1987). Fostering cooperative learning in middle and secondary level classrooms. *Journal of Reading, 31,* 10–17.

# PART II

# Instructional Alternatives

# 4

# Developing Vocabulary Knowledge and Concepts

"I hope you won't take umbrage," she said.
"No," he said, "I never take umbrage unless it's lying around and no one else wants it."

— *Sally of* Peanuts *fame, reading one of her compositions to her classmates.*

## ORGANIZING PRINCIPLE

How can anyone take umbrage with Sally's use of the word *umbrage?* She does what all of us do as we come to know words in the context of speaking, listening, writing, and reading. Language learners, like Sally, develop vocabulary knowledge and concepts by experimenting with language: using, testing, manipulating, and taking risks with words in different contexts and situations. The more experience and exposure that Sally has with unfamiliar words like *umbrage*, the more familiar and meaningful they will become to her.

Such is the case not only for words encountered in everyday discourse but also for words underlying the language of academic disciplines. Vocabulary is as unique to a content area as fingerprints are to a human being. A content area is distinguishable by its language, particularly the special and technical vocabulary terms that provide labels for the concepts undergirding subject matter. Teachers know they must do something with the language of their content areas, but they often have trouble with what that something should be. As a consequence, they reduce instruction to routines that have withstood the tradition of time and teacher-centered practice; namely, directing students to use glossaries and dictionaries to look-up, define, memorize, and use content-specific words in sentences. Such practices divorce the study of vocabulary from an exploration of the subject matter. Learning vocabulary becomes an activity in itself—a separate entity—rather than an integral part of learning academic content. In these instances, there is little awareness of the strong relationship that exists between conceptual knowledge and reading comprehension. Content area vocabulary must be taught *well enough* to remove potential barriers to students' understanding of texts as well as to promote a long-term acquisition of the language of a content area. The organizing principle underscores the main premise of the chapter: ***To teach words well means giving students multiple opportunities to learn how words are conceptually related to one another in the material they are studying.***

Study the Chapter Overview to get a feel for the major relationships among the key concepts and strategies that we will develop in this chapter. Try to verbalize these relationships by thinking aloud: What do you predict this chapter will be about? What ideas and strategies in the chapter are familiar to you? Somewhat familiar?

## CHAPTER OVERVIEW

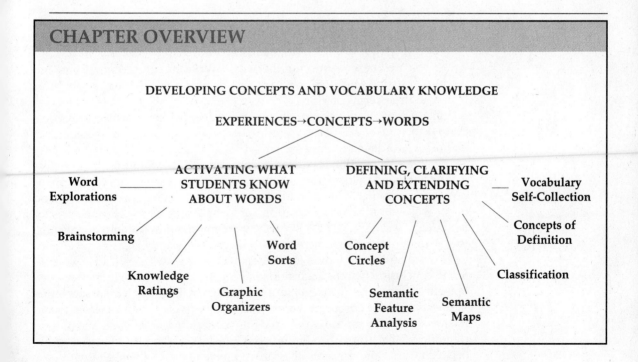

**DEVELOPING CONCEPTS AND VOCABULARY KNOWLEDGE**

**EXPERIENCES→CONCEPTS→WORDS**

**Word Explorations**

**ACTIVATING WHAT STUDENTS KNOW ABOUT WORDS**

**DEFINING, CLARIFYING AND EXTENDING CONCEPTS**

**Vocabulary Self-Collection**

**Brainstorming**

**Word Sorts**

**Concept Circles**

**Concepts of Definition**

**Knowledge Ratings**

**Graphic Organizers**

**Semantic Feature Analysis**

**Semantic Maps**

**Classification**

Also, take the time to put yourself in a frame of mind that will enable you to approach the chapter purposefully. The Frame of Mind questions raise expectations for the content presented in the chapter and will help to guide your search for information.

## FRAME OF MIND

1. Why should the language of an academic discipline be taught within the context of concept development?

2. What are the relationships among experiences, concepts, and words?

3. How can a teacher activate what students know about words and help them to make connections among related words?

4. How can a teacher support students in the definition of concepts as they are encountered in texts?

5. How do activities for vocabulary extension help students refine conceptual knowledge of special and technical vocabulary?

Fridays always seemed to be set aside for quizzes when we were students. And one of the quizzes most frequently given was the vocabulary test.

"Look up these words for the week. Write out their definitions and memorize them. And then use each one in a complete sentence. You'll be tested on these terms on Friday."

The extent of vocabulary study for us seemed consistently to revolve around the dull routines associated with looking up, defining, memorizing, and using words in sentences.

Such an instructional pattern soon became a meaningless, purposeless activity—an end in itself, rather than a means to an end. Although there was nothing inherently wrong with looking up, defining, memorizing, and using words in sentences, the approach in and of itself was too narrow for us to learn words in depth. Instead, we memorized definitions to pass the Friday quiz—and forgot them on Saturday.

Providing lists of words for students to learn sometimes leads to the ill-found conclusion that the acquisition of vocabulary is separate from the development of ideas and concepts in a content area. Teaching vocabulary often means assigning a corpus of words rather than exploring word meanings and relationships that contribute to students' conceptual awareness and understanding of the subject being studied. Once teachers clarify the relationship between words and concepts, they are receptive to instructional alternatives.

One clarification that's quickly made involves the types of reading vocabulary found in textbooks. Three types of vocabulary are evident. The first type, *general vocabulary*, consists of everyday words with widely acknowledged meanings in common usage. The second, *special vocabulary*, is made up of words from everyday, general vocabulary that take on specialized meanings when adapted to a particular content area. The third type, *technical vocabulary*, consists of words that have usage and application only in a particular subject matter field.

Special and technical terms are particularly bothersome when they're encountered in content material. Your participation in the demonstration in Box 4.1 will illustrate why special and technical terms are likely candidates for vocabulary instruction in content areas. If your responses are

---

**BOX 4.1    Vocabulary Demonstration: Words in Content Areas**

*Directions:* In each of the nine blanks, fill in the name of the content area that includes all the terms in the list below

**1.** _____

nationalism
imperialism
naturalism
instrumentalism
isolationist
radicalism
fundamentalist
anarchy

**2.** _____

forestry
ornithology
zoology
biology
entomology
botany
bacteriology
protista

**3.** _____

metaphor
allusion
irony
paradox
symbolism
imagery
simile

**4.** _____

prestissimo
adagio
larghetto
presto
allegro
largo
andante
tempo

**5.** _____

centimeter
milligram
deciliter
millisecond
kilometer
decimeter
kilogram
millimeter

**6.** _____

graffles
folutes
lesnics
raptiforms
cresnites
hygrolated
loors
chamlets

**7.** _____

polyunsaturated
glycogen
monosaccharide
hydrogenation
enzymes
lyzine
cellulose

**8.** _____

octagon
hemisphere
decagon
hexagon
bisect
equilateral
quadrilateral
pentagon

**9.** _____

auricle
ventricle
tricuspid
semilunar
apex
mitral
aorta
myocardium

similar to those of classroom teachers who have participated in this activity, several predictable outcomes are likely.

First of all, it is relatively easy for you to identify the content areas for several of the lists. Your knowledge and experience probably trigger instant recognition. You have a good working concept of many of the terms on these easy lists. You can put them to use in everyday situations that require listening, reading, writing, or speaking. They are your words. You own them.

Second, you probably recognize words in a few of the lists even though you may not be sure about the meanings of individual words. In lists 4 and 9, for example, you may be familiar with only one or two terms. Yet you are fairly sure that the terms in lists 4 and 9 exist as words despite the fact that you may not know what they mean. Dale (1975) comments that your attitude toward these kinds of words is analogous to your saying to a stranger, "I think I've met you before but I'm not sure." Several of the words from the lists may be in your "twilight zone"; you have some knowledge about them, but their meanings are a "bit foggy, not sharply focussed." *Polyunsaturated* in list 7 is a case in point for some of us who have heard the word used in television commercials and may even have sought polyunsaturated foods at the supermarket. Nevertheless, our guess is that we would be hard pressed to define or explain the meaning of *polyunsaturated* with any precision.

Finally, in one or two cases a list may have completely stymied your efforts at identification. There simply is no connection between your prior knowledge and any of the terms. You probably are not even sure whether the terms in one list really exist as words.

Which content area did you identify for list 6? In truth, the terms in this list represent nonsense. They are bogus words which were invented to illustrate the point that many of the content terms in textbooks look the same way to students that the nonsense words in list 6 look to you. You're able to pronounce most of them with little trouble but are stymied when you try to connect them to your knowledge and experience. Students are stymied this way every day by real words that represent the key concepts of a content area.

The words in these lists are actually taken from middle and high school textbooks. Just think for a moment about the staggering conceptual demands we place on learners daily as they go from class to class. Terminology that they encounter in content material is often outside the scope of their normal speaking, writing, listening, and reading vocabularies. Special and technical terms often do not have concrete referents; they are abstract and must be learned through definition, application, and repeated exposure.

Your participation in this activity leads to several points about word knowledge and concepts in content areas. The activity is a good reminder that every academic discipline creates a unique language to represent its important concepts. This is why teaching vocabulary in content areas is too important to be incidental or accidental. Key concept words need to be taught directly and taught well. Students shouldn't be left to their own devices or subjected to the vagaries of a look-up and define strategy as their only access to the long-term acquisition of language in an academic discipline.

The definitions of special and technical vocabulary terms can be learned by rote memorization without approaching a conceptual level of understanding. Looking up an unfamiliar word in a dictionary and learning it by rote is a far cry from encountering that word in a reading situation and constructing meaning for it based on a lifetime of prior knowledge and experience. For example, consider the term *edge*. An edge might be defined as "a 'region of abrupt change in intensity of the pattern of light waves reflected to the eye from a surface'. It should not be supposed that this kind of verbalizing would be very effective in bringing about the learning of a concept" (Gagne 1970, p. 177). Students need to experience how the word *edge* is used in a variety of contexts. They need to become aware that edge is related to other words that help define it conceptually. Although students may be able to verbalize a dictionary definition of the word *edge*, their ability to conceptualize it, to apply it in a variety of ways, may be limited.

In this chapter, we show how to teach words well within the framework of subject matter learning. Teaching words well removes potential barriers to reading comprehension and supports students' long-term acquisition of language in a content area. Teaching words well entails helping students make connections between their prior knowledge and the vocabulary to be encountered in text and providing them with multiple opportunities to define, clarify, and extend their knowledge of words and concepts during the course of study.

To begin, let's explore the connections that link direct experience to concepts and words. Understanding these connections lays the groundwork for teaching words, with the emphasis on learning concepts. As Anderson and Freebody (1981) suggest, "Every serious student of reading recognizes that the significant aspect of vocabulary development is in the learning of concepts, not just words" (p. 87).

## EXPERIENCES, CONCEPTS, AND WORDS

Words are labels—nothing more, nothing less—for concepts. A single concept, however, represents much more than the meaning of a single word. It might take thousands of words to explain a concept. However, answers to the question, "What does it mean to know a word?" depend on how well we understand the relationships among personal experiences, concepts, and words.

Concepts are learned through our acting upon and interaction with the environment. Edgar Dale's classic Cone of Experience in Figure 4.1 reminds us how students learn concepts best—through direct, purposeful experiences. Learning is much more intense and meaningful when it is first hand. However, in place of direct experience (which is not always possible), we develop and learn concepts through various levels of contrived or vicarious

**Figure 4.1    DALE'S CONE OF EXPERIENCE**

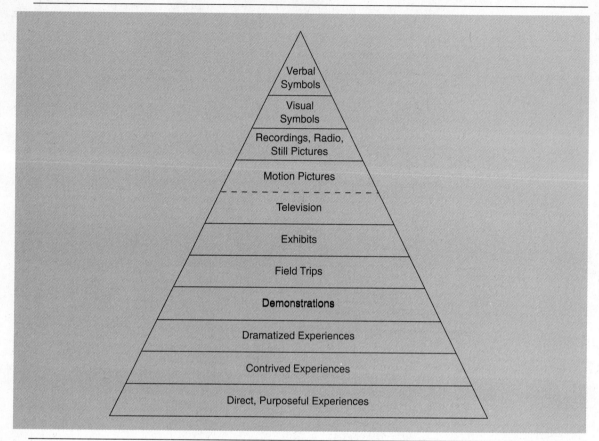

Verbal
Symbols

Visual
Symbols

Recordings, Radio,
Still Pictures

Motion Pictures

Television

Exhibits

Field Trips

Demonstrations

Dramatized Experiences

Contrived Experiences

Direct, Purposeful Experiences

**Source:** *Audiovisual Methods in Teaching,* 3rd ed., by Edgar Dale. Copyright © 1969 by Holt, Rinehart and Winston, Inc. Reprinted by permisssion of the publisher.

experience. According to Dale (1969), learning a concept through oral or written language is especially difficult because it is so far removed from direct experience.

Concepts provide mental images. These images may represent anything that can be grouped together by common features or similar criteria—objects, symbols, ideas, processes, or events. In this respect, concepts are similar in nature to schemata. A concept hardly ever stands alone, but instead is bound by a hierarchy of relations. As a result, "most concepts do not represent a unique object or event but rather a general class linked by a common element or relationship" (Johnson and Pearson 1978, p. 33).

Bruner, Goodnow, and Austin (1977) suggest that we would be overwhelmed by the complexity of our environment if we were to respond to each object or event that we encountered as unique. Therefore we invent categories (or form concepts) to reduce the complexity of our environment and the necessity for constant learning. For example, every feline need not have a different name to be known as a cat. Although cats vary greatly, the common characteristics that they share cause them to be referred to by the same general term. Thus, in order to facilitate communication, we invent words to name concepts.

Consider your concept for the word *ostrich*. What mental picture comes to mind? Your image of *ostrich* might differ from ours, depending on your prior knowledge of the ostrich or the larger class to which it belongs, known as *land birds*. Moreover, your direct or vicarious experiences with birds may differ significantly from someone else's. Nevertheless, for any concept we organize all our experiences and background knowledge into conceptual hierarchies according to *class, example,* and *attribute* relations.

The concept *ostrich* is part of a more inclusive class or category called *land birds,* which in turn is subsumed within an even larger class of animals known as *warm-blooded vertebrates.* These class relations are depicted in Figure 4.2.

In any conceptual network, class relationships are organized in a hierarchy consisting of superordinate and subordinate concepts. In Figure 4.2 the superordinate concept is *animal kingdom. Vertebrates* and nonvertebrates are two classes within the animal kingdom; they are in a subordinate position in this hierarchy. *Vertebrates,* however, divided into two classes, *warm blooded* and *cold blooded,* is superordinate to *mammals, birds, fish,* and *amphibians*— types or subclasses of vertebrates. The concept *land birds,* subordinate to *birds,* but superordinate to *ostrich,* completes the hierarchy.

For every concept there are examples of that concept. An *example* is a member of any concept being considered. A *nonexample,* conversely, is

**Figure 4.2**    SEMANTIC WORD MAP BASED ON CLASS RELATIONS

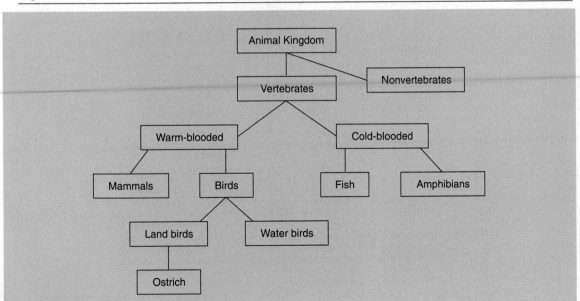

anything not a member of that concept. Class/example relations are complementary: vertebrates and nonvertebrates are examples within the *animal kingdom. Mammals, birds, fish,* and *amphibians* are examples of *vertebrates. Land birds* is one example of *birds,* and so on.

Let's make *land birds* our target concept. What are some other examples of land birds in addition to the ostrich? *Penguin, emu,* and *rhea* are a few which can be shown in relation to one another as in Figure 4.3. We could have listed more examples of land birds. Instead, we now ask, "What do the ostrich, penguin, emu, and rhea have in common?" This allows us to focus on their relevant attributes—those features, traits, properties, or characteristics common to every example of a particular concept. In this case the *relevant attributes* of land birds are the characteristics that determine whether the ostrich, penguin, emu, and rhea belong to the class of birds called *land birds.* An attribute is said to be *critical* if it is a characteristic that is necessary for determining class membership. An attribute is said to be *variable* if it is shared by some but not all examples of the class. An *irrelevant attribute* is any characteristic not shared by any examples of the class.

Thus we recognize that certain physical and social characteristics are shared by all land birds, but not every land bird has each feature. Virtually all land birds have feathers, wings, and beaks. They hatch from an egg and have two legs. They differ in color, size, habitat, and size of feet. Some land birds fly and others, with small wings that cannot support their bodies in the air, do not. In what ways is the ostrich similar to other land birds? How is the ostrich different?

This brief discussion of the concept *ostrich* was designed to illustrate an important principle: **Teachers can help students build conceptual knowledge of content area terms by teaching and reinforcing the concept words in relation to other concept words.** As you study how to devise activities that introduce and reinforce conceptual relations among words, keep in mind Goodman's (1976) proposition that "'Vocabulary' is largely a term for the ability . . . to sort out experiences and concepts in relation to words and phrases in the context of . . . reading" (p. 480).

**Figure 4.3**    CLASS/EXAMPLE RELATIONS FOR TARGET CONCEPT *LAND BIRDS*

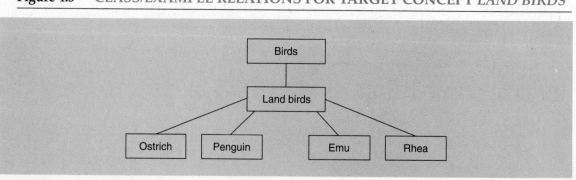

## ACTIVATING WHAT STUDENTS KNOW ABOUT WORDS

Imagine yourself in a tenth-grade biology class in which the teacher assigns a text selection, "Darwin's Theory of Natural Selection," for homework. Read the text in Box 4.2, and as you read, underline all the words of a special and technical scientific nature that contribute to an understanding of Darwin's theory.

In this short passage alone there are at least twenty terms of a scientific nature:

| | | |
|---|---|---|
| natural selection | competition | descendants |
| organism | necessities | reproduction |
| survival of the fittest | spores | ancestors |
| overpopulation | visible universe | spawn |
| variations | species | maturity |
| theory | transmit | electrons |
| offspring | overproduction | |

The biology teacher recognizes that the vocabulary of her subject matter can pose barriers to reading comprehension. As a result, she could have decided to teach the students every technical term that they would encounter in their reading of the Darwin passage. However, she knows that this would be impractical, time consuming, and fairly boring. She could have assigned the class to look up the words and write out their definitions. But this too makes little sense to her. She knows that this practice often leads to rote learning and empty verbalization that won't meet the needs of text learners. So what are her options? Her instructional alternatives?

The teacher puts into practice plans and procedures that will contribute to students' acquisition of vocabulary concepts. She knows that she can impact students' long-term acquisition of the language of biology *before*, *during*, and *after* reading. She uses five steps, recommended by Camille Blachowicz (1986), to make her class aware of and skilled in the use of categories for word knowledge and concept development:

### Before Reading

1. Activate students' prior knowledge of vocabulary words in a text selection.
   **Strategy Awareness:** Students need to learn how to ask the question: "What do I know about these words?"
   **Instructional Activities:** *word explorations, brainstorming, knowledge ratings, word sorts*

---

**BOX 4.2    Darwin's Theory of Natural Selection**

In 1859, Charles Darwin, an English scientist, published his *On the Origin of the Species by Means of Natural Selection*. His theory of natural selection, while confined to biology, has also influenced other branches of science. According to Darwin, the chief factors that account for the development of new species from a common ancestry can be summarized as follows:

1. All organisms produce more offspring than can actually survive.

2. Because of overproduction, there is a constant struggle for existence among individuals.

3. The individuals of a given species vary.

4. The fittest, or the best adapted, individuals of a species survive.

5. Surviving organisms transmit variations to offspring.

**Overproduction**

A fern plant may produce 50 million spores each year. If all the spores resulting from this overproduction matured, in the second year they would nearly cover North America. A mustard plant produces about 730,000 seeds annually. If they all took root and matured, in two years they would occupy an area 2000 times that of the land surface of the earth. The dandelion would do the same in ten years.

At a single spawning, an oyster may shed 114,000,000 eggs. If all these eggs survived, the ocean would be literally filled with oysters. Within five generations, there would be more oysters than the estimated number of electrons in the visible universe! There is, however, no such actual increase.

The elephant is considered to have a slow rate of reproduction. An average elephant lives to be 100 years old, breeds over a span of from 30 to 90 years, and bears about 6 young. Yet if all the young from one pair of elephants survived, in 750 years the descendants would number 19,000,000.

**Struggle for Existence**

We know that in actuality the number of individuals of a species usually changes little in its native environment. In other words, regardless of the rate of reproduction, only a small minority of the original number of offspring reaches maturity.

Each organism seeks food, water, air, warmth, and space but only a few can obtain these needs in struggling to survive. This struggle for existence is most intense between members of the same species, because they compete for the same necessities.

**Source:** James H. Otto and Albert Towle, *Modern Biology*. New York: Holt, Rinehart and Winston, 1973, pp. 206–207. Copyright © 1973.

2. Make connections between words, the main topic, and the structure of the text selection.
   **Strategy Awareness:** Students need to learn how to ask the question: "How are these words related to one another?"
   **Instructional Activities:** *graphic organizers, semantic maps, semantic feature analysis*

**During Reading**

3. Encounter words in context.
   **Strategy Awareness:** Students need to be aware that they build and clarify word knowledge by encountering words in their natural context while reading.
   **Instructional Activities:** *reading and constructing meanings based on the context in which words are used*

**After Reading**

4. Define and clarify word meanings and concepts.
   **Strategy Awareness:** Students need to learn how to ask the question: "How can I use what I read to confirm and clarify what I think these words mean?"
   **Instructional Activities:** *vocabulary self-collection, concept of definition word maps, word sorts, postgraphic organizers, vocabulary extension*

5. Refine, extend, and apply words.
   **Strategy Awareness:** Students must learn to recognize that "to make a word mine, I must know how to use it when I'm reading, writing, speaking, or listening."
   **Instructional Activities:** *reading, writing, discussion, listening*

The biology class has already studied changes in living populations through the ages. A comparison of ancient and modern organisms in fact led to the present unit on theories of evolution. Students in the class can bring a great deal of knowledge to the Darwin passage from previous study as well as their prior knowledge and experiences. The biology teacher knows the value of activating what the students know so that they can bring that knowledge to bear during reading.

So as part of initial preparation, the teacher has the class participate in a discussion of the *graphic organizer* in Figure 4.4 before assigning the Darwin passage to read for homework. She uses an overhead transparency to introduce the graphic organizer to the class. In the process of doing so, she asks good questions that allow the class to clarify the relationships among the concepts depicted in the graphic representation. The teacher draws on what the students know, but they do most of the talking during the discussion. Her job is to help the class members recognize what concepts they need to focus attention on as they read the assignment. "What do you need to know more about?" is the way she frames the question to the class.

## Depicting Spatial Relationships with Graphic Organizers

At the start of each chapter we have asked you to organize your thoughts around the main ideas in the text. These ideas are presented within the framework of a graphic organizer—a chart that uses content vocabulary to

**Figure 4.4    GRAPHIC ORGANIZER FOR PASSAGE ON DARWIN'S THEORY OF NATURAL SELECTION**

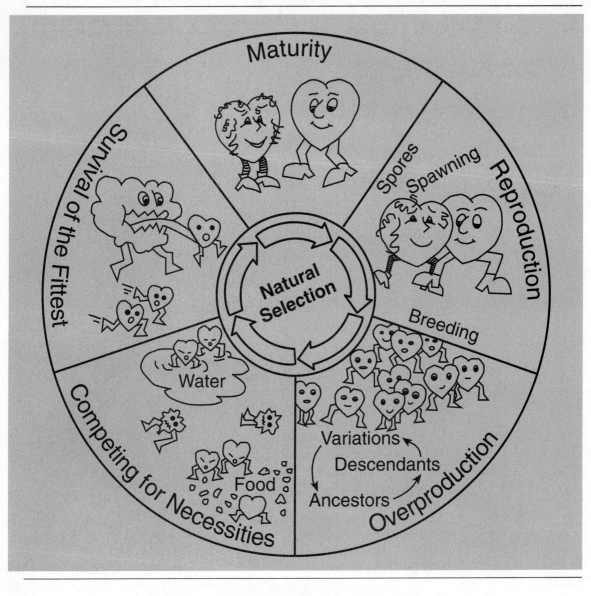

help students anticipate concepts and their relationships to one another in the reading material. These concepts are displayed by arranging key technical terms relevant to the important concepts to be learned.

Graphic organizers may vary in their format. A commonly used format is to connect concepts in a tree diagram so as to depict the hierarchical relationships among concept words, as explained earlier in the chapter. However, other formats, such as the one in Figure 4.4, depict spatial relationships according to the text patterns inherent in the material, for example, a causal chain of events. In Chapter 9, we will show how students can use a variety of formats to construct their own graphic organizers as an independent learning strategy for studying text material.

Thelen (1979) illustrates a hierarchical arrangement of mathematical concepts having similar attributes and characteristics. See Figure 4.5. The concept *quadrilateral* is subordinate to *polygon*, coordinate to *triangle*, and superordinate to *rhombus, square,* and *rectangle. Polygon* is the most inclusive concept and subsumes all of the others.

Keep in mind, a graphic organizer always shows vocabulary in relation to other vocabulary concepts. Let's take a closer look at its construction and application in the classroom.

**Constructing the Graphic Organizer.** Barron (1969) suggests the following steps for developing the graphic organizer and introducing the vocabulary diagram to students:

1. Analyze the vocabulary of the learning task and list all the words that you feel are important for the student to understand.

2. Arrange the list of words until you have a scheme that shows the interrelationships among the concepts particular to the learning task.

3. Add to the scheme vocabulary terms that you believe the students understand in order to show relationships between the learning task and the discipline as a whole.

4. Evaluate the organizer. Have you clearly shown major relationships? Can the organizer be simplified and still effectively communicate the idea you consider to be crucial?

5. Introduce the students to the learning task by showing them the scheme and tell them why you arranged the terms as you did.

**Figure 4.5    HIERARCHICAL ARRANGEMENT OF MATHEMATICAL CONCEPTS WITH SIMILAR ATTRIBUTES**

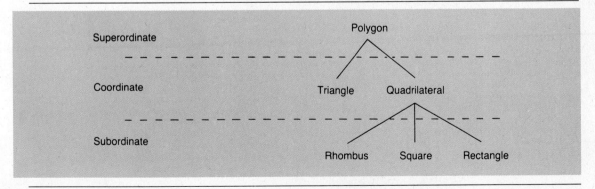

**Source:** From "Preparing students for content reading assignments" by Judie Thelen, *Journal of Reading,* March 1982. Reprinted with permission of Judie Thelen and the International Reading Association.

Encourage them to contribute as much information as possible to the discussion of the organizer.

6. As you complete the learning task, relate new information to the organizer where it seems appropriate.

Suppose you were to develop a graphic organizer for a text chapter in a high school psychology course. Let's walk through the steps involved.

1. *Analyze the vocabulary and list the important words.* The chapter yields these words:

| | | |
|---|---|---|
| hebephrenia | neurosis | personality disorders |
| psychosis | schizophrenia | catatonia |
| abnormality | mental retardation | phobias |

2. *Arrange the list of words.* Choose the word that represents the most inclusive concept, the one superordinate to all the others. Then choose the words classified immediately under the superordinate concept and coordinate them with one another. Then choose the terms subordinate to the coordinate concepts. Your diagram may look like Figure 4.6.

3. *Add to the scheme vocabulary terms that you believe the students understand.* You add the following terms: *antisocial, anxiety, intellectual deficit, Walter Mitty, depression, paranoia.* Where would you place these words on the diagram?

4. *Evaluate the organizer.* The interrelationships among the key terms may look like Figure 4.7 once you evaluate the vocabulary arrangement.

5. *Introduce the students to the learning task.* As you present the vocabulary relationships shown on the graphic organizer, create as much discussion as possible. Draw upon students' understandings and experiences with the concepts the vocabulary terms label. You might have students

**Figure 4.6     ARRANGEMENT OF WORDS IN PSYCHOLOGY TEXT**

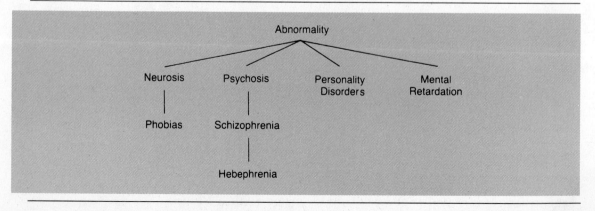

**Figure 4.7    ARRANGEMENT OF PSYCHOLOGY WORDS AFTER EVALUATION OF OVERVIEW**

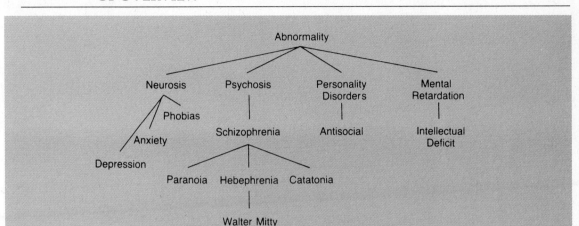

relate previous study to the terms. For example, *Walter Mitty* is subsumed within *hebephrenia*. If students were familiar with James Thurber's short story "The Secret Life of Walter Mitty," they would have little trouble bringing meaning to *hebephrenia*—a schizophrenic condition characterized by excessive daydreaming and delusions. The discussion might also lead to a recognition of the implicit comparison-contrast pattern among the four types of abnormality explained in the text. What better opportunity to provide direction during reading than to have students visualize the pattern. The discussions you will stimulate from the organizer will be worth the time it takes to construct it.

6. *As you complete the learning task, relate new information to the organizer.* This is particularly useful as a study and review technique. The organizer becomes a study guide that can be referred to throughout the discussion of the material. Students should be encouraged to add information to flesh out the organizer as they develop concepts fully.

**Classroom Examples.**  Use a graphic organizer to show the relationships in an entire text, in a unit covering several chapters, in one chapter, or in a subsection of a chapter. The classroom scenario that follows provides further insight into its utility as a prereading vocabulary activity.

An eighth-grade social studies teacher constructed the organizer in Figure 4.8 for 12 pages of his text. The purpose of the graphic organizer was to introduce students to the propaganda terms used in the textbook. Before having the class read the assigned pages, he placed the organizer on the board and asked his class to copy it into their notebooks for future reference. Then he explained that propaganda is a word used to describe one way people try to change the opinions of others. He gave an example or two

**Figure 4.8   GRAPHIC ORGANIZER**

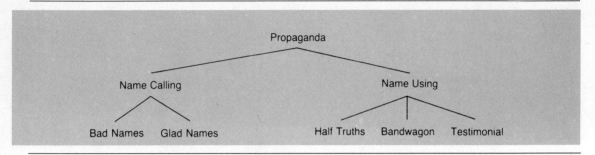

and then asked students to contribute other examples. As part of the development of the concept of propaganda, with the help and participation of students, he derived explanations for all the methods shown in the overview. As these explanations developed, students also saw how each method related to the two categories Name Calling and Name Using. The explanations which developed are as follows:

1. Bad names: calling a person an unpleasant name to make people feel angry or fearful. No facts are given about the person.

2. Glad names: calling a person a pleasant name to make people feel good. No facts are given about the person.

3. Half Truths: presenting only good or only bad information about something or someone. Only one side of the story is told.

4. Bandwagon: telling people that "everyone is doing it" to get them to follow the crowd.

5. Testimonial: getting a well-known person to say he or she likes or dislikes something or someone.

The students recorded these definitions in their notebooks. At this point they began to grasp the difference between methods and started to give examples of propaganda they saw being used in advertising. Then the teacher gave them nine sentences and asked them to identify the propaganda method used in each:

1. "Everyone in town is going to vote for Dan Ray."

2. "The present leaders are criminals and should be put in jail."

3. "She is a noble woman, capable in every way."

4. "As a football player, I know how important it is to use Brand X hair cream."

5. "The young fighter is faster than the champ and will win the fight."

6. "My opponent is a coward, afraid of solving problems."

7. "Before my TV show, I always use Brand X toothpaste."

8. "Come to the fair and see everyone you know."

9. "The new political party is well organized. It will win the election."

Sentences 2 and 6 prompted considerable discussion as to whether the method was Bad Names, Half Truths, or both. After completing this exercise the students read the assigned pages of the text. The reading went rapidly because the students quickly recognized the different methods of propaganda used in the textbook. The class discussion that followed was lively: The students were confident of their decisions and were eager to share them with their peers. According to the teacher, the lesson had a lasting effect on the students: In subsequent lessons not dealing specifically with propaganda they recognized the use of propaganda and shared it with the rest of the class.

So much for the testimonial of one teacher. As you study the following illustrations consider the adaptations that might be made if you were to develop a graphic organizer for material in your content area.

The organizer in Figure 4.9 was developed for a high school class in data processing. It introduced students to the different terms of data processing, delineating causes and effects.

With Figure 4.10 an art teacher showed the relationships among key concepts associated with firing ceramics.

**Adapting Graphic Organizers in Elementary Grades.** Graphic organizers are easily adapted to learning situations in the elementary grades. Often elementary teachers will construct organizers on large sheet of chart paper or on bulletin boards for class presentation. Other teachers have introduced vocabulary for content units by constructing mobiles they hang from the

**Figure 4.9    GRAPHIC ORGANIZER**

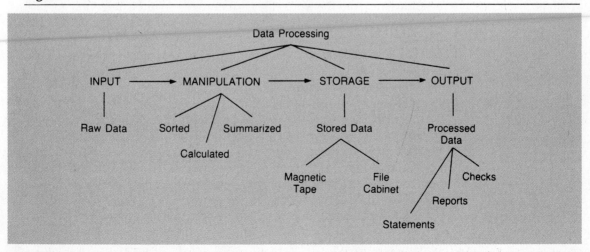

**Figure 4.10**    GRAPHIC ORGANIZER

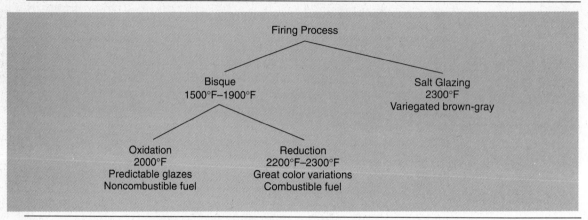

ceiling. Hanging mobiles are an interest-riveting way to attract students' attention to the hierarchical relationships among the words they will encounter. Still other elementary teachers draw pictures with words to illustrate the key concepts under study, similar in nature to the biology teacher's organizer in Figure 4.4.

The graphic organizer in Figure 4.11 revolves around a bear mobile, constructed by a second-grade teacher as part of an interdisciplinary unit on bears. She used the mobile with an informational book, *A Closer Look at Bears and Pandas* (Cook 1977).

## Exploring Word Meanings and Making Connections

In addition to graphic organizers, several procedures also help to activate what students know and help them to make connections between their existing knowledge and the words they are studying. Word exploration, for example, is a *writing to learn* strategy that works well in conjunction with the graphic organizer or as a prereading vocabulary activity in its own right. The biology teacher in the scenario above began the discussion of the graphic organizer in silence! That is to say, before asking students to make connections between the words and their prior knowledge, she asked them to explore what they knew about the concept of *natural selection*, by writing in their learning logs.

A learning log, as we explain in Chapter 8, is a content area journal that students use to record what they are learning. A variety of writing-to-learn activities may be initiated to help students to observe, speculate, make discoveries, question, and reflect on the learning events occurring in the classroom. A word exploration activity invites students to write quickly and spontaneously, a technique called *freewriting*, for no more than five or so minutes—without undue concern for spelling, neatness, grammar, or punctuation. The purpose of freewriting is to get down on paper everything that students know about the topic or target concept. Students write freely for

**Figure 4.11    WHAT BEARS EAT**

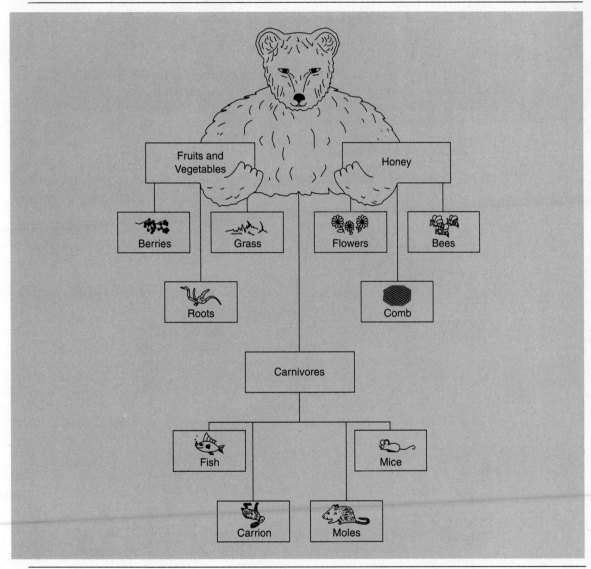

themselves, not for an audience, so that concerns for the mechanical, surface features of language, such as spelling, are not paramount.

Word explorations activate schema and jog long-term memory, allowing students to dig deep into the recesses of their minds to activate and gather thoughts about a topic. Examine one of the word explorations for the target concept, *natural selection*.

Natural selection means, I gues [sic] that nature selects, you know, kills off or does away with the week [sic] so only the strong make it. like we were saying in class last time everyting [sic] gets so competitive [sic] even among us for grades and jobs, etc. The homeless for instance, are having trouble living with no place to call home except the street and nothing to eat. Maybe that's as good example of natural selection as I can think of for now.

The teacher has several of the students share their word explorations with the class, either reading them verbatim or talking through what they have written, noting similarities and differences in the students' concepts. She then relates their initial associations with the concept to the graphic organizer and asks students to make further connections. "How do you personal understandings of the idea, *natural selection,* fit in with the organizer and some of the relationships that you see?"

**Brainstorming.** An alternative to word explorations, brainstorming is a procedure that quickly allows students to generate what they know about a key concept. Brainstorming creates a learning situation where the students can access their prior knowledge in relation to the target concept. Brainstorming involves two basic steps which can be adapted easily to content objectives: (1) identify a key concept that reflects one of the main topics to be studied in the text and (2) have students work in small groups to generate a list of words related to the concept in $x$ number of seconds.

These two steps help you instantly discover what knowledge your students possess about the topic they are going to study. Furthermore, Herber (1978) suggests:

> The device of having students produce lists of related words is a useful way to guide review. It helps them become instantly aware of how much they know, individually and collectively, about the topic. They discover quickly that there are no right or wrong answers. . . . Until the students reach the point in the lesson where they must read the passage and judge whether their predictions are accurate, the entire lesson is based on their own knowledge, experience, and opinion. This captivates their interest much more than the more traditional, perfunctory review. (p. 179)

In the next chapter, we will demonstrate how brainstorming can be used within a more inclusive strategy, called *PReP,* to serve the dual purposes of assessment and knowledge activation before reading.

**Semantic Word Maps.** Semantic word maps are similar to graphic organizers in that they may be used to depict spatial relationships among words. In addition, semantic word maps include brainstorming and the use of collaborative small groups. Mapping, as we explained earlier in the chapter, allows students to cluster words belonging to categories and to distinguish relationships among words. Here's how semantic mapping works:

1. The teacher or the students decide on a key concept to be explored.

2. Once the key concept is determined, the students, depending on what they have been studying and on their background knowledge and experiences, offer as many words or phrases as possible related to the concept term. These are recorded by the teacher on the chalkboard.

Once the list of terms is generated, the teacher may form small groups of students to create semantic maps and then share their constructions in class discussion. Such was the case in a sixth-grade class exploring the concept of *manufacturing*. Study the semantic map created by one of the small groups in the class (see Figure 4.12).

Teachers will need to model the construction of semantic maps once or twice so that students will get a feel for how to develop their own in small groups or individually. In Chapter 9, we will expand on the use of semantic maps as a postreading learning strategy used by students to outline content material as they study texts.

**Word Sorts.** Like brainstorming, word sorts require students to classify words into categories based on prior knowledge. However, unlike in brainstorming, students do not generate a list of words for a target concept.

**Figure 4.12    SEMANTIC MAP FOR MANUFACTURING**

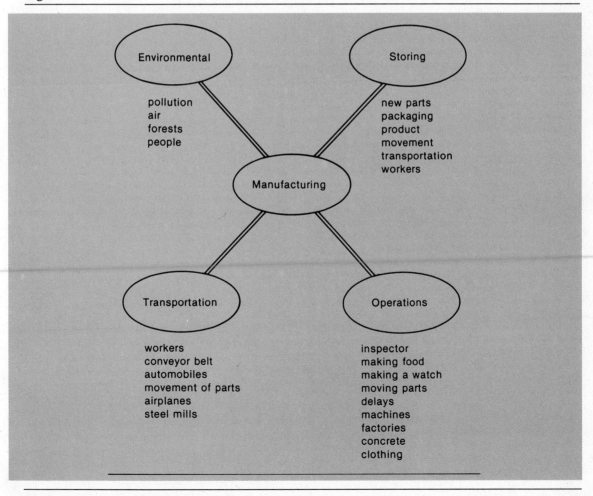

Instead, the teacher identifies the key words from the unit of study and invites the students to sort them into logical arrangements of two or more.

A word sort is a simple yet valuable activity to initiate. Individually or in small groups, students literally sort out technical terms that are written on cards or listed on an exercise sheet. The object of word sorting is to group words into different categories by looking for shared features among their meanings. According to Gillet and Kita (1979), a word sort activity gives students the opportunity "to teach and learn from each other while discussing and examining words together" (pp. 541–542).

Gillet and Kita also explain that there are two types of word sorts—the open sort and the closed sort. Both are easily adapted to any content area. In the closed sort students know in advance of sorting what the main categories are. In other words, the criterion the words in a group must share is stated. The closed sort reinforces and extends the ability to classify words, as we illustrate later in the chapter.

Open sorts, on the other hand, prompt divergent and inductive reasoning. No category or criterion for grouping is known in advance of sorting. Students must search for meanings and discover relationships among technical terms without the benefit of any structure. For example, if you were given the following list of names, how many different arrangements could be made by grouping together two or more names? You must be able to justify the reason or reasons for each arrangement.

| | |
|---|---|
| Washington | Susan B. Anthony |
| Alexander the Great | John Kennedy |
| Rembrandt | Edison |
| Columbus | De Gaulle |
| Hitler | Helen Hayes |
| Caesar | Napoleon |
| Cleopatra | Einstein |
| Henry Ford | Margaret Mead |

Your arrangements probably run the gamut from the obvious (men versus women) to the less obvious (names given to foods and cities).

Word sorts can be used before or after reading. Before reading, a word sort serves as an activation strategy to help learners make predictive connections among the words. After reading, word sorts enable students to clarify and extend their understandings of the conceptual relationships.

Study how an art teacher activated what students knew about words associated with pottery making by using the word sort strategy. She asked the high school students to work in collaborative pairs to arrange the words below into possible groups and to predict the concept categories under which the words would be classified:

| jordan | roka | cornwall stone |
| ball | lead | cone |
| antimony | chrome | wheel |
| cobalt | slip | bisque |
| mortar | scale | stoneware |
| sgraffito | kaolin | oxidation |
| | leather | |
| | hard | |

Several categories that students formed were *types of clay*, *pottery tools*, and *coloring agents*.

**Knowledge Ratings.** As the procedure implies, knowledge ratings get readers to analyze what they know about a topic. Blachowicz (1986) recommends that the teacher present students with a list of vocabulary in a survey-like format in which students must analyze each word individually as in the two examples in Box 4.3.

A follow-up discussion might revolve around questions such as these: Which are the hardest words? Which do you think most of the class doesn't know? Which are the easiest ones? Which will most of us know? Students should be encouraged within the context of the discussion to share what they know about the words. In this way the teacher can assess and get some idea of the state of knowledge the class brings to the text reading or a larger unit of study.

These procedures are all a part of prereading preparation. Naturally it would be foolhardy to use all of these procedures at one time, but one or two in combination set the stage for students to read with some confidence in and competence with the language of the text.

## DEFINING, CLARIFYING, AND EXTENDING CONCEPTS

Learners need many experiences, real and vicarious, to define, clarify, and extend word meanings and concepts. They need to use, test, and manipulate vocabulary in learning situations that capitalize on reading, writing, speaking, and listening activities. Vocabulary extension activities serve this purpose. Martha Rapp-Haggard Ruddell (1992) outlines five principles to guide the development of extension activities: (1) activities should allow students to use new words in a meaningful way, (2) activities should allow students opportunity to associate new words and concepts with their own experience, (3) activities should develop associations with other words, (4) activities should encourage high-level thinking, and (5) activities should lead students to many different text resources.

BOX 4.3     Two Examples of Knowledge Ratings

**Knowledge Rating***

How much do you know about these words?

|              | Can define | Have seen/heard | ? |
|--------------|:----------:|:---------------:|:-:|
| exponent     | x          |                 |   |
| intersection | x          |                 |   |
| domain       |            |                 | x |
| intercept    |            | x               | x |
| slope        |            | x               |   |
| parabola     |            |                 | x |
| origin       |            | x               |   |
| vertex       |            | x               |   |
| irrationals  | x          |                 |   |
| union        |            | x               |   |
| coefficient  |            | x               |   |

*From a unit on quadratic functions and systems of equations in a high school math class.

**Knowledge Rating†**

How much do you know about these words?

|              | A lot! | Some | Not much |
|--------------|:------:|:----:|:--------:|
| wire service |        | x    |          |
| AP           |        | x    |          |
| copy         |        | x    |          |
| dateline     | x      |      |          |
| byline       | x      |      |          |
| caption      | x      |      |          |
| masthead     |        |      |          |
| jumpline     |        |      | x        |
| column       | x      |      | x        |

†From a newspaper unit in a middle school language arts class.

Before considering a variety of extension activities that put students in the position of clarifying and refining their knowledge of words and concepts, consider two strategies that permit text learners to define words in relation to the contexts in which they are used: the Vocabulary Self-Collection Strategy (VSS) and Concept of Definition (CD) procedure.

## Defining Concepts in the Context of Their Use

The Vocabulary Self-Collection Strategy (VSS) and Concept of Definition (CD) are two instructional tactics that make students aware of and build learning strategies for concept definition. Both activities invite students to use their texts to determine how concepts are defined in their natural context.

**Vocabulary Self-Collection Strategy.** VSS was originated by Haggard (1986) to promote the long-term acquisition of language in an academic discipline. As a result of the repeated use of the strategy, students learn how to make decisions related to the importance of concepts and how to use passage context to determine what words mean. VSS begins once students read and discuss a text assignment. The teacher asks students, who are divided into teams, to nominate one word that they would like to learn more about. The word must be important enough for the team to share it with the class. The teacher also nominates a word.

Here are several suggested steps in the VSS:

1. Divide the class into nominating teams of two to five students. Together the students on a nominating team decide which word to select for emphasis in the text selection.

2. Present the word that each team has selected to the entire class. A spokesperson for each team identifies the nominated word and responds to the following questions:

   a. **Where is the word found in the text?** The spokesperson reads the passage in which the word is located or describes the context in which the word is used.

   b. **What do the team members think the word means?** The team decides on what the word means in the context that it is used. They must use information from the surrounding context and may also consult reference resources as well.

   c. **Why did the team think the class should learn the word?** The team must provide a rationale as to why the word is important enough to single out for emphasis.

To introduce VSS to the students, the teacher first presents his or her nominated word to the class, modeling how to respond to the questions above. During the team presentations, the teacher facilitates the discussion, writes the nominated words on the board with their meanings, and invites class members to contribute additional clarifications related to what the words mean.

To conclude the class session, students then record all the nominated words and their meanings in a section of their learning logs or in a separate vocabulary notebook. These lists may be used for review and study. As a consequence of VSS, the teacher has a set of student-generated words that can be incorporated into a variety of follow-up extension activities, some of which we will explain in the next section of this chapter.

**Concept of Definition.** Although VSS provides opportunities to define and explore the meanings of words used in the context of text readings, many students are not aware of the types of conceptual information that contribute to the meaning of a concept. Nor have they internalized a strategy for defining a concept based on the conceptual information available to them. In addition, words in a text passage often provide only partial contextual information for defining the meaning of a concept.

CD instruction provides a framework for organizing conceptual information in the process of defining a word (Schwartz and Raphael 1985; Schwartz 1988). As we explained earlier in the chapter, conceptual information can be organized in terms of three types of relationships: the general class or category in which the concept belongs, the attributes or properties of the concept and those that distinguish it from other members of the category, and the examples or illustrations of the concept. Students from elementary school through high school can use CD to better understand what it means to construct meaning for unknown words encountered while studying texts.

CD instruction supports vocabulary and concept learning by helping students to internalize a strategy for defining and clarifying the meaning of unknown words. The hierarchical structure of a concept exhibits an organizational pattern that is reflected in the general structure of a CD word map (see Figure 4.13).

In the center of the CD word map students write the concept being studied. Working outward, they then write the word which best describes the general class or superordinate concept that includes the target concept. The question "What is it?" is used to signal the general class or category. Students then provide at least three examples of the concept as well as three

**Figure 4.13   A GENERAL STRUCTURE FOR CD WORD MAP**

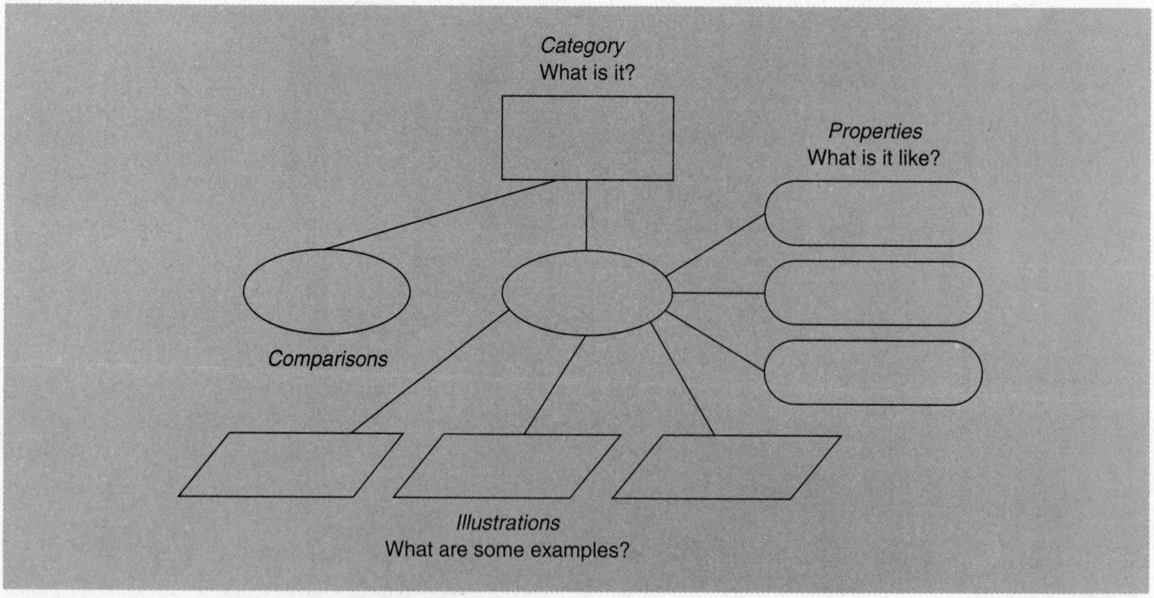

**Source:** Learning to Learn: Vocabulary in Content Area Textbooks by Robert Schwartz, *Journal of Reading, November, 1988.* Reprinted with permission of Robert Schwartz and the International Reading Association.

**Figure 4.14   CD MAP FOR TIGER**

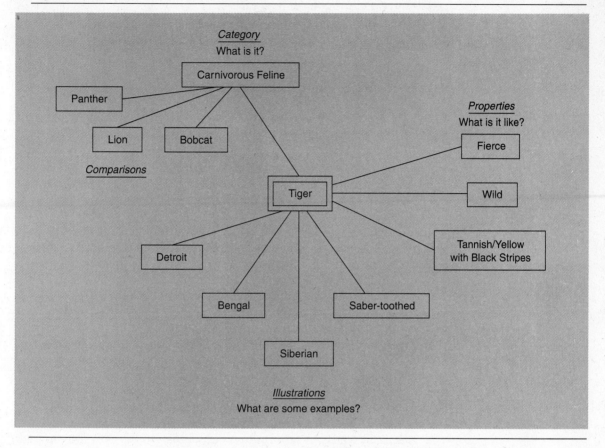

properties by responding respectively to the questions "What are some examples?" and "What is it like?" Comparison of the target concept is also possible when students think of an additional concept that belongs to the general class but is different from the concept being studied. Figure 4.14 depicts an example of a CD word map completed in a sixth-grade class.

Since students use the general CD word map as a framework for defining unknown concepts that they encounter during reading, a teacher can easily coincide CD instruction with VSS. Schwartz (1988) recommends a detailed plan for modeling CD with students. The plan includes demonstrating the value of CD by connecting its purpose to the way people use organizational patterns to aid memory and interpretation; introducing the general structure of a CD word map, explaining how the three probes define a concept, and walking students through the completion of a word map; and applying CD to an actual text selection.

Two caveats related to CD instruction: CD works best with concept words that function as nouns, but the procedure may be used, with some adaptation, with action words as well. Also, a potential misuse of CD occurs when teachers reproduce the general CD word map on dittos with the expectation that students will define lists of words at the end of a text chapter. This is not the intent of CD instruction. Instead, students should internalize the process through demonstration and actual use, applying it as they need it in authentic text learning situations. Ultimately, the goal of CD instruction is to have students own the strategy of defining unknown words in terms of category, property, and example relationships.

## Extending Vocabulary Knowledge and Concepts

When students manipulate technical terms in relation to other terms, they are thinking critically. Vocabulary activities can be designed to give a class the experience of *thinking about, thinking through,* and *thinking with* the technical vocabulary of a subject.

Students need many experiences, real and vicarious, to develop word meanings and concepts. They need to use, test, and manipulate technical terms in instructional situations which capitalize on reading, writing, speaking, and listening activities. In having students do these things, you will create the kind of natural language environment that is needed to extend vocabulary and concept development.

You can capitalize on the four basic cognitive operations associated with learning concepts and words (Henry 1974). The first involves **the act of joining,** or bringing together. Comparing, classifying, and generalizing are possible through the act of joining. When you ask students to explain how words are related or have them sort through word cards to group words together you are involving them in the act of joining.

The **act of excluding** is a second conceptual operation worth considering when teaching words in relation to other words. As the operation implies, students must discriminate, negate, or reject items because they do not belong within the conceptual category. When a student must decide which word does not belong in a set of other words, the process involves exclusion. In this case, students would search through their background knowledge to distinguish examples from nonexamples or relevant attributes from irrelevant attributes as we did with the ostrich example earlier in this chapter.

A third conceptual activity or operation involves the **act of selecting.** Students simply learn to make choices and to explain why based on what they experience, know, or understand. Synonyms, antonyms, and multiple-meaning words lend themselves well to the act of selecting.

A fourth aspect of thinking conceptually involves the **act of implying.** Are your students able to make decisions based on if-then, cause-effect relations among concept and words? Dupuis and Snyder (1983) suggest that the act of implying is such a complex cognitive activity that it actually requires the use of joining, excluding, and selecting processes.

As a rule of thumb, vocabulary extension activities should be completed individually by students and then discussed either in small groups or in the class as a whole. The oral interaction in team learning situations gives more students a chance to use terms. Students can exchange ideas, share insights, and justify responses in a nonthreatening situation. Barron and Earle (1973) suggest the following procedures for small-group discussion of reinforcement activities:

1. End small-group discussion only after the group has discussed each answer and every member of the group understands the reasons for each answer.

2. Encourage the active participation of all group members. A student who has trouble with a particular exercise can still make a valuable contribution by asking questions or asking someone to explain answers.

3. Limit talk to the particular exercise or to related questions.

4. Make sure that students use the words and their meanings in discussing the answers, rather than using letters and numbers (for example, "I think the answer to number 1 is C, 2 is F").

**Semantic Feature Analysis (SFA).**   SFA establishes a meaningful link between students' prior knowledge and words that are conceptually related to one another. The strategy requires that you develop a chart or grid to help students analyze similarities and differences among the related concepts. As the SFA grid in Box 4.4 illustrates, a topic or category is selected, and words related to that category are listed in a column down the left side of the grid. Features or properties shared by some of the words in the column are spaced across the top of the grid.

---

**BOX 4.4    SFA Grid for Early Civilizations**

| Early Civilizations | educated | monotheism | slavery | democratic | monarchy | naval power | baths | agriculture | builders | traders | theater | warlike |
|---|---|---|---|---|---|---|---|---|---|---|---|---|
| Roman | + | - | + | - | + | ? | + | + | + | + | + | + |
| Egyptian | + | - | + | - | + | + | + | + | + | + | ? | - |
| Viking | - | - | + | - | + | + | - | - | - | ? | - | + |
| Greek | + | - | + | + | - | ? | + | - | + | + | + | - |
| Frank | - | - | + | - | + | - | - | + | - | - | - | + |
| Assyrian | + | - | + | - | + | - | + | - | + | - | - | + |
| Anglo-Saxon | - | - | + | - | + | + | - | + | - | - | - | + |
| Byzantine | + | + | + | - | + | - | + | + | + | + | + | - |
| Moslem | + | + | + | - | + | - | + | + | + | + | + | + |
| Hun | - | - | + | - | + | - | - | - | - | - | - | + |

**Source:**   Figure, "SFA Grid for Early Civilizations" and excerpts from *Semantic Feature Analysis: Classroom Applications* by Susan D. Pittelman, Joan E. Heimlich, Roberta L. Berglund and Michael P. French. Reprinted with permission of the International Reading Association.

Students then analyze each word in the column, feature by feature, by recording a plus (+) or minus (–) on the grid. A plus indicates that the word possesses the feature; a minus means that the feature is not associated with the word. Students may use a question mark (?) to suggest their uncertainty about a particular feature.

As a teaching activity, SFA is easily suited to prereading or postreading situations. If you used it for prereading to activate what students know about words, then recognize that they can return to the SFA after reading to clarify and reformulate some of their initial responses on the SFA grid.

Pittelman, Heimlich, Berglund, and French (1991) suggest a two-day lesson plan in a seventh-grade social studies class for the SFA grid illustrated in Box 4.4. In the lesson plan, the SFA strategy serves as an extension activity toward the end of a unit of study. The lesson permits students to review and refine their conceptual knowledge of early civilizations as they sort through the relationships among the concept words and possible features.

**Day 1**

1. Draw a grid on an overhead transparency, chalkboard, or large sheet of chart paper.

2. Write Early Civilizations at the top of the left hand column. Along the top of the grid, write Features.

3. Ask students to recall the various early civilizations the class has studied in the unit (e.g., Roman, Egyptian). As students suggest the civilizations, list them down the left side of the grid.

4. Ask students to suggest features or characteristics of early civilizations (e.g., educated, monotheism, slavery). As each feature is mentioned, list it at the top of the grid.

5. Review the procedure for completing a grid by explaining to the students that if a civilization had a specific characteristic, they should put a plus in the box; if the characteristic did not apply to that civilization, they should put a minus in the box. Remind the students that if they are not sure, or if the class cannot agree on a rating, a question mark should be used.

6. Have the class help you fill in the appropriate marks for the first civilization listed on the grid (Roman). For each feature, discuss with the class whether there should be a plus, a minus, or a question mark in the box.

7. Distribute copies of a blank grid to students and have them copy the civilizations and the features onto their grids.

8. Instruct the students to use their notes and textbooks and work independently to complete the grid for the remaining civilizations. Encourage the students to add features they think would apply to any of the civilizations.

**Day 2**

1. Display the initial grid on the overhead projector, chalkboard, or chart. Review each civilization by asking students to share whether they had filled in a plus, minus, or question mark for each feature.

2. Encourage discussion about the responses, guiding the students to defend their decisions in cases of disagreement.

3. As responses are shared and consensus is reached, record the responses on the master grid. Provide an opportunity for students to modify their own grids as necessary.

4. Ask the students to share any additional features they have identified. Through discussion, have the class fill in the appropriate marks for each new feature.

5. Using the semantic feature analysis grid as a base, help students to generalize the similarities and differences among the civilizations.

6. Encourage students to use the completed grid as a study tool.

**Classification and Categorization.** Closed word sorts enable students to study words by requiring them to classify terms in relation to more general concepts. Examine how a business teacher helped extend students' knowledge of concepts from an assignment on types of resources. He directed the class to classify the list of terms under the three types of resources that they had read about.

| | | |
|---|---|---|
| tools | trees | power plants |
| minerals | wildlife | buildings |
| water | factories | |
| labor | tractors | |
| machinery | typewriters | |

| Natural Resources | Capital Resources | Human Resources |
|---|---|---|

Vocabulary extension exercises involving categorization require students to determine relationships among technical terms in much the same manner as word sorts. The difference, however, lies in the amount of structure students are given to make cognitive decisions. Put another way, students are usually given four to six words per grouping and asked to do something with them. That something depends on the format used in the exercise. For example, you can give students sets of words and ask them to circle the word in each set which includes the others. This exercise demands that students perceive common attributes or examples in relation to a more inclusive concept, to distinguish superordinate from subordinate terms. Study several sample exercises from different content areas:

**Social Studies**
*Directions:* Circle the word in each group that includes the others.

| | |
|---|---|
| government | throne |
| council | coronation |
| judges | crown |
| governor | church |

**English**
*Directions:* Circle the word that best includes the others.

| | |
|---|---|
| satire | humor |
| humor | satire |
| irony | irony |
| parody | tone |

**Geometry**
*Directions:* Circle the word that includes the others.

| | |
|---|---|
| closure | function |
| distributive | domain |
| property | range |
| associative | relation |
| commutative | preimage |

A variation on this format directs students to cross out the word that does not belong, and then explain in a word or phrase the relationship which exists among the common items.

**English**
*Directions:* Cross out the word in each set that does not belong. On the line above the set, write the word or phrase that explains the relationship among the remaining three words.

| _____ | _____ |
|---|---|
| drama | time |
| comedy | character |
| epic | place |
| tragedy | action |

Teachers find that they can construct categorization activities efficiently and effectively when the activities refer back to a previously constructed graphic organizer. The tie-in between an organizer and categories is logical:

Since graphic organizers depict superordinate-subordinate relationships among key terms, it is relatively easy to develop extension exercises involving categorization from them.

For example, turn to the organizer on abnormality in this chapter. Study the relationships shown among the key terms. If you were to construct categories in which students would circle the word in each set that included the others, which possible word groups might be formed? Probably groups similar to these:

| | | |
|---|---|---|
| neurosis | paranoia | depression |
| abnormality | schizophrenia | neurosis |
| mental retardation | catatonia | phobia |
| psychosis | hebephrenia | anxiety |

A quick perusal of the abnormality organizer would also give the ideas for categories in which students would cross out the word that didn't belong in each set. Examples:

| | | |
|---|---|---|
| depression | catatonia | neurosis |
| anxiety | mental retardation | psychosis |
| antisocial | paranoia | personality disorders |
| phobias | hebephrenia | schizophrenia |

The secret to constructing categories, of course, is to know the superordinate and subordinate relationships among terms in a unit or a chapter.

**Concept Circles.**  One of the more versatile activities we have observed in a wide range of grade levels is the concept circle. Concept circles provide still another format and opportunity to study words critically—for students to relate words conceptually to one another. A concept circle may simply involve putting words or phrases in sections of a circle and directing students to describe or name the concept relationship that exists among the sections. The example in Figure 4.15 is from a fourth-grade class; the circle was part of a geography lesson.

In addition, you might direct students to shade in the section of a concept circle which contains a word or phrase that *does not relate* to words or phrases in the other sections of the circle. Once students shade in the section, they must then identify the concept relationships that exist among the remaining sections. See Figure 4.16.

Finally, a concept circle can be modified by leaving one or two sections of the circle empty, as in Figure 4.17. Direct students to fill in the empty section with a word or two which relate in some way to the terms of the other sections of the concept circles. Students are then put in the position of justifying their word choice by identifying the overarching concept depicted by the circle.

**Figure 4.15    EXAMPLE OF CONCEPT CIRCLE**

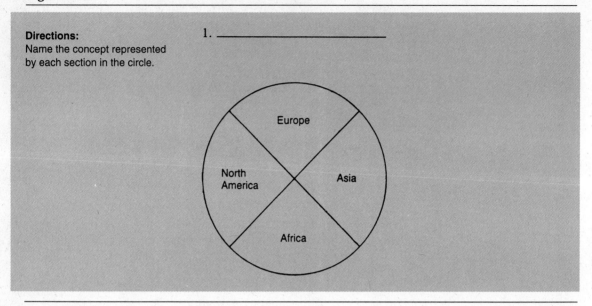

**Directions:**
Name the concept represented by each section in the circle.

1. _____

As you can see, concept circles serve the same function as categorization activities. However, students respond positively to the visual aspect of manipulating sections in a circle. Whereas categorization exercises sometimes appear like tests to students, concept circles are fun to do.

**Figure 4.16    VARIATION ON CONCEPT CIRCLE**

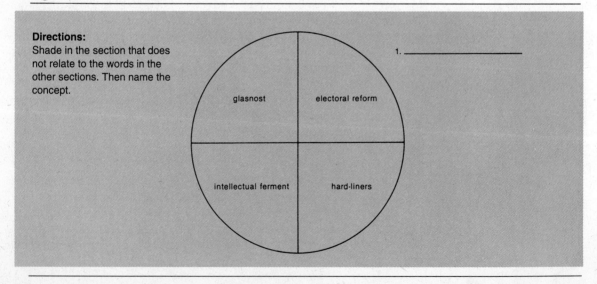

**Directions:**
Shade in the section that does not relate to the words in the other sections. Then name the concept.

1. _____

**Figure 4.17     ANOTHER VARIATION ON CONCEPT CIRCLE**

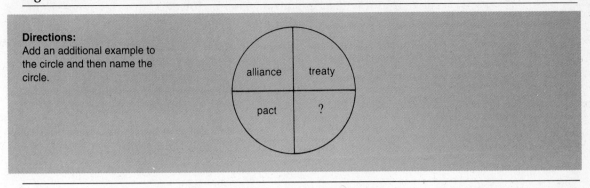

**Directions:**
Add an additional example to the circle and then name the circle.

alliance | treaty | pact | ?

**Post Graphic Organizers.** Earlier in the text, we described the graphic organizer as a technique to introduce students to the important interrelationships among the key concepts they are about to study. Along with semantic mapping, graphic organizers provide visual displays of how words are related to other words. Barron and Stone (1973) have also reported the value of *post graphic organizers*, which students construct after reading. Post graphic organizers allow students to work in groups to relate important content area terms in a spatial arrangement. To do this, students must analyze the relationships among the words.

The post graphic organizer as a reinforcement activity presumes that students are aware of the idea behind a graphic organizer. If they are not, you will need to provide them with an example or two. You can then introduce the class to a post graphic organizer by following these steps from Barron and Stone:

1. Type the key words on a ditto master.

2. After they read and study the material to be learned, place students into small groups of about two or three students each.

3. Distribute the list of terms and a packet of three-by-five-inch index cards to each group.

4. Students write each word from the list on a card. They then work together to decide upon a spatial arrangement among the cards which depicts the major relationship among the words.

5. As students work, provide assistance as needed.

6. Initiate a discussion of the constructed organizer.

Before actually assigning a post graphic organizer to students, the teacher should prepare for the activity by carefully analyzing the vocabulary of the material to be learned. List all the terms that are essential for students to understand. Then add relevant terms which you feel the students already understand and which will help them relate what they know to the new material. Finally, construct your own organizer.

The form of the student-constructed graphic organizer will doubtless differ from the teacher's arrangement. However, this difference in and of itself should not be a major source of concern. According to Herber (1978),

> Form is not the issue; substance is, and that is demonstrated by a clear portrayal of the implicit relationships among key words. . . . Students will see things differently than teachers and from one another. It is good . . . for the teacher to have thought through his or her own arrangement of the words for purposes of comparison, clarification and confirmation. (p. 149)

What is important, then, is that the post graphic organizer reinforce students' ability to relate essential ideas to one another through the key vocabulary terms in content materials.

## LOOKING BACK, LOOKING FORWARD

A strong relationship exists between vocabulary knowledge and reading comprehension. In this chapter, we provided numerous examples of what it means to teach words well: giving students multiple opportunities to build vocabulary knowledge, learning how words are conceptually related to one another, and how they are defined contextually in the material that students are studying. Vocabulary activities provide students the multiple experiences they need to use and manipulate words in differing situations. Conceptual activities provide the framework needed to study words critically. Various types of concept extension activities, such as vocabulary self-collection, semantic feature analysis, semantic maps, concept of definition, word sorts, categories, concept circles, and post-graphic organizers reinforce and extend student's abilities to perceive relationships among words they are studying.

In the next chapter, our emphasis turns to kindling student interest in text assignments and preparing them to think positively about what they will read. The importance of the role of prereading preparation in learning from text has often been neglected or underestimated in the content area classroom. Yet, prereading activity is in many ways as important to the text learner as warm-up preparation is to the athlete. Let's find out why.

## SUGGESTED READINGS

Blachowicz, C. L. Z. (1986). Making connections: Alternatives to the vocabulary notebook. *Journal of Reading, 29,* 643–49.

Graves, M. & Prenn, M. C. (1986). Costs and benefits of various methods of teaching vocabulary. *Journal of Reading, 29,* 596–602.

Hagard, M. 1986. The vocabulary self-collection strategy: Using student interest and word knowledge to enhance vocabulary growth. *Journal of Reading, 29,* 634–38.

Heimlich, J. & Pittelman, S. D. (1986). *Semantic mapping: Classroom applications.* Newark, DE: International Reading Association.

Johnson, D. & Johnson, B. 1986. Highlighting vocabulary in inferential comprehension instruction. *Journal of Reading, 29,* 622–25.

Marzano, R. and Marzano, J. (1988). *A Cluster approach to elementary vocabulary instruction.* Newark, DE: International Reading Association.

McKeown, M. 1985 The Acquisition of word meaning from context by children of high and low ability. *Reading Research Quarterly, 20,* 482–96.

McKeown, M., Beck, I. Omanson, R. & Pople, M. (1985). Some effects of the nature and frequency of vocabulary instruction on the knowledge and use of words. *Reading Research Quarterly, 20,* 222–35.

Nagy, W., Herman, P., & Anderson, R. C. (1985). Learning words from context. *Reading Research Quarterly, 20,* 233–53.

Nagy, W. (1988). *Teaching vocabulary to improve reading comprehension.* Newark, DE: International Reading Association.

Ryder, R. (1985). Student activated vocabulary instruction. *Journal of Reading, 28,* 254–59.

Stahl, S. (1986). Three principles of effective vocabulary instruction. *Journal of Reading, 29,* 662–68.

# 5

# Activating Prior Knowledge and Interest

> When the student is ready, the teacher appears.
>
> —*Author unknown*

## ORGANIZING PRINCIPLE

More often than not, content area teachers are perplexed by the behavior of learners who are capable of acquiring content through lecture, discussion, and other modes of classroom presentation, but who appear neither ready nor willing to learn with texts. The wisdom in the saying "When the student is ready, the teacher appears" is self-evident; yet teachers who want to use texts often find themselves waiting in the wings to make their appearance and wondering, "*When* is the student ready?"

Certainly preparing students for the language of a content area, as we discussed in the previous chapter, readies them for learning with texts. The more learners connect what they know to the vocabulary of a content area, the more familiar and confident they are likely to be with the material being studied. To be ready, for sure, is a state of mind; a mental preparation for learning; a psychological predisposition. But content area teachers know that readiness also entails an emotional commitment; an emotional stake in the ideas under scrutiny in an academic content area; a willingness on the part of the students to *want* to engage in learning. Most students, we believe, would like to use reading to learn, but don't believe that they have much chance for success. So some find any excuse to avoid reading. Others go through the motions—reading assigned material purposelessly—to satisfy the teacher's requirements rather than their own as learners.

When are students ready? We're tempted to say: when they are willing. Students *will* want to read to learn, first and foremost, when they develop a sense of confidence with texts. Ability alone is no guarantee that students will use reading to learn. Neither is knowledge of the subject. Competence and confidence go together like Astaire and Rogers or Laurel and Hardy. As Virgil, the ancient Roman poet, affirmed all things are within the realm of human possibility when people have confidence in their ability to succeed. "They can," Virgil mused, "because they think they can."

Confident readers think and learn with texts, but also they think positively about the process of learning with texts. They generate interest in the task at hand; their goals are in front of them. If there is an imperative in this chapter, it is to kindle student interest in text assignments and prepare them to think positively about what they will read.

Preparing students to read can easily be neglected in a teacher's rush to cover the content of the curriculum. Yet the payoffs of prereading activation, as suggested in the organizing principle of the chapter, will make your efforts worthwhile: *Piquing interest and raising expectations about the meaning of texts create a context in which students will read with purpose and anticipation.*

Study the Chapter Overview before you begin reading to gain direction and help in organizing what you already know and will need to know.

## CHAPTER OVERVIEW

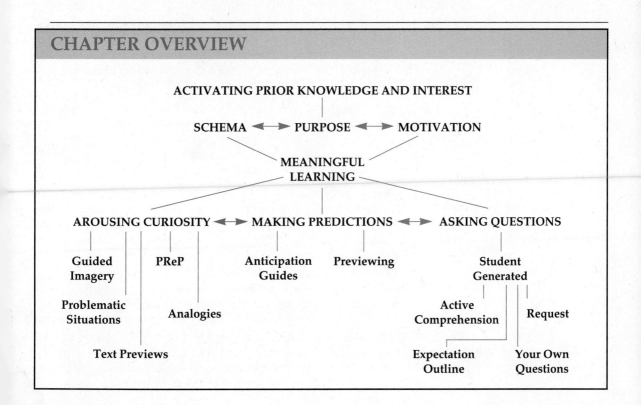

## FRAME OF MIND

1. Why does activating prior knowledge and interest prepare students to approach text reading in a critical frame of mind?

2. How can meaningful learning be achieved in content area reading situations?

3. What are the relationships between curiosity arousal, conceptual conflict, and motivation?

4. How and why do prediction strategies such as previewing and the use of anticipation guides facilitate reading comprehension?

5. What is the value of student-generated questions and how might teachers help students to ask questions as they read?

6. Which prereading strategies seem to be the most useful for your content area? Least useful? Why?

Explanations of reading tend to be complex. Yet as intricate a process as reading may be, it's surely just as magical and mysterious to most of us. After all, who ever really knows a covert process—one that takes place in the head?

Huey (1908) tells a fascinating tale about the adventurer Livingstone in Africa:

> Livingstone excited the wonder and awe of an African tribe as he daily perused a book that had survived the vicissitudes of travel. So incomprehensible, to these savages, was his performance with the book, that they finally stole it and *ate* it, as the best way they knew of "reading" it, of getting the white man's satisfaction from it (p. 2).

The preliterate natives wanted what Livingstone had. They were so motivated by his sense of pleasure and satisfaction with texts that they wanted to exercise some control over the rather mystical and mysterious process of which they had little concept. So they acted in the only way they knew how. Eating Livingstone's book was a response, somewhat magical, to their uncertainty and lack of control over the process that we call reading. Teachers should be so fortunate as to have students who want to devour texts, metaphorically speaking, in the pursuit of knowledge!

Magic and uncertainty go hand in hand. According to Malinowski (1954), people resort to magic in situations where they feel they have limited control over the success of their activities. This is so in primitive cultures such as the African tribe described by Huey or in highly technological societies such as ours.

We believe an element of mystery will always be a part of reading, even though it appears to be second nature to many of us. For most teachers reading just happens, particularly when there is a strong purpose or need to read in the first place. However, a great deal of uncertainty pervades reading for many students. The reading process remains a mystery, a lot of hocus-pocus, for students who believe they have limited control over their chances for success with a reading assignment.

As a result, some students resort to a special kind of "magic" to achieve control over the information and concepts communicated in a text. Magic, in this case, often involves bypassing the text altogether. In its place, students might resort to memorizing class notes, reading "Cliff-note" summaries, or praying for an easy exam that doesn't require text reading.

You can do a great deal to reduce the lack of control and the uncertainty that students bring to text learning situations. You can take the mystery out of learning with texts by generating students' interest in what they are reading, convincing them that they know more about the subject under study than they think they do, helping them to actively connect what they do know to the content of the text, and making them aware of the strategies they need in order to construct meaning.

Certainly preparing students for the language of a content area, as we discussed in the previous chapter, readies them for learning with texts. The more learners connect what they know to the vocabulary of a content area, the more familiar and confident they are likely to be with the material being studied. To be ready for sure is a state of mind, a mental preparation for learning, a psychological predisposition. But content area teachers know that readiness also entails an emotional commitment, an emotional stake in the ideas under scrutiny in an academic content area, a willingness on the part of students to *want* to engage in learning.

Most students, we believe, would like to use reading to learn, but don't believe that they have much of a chance of success. So some find any excuse to avoid reading. Others go through the motions—reading assigned material purposelessly—to satisfy the teacher's requirements rather than their own as learners.

The challenge content area teachers face with reading to learn is not necessarily related to students' inability to handle the conceptual and stylistic demands inherent in academic texts. What students can do and what they choose to do are related but different instructional matters. This is why you need to create conditions that not only allow students to read effectively but also motivate them to want to read in ways that are purposeful and meaningful.

## MEANINGFUL LEARNING, SCHEMA, AND MOTIVATION

Return to the questions "When is the student ready to read? To learn with texts?" First, recognize that readiness is a conditional concept. *If,* for example, learning is to be meaningful, *then* students must approach a reading task with purpose and commitment. More than 20 years ago, two of our professional heroes, Jerome Bruner and Eliot Eisner, celebrated the inseparability of thought and feeling in matters pertaining to the mind and the school curriculum. Bruner (1970), a pioneer in the psychology of the mind, suggested that the mind doesn't work apart from feeling and commitment. The learner makes meaning when he or she exhibits an "inherent passion" for what is to be learned. That is to say, *if* knowledge is to be constructed, *then* it must be put into a context of action and commitment. Willingness is the key; action, the instrument for learning.

At about the same time, Eisner (1969), a curriculum revisionist, expressed sentiments similar to Bruner's, but from a curriculum rather than a cognitive perspective: "It may be that the most important goal of education is to enable people to think in such a way that the kind of experience they undergo is a feelingful experience" (p. 28). Today, Bruner and Eisner remain steadfast in their conviction that meaningful learning is inspired by the inseparability of feeling and thought in action.

In his latest book, *Acts of Meaning,* Bruner (1990) champions a renewed cognitive revolution that is sensitive to meaning-making within a cultural context. How people construct meaning depends on their beliefs, mental states, intentions, desires, and commitments. Likewise, Eisner (1991) calls us to celebrate thinking in schools by reminding us that brains may be born, but minds are made. Schools do not pay enough attention to students' curiosity and their imagination. As a result, students disengage from active participation in the academic life of the classroom because there is little satisfaction to be gained from it. Unless the student receives satisfaction from school work, Eisner argues, there is little reason or motive to continue to pursue learning: "Thinking . . . should be prized not only because it leads to attractive destinations but because the journey itself is satisfying" (p. 40).

In exploring matters of the mind, cognitive activity cannot be divorced from emotional involvement. Schema and motivation are intertwined with students' reasons for reading. Meaningful learning with texts occurs when students reap a feeling of satisfaction with texts and a sense of accomplishment.

In previous chapters we have underscored the important role that schema plays in meaningful learning, so we won't belabor the point here, other than to reaffirm that prior knowledge activation is inescapably bound to one's purposes for reading and learning. As students ready themselves to learn with texts, they need to approach upcoming material in a critical frame of mind for potentially meaningful but new material that they will encounter while reading. This is why we initiate each chapter of this book with an Organizing Principle, a Chapter Overview in the form of a graphic organizer, and Frame of Mind questions. These instructional aids should make readers receptive to meaningful learning by creating a reference point for connecting the given—what one knows—with the new—the material to be learned. A frame of reference signals the connections students must make between the given and the new. They need to recognize how new material fits into the conceptual frameworks they already have.

Thelen (1984) likens an individual's store of knowledge to a personal filing cabinet. She noted that "As students encounter new ideas, they need appropriate filing systems for storing the information" (p. 12). In other words, helping students to organize what they know is a critical step in preparing them to read. Moreover, showing them *where* and *how* new ideas fit into existing knowledge structures is essential for active learning to take place. This is why graphic organizers, semantic maps, and other conceptually related instructional activities presented in the previous chapter induce a cognitive set for learning. These activities provide a frame of reference for what students know and what they will need to learn.

Two of the most appropriate questions that students can ask about a reading selection are "What do I need to know?" and "How well do I already know it?" "What do I need to know?" prompts readers to activate their prior knowledge to make predictions and set purposes. It gets them thinking positively about the reading material. "How well do I already know it?" helps readers to search their experience and knowledge to give support to tentative predictions and to help make plans for reading.

As simple as these two questions may appear on the surface, maturing readers rarely *know enough* about the reading process to ask them. "What do I need to know?" and "How well do I already know it?" require, as we discussed in Chapter 2, *metacognitive awareness* on the part of learners. However, these two questions, when consciously raised and reflected upon, put students on the road to regulating and monitoring their own reading behavior. It is never too early (or too late) to begin showing students how to set purposes by raising questions about text.

Nevertheless, the old expression "You can lead a horse to water, but you can't make it drink" reflects the role that commitment and motivation play in purposeful learning. Students may be skilled in their ability to read and knowledgeable about a subject, but they may not bring that skill and knowledge to bear in a learning situation. The apathetic stares and the groans of dissatisfaction are sledgehammerlike signs that students aren't willing to attend to the learning situation at hand. It often takes more than ability to get students to open their books.

Motivation has been described by psychologists as those processes that arouse behavior, give direction or purpose to behavior, and continue to allow behavior to persist (Wlodkowski, 1982). When a teacher creates conditions that allow students to establish *within themselves* motives for reading, readiness to learn is affected.

Curiosity, prediction, and question-asking are intrinsic to learning and one's desire to learn. Teachers can use these epistemic, knowledge-seeking processes as pedagogical tools to activate what students know and to capture their interest in content area reading. The more students predict as they read, the more they will read with certainty, confidence, and commitment; the greater their curiosity, the greater their motivation to read; the more they generate questions for reading, the more active their search for meaning will be.

Prediction, curiosity, and self-questioning underscore one of the most important functions of reading, which is to solve problems. Text learners will recognize that there are problems—conceptual conflicts—to be resolved that they can best resolve through reading. Conceptual conflicts are the key to creating motivational conditions in the classroom (Berlyne 1965). Should students be presented with prereading situations that take the form of puzzlement, doubt, surprise, perplexity, contradiction, or ambiguity, they will be motivated to seek resolution. Why is this the case? The need within the learner is to resolve the conflict. As a result, the search for knowledge becomes a driving motivational force. When a question begins to gnaw at a learner, searching behavior is aroused; learning occurs as the conceptual conflict resolves itself.

# AROUSING CURIOSITY

Arousing curiosity and activating prior knowledge are closely related instructional activities. Curiosity arousal gives students the chance to consider what they know already about the material to be read. Through your guidance they are encouraged to make connections—to relate their knowledge to the text assignment. And further, they will recognize that there are problems—conceptual conflicts—to be resolved through reading. Arousing curiosity helps students raise questions that they can answer only by giving thought to what they read.

## Establishing Problematic Situations and Perspectives

Creating problems to be solved or perspectives from which readers approach text material provides an imaginative entry into a text selection. For example, the teacher's role in creating problematic situations is one of (1) providing the time to discuss the problem, raising questions, and seeking possible solutions prior to reading, and then (2) assigning the reading material that will help lead to resolution and conceptual development.

Collette (1973) offers an excellent example of a teachable moment that helped students get "curiouser" about reading science materials:

An unusual fall thunderstorm killed one of two men who sought shelter under a tree. The ninth-grade students immediately were curious about the reason for the death of only one man while his companion only a couple of feet away was unharmed. The science teacher explained that man did not know much about the action of lightning and suggested that the pupils make a list of questions that would likely be answered by looking in books and other references.

In addition to the teachable moment, consider keying a problematic situation directly to specific text selections. For example, a social studies teacher and her students were exploring the development of early American settlements in a unit on Colonial life. She presented the problematic situation to students, as shown in Box 5.1. The series of questions promoted in interest-filled discussion, putting students into a situation in which they had to rely on prior knowledge for responses.

Asking the students in the social studies class to approach reading by imagining that they were early European settlers placed them in a particular role. With the role comes a perspective. Creating such a perspective has its underpinnings in a schema-theoretical view of the reading process.

One of the earlier studies from the Center for the Study of Reading at the University of Illinois pointed to the powerful role of perspective in comprehending text (Pichert and Anderson 1977). The researchers showed just how important the reader's perspective can be. Two groups of readers were asked to read a passage about a house from one of two perspectives, that of either a burglar or a house buyer. When readers who held the perspective of a house burglar read a story about going through a house, they recalled different information than those readers who approached the story from the perspective of a house buyer.

Creating a perspective (a role) for the student is one way to get into reading. Students in these roles find themselves solving problems that force them to use their knowledge and experience.

In Box 5.2, a high school teacher created a perspective for students before assigning a reading selection from an auto mechanics manual.

In preparation for reading the short story "Alas Babylon," an English teacher set up a perspective in which students' curiosity was aroused and expectations for the story raised:

> The year is 1990. We are on the verge of a nuclear disaster. Through inside sources you hear that the attack will occur within five days. What preparations will you consider making before the nuclear attack occurs?

---

**BOX 5.1    Problematic Situation in American History Class**

Suppose the time is 1680 and the place Massachusetts. Imagine that you are early European settlers. You will want to try to think as you believe they may have thought, act as they might have acted. You and your group have petitioned the Great and General Court to be allowed to form a new town. After checking to make sure you are of good character and the land is fertile and can be defended, the court says yes. They grant you a five-mile square of land. As proprietors of this land, you must plan a town. What buildings would you put in first? Second? Third? Later? Why? How would you divide the land among the many people who want to live there? Why? As proprietors would you treat yourselves differently from the way you treated the others? Why? How would you run the government?

---

**BOX 5.2    Creating a Perspective in an Auto Mechanics Class**

**The Perspective:**

You are the only mechanic on duty when a four-wheel-drive truck with a V-8 engine pulls in for repair. The truck has high mileage, and it appears that the problem may be a worn clutch disk. What tools do you think you will need? What procedures would you follow? Put your answers to these questions under the two columns below.

**Tools needed**                              **Procedures**

---

The class considered the orienting question. After some discussion, the teacher initiated the activity in Box 5.3. The students then formed small groups in which each group was directed to come to consensus on the twelve items they would choose. Those items were chosen from the list in Box 5.3.

From the small-group discussions came the recognition that the values, beliefs, and attitudes readers bring to text shape their perspective as much as their background knowledge of a topic. For this reason, we suggest that building motivation for text to be read take into account, where appropriate, the examination of values, attitudes, and controversial issues related to the subject matter under study.

## Guided Imagery

Guided imagery allows students to explore concepts visually. Samples (1977) recommends guided imagery, among other things, as a means for:

1. building an experience base for inquiry, discussion, and group work,

2. building self-image,

3. exploring and stretching concepts,

4. solving and clarifying problems,

5. exploring history and the future,

6. exploring other lands and worlds;

---

**BOX 5.3    Creating a Perspective in an English Class**

Assuming that your town and house will not be destroyed by the bomb and that you have enough time to prepare for the attack, which twelve items from the list provided will you choose?

_____ a.  buy a gun and ammunition to protect against looters

_____ b.  cash in all savings bonds and take all the money out of your checking and savings accounts

_____ c.  build a fireplace in your house

_____ d.  buy firewood and charcoal

_____ e.  buy extra tanks of gasoline and fill your car up

_____ f.  purchase antibiotics and other medicines

_____ g.  dig a latrine

_____ h.  buy lumber, nails, and various other supplies

_____ i.  plant fruit trees

_____ j.  notify all your friends and relatives of coming nuclear attack

_____ k.  invest in books on canning, making candles, and soap

_____ l.  buy a few head of livestock from a farmer

_____ m. buy fishing equipment and a boat

_____ n.  buy seeds of several different kinds of vegetables for a garden

_____ o.  make friends with a farmer who has a horse and wagon

_____ p.  shop at antique stores for kerosene lamps and large cooking pots

_____ q.  buy a safe to hide your money in

_____ r.  buy foodstuffs

---

Guided imagery works like this. The teacher, according to Samples, structures a daydream: "You use *words* to get into the process—but once there, images take over" (p. 188). After you read the illustration in Box 5.4 close your eyes and do it.

You may wish to have students discuss their "trips" which, of course, parallel in some way the content of the reading selection to be assigned. In the classroom where this example was devised, students in a literature class participated in the imagery discussion prior to reading a short story on space travel. Discussion questions included: "How did you feel just before entering the space capsule?" "What were the reactions of your companions?" "Where did your exploration take you?" "Were there things that surprised you on the trip? Colors? Sounds?"

Samples (1977) provides these tips as he explains the imagery strategy:

Relaxed positions are helpful. . . . As few distractions as possible will make the first few experiences easier. A soothing but audible voice is best. For those who can't get themselves to participate, an alternative quiet activity will cut down on embarrassed giggles. Leave lots of "empty" space both in terms of specific content and time to visualize. . . . (p. 188)

BOX 5.4    **Guided Imagery Illustration**

Close your eyes . . . tell all your muscles to relax. You are entering a space capsule ten minutes before takeoff. Soon you feel it lift off . . . you look over at your
companions and check their reactions. Now you are ready to take a reading of
the instrument panel. As you relay the information to ground control, it is 11
minutes into the flight . . . you settle back into your chair and tell your fellow
astronauts about your thoughts . . . about what you hope to see when the vehicle
lands . . . about what you might touch and hear as you explore the destination.
Finally, you drift off to sleep . . . picturing yourself returning to earth . . . seeing
once again your friends and relations. You are back where you started . . . tell
your muscles to move . . . open your eyes.

Guided imagery isn't for everyone. Some teachers will find themselves
uncomfortable using it; other will not. As a prereading alternative, however, it gives you an additional option that will help students connect, in this
case, what they "see " to what they will read.

## Analogies and Text Previews

An analogy establishes a comparison-contrast between concepts familiar to
the reader and unfamiliar ideas which will be encountered in text. For
example, in the Hayes and Tierney (1982) study, readers compared what
they already knew about the game of baseball with information from a text
passage on the English sport cricket. Activating readers' knowledge of baseball served as a frame of reference for understanding the cricket passage.

In everyday terms, analogies often have been devised as part of a verbal
presentation. Analogies can be created for almost any content area. In reading a literary work, for example, an English or language arts teacher may
devise an analogous situation in which students compare their approach to
a problem with a problem that the protagonist of the story must resolve. Or
the teacher may create an analogy around the theme of the selection. If students were to read "The Gift of the Magi" they might examine their own
beliefs and understandings about giving and receiving in relation to the
story's theme.

We recommend the following guidelines for constructing analogies
during prereading preparation:

1. Construct an analogy for difficult text material only.

2. Devise the analogy so that it reflects the main ideas in the text to be
   assigned. Make sure that these ideas are prominent and easily identifiable in the analogy.

3. In the analogy, use real-life incidents, anecdotes, familiar examples, or
   illustrations to which readers can relate. These devices serve as a basis

for comparing or contrasting what readers know already with unfamiliar material.

4. Raise a question or two in the analogy that will engage students in thinking about the text to be read.

Study the analogy in Box 5.5, which was prepared for a junior high school science lesson on the Earth's physical makeup.

As the students discussed the analogy in Box 5.5, the teacher used an orange and a facsimile of the Earth as props. The discussion led to the clarification of key concept words introduced in the analogy passage. It also created the organizational framework that students needed to fit new information into existing knowledge.

Mathiason (1989) shows how a sixth-grade teacher, Mrs. Johnson, used an analogy to activate prior knowledge and interest for a text assignment on keeping the heart healthy. Mrs. Johnson's class was studying the organs of the body and their functions. Working with an overhead projector, she displayed the transparency in Figure 5.1. The overhead transparency is a rough sketch of a city map of downtown Indianapolis.

Before assigning the text reading, "Keeping Your Heart Healthy," Mrs. Johnson asked the class to identify the heart of the city. As students responded, she drew a heart shape over the center of the city. As the discussion continued, she invited the students to locate the major roadways leading into

---

**BOX 5.5     An Example of an Analogy**

**The Orange and the Earth**

The Earth's physical makeup is very similar to the makeup of an orange. Sometimes an orange has one seed at its center. The Earth's single central "giant seed," about 760 miles in radius, is called the inner solid iron core. This inner core serves to give our planet life just as the orange's seed gives life.

Earth's interior is as liquid as the interior of an orange. However, the liquid in an orange is what we call orange juice, while the liquid in the Earth is liquid iron and is known as the outer liquid core. This liquid core is about 1400 miles in depth. The liquid iron is confined by what is called a rocky mantle; the juice of the orange is confined by a white spongy cellulose material. The difference is that the white cellulose is only a small fraction of the orange's radius, while the mantle of the Earth accounts for about a third of the Earth's radius, about 1300 miles.

As you may have guessed by now, both the orange and the Earth have a crust or skin which serves to protect the interior. The Earth's skin actually has two components: the asthenosphere, a layer of fudgelike consistency that extends about 300 miles, and the lithosphere, which is the Earth we walk on and see. The Earth's lithosphere is as thin as the skin of an orange by comparison. As you read more about the Earth's physical makeup, what other comparisons can you make between the orange and the Earth?

**Figure 5.1    AN ANALOGY FOR THE HEART USING A CITY MAP**

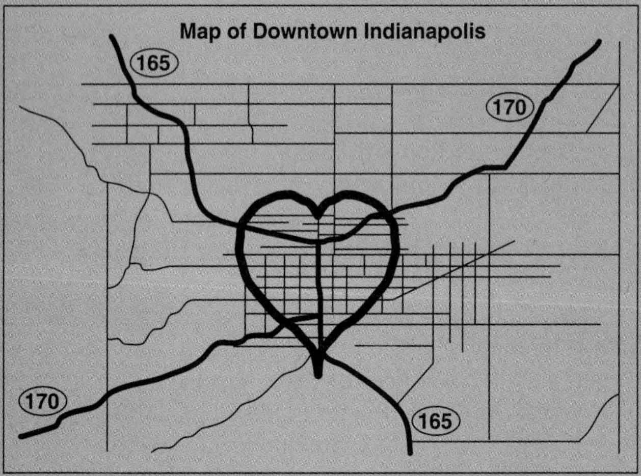

Map of Downtown Indianapolis

**Source:** From "Activating student interest in content area reading" by Carla Mathison, *Journal of Reading*, December 1989. Reprinted by permission of the International Reading Association.

and out of center-city. As they did so, she highlighted them on the transparency. The analogy took shape as students reflected on the question, "In what ways does the map remind you of the heart?"

With the analogy set, the prereading discussion was off and running. Issues were raised in terms of the familiar and the unfamiliar: the slowdown of traffic during the rush hour versus the slowing down of the blood supply from clogging of the heart's veins and arteries; a car wreck and a heart attack. The discussion concluded with Mrs. Johnson setting the stage for reading: "Tonight, for your homework, you're going to be reading about some things that make it hard for your veins and arteries to get all the blood to the heart that it needs. Why is that important information for you to know?"

Text previews are similar to analogies in that they also provide students with a frame of reference in which to understand new material. Previews should be used, like analogies, for difficult short stories. They may also be adapted for expository materials.

The preview passage should provide much more substantive information than the brief introductory statements which usually accompany selections found in literature textbooks. However, the real value of previews is that they build a frame of reference for the story.

To construct a preview, follow these guidelines:

1. Begin with a series of short statements and one or more questions that spark interest, provide a link between a familiar topic and the topic of the story, and encourage students to actively reflect upon the theme.

2. Provide a synopsis of the story that includes key elements in the story structure (without signaling the resolution or outcome of the plot).

3. Define several key terms within the context of the preview passage.

According to Graves, Prenn, and Cooke (1985), using a preview for pre-reading instruction is a relatively straightforward procedure. They recommend the following steps:

1. Tell students you're going to introduce the upcoming selection.

2. Read the first few sentences of the preview.

3. Given students two or three minutes to discuss the question or questions.

4. Read the remainder of the preview.

5. Have students begin reading immediately after you complete the preview (p. 597).

Study the example in Box 5.6 of a preview developed for Robert Cormier's short story, "In the Heat." If you teach (or are planning to teach) in a content area other than English, you might consider adopting the preview for nonnarrative material. Examine the preview in Box 5.7. It was developed by a vocational education teacher for a text chapter explaining the chemistry of cosmetics.

Notice how the teacher's preview begins by *establishing the main idea* of the text to be read. She then attempts to have students *build and share prior knowledge and experiences* relating to the chemicals in cosmetics that they have used. The final section of the preview helps students *make connections* between the text to be read and the knowledge they already have. *Key questions* are raised to provide students with expectations as to what is important material upon which to focus attention as they read.

Previews and analogies make excellent student writing assignments. Consider assigning students to write a preview in order to advertise a reading assignment for future groups of students. You might suggest that students put themselves in the shoes of the teacher or the author. The writing task might be introduced in this manner: "If you were the author of (*title of text selection*) how would you introduce readers to the major ideas in the reading selection?" To accompany the written passage, students may use pictures, posters, book jackets, slogans, or bumper stickers to capture the unifying idea of the text selection and to arouse interest. As students compose, they should be aware of their audience—other students. Impress upon students that their passages will be read and used by students in future classes.

The teacher may need to model how previews or analogies are constructed as part of prewriting discussion. This perhaps may entail reflecting upon a teacher-constructed passage that students had previously experienced. Which major ideas received the most prominence? Why did the teacher select these over others? Why were questions or examples included in the model passage?

BOX 5.6    **Preview for "In the Heat," by Robert Cormier**

Have you ever heard a bell ring and immediately remembered someone special? Has an aroma ever triggered a memory either painful or pleasant? Have you ever seen an object that suddenly reminds you of a loved one? Sometimes sounds, smells, and objects can spark our dusty long-ago memories. Think for a minute. Does seeing your old Little League baseball glove bring back memories? Or how about seeing your favorite doll peering through the top of an old attic box? Can you think of any examples where sounds, smells, sights, taste, or touch can bring old memories to life? (*Pause, wait for student responses.*) Of course, just because something touches off our memories doesn't mean that what we remember will always be pleasant. Sometimes memories can be painful. But who chooses what to remember?

In the beginning of our short story, "In the Heat," the main character is a father with a difficult task ahead of him. But before he begins this most unwanted, but necessary, task, he has a flashback—the heat from the scorching summer day reminds him of a time long ago when he could hear his father yelling up the stairs to all the kids, "Hell, come on down here. Who wants to go to sleep in this heat?" Yes, in his flashback it was his father who understood about the heat and "how a kid never wants to go to bed."

But the flashback ends quickly. Now, the father of our story realizes the task at hand and all the things that must be done. He says out loud, to no one in particular; "Yes, there are other things to think about . . . Not things, really. Only one: the fact of my wife's death." (*Pause.*)

As the father prepares to go to the services, he thinks to himself, "What I dread most are the *reminders,* waiting like unexploded time bombs in unexpected places. This morning, I *discovered* one of her bobby pins on the mantel. I stared at it awhile, *remembering* last winter's fires." But the father is not concerned about *his* memories, only. You see, this father has a teenage son, Richy. And the father is worried about what kind of memories Richy is going to have about his mother. Whenever Richy feels the scorching sun in the middle of summer, what will he remember about this day?

As you read this story, pay close attention to the development of the two characters: the father and Richy. Does the father need a name? Without a name, is the father still a believable character? Why or why not? Also, as you read this passage, be alert for metaphors, for example, "the sun now hemorrhaging to death . . . " or "my heart is Hiroshima." How do these and other metaphors affect the tone of the story? The author seems to convey a great deal of sadness, but at the same time the story seems uplifting. Why do you think?

## PReP

Brainstorming is a key feature of the *Prereading Plan (PReP)*, which may be used to generate interest in content area reading and to estimate levels of background knowledge that students bring to the text assignments. Judith Langer (1981) recommends PReP as an assessment/instructional activity

---

BOX 5.7    **Preview for "Chemistry of Cosmetics"**

A knowledge of chemistry is essential to making intelligent decisions about the use of cosmetics and other products. When we think of chemistry we often think of test tubes in a science lab with formulas bubbling and scientists experimenting. It is exactly that kind of setting where shampoos, cosmetics, perms, and hair coloring are developed. Did you ever use the wrong color or perm formula, making your hair look like a haystack? By learning some basics of chemistry we can avoid some of those mistakes.

   Chapter 32 first provides some general science information. For example, what are molecules? What is matter? The chapter then develops some important concepts about *cosmetic chemistry*. What do you need to know about mixtures and changes—physical and chemical (page 434)? What are the most common elements that you need to know about (pages 435 and 436)? Be sure that you will know how to explain pH scale (pages 436–439).

---

which fosters group discussion and an awareness of the topics to be covered. She suggested that PreP works best with groups of about ten students.

   Before beginning the PreP activity, the teacher should examine the text material for key words (which represent a major concept to be developed), phrases, or pictures, and then introduce the topic that is to be read, following the three-phase plan that Langer (1981, p. 154) outlines.

1. *Initial associations with the concept.* In this first phase the teacher says, "Tell anything that comes to mind when . . ." (e.g., ". . . you hear the word *Congress*"). As each student tells what ideas initially came to mind, the teacher jots each response on the board. During this phase the students have their first opportunity to find associations between the key concept and their prior knowledge. When this activity was carried out in a junior high school class, one student, Bill, said "important people." Another student, Danette, said "Washington, D.C."

2. *Reflections on initial associations.* During the second phase of the PreP the students are asked, "What made you think of . . . [the response given by a student]?" This phase helps the students develop awareness of their network of associations. They also have an opportunity to listen to each other's explanations, to interact, and to become aware of their changing ideas. Through this procedure they may weigh, reject, accept, revise, and integrate some of the ideas that came to mind. When Bill was asked what made him think of important people, he said, "I saw them in the newspaper." When Danette was asked what made her think of Washington, D.C., she said, "Congress takes place there."

3. *Reformulation of knowledge.* In this phase the teacher says, "Based on our discussion and before we read the text, have you any new ideas about . . . [e.g., Congress]?" This phase allows students to verbalize

associations that have been elaborated or changed through the discussion. Because they have had a chance to probe their memories to elaborate their prior knowledge, the responses elicited during the third phase are often more refined than those from phase one. This time Bill said, "lawmakers of America," and Danette said, "U.S. government part that makes the laws."

Through observation and listening during the PreP, content area teachers will find their students' knowledge can be classified into three broad levels. On one level are students who have *much* prior knowledge about the concept. These students are often able to define and draw analogies, make conceptual links, and think categorically. On another level are students who may have *some* prior knowledge. These students can give examples and cite characteristics of the content but may be unable to see relationships or make connections between what they know and the new material. On the third level are students who have *little* background knowledge. They often respond to the PreP activity with words that sound like the concept word and may attempt to make simple associations, often misassociating with the topic.

## MAKING PREDICTIONS

Prediction strategies activate thought about the content before reading. Students must rely on what they know through previous study and experience to make educated guesses about the material to be read.

Why an educated guess? Smith (1978) defines predicting as the prior elimination of unlikely alternatives. He suggested:

> Readers do not normally attend to print with their minds blank, with no prior purpose and with no expectation of what they might find in the text. . . . The way readers look for meaning is not to consider all possibilities, nor to make reckless guesses about just one, but rather to predict within the most likely range of alternatives. . . . Readers can derive meaning from text because they bring expectations about meaning to text (p. 163).

You can facilitate student-centered purposes by creating anticipation about the meaning of what will be read.

### Anticipation Guides

An anticipation guide is a series of statements to which students must respond individually before reading the text. Their value lies in the discussion that takes place after the exercise. The teacher's role during discussion is to activate and agitate thought. As students connect their knowledge of the world to the prediction task, you must remain open to a wide range of responses. Draw upon what students bring to the task, but remain nondirective in order to keep the discussion moving.

**An Anticipation Guide Demonstration.**  Sidney Harris wrote an article for his *Strictly Personal* column concerning an air crash that killed 75 persons returning from a college football game. Complete the anticipation guide Box 5.8 and then read the article.

This demonstration shows how strongly anticipation is founded on what the reader brings to the reading selection. Your response to each statement reflects what you know and believe already about the two concepts, tragedy and catastrophe. Notice that the opportunity to discuss your responses with other class members may have broadened your conceptual base or helped to further articulate and clarify the difference between the two terms.

By contrasting You and Harris, you probably read the selection more attentively, with purpose, to determine how accurate your predictions were and how similar or different your choices were from those of the author.

If there are differences between your choices for tragedy and Harris's, you have the opportunity to justify the reasons for your choices against those Harris provided. What better critical reading experience could you have?

Anticipation guides may vary in format but not in purpose. In each case, the reader's expectations about meaning are raised prior to reading the test. Keep these guidelines in mind in constructing and using an anticipation guide:

1. Analyze the material to be read. Determine the major ideas—implicit and explicit—with which students will interact.

2. Write those ideas in short, clear declarative statements. These statements should in some way reflect the world that the students live in or know about. Therefore, avoid abstractions whenever possible.

3. Put these statements into a format that will elicit anticipation and prediction making.

4. Discuss readers' predictions and anticipations prior to reading the text selection.

5. Assign the text selection. Have students evaluate the statements in light of the author's intent and purpose.

6. Contrast readers' predictions with author's intended meaning.

**Classroom Examples.**  A junior high social studies teacher prepared students for a reading assignment that contrasted the characteristics of Northern and Southern soldiers in the Civil War. She began by writing *Johnny Reb* and *Billy Yank* in two columns on the chalkboard. She asked students to think about what they already knew about the two groups of soldiers. How do you think they were alike? How were they different? After

## BOX 5.8     Anticipation Guide Demonstration: "Crash Was No Tragedy"

*Directions:* Before you read Harris's article, check those incidents you think should be classified as tragedies in the column headed You. Discuss your responses with class members, providing reasons for your choices. After reading the article, check in the column headed Harris those incidents that Harris could label as tragedy.

**You        Harris**

_____  _____  1. In his desire to remain in office, a law-and-order president authorizes breaking the law (for political and national security reasons) and is ultimately driven from office.

_____  _____  2. During the Master's Tournament, a golfer leading by ten strokes on the sixteenth hole of the last round is struck and killed by lightning.

_____  _____  3. In Guatemala, an earthquake kills 16,000 persons and leaves five times as many homeless.

_____  _____  4. A mass murderer slips and falls to his death as police close in on him.

_____  _____  5. A community spends one million dollars to upgrade its football program instead of its airport, and then its football team dies in a crash at that airport.

_____  _____  6. An understudy for an ill leading lady breaks her leg hurrying to meet her cue in her debut in a leading role.

_____  _____  7. A father and mother of three die in a head-on auto accident on the way home from a New Year's Eve party. The father was heard to brag about his capacity for alcohol and his ability to drive after drinking heavily.

_____  _____  8. A soccer team crashes in the Andes, and those who are left are forced to eat the flesh of the victims in order to have a chance to live. Only seven of thirty-six survive.

_____  _____  9. As his defenses crumble before the onslaught of the allies, a ruthless dictator shoots and kills himself and has his body cremated.

_____  _____  10. The week before the Master's Tournament, the golfer in statement 2 laughed at a near miss and asserted that as long as he wore a band-aid on his arm, nothing could happen to him. He refused to get off the course during a violent thunderstorm.

some discussion, the teacher invited the students to participate in the anticipation activity in Box 5.9.

Of course, each of the points highlighted in the statements was developed in the text selection. Not only did the students get a sense of the major ideas they would encounter in the text selection, but they also read to see how well they predicted which statements more accurately represented soldiers from the South and the North during the Civil War.

A science teacher began a weather unit by introducing a series of popular clichés about the weather. He asked students to anticipate whether or not the clichés had a scientific basis. See Box 5.10.

### Crash Was No Tragedy

### Sydney J. Harris

We say that differences in words are "just semantical" and so we fail to understand the important distinctions between words that we use interchangeably. But if we use the wrong word, it is hard to think properly.

For a few days last November, the newspapers were filled with the story of "the Marshall University air tragedy" that killed 75 persons returning from a football game to Huntington, W. Va.

If I said it was not a tragedy but a catastrophe, you would retort that I was quibbling about words, or that I am being shallow and unfeeling. I think I can show you that you would be wrong on both counts.

An airplane crash is a catastrophe (literally, from the Greek, an "overturning"), like a sudden flood, a fire, a falling girder. Such accidents are part of the natural order and of the human condition; they result from the contingency of things, and are sad or shocking or pitiful—but they are not tragic. There was, however, a tragic element in the Marshall University air crash; and we can recognize it only if we comprehend the difference between the two words. The tragedy lay in the community's frantic effort to have a winning football team, coupled with its indifference to an unsafe airport.

The school's and the city's hunger for football fame prompted the formation of a booster organization, the Big Green Club, made up of wealthy local business and professional men, who collected funds to help pay for the college's athletic program.

Two years ago, the athletic department's budget began to boom. A new coach was hired, players were recruited from other states, and the college's president resigned under pressure from sports buffs. Vigorous lobbying attempts were made in the state legislature to obtain $1 million for the building of an athletic field and facilities.

Meanwhile, the president of the Tri-State Airport Board confessed the day after the crash: "I've been sleeping with this possibility for the last eight years."

He blamed the lack of funds for the airport failure to have either radar or a warning light system—which would cost about $1 million, the price of the proposed athletic field.

In the classic Greek conception of tragedy, hubris, or false pride, is followed by hamartia, or sin, and this in turn is followed by nemesis, the fate that catches up with human pride and folly.

When having a victorious football team means more to the citizens than having a safe airport, then community hubris is riding for a terrible fall.

The players paid with their lives for this sin, but only if we understand the true nature of their "tragedy" will they not have died in vain.

**Source:** "Crash Was No Tragedy" by Sydney Harris from *Strictly Personal*. Reprinted with special permission of King Features Syndicate.

The prereading discussion led students to review and expand their concepts of scientific truth. Throughout different parts of the unit, the teacher returned to one or two of the clichés on the anticipation guide and suggested to the class that the textbook assignment would explain whether or not there was a scientific basis for each saying. Students were then directed to read to find out what the explanations were.

A final example of how an anticipation guide may be used as a prereading strategy is evident in a high school English teacher's presentation of Richard Brautigan's poem "It's Raining in Love." The poem is a good example of a contemporary poem that discusses love in a not so typical way. It is

---

**BOX 5.9     Anticipation Guide for Civil War Lesson**

Johnny Reb and Billy Yank were common soldiers of the Civil War. You will be reading about some of their basic differences in your textbook. What do you think those differences will be? Before reading your assignment, place the initials JR in front of the phrases that you think best describe Johnny Reb. Place initials BY in front of those statements which best describe Billy Yank. Do not mark those statements common to both sides.

_____     1. more likely to be able to read and write
_____     2. best able to adjust to living in the open areas
_____     3. more likely to be from a rural setting
_____     4. took a greater interest in politics
_____     5. more deeply religious
_____     6. often not able to sign his name
_____     7. disliked regimentation of army life
_____     8. more likely to speak more slowly and with an accent
_____     9. more probably a native American
_____    10. common man in the social order

---

the kind of poem that captures the way many high school students feel. Note the format used for the teacher's anticipation activity in Box 5.11.

## Previewing

Students who know how to preview text are in a strategic position to take charge of their own learning. Previewing is the type of cursory learning activity that helps readers to analyze the task at hand and make plans for reading.

To analyze the reading task and make plans, a student must ask questions such as these:

- What kind of reading is this?
- What is my primary goal or purpose?
- Should I try to remember details or read for the main ideas only?
- How much time will I devote to the reading assignment?
- What do I already know about the topic? What do I need to know?

In essence, questions such as these will make students aware of the purposes for a reading assignment so that they can adapt their reading and study to the task.

A strategy such as previewing gives students some idea of what a text selection is about before reading it. It prepares them for what is coming. Students' tendency, of course, is to jump right into an assignment, often without rhyme or reason, and plow though it. Not so, however, when they learn how to preview material. This prereading technique helps them to raise questions and set purposes.

---

**BOX 5.10    Anticipation Guide for Clichés About Weather**

Directions: Put a check under Likely if you feel that the weather saying has any scientific basis; put a check under Unlikely if you feel that it has no scientific basis. Be ready to explain your choice.

**Likely        Unlikely**

_____  _____  1. Red sky at night, sailors delight; red sky at morning, sailors take warning.
_____  _____  2. If you see a sunspot there is going to be bad weather.
_____  _____  3. When the leaves turn under it is going to storm.
_____  _____  4. If you see a hornet's nest high in a tree a harsh winter is coming.
_____  _____  5. Aching bones mean a cold and rainy forecast.
_____  _____  6. Groundhog sees his shadow—six more weeks of winter.
_____  _____  7. Rain before seven, sun by eleven.
_____  _____  8. If a cow lies down in a pasture, it means that it is going to rain soon.
_____  _____  9. Sea gull, sea gull sitting on the sand; it's never good weather while you're on land.

When students raise questions about content material that they preview, they are likely to examine the extent of their own uncertainty and to find out what they don't know about the information they will acquire during reading. As a result of previewing and questioning, students become involved in a search for answers during reading. However, previewing and questioning require active participation by students; this is why high-powered as well as low-powered readers have trouble previewing on their own. They need teachers who will provide explicit instruction in how to preview and activate questions. Where does the teacher start?

---

**BOX 5.11    Anticipation Guide for "It's Raining in Love"**

_Directions:_ We have already read several poems by Richard Brautigan. Before reading "It's Raining in Love," place a check in the You column next to each statement that you think expresses a feeling the poet will deal with in the poem. Discuss your choices in small groups and explain why you checked the statements you did. Then I'll assign the poem. After reading the poem, check the statements in the poet column that express the feelings that the poet did deal with in his poem.

**You        Poet**

_____  _____  Being in love is a painful experience.
_____  _____  Boys can be just as nervous as girls when they like a member of the opposite sex.
_____  _____  It is OK for a girl to call a boy and ask him out.
_____  _____  It's better to be friends with members of the opposite sex than to be in love with them.
_____  _____  Poetry about love must be mushy to be effective.
_____  _____  Once a person has been in love, he's (or she's) much more sensitive to another person's feelings when he finds out that person likes him.

Start the way a Harvard professor did. William Perry conducted an experiment with 1500 freshmen who were probably among the "finest readers in the country." He assigned a chapter from a history book, instructing the students to use their best strategies to read and study it. After approximately 20 minutes he asked them to stop reading and answer multiple-choice questions on the details of the chapter. Not surprisingly, the vast majority of the students scored high on the test. Yet, when they were asked to write a short essay summarizing the main idea of the chapter, only 15 students did so successfully. Why? Because these 15 freshmen, about one percent of the students in the experiment, took the time to preview the chapter before plunging into the details of the material.

Use this anecdote, as well as observations from an assessment of how students actually approach a text selection, to drive home the importance of sizing up the material before reading it. Discuss the reasons why most readers just plow through the material. And through give-and-take exchanges, begin to develop a rationale for previewing.

Previewing works well when content materials contain textbook aids that are organizational, typographic, or visual in nature. Textbook writers use these aids as guideposts for readers.

Certain organizational aids, such as the table of contents, preface, chapter introductions and/or summaries, and chapter questions, give readers valuable clues about the overall structure of a textbook or the important ideas in a unit or chapter. Previewing a table of contents for example, not only creates a general impression, but also helps readers to distinguish the forest from the trees. The table of contents gives students a feel for the overall theme or structure of the course material so that they may get a sense of the scope and sequence of ideas at the very beginning of the course. The teacher can also use the table of contents to build background and discuss the relatedness of each of the parts of the book. Model for students the kinds of questions that should be raised. "Why did the authors sequence the material this way?" "Why do the authors begin with _____ in Part One?" "If you were the author, would you have arranged the major parts in the text differently? Why?"

The table of contents can also be used to introduce a chapter or unit. The teacher might ask students to refer to Part One on the table of contents. "What do you think this part of the book is about?" "Why do you think so?" Key words can also be highlighted for discussion. For example, key terms in the table of contents of a business textbook may lead to questions such as these: "What do you think the author means by *values?*" "What does *budgeting* mean? What does it have to do with *financial planning?*" Open-ended questions such as these help readers to focus attention on the material and also illustrate the value of predicting and anticipating content.

As students zero in on a particular chapter, they can make use of additional organizational aids such as the introduction, summary, or questions at the end of the chapter. These aids often create a frame of reference for the important ideas in the chapter.

Typographical and visual aids within a chapter are also invaluable devices for previewing. Students can survey chapter titles; headings and subheadings; words, phrases, or sentences in special type; and pictures, diagrams, illustrations, charts, and graphs in advance of reading to get a general outline—an agenda, so to speak—of what to expect.

An author, for example, has a definite purpose in mind in using visual aids to enhance text material. In some cases, an aid is used to expand upon a concepts developed in the main text. In other cases, a graphic might be inserted to serve as an example or an illustration of an idea the writer has introduced.

Visual aids, particularly charts and tables, also help readers by summarizing and organizing information. Moreover, many aids, such as photographs and pictures, are experience builders in the sense that they add a reality dimension to expository material.

As a result, visual aids provide an important resource for building students' expectations before they read by providing a basis for group predictions. The stream chart shown in Figure 5.2, for example, could be used as part of a discussion to arouse interest and focus students' attention before reading the text. The chart might be the stimulus for questions such as:

- Where was bartering first used?
- What precious metal was first used for coins?
- Why were sheep so valuable?
- When was paper money first printed?
- Is bartering still used?
- Why don't we still use gold coins?

In general, students should learn and follow these steps when previewing:

1. Read the title. Convert it to a question.

2. Read the introduction, summary, and questions. What seem to be the author's main points?

3. Read the heads and subheads. Convert them to questions.

4. Read print in special type. Why are certain words, phrases, or sentences highlighted?

5. Study visual materials such as pictures, maps, diagrams. What do the graphics tell you about the chapter's content?

The teacher demonstrates the preview and then models effective previewing/questioning behaviors. This entails walking students through the process. Select several pages from the assigned reading and develop transparencies in which you annotate the types of questions students should ask while previewing. Then share the overhead transparencies with the class, explaining the reasons for your annotations. You might then have students open their textbooks to another section of the chapter. Take turns asking the kinds of questions that you modeled, paying attention to the organizational,

**Figure 5.2    STAGES IN THE DEVELOPMENT OF MONEY**

1. barter

2. objects used as a measure of value

3. valuable items used as a medium of exchange

4. money coined from precious metals

5. paper money printed

**Source:**  Robert Carter and John Richards. *Of, By and For the People*, Westchester, Ill.:
Benefic Press, 1972, p. 360.

typographical, and visual aids in the assigned material. Finally, as students develop metacognitive awareness, have them raise their own questions while previewing

## STUDENT-GENERATED QUESTIONS

Teaching students to generate their own questions about material to be read is one of the major instructional goals of prereading preparation. Harry Singer (1978) contends that whenever readers are involved in the process of asking questions, they are engaged in "active comprehension." Teachers encourage active comprehension when they *ask questions that beget questions in return.* You might, for example, focus attention on a picture or an illustration from a story or book and ask a question that induces student questions in response: "What would you like to know about the picture?" In return, invite the students to generate questions that might focus on the details in the picture or its overarching message.

Or you might decide to read to students an opening paragraph or two from a text selection, enough to whet their appetite about the selection. Then ask, "What else would you like to know about _____?" Complete the question by focusing attention on some aspect of the selection that is pivotal to students' comprehension. It may be a main character of a story or the main topic of an expository text.

Active comprehension questions not only will arouse interest and curiosity but also will draw learners into the material. As a result, they will read to satisfy purposes and resolve conceptual conflicts that they have identified through their own questions. Examine in the next several sections additional instructional strategies for engaging students in asking questions for reading.

### ReQuest

ReQuest was originally devised as a one-on-one remedial procedure involving the student and teacher. Yet this strategy can easily be adapted to content classrooms to help students think as they read. ReQuest encourages students to ask their own questions about the content material under study. Self-declared questions are forceful. They help students establish reasonable purposes for their reading. Betts (1950) describes a "highly desirable learning situation" as one in which the student does the questioning: "That is, the learner asks the questions, and sets up the problems to be solved during the reading activity" (p. 450).

ReQuest fosters an active search for meaning. The rules for ReQuest, as described by Manzo (1969), follow:

The purpose of this lesson is to improve your understanding of what you read. We will each read silently the first sentence. Then we will take turns asking questions about the sentence and what it means. You will ask questions first, then I will ask questions. Try to ask the kind of questions a teacher might ask, in the way a teacher might ask them. You may ask me as many questions as you wish. When you are asking me questions, I will close my book (or pass the book to you if there is only one between us). When I ask questions, you close your book. . . . Any question asked deserves to be answered as fully and honestly as possible. It is cheating for a teacher to withhold information or play dumb to draw out the student. It is unacceptable for a student to answer with "I don't know," since he can at least attempt to explain why he cannot answer. If questions are unclear to either party, requests for rephrasing or clarification are in order. The responder should be ready (and make it a practice) to justify his answer by reference back to the text or to expand on background that was used to build or to limit an answer. Whenever possible, if there is uncertainty about an answer, the respondent should check his answer against the text (pp. 124–125).

Although the rules for ReQuest were devised for one-on-one instruction, they can be adapted for the content classroom. If you decide to use ReQuest in your class, consider these steps:

1. Both the students and the teacher silently read a common segment of the text selection. Manzo recommends one sentence at a time for poor comprehenders. However, text passages of varying length are suitable in applications to a classroom. For example, both teacher and students begin by reading a paragraph or two.

2. The teacher closes the book and is questioned about the passage by the students.

3. Next there is an exchange of roles. The teacher now queries the students about the material.

4. Upon completion of the student-teacher exchange, the class reads the next segment of text. Steps 2 and 3 are repeated.

5. At a suitable point in the text, when students have processed enough information to make predictions about the remainder of the assignment, the exchange of questions stops. The teacher then asks prediction questions: "What do you think the rest of the assignment is about?" "Why do you think so?" Speculations are encouraged.

6. Students are then assigned the remaining portion of the selection to read silently.

7. The teacher facilitates follow-up discussion of the material.

You can modify the ReQuest procedure to good advantage. For example, consider alternating the role of questioner after each question. By doing so you will probably involve more students in the activity. Once students sense the types of questions that can be asked about a text passage, you might also try forming ReQuest teams. A ReQuest team composed of three or four students is pitted against another ReQuest team. Your role is to facilitate the multiple action resulting from the small-group formations.

Our own experiences with ReQuest suggest that students may consistently ask factual questions to stump the teacher. Such questions succeed brilliantly because you are subject to the same restrictions imposed by short-term memory as the students. That you miss an answer or two is actually healthy—after all, to err is human.

However, when students ask only verbatim questions because they don't know how to ask any others, then the situation is unhealthy. The sad fact is that some students don't know how to ask questions that will stimulate interpretive or applied levels of thinking. Therefore, your role as a good questioner during ReQuest is to provide a model that students will learn from. Over time you will notice the difference in the quality of student questions formulated.

## Expectation Outline

Spiegel (1981) suggests the development of an Expectation Outline to help students ask questions about text. She recommends the Expectation Outline for factual material, but the strategy can be adapted to narrative studies as well. The Expectation Outline is developed on the chalkboard or an overhead projector transparency as students simply tell what they expect to learn from a reading selection.

If students are reading a factual selection, you may have them first take several minutes to preview the material. The ask, "What do you think your assignment is going to be about?" Ask students to state their expectations in the form of questions. As they suggest questions, the teacher groups related questions on the chalkboard or transparency. You also have the opportunity to ask students what prompted them to ask these questions in the first place. At this point, students may be encouraged to refer back to the text to support questions.

Once questions have been asked and grouped, the class labels each set of questions. Through discussion, students begin to see the major topics which will emerge from the reading. Lead them to recognize that gaps might exist in the Expectation Outline for the assignment. For example, you may add a topic or two to the outline for which there were no questions raised. Upon completion of the Expectation Outline, students read to answer the questions generated.

For narrative materials, students may use the title of the selection, pictures, or key words and phrases from the selection to ask their questions. For example, direct students to preview a story by skimming through it quickly, studying the pictures and illustrations (if any) and jotting down five to ten key words or phrases that appear to indicate the main direction of the story. As students suggest key words and phrases, write these on the board and categorize them. Then ask students to state what they expect to find out from the story. Have them raise questions about its title, setting and characters, plot and theme. As an alternative to questions, students may summarize their expectations by writing a paragraph about the story using the key words and phrases that were jotted down and categorized.

A variation on the Expectation Outline is a strategy called *Your Own Questions*. Here's how it works:

1. Have students listen to or read a portion of text from the beginning of a selection.

2. Ask students to write five to ten questions that they think will be answered by reading the remainder of the selection.

3. Discuss some of the questions asked by the students before reading. Write the questions on the board.

4. Students then read to see if questions are answered.

5. After reading, which questions were answered? Which weren't? Why not?

Strategies such as an Expectation Outline or Your Own Questions teach students how to approach reading material with an inquisitive mind. These instructional strategies and the others presented in this chapter form a bridge between teacher-initiated guidance and independent learning behavior on the part of students.

## LOOKING BACK, LOOKING FORWARD

Meaningful learning with texts occurs when students experience a sense of satisfaction with text and a feeling of accomplishment. In this chapter, the role that commitment and motivation play in purposeful learning was emphasized. Although some students may be skilled in their ability to read, and knowledgeable about the subject, they may not bring that skill and knowledge to bear in learning situations. It takes motivation, a sense of direction and purpose, and a teacher who knows how to create those conditions in the classroom that allow students to establish within themselves motives for reading. One way that you arouse curiosity about reading material is by creating conceptual conflict. Students will read to resolve conflicts arising from problem situations and perspectives, and will used guided imagery to explore ideas to be encountered during reading.

To reduce any uncertainty that students bring to reading material, you can help them raise questions and anticipate meaning by showing students how to connect what they know already to the new—to the ideas presented in the text. Instructional activities involving analogies and text previews can also help to generate and activate prior knowledge and interest in reading.

The questions students raise as a result of predicting will feed them into the reading material and keep them on course. Anticipation guides,

ReQuest, expectation outlines, self-questioning, and previewing techniques are strategies for stimulating predictions in anticipation about the content.

In the chapter that follows, you will study the topic of student engagement; that is, how do you engage students in active reading and in discussions about what they have read? Since readers respond to texts at different levels of comprehension, they must become aware of information sources they can rely on to answer questions. As a result, you will examine a metacognitive teaching strategy called Question-Answer Relationships (QARs). QARs will make students aware of information sources, that is, where they can find answers to questions about text under study.

## SUGGESTED READINGS

Anderson, R. C., & Pearson, P. D. (1984). A schema-theoretic view of basic processes in reading comprehension. In P. D. Pearson (ed.), *Handbook of reading research.* New York: Longmans, Green.

Bransford, J. (1983). Schema activation-schema acquisition. In R. C. Anderson, J. Osborn, and R. Tierney (eds.), *Learning to read in american schools.* Hillsdale, NJ: Erlbaum.

Estes, T., & Vaughan, J., Jr. (1985). Prereading anticipation (Chapter 9). *Reading and learning in the content classroom* (2nd ed.). Boston: Allyn and Bacon.

Herber, H. (1978). Prediction as motivation and an aid to comprehension (Chapter 7). *Teaching reading in content areas* (2nd ed.). Englewood Cliffs, NJ: Prentice Hall.

Langer, J. (1982). Facilitating text processing: The elaboration of prior knowledge. In J. Langer and M. T. Smith-Burke (eds.), *Reader meets author/bridging the gap.* Newark, DE: International Reading Association.

Mathison, C. (1989). Stimulating and sustaining student interest in content area reading. *Reading research and instruction. 28,* 76–83.

Moore, D. W., Readence, J., & Rickelman, R. (1988). *Prereading activities for content area reading* (2nd ed.). Newark, DE: International Reading Association.

Stipek, D. (1988). *Motivation to learn: From theory to practice.* Englewood Cliffs, NJ: Prentice-Hall.

Thelen, J. (1984). Prereading strategies for teaching science (Chapter 3). *Improving reading in science* (2nd ed.). Newark, DE: International Reading Association.

Vacca, R. T. (1977). Readiness to read content area assignments. *Journal of Reading. 20,* 387–392.

# 6

# Guiding Reader-Text Interactions

You can ask a baby frog if he remembers how you taught him to catch a fly, but there is no quest in that question.

—*Lu Po Hua*

## ORGANIZING PRINCIPLE

Questions get teachers where they want to go. More than any other single instructional tool, they help you to achieve your objectives. Teaching without asking questions is like gardening without a hoe or a spade. Questions dominate instructional time in most classrooms. Questions, after all, are the tools of our trade. Reflect for a moment on the number of times you have asked students to respond to questions. If you have yet to teach, recall the number of times you have been asked questions by instructors. Questions are important. When used effectively in lessons that require reading, questions promote thinking and light the way to productive learning and retention of content material. But questions can also be counterproductive when used habitually in the classroom with little forethought or preparation. The success or failure of text discussions often rests with the quality of the questions asked during question-answer exchanges.

It has been said that a good question is half the answer. What, then, is a bad question? Probably a question in and of itself is neither good nor bad. Questions are tools in the hands of the teacher. A question is only as effective as the context in which it is asked. An effective question, to our way of thinking, is any question that sets up a quest, that agitates thought and stirs the imagination. If you ask students questions that create a quest and require thought and imagination, you're more likely to get answers that are thoughtful and imaginative. On the other hand, if you ask pseudoquestions,

questions whose answers you already know, then you're bound to get straight and narrow responses in which students, more often than not, try to guess what's in your head.

The organizing principle of this chapter makes a distinction between questions that quiz readers' understanding of text and questions that actively engage students in a search for meaning: *There's a critical difference between asking questions that evaluate a product (what students learn and remember as a result of their interactions with texts) and questions that guide a process (engaging and sustaining students in their efforts to think and learn as they interact with texts and with one another).*

As you prepare to read, study the graphic organizer in the Chapter Overview. Then read the questions in the Frame of Mind. Both the Overview and the Frame questions allow you to anticipate the content to be presented.

## CHAPTER OVERVIEW

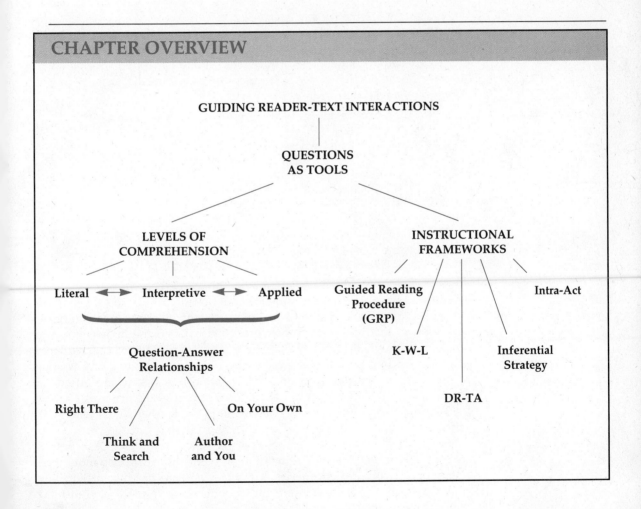

GUIDING READER-TEXT INTERACTIONS

QUESTIONS AS TOOLS

LEVELS OF COMPREHENSION

INSTRUCTIONAL FRAMEWORKS

Literal ⟷ Interpretive ⟷ Applied

Guided Reading Procedure (GRP)

Intra-Act

Question-Answer Relationships

K-W-L

Inferential Strategy

Right There          On Your Own

DR-TA

Think and Search          Author and You

---

## FRAME OF MIND

1. When are questions tools for learning? When are they threats to learning?

2. What does it mean to interact with texts at different levels of comprehension and response?

3. Why and how does an awareness of question-answer relationships help students to comprehend texts?

4. Which instructional frameworks for guiding reader-text interactions seem most appropriate for use in your content area? Why?

---

The strategic use of questions, as shown in the previous chapter, is one of the best ways we know to activate students' prior knowledge for reading, create conceptual conflict, and arouse interest and curiosity in a topic to be studied. Questions that gnaw at students are questions that usually propel them into the reading.

The practical concern in this chapter is with *student engagement:* How does a teacher engage students in reading and in discussions about what they have read? When used effectively, questions guide the interactions readers have with texts and keep them on course during reading. Questions also are powerful springboards into discussion and facilitate students' interactions and transactions with one another.

## QUESTIONS AS TOOLS FOR LEARNING

It is hard to imagine a class session without questions. It is no exaggeration to suggest that in text learning situations, teachers talk to students in questions most of the time. And students respond by speaking in answers. The problem arises when a teacher's questions are so narrowly cast that students engage in reading to find the right answers only. In these situations, would-be text discussions soon turn into interrogation sessions, where questions are used to check on whether or not students have read the material.

When questioning becomes interrogating, the teacher's goal usually is veridicality ("the truth, the whole truth, and nothing but the truth"): Do readers grasp the facts and details explicitly stated in the text? As a result, the teacher fires one question after another, typically pausing no more than a second or two between queries. The questions are narrow in that they require verbatim text responses from students and are more likely to test comprehension than to guide its development.

The artful use of questions, however, not only triggers a search for meaning but also encourages elaborative thinking. Questions are capable of transforming students from information seekers to information users. An information seeker is the student who asks, "What do I already know about the topic? What do I need to learn more about?" Questions such as these engage students in reading and guide their interactions with texts as they search for information. Information users, on the other hand, are students who know how to integrate information and put it to work for them—to solve problems, to reflect on what they have read, to make judgments, or to invent new ways of looking at the world. An information user asks, "So what? How can I use what I have read?" Questions such as these are the basis for elaborative and reflective thinking.

The positive side of questions is that they work. The issue isn't whether to use or not use questions to guide students' interactions with text. Rather, the issue is how, when, and where questions ought to be used (Pearson and Johnson 1978). Questions can be tools, but they can also become weapons that interfere with learning.

When do questions become weapons? Samples (1977) likens questions to conversational acts of aggression when they wittingly or unwittingly put students on the spot.

Do you recall ever being put on the spot by a question? In that interminable second or two between question and response, between pounding heart and short gasps for air, do you remember asking yourself, "What's *the* right answer—the one this instructor expects?"

When questions are used to foster a right-answer-only atmosphere in class they will not focus thinking about what has been read, nor will they prompt the processes by which students construct knowledge from text material. Instead they make the response—the correct answer—the all-important concern. Some students even become the classroom "answer machines." (An answer machine is easily recognizable. Usually one arm is several inches longer than the other—from constantly shooting the arm skyward in a quick, jerky motion to gain attention during a question-answer interchange.) The danger of putting students on the spot is that we run the risk of losing most of the class during discussion by actively seeking responses from students who will give us what we want to hear—the right answer.

When students are on the spot, they often resort to guessing what is inside the teacher's head. One need only read Judy Blume's devastating parody of a music teacher's question to her class in Box 6.1 to appreciate how paltry and nonproductive it is to wittingly or unwittingly involve students in playing "Guess What's in My Head." Unfortunately, some students learn to play the game with consummate skill. They will read everything but the text to answer the teacher's question "correctly." They scrutinize the teacher's gestures for the slightest of indications that they are on the right track. As they respond to facial gestures and body language, some students skillfully verbalize under, over, and around a question until they strike the responsive chord they seek—a nod of approval.

---

**BOX 6.1     Guess What's in My Head**

When she finished her song she was right next to Wendy. "Wendy . . . can you tell me what was coming out of my mouth as I sang?"

"Out of your mouth?" Wendy asked.

"That's right," Miss Rothbelle told her.

"Well . . . it was . . . um . . . words?"

"No . . . no . . . no," Miss Rothbelle said.

Wendy was surprised. She can always give teachers the answers they want.

Miss Rothbelle moved on. "Do you know, Caroline?"

"Was it sound?"

"Wrong!" Miss Rothbelle said, turning, "Donna Davidson, can you tell me?"

"It was a song," Donna said.

"Really Donna . . . we all know that!" Miss Rothbelle looked around. "Linda Fischer, do you know what was coming out of my mouth as I sang to the class?"

Linda didn't say anything.

"Well, Linda . . ." Miss Rothbelle said.

"I think it was air." Linda finally told her. "Either that or breath."

Miss Rothbelle walked over to Linda's desk. "That was not the correct answer. Weren't you paying attention?" She pulled a few strands of Linda's hair. . . .

She walked up and down the aisles until she stopped at my desk. . . .

"We'll see if you've been paying attention . . . suppose you tell me the answer to my question."

I had no idea what Miss Rothbelle wanted me to say. There was just one thing left that could have been coming out of her mouth as she sang, so I said, "It was spit."

"What?" Miss Rothbelle glared at me.

"I mean, it was saliva," I told her.

Miss Rothbelle banged her fist on my desk. "That was a very rude thing to say. You can sit in the corner for the rest of the period." . . .

At the end of the music period Robby Winters called out, "Miss Rothbelle . . . Miss Rothbelle . . ."

"What is it?" she asked.

"You never told us what was coming out of your mouth when you sang."

"That's right," Miss Rothbelle said. "I didn't."

"What was it?" Robby asked.

"It was melody," Miss Rothbelle said. Then she spelled it. "M-e-l-o-d-y. And every one of you should have known." She blew her pitchpipe at us and walked out of the room.

**Source:** Reprinted with the permission of Bradbury Press, an affiliate of Macmillan, Inc. from *Blubber* by Judy Blume. Copyright © 1974 by Judy Blume.

Seeking right answers only, putting students on the spot, and reinforcing Guess What's In My Head behavior are tied to what some consider the prevalent instructional model in American schooling, *turn taking* (Duffy 1983). Turn taking occurs whenever the teacher asks a question or assigns a turn, the student responds, and the teacher gives feedback by correcting or reinforcing the response. Teachers often depend on turn taking to "discuss" the content of textbook assignments. Yet what results is hardly a discussion at all. During turn-taking routines, questions usually forestall or frustrate discussion. Question-answer exchanges are brief, usually three to five seconds in duration, sometimes less, sometimes more. Rather than characterize these question-answer exchanges as discussion, it is more appropriate to view them as recitation.

Turn taking almost always involves some form of recitation. The striking feature of recitation is that the teacher's speech consists of questions. Dillon (1983) noted that during a recitation, "we might judge that *too many* questions are being asked at *too fast* a pace. But the exchanges take the form they do because the teacher speaks in question-form, not because of the number of questions he asks in a brief time" (p. 11). To illustrate this point, Dillon (1983, pp. 10–11) provided a transcript from a typical recitation conducted by a high school teacher of United States history:

> T: OK, so we've kind of covered leadership and some of the things that Washington brought with it. Why else did they win? Leadership is important, that's one.
>
> S: France gave 'em help.
>
> T: OK, so France giving aid is an example of what? France is an example of it, obviously.
>
> S: Aid from allies.
>
> T: Aid from allies, very good. Were there any other allies who gave aid to us?
>
> S: Spain.
>
> T: Spain. Now, when you say aid, can you define that?
>
> S: Help.
>
> T: Define "help." Spell it out for me.
>
> S: Assistance.
>
> T: Spell it out for me.
>
> S: They taught the men how to fight the right way.
>
> T: Who taught?
>
> S: The allies.
>
> T: Where? When?
>
> S: In the battlefield.
>
> T: In the battlefield?

In the exchanges above, the students take turns answering questions about the success of Washington's revolutionary army. The eight question-answer exchanges lasted a little more than thirty seconds, or four to five seconds per exchange. Each student addressed a response to the teacher, not other students. The nature of turn taking is such that it is *verboten* for another student to jump in to the exchange, unless first recognized by the teacher to take a turn.

In turn-taking situations, as you can infer, certain rules accompany classroom discourse. One was alluded to earlier: The teacher speaks in questions; the students speak in answers. And the form of their answers indicates another rule of turn taking: Give just enough information specified by the question to satisfy the teacher. No wonder question-answer exchanges are brief. Interestingly, as part of the exchange, students invariably address their responses to the teacher. The implicit rule is never address other students because only the teacher gives feedback. Each respondent, thus, awaits his or her turn to answer further questions. Any attempts at conversation or discussion are stifled.

A teacher's language and actions signal to students what their roles are to be within a lesson. While recitation serves several legitimate educational purposes (quizzing, reviewing), it may produce negative effects on students' cognitive, affective, and expressive processes. Given the rules that operate during turn taking, teachers may very well increase student passivity and dependence. Furthermore, turn taking leads to limited construction of meaning with text. Because the pace of questions is often rapid, readers hardly have the time to think, clarify, or explore their understanding of the text material undergoing questioning. When teachers ask predominantly "quiz show" questions, students soon engage in fact-finding behavior rather than thinking about the ideas the author communicates. Questions become weapons that thwart active text learning under these conditions. The inherent danger to text learners is subtle but devastating: Mistaken signals may be telegraphed to students about what it means to comprehend text and what their roles are as comprehenders. Finding bits and pieces of information becomes the end-all and be-all of reading.

So how might questions guide reader-text interactions and engage students in active text learning and discussion? Part of the answer lies in helping students to understand that they respond to texts at different levels of comprehension and making them aware of information sources they can rely upon to answer questions.

## LEVELS OF COMPREHENSION

Because reading is a thoughtful process, it embraces the idea of levels of comprehension. Readers respond to meaning at various levels of abstraction and conceptual difficulty. Figure 6.1 shows the major aspects of levels of comprehension.

The literal level is another way of saying students can read the lines of your content material. They can stay with print sufficiently to get the gist of the author's message. In simple terms, a literal recognition of that message determines what the author says.

**Figure 6.1**    MAJOR ASPECTS OF LEVELS OF COMPREHENSION

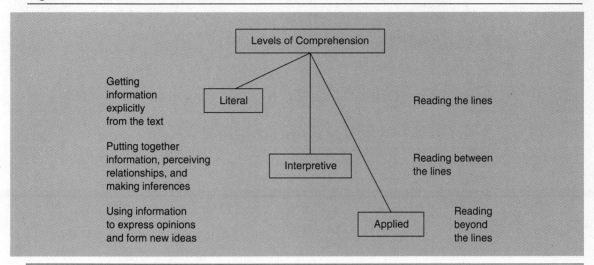

Try to recall your freshman year in college, when you probably learned the universal strategy of coping with the literal level of your first five-pound text. Probably after careful observation of a model, that stoic sophomore or junior struggling with a textbook in a library carrel, you rushed to the nearest bookstore and purchased your first felt-tip marker. Its ink was pink or yellow, wasn't it? Then you began to get the gist as you underlined the essential information in your text readings.

If you were like us, your yellow felt-tip pen soon became as comfortable as Linus's blanket. The only trouble, of course, is that soon into the business of underlining, you moved from selective markings to full-scale assaults on the printed page. You probably began to change entire pages of white background to yellow background as your marker ran amuck with indiscriminate frenzy. You were learning. Or so you thought.

The trouble is that searching for important literal information isn't an easy chore, particularly if readers haven't matured enough to know how to make the search, or even worse, haven't determined why they are making it in the first place. Most students can and will profit handsomely from being shown how to recognize the essential information in text.

Knowing what the author says is necessary but not sufficient in constructing meaning with text. Good readers search for conceptual complexity in material. They read between the lines. They focus not only on what authors say but also on what authors mean by what they say. Herber (1978) clarifies the difference between literal and interpretive levels this way: "At the literal level readers identify the important information. At the interpretive level readers perceive the relationships that exist in that information, conceptualizing the ideas formulated by those relationships. . . . " (p. 45)

The interpretive level reflects the author's intended meaning. How the reader conceptualizes implied ideas by integrating information in light of what they already know is part and parcel of the interpretive process. Recognizing the thought relationships that the author weaves together helps the reader to make inferences that are implicit in the material.

For example, study the following passage, which is organized according to cause-effect relationships. Figure 6.2 shows how a cause combines with several effects to form a logical influence that is implicit in the text passage.

> As part of an experiment, young monkeys were taken away from their mothers when they were born and each was raised in complete isolation. When these monkeys were brought together for the first time, they didn't want to play with each other as monkeys usually do. They showed no love for each other. And in fact they never learned to live together. It seemed that living apart from their mothers and from each other from the very beginning had some unusual side effects on these growing monkeys.

From time to time throughout the book you have probably been trying to read us—not our words but us. And in the process of responding to our messages, you probably raised questions similar to these: So what? What does this information mean to me? Does it make sense? Can I use these ideas for content instruction? Your attempt to seek significance or relevance in what we say and mean is one signal that you are reading at the applied level. You are reading beyond our lines.

Reading at the applied level is undoubtedly akin to the act of discovery. It underscores the constructive nature of reading comprehension. Bruner (1961) explains that discovery "is in its essence a matter of rearranging or transforming evidence in such a way that one is enabled to go beyond the evidence so reassembled to additional new insights" (p. 21). When students respond to text at the applied level they know how to synthesize information—lay that synthesis alongside what they know already—to express opinions about and to draw additional insights and fresh ideas from content material.

**Figure 6.2    LOGICAL INFERENCE FROM CAUSE-EFFECT RELATIONSHIPS**

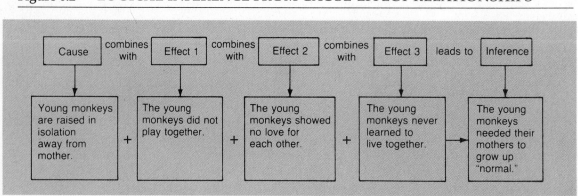

## Creating Awareness of Information Sources

The type of question asked to guide comprehension should be based on the *information readers need to answer the question*. As a result, teachers must help students *become aware of* likely sources of information as they respond to questions (Pearson and Johnson 1978).

Readers draw upon two broad information sources to answer questions: information in the text and information inside the reader's head. For example, some questions have answers that can be found directly in the text. These questions are *textually explicit* and lead to answers that are "right there" at the literal level of comprehension.

Other questions have answers that require students to think about the information they have read in the text. They must be able to search for ideas that are related to one another, and then put these ideas together, to answer questions. These questions are *textually implicit* and lead to "think and search" answers at an interpretive level of response.

Still other questions require students to rely mainly on prior knowledge and experience. In other words, responses to these questions are more inside the reader's head than in the text itself. These questions are *schema based* and lead to "author and you" and "on my own" answers that reflect thinking with text at an applied level.

"Right There," "Think and Search," "Author and You," and "On Your Own" are mnemonics for question-answer relationships (Raphael 1982, 1984, 1986). Many kinds of responses can be prompted at the literal level by textually explicit questions, at the interpretive level by textually implicit questions, and at the applied level by schema-based questions. However, the success that students experience when responding to a certain type of question depends on their ability to recognize the relationship between the question and its answer. Let's explore in more detail how students can be taught to be more strategic in their awareness and use of question-answer relationships.

## Question-Answer Relationships (QARs)

QAR is a technique that teaches students the relationships that exist among the type of question asked, the text, and the reader's prior knowledge. In the process of teaching QARs, you help students to become aware of and skilled in the use of learning strategies to find information they need to comprehend at different levels of response to text.

Procedures related to learning QARs can be taught directly to students by reading teachers and reinforced by content area specialists. Keep in mind, however, that students may come to your class totally unaware of what information sources are available for seeking an answer; or they may not know when to use different sources. If this is the case, then it is worth the effort over several days to teach students the relationship between questions and answers. It may take up to three days to show students how to identify the information sources necessary to answer questions. The following steps, which we have adapted for content area situations, are suggested for teaching QARs.

1. Introduce the concept of QARs by showing students a chart or an overhead transparency containing a description of the four basic question-answer relationships. (We recommend a chart that can be positioned in a prominent place in the classroom. Students may then refer to the chart whenever needed during content area lessons.) Point out that there are two broad categories of information sources: In the Text and In My Head. Figure 6.3 is adapted from a chart recommended by Raphael (1986).

2. Begin by assigning students several short passages from the textbook (no more than two to five sentences in length). Follow each reading with one question from each of the QAR categories on the chart. Then discuss the differences between a "Right There" question and answer, a "Think and Search" question and answer, an "On My Own" question and answer, and an "Author and You" question and answer. Explanations should be clear and complete. Reinforce the discussion by assigning several more short text passages and asking a question for each. Students will soon begin to catch on to the differences among the four QAR categories. The example in Box 6.2 illustrates how a science teacher in the middle grades introduced the QAR categories to her students.

3. Continue the second day by practicing with short passages—with one question for each QAR category per passage. First, give students a passage to read with questions *and* answers *and* identified QARs. Why do the questions and answers represent one QAR and not another? Second, give students a passage with questions and answers; this time they have to identify the QAR for each. Finally, give students passages, decide together which strategy to use, and have them write their responses.

4. Review briefly on the third day. Then assign a longer passage (75–200 words) with up to six questions (at least one each from the four QAR categories). First have students work in groups to decide the QAR category for each question and the answers for each. Next, assign a second passage, comparable in length, with five questions for students to work on individually. Discuss responses either in small groups or with the whole class. You may wish to work with several class members or colleagues to complete the QAR exercise in Box 6.3. It was developed by a high school English teacher as part of a short story unit.

5. Apply the QAR strategy to actual content area assignments. For each question asked, students decide on the appropriate QAR strategy and write out their answers.

Once students are sensitive to different information sources for different types of questions and know how to use these sources to respond to questions, variations can be made in the QAR strategy. For example, you might consider having students generate their own questions to text assignments—perhaps two for each QAR strategy. They then write down the answers to

**Figure 6.3    INTRODUCING QARS**

Where are Answers to
Questions Found?

In  the Text:

Right There!

The answer is in the text. The words
used in the question and words used
for the answer can usually be found
in the same sentence.

Think and Search!

The answer is in the text but the
words used in the question and those
used for an answer would not be in
the same sentence. You need to think
about different parts of the text and
how ideas can be put together before you
can answer the question.

Or

In My Head:

On My Own

The text got you thinking, but the
answer is inside your head. The
author can't help you much. So think
about it and use what you know
already to answer the question.

Author and You

The answer is not in the text. You
need to think about what you know,
what the author says, and how they
fit together.

---

**BOX 6.2     Introduction to QARs in a Science Class**

1.  Everyone has some idea of what growth means. People, plants, and animals grow. But what changes occur when a person or a plant grows? Two changes usually occur during the growth process. There is an increase in height and a gain in weight.
    *Question:* How many changes usually occur in the growth process?
    *Answer:* two

    *QAR:*  RIGHT THERE             __x__
            THINK AND SEARCH     _____
            ON MY OWN              _____
            AUTHOR AND YOU     _____

    *Rationale (developed during class discussion):* This is an example of a *Right There* question because the answer is easy to find and the words used to make the question are also in the answer.

2.  New cells must be added as an organism grows. Cells that die or are worn away must be replaced. New cells are produced by a process called *mitosis*. During mitosis, one cell divides to become two cells.
    *Question:* What would happen if our cells stopped dividing?
    *Answer:* Our bodies would stop growing and we would eventually die because cells that died or were worn away would not be replaced.

    *QAR:*  RIGHT THERE             _____
            THINK AND SEARCH     __x__
            ON MY OWN              _____
            AUTHOR AND YOU     _____

    *Rationale (developed during class discussion):* The answer is in the text but harder to find. The words to the question and answer are not in the same sentence.

3.  Growth in height is not steady during the life of a human. There are times when you grow very fast. At other times, you grow slowly. Adults do not grow in height at all. Your most rapid growth took place before you were born. Rapid growth continues through the first two years of life.

the questions as they understand them, except that they leave one question unanswered from the Think and Search category and one from the On My Own or Author and You category. These are questions on which the student would like to hear the views of others. During the discussion students can volunteer to ask their unanswered questions. The class is invited first to identify the question by QAR category and then to contribute answers, comments, or related questions about the material.

A second variation involves discussions of text. During question-answer exchanges, consider prefacing a question by saying, "This question is *right there* in the text." Or, "You'll have to *think and search* the text to answer." Or, "You're *on your own* with this one." Or, "The answer is a combination of the *author and you.* Think about what the author tells us and what we already know to try and come up with a reasonable response." Make sure that you pause several seconds or more for "think time." Think time, or "wait time," is critical to responding to questions at interpretive or

*Question:* What were the times in your life when you or someone you know grew rapidly?
*Answers:* My 9-year-old brother (pants needed hemming); young babies; themselves at puberty; high school students.

*QAR:*  RIGHT THERE         _____
        THINK AND SEARCH _____
        ON MY OWN            __x__
        AUTHOR AND YOU   _____

*Rationale (developed during class discussion):* To answer a question like this you have to use what you know already. The answer is in your head, not the text. You're "on your own."

4. Two provisions are necessary for a tree to grow more than one kind of fruit. First, the branches of different fruit trees must be properly spliced onto the original tree. Second, the different fruit of all of the branches must belong to the same genus. Many orange trees, for example, have produced grapefruits, lemons, and limes.
*Question:* If you were a fruit grower, would you be able to grow bananas on an apple tree?
*Answer:* It's impossible. Bananas are a tropical fruit. I know that bananas and apples are not related to one another like oranges, grapefruits, and lemons, which are citrus fruits.

*QAR:*  RIGHT THERE         _____
        THINK AND SEARCH _____
        ON MY OWN            _____
        AUTHOR AND YOU   __x__

*Rationale (developed during class discussion):* To answer this question you need to take what the author tells you and connect it to what you know. The answer's not in the text but in your head. However, you need to use information in the text and link it to what you know to respond to the question.

applied levels of comprehension. Gambrell (1980) found that increasing think time to five seconds or longer increases the length of student responses as well as the quality of their speculative thinking.

QARs permit students to respond strategically to text at different levels of comprehension. Explicit instruction in the use of QARs puts students on the road to independent text learning. Once students are familiar with QARs, they can be used in combination with a variety of interactive strategies.

# FRAMEWORKS FOR READER-TEXT INTERACTIONS

Asking questions within an instructional framework creates the conditions necessary to maintain and sustain readers' interactions with texts. An instructional framework provides a structure through which students actively engage

## BOX 6.3     QAR Awareness in an English Class

"Got your glove?" asked Glennie after a time. Scho obviously hadn't..

"You could give me some easy grounders," said Scho. "But don't burn 'em."

"All right," Glennie said. He moved off a little, so the three of them formed a triangle, and they passed the ball around for about five minutes, Monk tossing easy grounders to Scho, Scho throwing to Glennie, and Glennie burning them into Monk. After a while, Monk began to throw them back to Glennie once or twice before he let Scho have his grounder, and finally Monk gave Scho a fast, bumpy grounder that hopped over his shoulder and went into the brake on the other side of the street.

"Not so hard," called Scho as he ran across to get it.

"You should've had it," Monk shouted.

It took Scho a little while to find the ball among the ferns and dead leaves, and when he saw it, he grabbed it up and threw it toward Glennie. It struck the trunk of the apple tree, bounced back at an angle, and rolled steadily and stupidly onto the cement apron in front of the firehouse, where one of the trucks was parked. Scho ran hard and stopped it just before it rolled under the truck, and this time he carried it back to his former position on the lawn and threw it carefully to Glennie. *(from "A Game of Catch," by Richard Wilbur)*

1. Question: What are the three boys doing?
   Answer: _____
   _____
   QAR: _____
   _____

2. Question: Why did Monk throw the ball so hard to Scho?
   Answer: _____
   _____
   QAR: _____
   _____

3. Question: Who was throwing the ball to Monk?
   Answer: _____
   _____
   QAR: _____
   _____

4. Question: How would you describe Scho's throwing ability?
   Answer: _____
   _____
   QAR: _____
   _____

5. Question: How would you characterize Monk?
   Answer: _____
   _____
   QAR: _____
   _____

6. Question: Why do friends sometimes get frustrated with one another?
   Answer: _____
   _____
   QAR: _____
   _____

in text learning and discussion. Instructional frameworks in general, as we discussed in Chapter 3, make provisions for prereading, during reading, and post-reading activities. In this section, we describe several frameworks that prepare students for reading, guide their interactions with texts, and help them to clarify and extend meaning. These frameworks include the following: (1) K-W-L (What Do You *Know*? What Do you *Want* To Know More About? What Did You *Learn*?, (2) Directed Reading-Thinking Activity (DR-TA), (3) Inferential Strategy, (4) Guided Reading Procedure (GRP), and (5) Intra-Act.

Note the differences as well as the commonalities among the various instructional frameworks emphasized in this section. Each can be adapted to meet the demands inherent in any subject matter material, narrative or expository in nature. Think about the kinds of adaptations you will have to make to meet particular needs.

## The K-W-L Strategy (What Do You Know? What Do You Want to Know? What Did You Learn?)

K-W-L is a meaning-making strategy that engages students in active text learning. The strategy creates an instructional framework that begins with what students **know** about the topic to be studied, moves to what the students **want to know** as they reflect on their knowledge and generate questions about the topic, and leads to a record of what students **learn** as a result of their engagement in the K-W-L strategy. Follow-up activities to K-W-L often include discussion, the construction of graphic organizers, and summary writing to clarify and internalize what has been read.

K-W-L may be initiated with small groups of students or the whole class. When they develop confidence and competence with the K-W-L strategy, students may begin to use it as an independent learning strategy. K-W-L makes use of a strategy sheet, such as the one in Figure 6.4. The steps in K-W-L revolve around the completion of the strategy sheet as part of the dynamics of class interaction and discussion.

**Steps in the K-W-L Strategy.**  Here's how the K-W-L strategy works:

1. **Introduce the class to the K-W-L strategy in conjunction with a new topic or text selection to be studied.** Prior to assigning a text to be read, explain the strategy. Donna Ogle (1992), the originator of K-W-L, suggests that dialogue begin with the teacher saying:

   > It is important to first find out what we think we know about this topic. Then we want to anticipate how an author is likely to present and organize the information. From this assignment we can generate good questions to focus on reading and study. Our level of knowledge will determine to some extent how we will study. Then as we read we will make notes of questions that get answered and other new and important information we learn. During this process some new questions will probably occur to us; these we should also note so we can get clarification later (p. 271).

**Figure 6.4    K-W-L STRATEGY SHEET**

| K—What I Know | W—What I Want to Know | L—What I Learned and Still Need to Learn |
| --- | --- | --- |
|  |  |  |

**Categories of Information I Expect to Use**

A.                                      E.

B.                                      F.

C.                                      G.

D.

**Source:** From K-W-L: A teaching model that develops active reading of expository text by Donna Ogle. *The Reading Teacher*, February 1986. Reprinted with permission of Donna Ogle and the International Reading Association.

In the process of explaining K-W-L, be sure that students understand *what* their role involves and *why* it is important for learners to examine what they know and to ask questions in relation to topics that they will be reading and studyng.

The next several steps allow you to model the K-W-L strategy with a group of learners or the entire class. Some students will find it difficult to complete the K-W-L strategy sheet on their own. Others will avoid taking risks or revealing what they know or don't know about a topic. Others just won't be motivated in a positive direction. Modeling the K-W-L strategy lessens the initial risk and creates a willingness to engage in the process. Students who experience the modeling of the strategy quickly recognize its value as a learning tool.

2. **Identify what students think they know about the topic.** Engage the class in brainstorming, writing their ideas on the board or on an overhead transparency. Use the format of the K-W-L strategy sheet as you record students' ideas on the chalkboard or transparency. It's important to record everything that the student *think* they know, including their misconceptions about the topic. The key in this step is to get the class actively involved in making associations about the topic, not to evaluate the rightness or wrongness of the associations. Students will sometimes challenge one another's knowledge base. The teacher's role is to help learners to recognize that differences exist in what they think they know. These differences can be used to help students frame questions.

3. **Generate a list of student questions.** Ask, "What do you want to know more about?" "What are you most interested in learning about?" As you write their questions on the chalkboard or transparency, recognize that you are again modeling for students what their role as learners should be—to ask questions about material to be studied.

   When you have completed modeling the brainstorming and question-generation phases of K-W-L, have the students use their own strategy sheets to make decisions about what they personally think they know and what they want to know more about. Students, especially those who may be at risk in academic situations, may refer to the chalkboard or overhead transparency to decide what to record in the first two columns.

4. **Anticipate the organization and structure of ideas that the author is likely to use in the text selection.** As part of preparation for reading, have students next consider their knowledge of the topic and the questions that have been generated to make predictions about the organizational structure of the text. What are the major categories of information that are likely to be used by the author to organize his/her ideas?

   The teacher might ask: "How do you think the author of a text or article on _____ is likely to organize the information?" (Ogle 1992) Have students focus on the ideas they have brainstormed and the questions they have raised to predict possible categories of information. As students make their predictions, record these on the board or transparency in the area suggested by the K-W-L strategy sheet. Then have students make individual choices on their strategy sheets.

5. **Read the text selection to answer the questions.** As they engage in interactions with the text, the students write answers to their questions and make notes for new ideas and information in the L column of their strategy sheets. Again, the teacher's modeling is crucial to the success of this phase of K-W-L. Students might need a demonstration or two to understand how to record information in the L column.

   Debrief students after they have read the text and completed writing responses in the L column. First invite them to share answers, recording these on the chalkboard or transparency. Then ask, "What new ideas did you come across that you didn't think you would find in the text?" Record and discuss student responses.

**6. Engage students in follow-up activities to clarify and extend learning.**
Use K-W-L as a springboard into post-reading activities to internalize student learning. Activities may include the construction of graphic organizers to clarify and retain ideas encountered during reading or the development of written summaries. Each serves an important study function, as we will discuss in Chapter 9.

**A K-W-L Illustration.** In Christa Chaney's U.S. history class, students were beginning a study of the Vietnam War. Christa realized that her students would have some, if not much, prior knowledge about and attitudes toward the Vietnam War, because it has remained "a strong part of our national consciousness." The students, in fact, were acutely aware of the war from recent popular movies, and also from fathers and other relatives who had participated in it.

However, Christa realized that while students might know something about the Vietnam War, they probably had had little opportunity to study about it from the perspective of historians. This, then, was Christa's objective as a teacher of history: to help students approach the study of the Vietnam War—and better understand the social, economic, and political forces surrounding it—from a historian's perspective.

As a result, Christa felt that the K-W-L strategy would be an appropriate way to begin the unit. She believed that it would help students get in touch with what they knew (and didn't know) about the Vietnam War and to begin to raise questions that would guide their interactions with the materials that they would be studying.

Christa began K-W-L knowing that students were familiar with its procedures, having participated in the strategy on several previous occasions in the class. Following the steps suggested in the previous section, the class as a whole participated in brainstorming what they knew about the war and raising questions that reflected what they wanted to know. Christa recorded their ideas and questions on an overhead transparency and encouraged students' participation by asking such questions as "What else do you know? Who knows someone who was in the war? What did they say about it? Who has read about the Vietnam War or seen a movie about it? What did you learn?"

As ideas and questions were recorded on the transparency, Christa asked students to study the K column to anticipate categories of information that they might study in their textbook and other information sources that they would be using: "Do some of these ideas fit together to form major categories we might be studying?" She also asked the students to think about other wars they had studied—World Wars I and II, the War Between the States, and the American Revolution: "When we study wars, are there underlying categories of information that historians tend to focus on?"

Upon completion of the whole class activity, Christa invited students to complete their strategy sheets, recording what they knew, what they wanted to find out more about, and the categories of information they expected to use.

Then, for homework, she assigned several sections from the textbook covering the Vietnam War and asked students to work on the L column on their own. Box 6.4 shows how one student, Clayton, completed his strategy sheet.

## BOX 6.4   Clayton's K-W-L Strategy Sheet on Vietnam War

| K—What I Know | W—What I Want to Know | L—What I Learned and Still Need to Learn |
|---|---|---|
| U.S. lost war<br>protest marches<br>and riots<br>movies made 1960s<br>Jungle fighting<br>POWs<br>gorilla fighting<br>North and South<br>fighting each other<br>U.S. soldiers suffered<br>The wall in<br>Washington | Why did we go<br>to war?<br>Why did we<br>loose?<br>How many soldiers<br>died?<br>Who helped us?<br>Who was president<br>during war?<br>Whose side were<br>we on? | Gulf of Tonkin<br>Revolution made it<br>legal for war<br>but war was not<br>legally declared.<br>French helped U.S.<br>Nixon withdrew<br>troops because<br>of fighting at home<br>Lottery used to<br>draft soldiers<br>Anti-war movement<br>at home<br>55,000 Americans died<br>plus thousands of<br>innocent people<br>Kennedy, Johnson and<br>Nixon were the<br>presidents<br>Fought war to stop<br>Communism |

Categories of Information I Expect to Use

A. cause                E.

B. results              F.

C. U.S. Involvement     G.

D. Type of fighting

As part of next day's class, Christa asked the students to work in groups of four to share what they had found out about the war. They focused on the questions they had raised, as well as new ideas that they had not anticipated. When the groups completed their work, Christa brought the class together. She directed them to open their learning logs and write a summary of what they had learned from participating in K-W-L. Students used the L column on their strategy sheets to compose the summary. Clayton's summary is depicted in Figure 6.5.

In Christa's class, the learning logs serve as a history notebook, where students can record what they are learning, using a variety of writing to learn activities. In Chapter 8, we explain learning logs and their uses more fully.

## Directed Reading-Thinking Activity (DR-TA)

The DR-TA fosters critical awareness by moving students through a process that involves prediction, verification, judgment, and ultimately extension of thought. The teacher guides reading and agitates thinking through the judicious use of questions. These questions will prompt interpretation, clarification, and application.

The atmosphere created during a DR-TA questioning episode is paramount to the strategy's success. You must be supportive and encouraging so as not to inhibit students' free participation. Never refute any predictions that students offer—to do so is comparable to pulling the rug out from under them.

**Figure 6.5     CLAYTON'S SUMMARY IN LEARNING LOG**

We fought the Vietnam War to stop communism. The U.S. Congress passed the Gulf of Tonkin Resolution which said it was O.K. to go to war there, but the war was never declared a war, it was called just a conflict. The French and South Vietnamese people helped us, but it didn't matter. 55,000 Americans died fighting. People protested in the U.S. Nixon withdrew the troops because of the pressure to end the war at home.

Think time is again important. When you pose an open-ended question, is it reasonable to pause no more than two, three, five, or even ten seconds for a response? If silence pervades the room for the several seconds or more that have lapsed from the time a question has been asked, simply wait a few more seconds. Too often, the tendency is to slice the original question into smaller parts. Sometimes a teacher starts slicing too quickly out a sense of frustration or anxiousness (after all, three seconds of lapsed time can seem an eternity in the midst of a questioning foray) rather than the students' inability to respond. Silence may very well be an indication that hypothesis formation or other cognitive activities are taking place in the students' heads. So wait—and see what happens.

To prepare for a DR-TA with narrative or expository text, analyze the narrative material for its story structure or the expository material for its superordinate and subordinate concepts. For expository texts, what do you see as relevant concepts, ideas, relationships, information in the material? The content analysis will help you decide on logical stopping points as you direct students through the reading.

For short stories and other narrative material, it is best to develop a *story analysis* (see Chapter 2). A story analysis allows the teacher to determine the key elements of a story: the *setting* (time and place, major characters) and the *events within the plot* [the initiating events or problem-generating situation, the protagonist's reaction to the event and his/her goal to resolve the problem, the set of attempts to achieve the goal, outcome(s) related to the protagonist's attempts to achieve the goal and resolve the problem, the character's reaction].

Once these elements have been identified, the teacher has a framework for deciding on logical stopping points within the story. In Figure 6.6 we indicate a general plan that may be followed or adapted for specific story lines.

As you examine Figure 6.6, notice that the suggested stopping points come at key junctures in a causal chain of events in the story line. Each juncture suggests a logical stopping point in that it assumes that the reader has enough information from a preceding event(s) to predict a future happening or event.

**Figure 6.6**    POTENTIAL STOPPING POINTS IN A DR-TA FOR A STORY LINE WITH ONE EPISODE

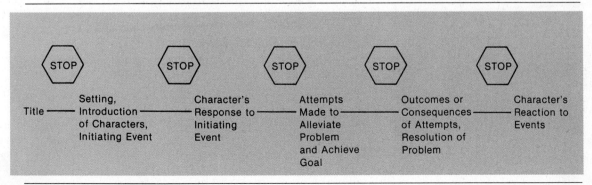

**Steps in the DR-TA.** Set the climate and guide the DR-TA by the frequent use of three questions:

What do you think? or What do you think will happen next?

Why do you think so? or What part of the story gave you a clue?

Can you prove it? or What else might happen?

The following may be considered general steps in the DR-TA:

1. **Begin with the title of the narrative or with a quick survey of the title, subheads, illustrations, and so forth in expository material.** Ask: "What do you think this story (or section) will be about?" Encourage predictions. Ask, "Why do you think so?"

2. **Ask students to read silently to a predetermined logical stopping point in the text.** A five-by-eight-inch index card or blank sheet of paper placed on the page will guide students and slow down those who want to read on before answering the questions.

3. **Repeat questions as suggested in step 1.** Some predictions will be refined; new ones will be formulated. Ask, "How do you know?" to encourage clarification or verification. Redirect questions.

4. **Continue silent reading to another suitable point.** Ask similar questions.

5. **Continue this way to the end of the material.** A note of caution: Too frequent interruption of reading may detract from the focus of attention, which needs to be on larger concepts. As readers move through the DR-TA process, encourage reflection and thoughtful responses to the text.

How do you apply the DR-TA to expository text situations? The steps below specify the following procedures:

1. **Identify purposes for reading.** Individual or group purposes set by students based on some limited clues in material and their own background of experience.

   a. "From only reading the chapter title (subtitles, charts, maps, etc.) what do you think the author(s) will present in this chapter (passage, next pages, etc.)?"

   b. Record speculations on chalkboard and augment by the query, "Why do you think so?"

   c. Encourage a guided discussion. If speculations and statements of proof yield an inaccurate or weak knowledge base, review through discussion. Frequently, terminology will be introduced by students in their predictions (especially from those more knowledgeable). The teacher may choose to capitalize on such situations by further clarifying significant concepts, etc. If done, this should be accomplished in a way that enhances pupil discussion and inquiry through discovery techniques.

   d. A poll can be taken to further intensify the predictive process. A debatelike setting may naturally ensue at this point pending the outcome of the poll count. Additional proof may be needed from available reference books.

2. **Adjust rate to purposes and material.** Teacher adjusts amount of reading depending upon the purposes, nature, and difficulty of the reading material; skimming, scanning, and studying are involved.

   a. "Read to find out if your predictions were correct." The reading task may be several pages within a chapter, an entire chapter, a few passages, etc. If the teacher designates numerous stopping points within the reading task, then the same steps for "identifying purposes" should be executed at each stopping point.

3. **Observe the reading.** The teacher observes the reading by assisting students who request help and noting abilities to adjust rate to purpose and material, to comprehend material, and to use word-recognition strategies.

4. **Guide reader-text interactions.** Students check purposes by accepting, rejecting, or redefining purposes. This can be accomplished by providing discussion time after having read a predetermined number of pages or by encouraging students to rework predictions as they read. Revised predictions and hypotheses can be written on paper by the students during the reading.

5. **Extend learning through discussion, further reading, additional study, or writing.** Students and teacher are identifying these needs throughout the strategy.

   a. After the reading, students should be asked (1) if their predictions were inaccurate, (2) if they needed to revise or reject predictions during the reading, (3) how they knew revision was necessary, and (4) what were their newly created predictions.

   b. Discussion in small groups is most reflective for this step. A recorder can be appointed by the group. It is this person's responsibility to share the groups' reading-thinking processes with the total class. These should be compared with original predictions.

   c. The teacher should ask open-ended questions that encourage generalization and application relevant to students' predictions and significant concepts presented. In any follow-up discussion or questioning the demand for proof should always prevail. "How do you know that?" "Why did you think so?" "What made you think that way?" Encourage students to share passages, sentences, etc., for further proof (Homer 1979).

**A DR-TA Illustration.** In an eighth-grade science class, a group of eight students was engaged in a study of a textbook chapter about the light spectrum, while their classmates were involved in individual projects (Davidson and Wilkerson 1988). The teacher guided the students' interactions with the text material using a DR-TA framework. Study an excerpt of the transcript from the beginning cycle of the DR-TA in Box 6.5.

As you examine the transcript, note that teacher-student interactions are recorded in the left-hand column of the box. The teacher's questions and comments are printed in capital letters, followed by the students' responses in lower case letters. An analysis of the DR-TA lesson as it evolved is printed in italics in the right-hand column.

The transcript shows how the students used prior knowledge to anticipate the information that the text would reveal. As they shared what they expected to find, the students engaged in analyzing their pooled ideas. Their interactions with the teacher illustrate how a DR-TA instructional framework creates a need to know and helps readers declare purposes through anticipation and prediction-making.

Once purposes were established, the teacher assigned a section of the text chapter to be read. According to Davidson and Wilkerson, two observers of the lesson:

> When students read the portion of the text they were directed to read, they read that infrared waves are invisible and that they are heat waves. Discussion, involving text ideas, students' previous ideas, and their reasoning abilities, showed that they discovered that infrared light is *not* one of the hottest colors because it is not a color. They also discovered that infrared waves are

---

**BOX 6.5    An Excerpt of a DR-TA Transcript from a Science Lesson on the Light Spectrum**

| Teacher-Student Interactions | Analysis of Lesson |
|---|---|
| I'D LIKE FOR YOU TO BEGIN BY JUST READING THIS ACTIVITY IN THIS SECTION. THEN TELL ME WHAT YOU EXPECT TO FIND IN THIS PASSAGE. YOU KNOW IT'S ABOUT LIGHT AND COLOR AND SPECTRUMS. WHAT ELSE DO YOU EXPECT THAT YOU WILL FIND?<br>s: Heat.<br>WHY DO YOU SAY HEAT?<br>s: Well, some of the colors are cooler. | *The teacher directs students to read a description of an activity designed to produce a sun's spectrum with a prism. The activity includes holding a thermometer in the spectrum produced, placing a flourite substance near the spectrum, and anticipating changes.*<br><br>*The student's response is based on prior knowledge which she judges will be relevant.* |
| DO YOU KNOW WHICH ONES WILL BE COOLER? | *The teacher encourages the student to extend the response.* |
| s: I think the darker ones.<br>WHY DO YOU SAY THAT?<br>s: They look cooler.<br>THEY LOOK COOLER? OKAY. | *Teacher asks for justification.*<br><br>*Teacher accepts response, recognizing that the student has, in fact, generated a question to be answered in reading the text.* |
| WHAT ELSE? DO YOU AGREE OR DISAGREE?<br><br>s: Well, I agree with her on infrared and ultraviolet. They are probably the hottest colors you can get of the spectrum.<br>ALL RIGHT. ANYBODY ELSE? | *The teacher encourages other students to analyze this hypothesis or generate a different one.*<br>*The student's response shows that he is evaluating the other student's response. Also, he uses specific vocabulary from his prior knowledge to extend the prediction.*<br>*The teacher does not make a judgment about the validity of the predictions since that is the responsibility of the students as they read and discuss.* |

hot, since they are heat waves. The text supplied literal information. The discussion facilitated concept development and critical thinking (1988, p. 37).

Although the students' predictions were amiss in the initial cycle of questioning, the teacher chose not to evaluate or judge the predictions. She recognizes that as readers interact with the text, more often than not they are able to clarify their misconceptions for themselves.

## Inferential Strategy

Hansen (1981b) created the Inferential Strategy for elementary children. Yet with some adaptation it can also be used in secondary content area instructional situations. Note that the use of questions in a DR-TA puts the spotlight on students' background experiences and their ability to make

| | |
|---|---|
| s: I think he is wrong.<br>WHY?<br>s: Because whenever you melt steel, steel always turns red before it turns white. When it turns white, it melts completely. | *A student disagrees.*<br>*Teacher asks for justification.*<br>*The student analyzes the prior student's prediction and explains in terms of his own experience.* |
| OKAY.<br>s: You can't see infrared.<br>AND HOW WOULD THAT MAKE A DIFFERENCE IN WHAT HE JUST SAID?<br>s: Well, he just said that it turned red before it turned white. And you can't see white, it's just a shade. Infrared you can't see—which would be just like sunlight. You can't see sunlight. So, I think it would be hotter. | *As stated, the student's response is a literal statement. The teacher assumes that there is a connection with the discussion and asks for explanation.*<br><br>*In his extended response the student disagrees with the prior student's conclusion and explanation and uses an illustration from his prior knowledge which he feels is relevant to "prove" his point.* |
| YOU THINK IT WOULD BE HOTTER? OKAY.<br><br>ANYBODY ELSE?<br><br>WELL, LET ME GIVE YOU THIS WHOLE FIRST PARAGRAPH. I WANT YOU TO READ TO THE BOTTOM OF THE PAGE AND THEN I WANT YOU TO GO OVER ON YOUR PAGE. IT WILL BE THE VERY TOP PARAGRAPH. COVER UP WHAT'S BELOW IT WITH YOUR PAPER. READ THAT FAR AND THEN STOP. | *The teacher does not point out the validity or lack of validity or either student's logic. She recognizes that both students are thinking critically and that they and others in the group will read to find clues to justify the concepts they are hypothesizing. She is consistent in her role as a facilitator of student discussion.* |
| (Students read silently.) | |

**Source:** Reprinted with permission of Jane Davidson and Bonnie Wilkerson.

predictions. This is precisely the case with the Inferential Strategy as well. The strategy is based on the notion that students comprehend better when they possess appropriate background knowledge about a topic and can relate new text information from their readings to familiar experiences. According to Hansen, "Young children seldom draw inferences spontaneously," but need to be taught the process at an early age. Older readers also benefit handsomely from instruction that shows them how to connect previous experience and knowledge to new information from the material.

Unlike the DR-TA, the Inferential Strategy does not require stopping points throughout the reading selection. Instead, it relies on a line of questions prior to reading and discussion afterwards.

**Steps in the Inferential Strategy.** Consider the following steps in the Inferential Strategy:

1. **Analyze the content selection for important ideas central to the material.** Before assigning the class to read the material, select *three* or *four* ideas that are important or might be difficult to understand.

2. **Plan prereading questions.** Develop *two* questions for *each idea* identified in the content analysis. One question is posed to tap background knowledge relative to the idea; the other, prediction. For example, a *background question:* "How do you react when you feel uncomfortable in a social situation?" Or a *prediction question:* "In the selection you are about to read, Tim feels unsure of himself on his first blind date. How do you think Tim will react when he meets his date?" Ask students to write predictions before discussion takes place.

3. **Discuss responses to background and prediction questions** *before* **reading.** Discuss both students' previous experiences with the topic and their predictions for the selection.

4. **Upon finishing the prereading discussion, assign a selection to be read.**

5. **After reading, relate predictions to what actually happened in the selection.** Evaluate the three or four ideas that motivated background and prediction questions.

An English teacher implemented the Inferential Strategy for a short story called "August Heat" by W. F. Harvey. A story map prepared by the teacher outlines the key elements in the story that students would need to perceive. Figure 6.7 depicts the main events in the story.

Given the story line, the teacher decided on the following ideas, which she felt were important enough or difficult enough for students to warrant close attention:

1. Not everything that happens can be explained by reason and logic.

2. In many cases, the way an incident or event is reported depends on who is doing the reporting.

3. Some stories are open ended. The reader's imagination will determine the outcome.

The class explored each of those ideas through a guided discussion before reading, which focused on (a) a background question and (b) a prediction question for each idea:

Idea 1: (a) Have you ever had anything happen to you that seemed like an unusual coincidence or a case of ESP?

(b) "August Heat" is about an artist who draws a picture of a man he has never seen who is on trial in a courtroom. Knowing just this much information and the title of the story, can anyone predict what this story is going to be about?

**Figure 6.7    STORY MAP FOR "AUGUST HEAT"**

The Setting

Time and Place: A hot, oppressive, steamy day in an English city on August 20, 190_.
Character: James Withencroft, an artist

The Problem

On impulse, Withencroft draws a picture of a sweaty, guilty-looking fat man who is on trial and sitting in the defendant's box. The artist doesn't know what possessed him to draw the work, but he feels it is his best work ever.

The Goal

To figure out why he, the artist, drew the picture.

| | |
|---|---|
| Event 1: | The artist goes for a walk and encounters Atkinson, the very man whose picture he has drawn. |

| | |
|---|---|
| Event 2: | The artist discovers that Atkinson, a tombstone engraver, has had an impulse to carve a name unknown to him on a tombstone. |

| | |
|---|---|
| Event 3: | The name on the tombstone is revealed to be that of the artist, with the date of death being August 20, 190_. |

| | |
|---|---|
| Event 4: | The artist is persuaded to stay the evening at the engraver's house, lest he meet his demise on the way home. |

| | |
|---|---|
| Event 5: | The artist suspects that the tombstone engraver is fated to murder him. |

The Resolution

The story ends with the reader left to resolve the outcome.

Idea 2: (a) Have you ever talked with two people, both of whom witnessed the same incident, and found that their versions of the same event were different?

(b) This story is told to you by the main character himself. How do you think this might influence the way you read the story?

Idea 3: (a) Can you think of any movies you have seen that left you totally hanging at the end? You never did find out what happened. Did this leave you frustrated and disappointed, or do you prefer to decide for yourself what happens?

(b) This story is also a cliffhanger. You will have to decide for yourself what happens. Knowing this ahead of time, what might you be looking for as you read that will help you to determine your own conclusion?

Class members wrote down their predictions about the story before reading. Several students volunteered to share theirs with the class. The predictions were later contrasted with inferences derived from the story during a postreading discussion. As a follow-up to the discussion, the students formed pairs to decide on a possible ending. Each pair's first task was to skim through the story and list clues that would support their ending. If enough pairs of students believed that the engraver killed the artist, they could opt to set up a mock trial to try the engraver. Other pairs of students had the option of collaboratively writing the ending of the story.

The DR-TA and Inferential Strategy share several common premises. The next strategy, however, is founded on a different set of assumptions. As you read about the GRP, contrast it with the DR-TA and Inferential Strategy.

## Guided Reading Procedure (GRP)

The GRP emphasizes close reading (Manzo 1975). It requires that students gather information and organize it around important ideas, and it places a premium on accuracy as students reconstruct the author's message. With a strong factual base, students will work from a common and clearer frame of reference. They will then be in a position to elaborate thoughtfully on the text and its implications.

Steps in the GRP. The GRP is a highly structured activity and therefore should be used sparingly as a training strategy—perhaps once a week at most. These steps are suggested:

1. **Prepare students for reading:** Clarify key concepts; determine what students know and don't know about particular content to be studied; build appropriate background; give direction to reading.

2. **Assign a text selection:** 500–900 words in the middle grades (approximately five to seven minutes of silent reading); 1000–2000 words for high school (approximately ten minutes). Provide general purpose to direct reading behavior. Direction: Read to remember all you can.

3. **As students finish reading, have them turn books face down.** Ask them to tell what they remember. Record it on the chalkboard in the fashion in which it is remembered.

4. **Help students recognize that there is much that they have not remembered or have represented incorrectly.** Simply, there are implicit inconsistencies which need correction and further information to be considered.

5. **Redirect students into their books and review the selection to correct inconsistencies and add further information.**

6. **Organize recorded remembrances into some kind of an outline.** Ask guiding, nonspecific questions: "What were the important ideas in the assigned reading?" "Which came first?" "What facts on the board support it?" "What important point was brought up next?" "What details followed?"

7. **Extend questioning to stimulate an analysis of the material and a synthesis of the ideas with previous learnings.**

8. **Provide immediate feedback, such as a short quiz, as a reinforcement of short-term memory.**

**A GRP Illustration.**  Middle grade students in a music class were assigned an article from the music education magazine *Pipeline*. The selection, "Percussion—Solid as Rock," concerns the development and uses of percussion instruments from ancient to modern times.

The teacher introduced the selection by giving some background. She then began a discussion by asking students to remember as much as they could as they read the assignment silently. The teacher recorded the collective memories of her students on a transparency, projecting responses onto an overhead screen. Then she asked, "Did you leave out any information that might be important to know about?" Students were directed to review the selection to determine if essential information was missing from the list on the screen. The teacher also asked, "Did you mix up some of the facts on the list? Did you misrepresent any of the information in the author's message?"

These two questions are extremely important to the overall GRP procedure. The first question—"Did you leave out any information that might be important?"—encourages a review of the material. Students sense that some facts are more important than others. Further questioning at this point will help them distinguish essential from nonessential information. The second question—"Did you misrepresent any facts?"—reinforces the importance of selective rereading and rehearsal because of the limitations imposed by short-term memory.

Next the teacher asked the class to study the information recorded on the screen. The teacher requested the students to form pairs and then assigned the following task: "Which facts on the overhead can be grouped together? Organize the information around the important ideas in the selection. You have five minutes to complete the task."

Upon completion of the task the teacher encouraged students to share their work in whole-group discussion. Their groupings of facts were compared, refined, and extended. The teacher served as a facilitator, keeping the discussion moving, asking clarifying questions, provoking thought. She then initiated the next task: "Let's organize the important ideas and related information. Let's make a map."

Figure 6.8 shows what the students produced.

Outlining the mass of information will make students aware of the text relationships developed by the author. In Chapter 9 we will explore several outlining procedures that help students produce the author's main ideas in relation to one another. Producing the author's organizational structure leads to more efficient recall at a later time and lays the groundwork for interpreting and applying the author's message. Once this common framework is developed, your questioning should lead to more divergent and abstract responding by the students.

The discussion took off after the outline was completed. The teacher asked several reflective questions that helped students associate their previous experiences and beliefs about drumming to the content under discussion. Cognitive performance centered on evaluation and application as students linked what they knew to what they were studying.

The final suggested step in the GRP is a short quiz—mainly to demonstrate in a dramatic way how successful the students can be with the reading material. The quiz should be viewed as positive reinforcement, not an interrogation check. Most of the students in this class earned perfect or near-perfect scores on the quiz—and this is as it should be.

## Intra-Act

Intra-Act lays the groundwork for reflective discussion following the reading of text material. Pivotal to the Intra-Act procedure is the notion that students engage in a process of valuing as they reflect on what they have read. Hoffman (1979) suggests Intra-Act to provide readers with "the opportunity to experience rather than just talk about critical reading" (p. 608). According to Hoffman, students are more likely to read critically when they engage in a process of valuing. The valuing process allows students to respond actively to a text selection with thought and feeling. In cognitive terms, valuing places a heavy premium on integrating and using knowledge.

The Intra-Act procedure can be used with a variety of reading materials—content area text assignments, historical documents, newspaper and magazine articles, narrative and poetic material. The procedure requires the use of small groups whose members are asked to react to value statements based on the content of the text selection. There are four phases in the Intra-Act procedure, which roughly parallel those phases identified in value clarification activities. These phases include (1) *comprehension* (understanding of the topic under discussion), (2) *relating* (connecting what has been learned about the topic to what students already know and believe), (3) *valuation* (expressing personal values and feelings related to the topic), and (4) *reflection* (reflecting on the values and feelings just experienced).

**Figure 6.8    SEMANTIC MAP OF "PERCUSSION—SOLID AS A ROCK"**

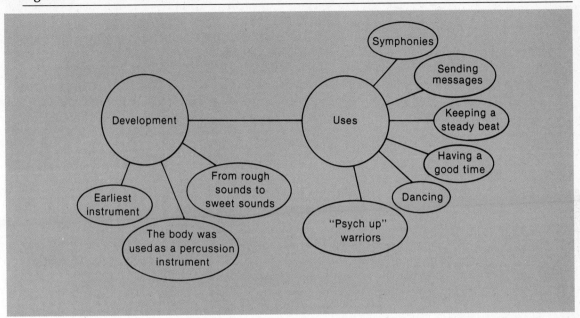

**Steps in Intra-Act.** Here's how Intra-Act works:

**Comprehend:** The comprehension phase promotes an understanding of the reading material to be learned. To begin this phase, the teacher follows effective prereading procedures by introducing the text reading, activating and building background knowledge for the ideas to be encountered during reading, and inviting students to make predictions and speculate on the nature of the content to be learned. Building a frame of reference for upcoming text information is crucial to the overall success of the Intra-Act procedure.

Prereading preparation paves the way for readers to interact with the text. Before inviting students to individually read the selection, the teacher forms small groups—Intra-Act teams—of *four to six* members. Assign a student from each group to serve as the team leader. The comprehension phase depends on the team leader's ability to initiate and sustain a discussion of the text. The team leader's responsibility is to lead a discussion by first summarizing what was read. The group members may contribute additional information about the selection or ask questions which seek clarification of the main ideas of the selection. The comprehension phase of the group discussion should be limited to *seven to ten* minutes.

**Relate:** The team leader is next responsible for shifting the discussion from the important ideas in the selection to the group's personal reactions and values related to the topic. Many times, this shift occurs naturally. However, if this is not the case, members should be encouraged by the team leader to contribute their own impressions and opinions. Discussion should also be limited to *seven to ten* minutes.

**Value:** Once group members have shared their personal reactions to the material, they are ready to participate in the valuation phase of the discussion. Here's how this aspect of the Intra-Act procedure works: The teacher or team leader for each group distributes a game sheet. This game sheet contains a valuing exercise—a set of four declarative statements based on the selection's content. These value statements reflect opinions about the text selection and draw insights and fresh ideas from it. The purpose of the valuing exercise is to have students come to grips with what the material means to them by either agreeing (A) or disagreeing (D) with each statement. Figure 6.9 displays a game sheet that is part of the Intra-Act illustration in the next section.

Study the game sheet in Figure 6.9. Note that students must first indicate on the game sheet their own reactions to the four value statements. Then, based on the previous discussion, they must *predict* how each of the other members of their group would respond. In the example of Figure 6.9, Joe disagreed with three of the statements. His predictions as to how other team members would respond are indicated by the circled letters underneath the individual names. Once the responding is complete, the students are ready for the reflective phase of the Intra-Act procedure.

**Reflect:** Begin the reflection phase of Intra-Act by scoring the game sheet. Group members take turns revealing how each responded to the four statements. As each member tells how he or she responded, the other members check whether their predictions agreed with that member's actual responses. During this phase the teacher acts as a facilitator, noting how students responded but refraining from imposing a particular point of view upon students. Instead, encourage students to reflect on what they have learned. According to Hoffman (1979), "It is very important that during this period students be allowed ample time to discuss, challenge, support and question one another's response. This interaction serves to separate opinions quickly arrived at from sound evaluative thinking" (p. 607).

Intra-Act will require several classroom applications before students become accustomed to their roles during discussion. Repeated and extensive participation in Intra-Act will help students become fully aware of the task demands of the procedure. In the beginning, we recommend that upon completion of an Intra-Act discussion students engage in a whole-class discussion of the process in which they participated. Help students debrief: What did we learn from our participation in Intra-Act? Why must all members of a group participate? How might discussion improve the next time we use Intra-Act? Questions such as these make students sensitive to the purpose of the Intra-Act procedure (problem solving) and the role of each reader (critical analysis).

**An Intra-Act Illustration.** After students in one junior high class read the article "Getting Hooked on Tobacco," four students, Joe, Sharon, Katie, and Paul, met as a group to discuss their impressions. Joe, who was the group's team leader, began with a summary of the article and then gave his own reactions. Here's how Joe summarized the article's main ideas: "Well, basically the article says that the government says that tobacco makes you, you know,

**Figure 6.9    JOE'S GAME SHEET**

Name _____
Date _____
Total Score _____
Percentage
of Correct Predictions _____

| Names | Joe | | Sharon | | Paul | | Katie | |
|---|---|---|---|---|---|---|---|---|
| Tobacco companies should be held responsible for the deaths of smokers from heart attacks and lung cancer. | A | (D) | A ____ + | D | A ____ + | D | A ____ − | D |
| Smokers should be able to quit. They just need to really want to. | (A) | D | A ____ + | D | A ____ + | D | A ____ + | D |
| The sale of cigarettes should be illegal just like the sale of cocaine or heroin. | A | (D) | A ____ + | D | A ____ + | D | A ____ + | D |
| The government should spend money on programs to help people stop smoking. | A | (D) | A ____ − | D | A ____ + | D | A ____ − | D |

+ : Joe's predictions were correct.
− : Joe's predictions incorrect.

a drug addict, or something like that. It's like using cocaine or heroin. They say that people can't quit and they need more and more, so cigarettes should be like liquor and you have to get a license to sell them. The cigarette companies don't agree. Me, too. I don't think a guy is going to go out and rob people just to get cigarettes. I mean, if he is that hard up, he would just quit."

After some clarifying discussion of what the article was about, the discussion shifted gears into the relational phase. Sharon reacted to the article this way: "Well, I don't think that a company should be allowed to sell stuff that kills people. And if all the people quit, the company would go out of business anyway, so they should just go out of business now because of a law."

Paul entered the conversation: "I think the guy was right that said if cigarettes were illegal the gangs would have gang wars to see who would get to sell them—just like they do with crack and cocaine right now. Besides, if people really want to kill themselves with smoking they should be allowed. And if they don't, they should just quit. Right on the pack it says *quit.*"

Katie replied: "It ain't so easy to quit. My dad tried like five times, and he finally had to get hypnotized to quit. And he wouldn't have started if he had to buy them from some gang or something. You get them from a store, and nobody ever asks you how old you are. Besides, who reads the warnings?"

When time for discussion was over, the valuation phase was initiated. Students were given a game sheet with these four value statements:

1. Tobacco companies should be held responsible for the deaths of smokers from heart attacks and lung cancer.

2. Smokers should be able to quit. They just need to really want to.

3. The sale of cigarettes should be illegal just like the sale of cocaine or heroin.

4. The government should spend money on programs to help people stop smoking.

Each student was asked to individually respond to the statements and then predict whether the other members of the group would agree or disagree with each statement. Joe's sheet is reproduced in Figure 6.9. From the discussion, he was pretty sure that Sharon would agree with the first statement because she had said that they "shouldn't be allowed to kill people." Similarly, he thought Paul would disagree because he thought people should "just quit." He was also pretty sure that Katie would agree since she seemed to think it was bad that you could just go into a store and buy cigarettes. He used similar reasons to predict the group members' reactions to the other statements.

As part of the reflective phase of Intra-Act, the group shared what they had learned. Joe found that most of his predictions were correct. He was surprised to find out that Katie did not agree with statement one, but she explained that, "It's not the company's fault that they sold something that's not illegal. First, they should make it illegal, then it's the company's fault." Other members argued that her reasoning "didn't make sense" since the tobacco companies know that cigarettes are harmful. That debate was typical of the discussion that went on in all the groups as students worked out the ways in which the ideas presented in the text fit in with their own attitudes and beliefs.

## LOOKING BACK, LOOKING FORWARD

Students engage in a full range of cognitive activity when they interact with text at different levels of comprehension: literal, interpretive, and applied. One way to help students experience levels of comprehension is to provide explicit instruction in Question-Answer Relationships (QARs). QARs sensitize readers to two likely sources of information where answers to textually explicit and textually implicit and schema-based questions can be found.

An instructional framework provides a structure (1) for asking questions and (2) through which students can actively engage in text learning and discussion. In this chapter, several frameworks that prepare students for reading, guide their interaction with texts, and help them to clarify and extend meaning were described.

K-W-L is a meaning-making strategy that engages students in active text learning and that may be initiated with small groups of students or with the whole class. K-W-L revolves around several steps that help students to examine what they know, what they want to know more about, and what they have learned from reading. The Directed Reading-Thinking Activity was also described. This strategy revolves around the use of three guiding questions: (1) What do you think? (2) Why do you think so? (3) Can you prove it? The Inferential Strategy allows readers to use prior knowledge to make inferences about the content under investigation. The GRP or Guided Reading Procedure requires that students gather information and organize it around important ideas, placing a premium on accuracy as students construct the author's message. Intra-Act, based on the notion that students engage in a process of valuing as they reflect on what they have read, lays the groundwork for reflective discussion following the reading of text material.

In the next chapter, we will explore the concept of *scaffolding* with the use of three-level reading guides, text pattern guides, and selective reading guides. These guides bridge the gap between difficult materials in textbooks and the ability of students to comprehend the material independently. The guides provide the immediate support students need to learn from text as they are discovering how to take charge of their own learning.

## SUGGESTED READINGS

Alvermann, D., Dillon, D., & O'Brien, D. (1987). *Using discussion to promote reading comprehension.* Newark, DE: International Reading Association.

Carr, E., & Ogle, D. (1987). K-W-L plus: A strategy for comprehension and summarization. *Journal of Reading, 30,* 626–631.

Dillon, J. (1984). Research on question and discussion. *Educational Leadership, 42,* 50–56.

Dillon, J. (1983). *Teaching and the art of questioning.* Bloomington, IN: Phi Delta Kappa.

Dillon, J. (1985). Using questions to foil discussion. *Teaching and teacher education,* 109–121.

Gall, M., & Gall, J. (1976). The discussion method. In N. Gage (ed.), *The psychology of teaching method. 75th yearbook of the NSSE.* Chicago: University of Chicago Press, 166–216.

Pennock, C. (ed.). (1979). *Reading comprehension at four linguistic levels.* Newark, DE: International Reading Association.

Roby, T. (1987). Commonplaces, questions, and modes of discussion. In J. Dillon, *Classroom questions and discussion.* Norwood, NJ: Ablex.

Stauffer, R. (1969). *Directing reading maturity as a cognitive process.* New York: Harper & Row.

Vacca, J. L., Vacca, R. T., & Gove, M. K. (1991). *Reading and learning to read.* (2nd ed.). New York: HarperCollins.

# 7

# Scaffolding Learning with Reading Guides

There's no limit to how complicated things can get, on account of one thing always leading to another.

—*E.B. White*

## ORGANIZING PRINCIPLE

Reading is an act of maturity. From the very first day we pick up books, we are reading to learn and learning to read. We grow *in* reading and *through* reading. As children learn to read, they become more fluent and their ability to handle the mechanics of the process becomes more automatic. But automatically doesn't necessarily mean that reading to learn gets easier as readers grow older. To paraphrase E.B. White, there's no limit to how complicated reading can get.... This is particularly so if the ideas we encounter are beyond our level of knowledge and experiential grasp. Many students find that reading gets complicated in academic disciplines when they have trouble handling the conceptual demands of difficult texts.

Teachers can contribute to the reading maturity of students within the context of subject matter instruction. While the raison d'être of content area reading is to show students how to learn with texts independently, many students may have trouble handling the conceptual demands inherent in difficult texts. This is often the case, for example, when they have difficulty responding to what they're reading at different levels of comprehension. Our task, then, is to help students experience what it is to respond to difficult texts. So a teacher supports readers' efforts to make meaning by *scaffolding* their interactions with texts. Scaffolding takes many forms. The organizing principle of this chapter reflects one of the most basic approaches to scaffolding difficult material: *Reading guides scaffold learning by providing the kind of instructional support that allows students to interact with and respond to difficult texts in meaningful ways.*

As the Chapter Overview shows, there are three types of reading guides you will learn about. The first type, a *three-level reading guide,* reflects the concept of levels of comprehension. *Text pattern guides* are similar to three-level guides but they make a concerted effort to help students recognize the organizational structure underlying the author's text. The third type of reading guide, a *selective reading guide,* models the way a strategic reader responds to text that is difficult to read. There are many more types of reading guides you can devise to scaffold students' learning. However, those that you will read about in this chapter reflect some of the possibilities for guided instruction.

## CHAPTER OVERVIEW

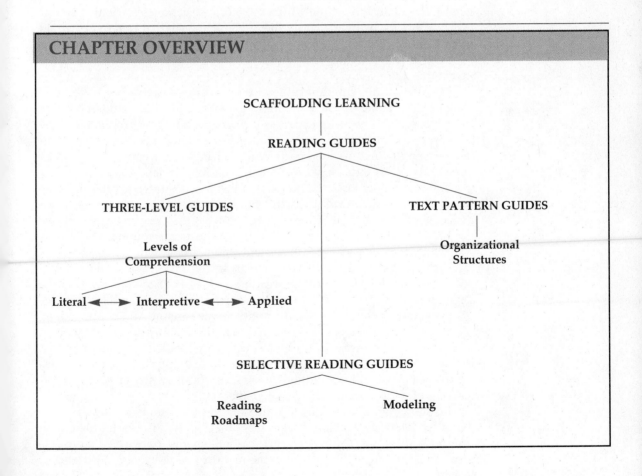

## FRAME OF MIND

1. How do reading guides scaffold learning?

2. What are the purpose and value of three-level guides?

3. What are the purpose and value of text pattern guides?

4. What are the purpose and value of selective reading guides?

5. How can you use and adapt different kinds of reading guides in your content area?

Used in construction, scaffolds serve as supports, lifting up workers so that they can achieve something that otherwise would not have been possible. In teaching and learning contexts, scaffolding means helping learners to do what they cannot do at first (Bruner 1986). Instructional scaffolds support text learners by helping them achieve literacy tasks that otherwise would have been out of reach. All the chapters in this book, in one way or another, suggest ways to provide enough instructional support for students to grow in and through reading.

Reading guides simplify difficult text for students (Herber 1978). As a result, guides make textbook life in the classroom easier for students. Don't think by "easier" that we mean "less challenging" or "less productive." Just the opposite is intended. Reading guides are used in content classes primarily because the text material is difficult and important enough to warrant scaffolding. Their judicious use will make learning easier.

The conceptual load of content area textbooks is often greater than the levels of reading maturity that students bring to the task. As a result, students experience difficulty comprehending what they read. They simply do not know what ideas are important enough to merit concentrated study. The whole idea of a guide is to provide enough instructional support and direction for students to learn with texts. In the process of doing so, they will gain confidence. Over time, reading guides help to contribute to the development of strategies that lead to independent reading and learning.

To some teachers the use of guides is tantamount to spoon-feeding. Maybe it is. However, spoon-feeding doesn't necessarily mean that you are giving the content away. It means that you simplify the tough sledding that is ahead for students when the information in text appears too overwhelming to read on their own. Without some simplification, students' only alternative is often to avoid textbooks altogether.

Reading guides are firmly grounded in the here and now, assisting students to comprehend texts better than they would if left to their own resources. Over time, however, text learners should be weaned from this type of scaffolding as they develop the maturity and the learning strategies to interact with difficult texts without teacher intervention in the form of guide material. So with this caveat in mind, let's explore the use of *three-level reading guides*, *text pattern guides*, and *selective reading guides*.

## THREE-LEVEL READING GUIDES

The levels of comprehension model presented in the previous chapter lends itself well to the preparation of guide material to scaffold reader-text interactions. Recall, if you will, that when a reader interacts with text, he or she constructs meaning at different levels of abstraction and conceptual complexity: at the *literal level,* where the reader reads the lines; at the *interpretive level,* where the reader reads between the lines; and at the *applied level,* where the reader reads beyond the lines. A three-level reading guide provides the scaffold from which students can interact with difficult texts at these levels. One of the best ways to become familiar with the three-level guide as an instructional scaffold is to experience one. Therefore, we invite your participation in the following demonstration.

First preview the three-level guide in Box 7.1, and then read "The Case of the Missing Ancestor," which originally appeared in a chapter in *Silver Burdett Biology* (1986). After reading the text, complete the guide.

Several comments are in order on your participation in the three-level guide demonstration. First of all, note that the three-level format gave you a "conscious experience" with comprehension levels as a process (Herber 1978). Consider also that as you walked through the process you responded to and manipulated the important explicit and implicit ideas in the material. You may have sensed the relatedness of ideas as you moved within and among the levels.

Why did we direct you to first preview the guide and then read the material? Because previewing helps create a predisposition for reading the material. As you recall from Chapter 5, previewing helps to reduce the reader's uncertainty about the material to be read. You know what is coming. When we asked you to read the guide first, we hoped to raise your expectations about the author's message. By encountering some of the ideas before reading, you are in a better position to direct the search for information that may be relevant in the reading material.

You probably noted also that the declarative statements did not require you to produce answers to questions. Rather, you had to make decisions among likely alternatives; it's easier to recognize possible answers than to produce them.

Notice, too, that in a very positive way the statements can serve as springboards for discussion and conversation about the content. Were students to react to guides without the opportunity to discuss and debate responses, the adjunct material would soon deteriorate into busywork and paper shuffling.

A final comment: your maturity as a reader probably is such that you didn't need structured guidance for this selection, particularly at levels I

---

**BOX 7.1    Three-Level Reading Guide**

**"The Case of the Missing Ancestor"**

I. *Directions:* Check the statements that you believe say what the author says. Sometimes the exact words are used; other times other words may be used.

_____ 1. The Germans discovered the fossilized remnants of the Neanderthal man and the Heidelberg man.

_____ 2. Charles Dawson found a human skull in a gravel pit in Piltdown Common, Sussex.

_____ 3. Charles Dawson was a professional archaeologist.

_____ 4. The fossil, *Eoanthropus dawsoni*, became known as the Piltdown man.

_____ 5. The discovery of the Piltdown man was acclaimed as an important archaeological find.

_____ 6. Dental evidence regarding the Piltdown man was ignored.

II. *Directions:* Check those statements which you feel represent the author's *intended* meaning.

_____ 1. The English scientific community felt left out because important fossils were found in other countries.

_____ 2. Good scientific practices were ignored by men working with the Piltdown fossils.

_____ 3. Many scientists said that Piltdown was important because they wanted England to be important.

_____ 4. Dawson wanted to make himself famous, so he constructed a hoax.

III. *Directions:* Check those statements you agree with and be ready to support your choices with ideas from the text as well as your own knowledge and beliefs.

_____ 1. Competition in scientific research may be dangerous.

_____ 2. Scientists, even good ones, can be fooled by poorly constructed hoaxes.

_____ 3. People often see only what they want to see.

_____ 4. A scientific "fact" is not always correct just because many scientists believe strongly in it; theories are always open to question.

---

and II. If you make the decision that certain segments of your text can be handled without reading guidance, then don't construct guide material. A three-level guide is a means to growth in reading and growth through reading. It is not an end in itself.

## A Three-Level Reading Guide in Action

In order to get a feel for how a three-level reading guide may be used in a content classroom, study the lesson below from a senior-level economics class. The lesson revolves around an instructional framework that includes a *prereading* component, a *during reading* component in which the three-level guide is used to scaffold reader-text interactions, and a *postreading* component.

The text assignment, from *Invitations to Economics* (Scott, Foresman 1982), was six pages in length and dealt with the topic Trade Offs. The following major ideas were presented in the text:

### The Case of the Missing Ancestor

From the mid-1800s to the early 1900s, Europeans were actively searching for early ancestors. The Germans dug up the fossilized remnants of Neanderthal man and Heidelberg man. The French discovered not only ancient bones but also cave paintings done by early humans.

England, Charles Darwin's home, had no evidence of ancient ancestors. English scientists—both professionals and amateurs—began searching for fossils. Scarcely a cave was left unexplored, scarcely a stone was left unturned. Many scientists asked workers in gravel pits to watch for fossils.

In 1912, Charles Dawson, a part-time collector of fossils for the British Museum, wrote to Dr. Arthur Smith Woodward, keeper of the Natural History Department at the British Museum. Dawson claimed that a human skull he had found in a gravel pit in Piltdown Common, Sussex, "would rival Heidelberg man." Soon Woodward was digging in the gravel pit with Dawson and other eager volunteers. They found a separate jaw that, though apelike, included a canine tooth and two molars, worn down as if by human-type chewing. Flints and nonhuman fossils found at the same dig indicated that the finds were very old.

Despite arguments by some scientists that the jaw came from a chimpanzee or an orangutan, the discoverers reconstructed the skull and connected the jaw to it. They named the fossil *Eoanthropus dawsoni*, Dawson's "Dawn man," and said that it was much older than Neanderthal man. The find came to be known as Piltdown man.

The finds were X-rayed. One dental authority was suspicious of the canine; he said it was too young a tooth to show such wear. However, such contrary evidence was ignored in the general surge of enthusiasm. So the Piltdown man was acclaimed as an important find, a human in which the brain had evolved more quickly than the jaw.

Beginning in the 1940s, the bones were subjected to modern tests. It is now believed that the skull was from a modern human and the jaw was from a modern ape, probably an orangutan. The animal fossils and flints were found to be very old, but not the types that have been found in England. Apparently, they had been placed in the gravel pit to make the finds more convincing. Why were the scientists and others fooled so easily? Perhaps the desire to find an "ancestor" may have interfered with careful scientific observation.

1. When resources are used to produce one economic good or service, those same resources cannot be used simultaneously to produce another good or service: this opportunity has been traded off.

2. In answering the basic economic questions, all countries must consider the question of (relative) value.

3. The trade offs that a consumer must make when buying different quantities of two items is shown graphically by a budget line.

4. The trade offs that a nation must make when producing different quantities of two items is shown graphically by the production-possibility frontier.

5. If the opportunity cost between two items is constant, this will be portrayed graphically by a straight line on a budget line or the production-possibility frontier.

6. If the opportunity cost between two products varies, this will be shown graphically by a curved line on the production-possibility frontier.

7. Any point (representing a combination of two items) that lies within or on a budget line is attainable with a given income; any point lying beyond the line is not attainable with that income.

8. Any point (representing a combination of two products) that lies within or on the production-possibility frontier for a particular nation is attainable, given that nation's existing amount of resources. Any point lying beyond the frontier is not attainable, given the existing amount of resources.

9. An increase in a nation's amount of resources or level of technology will push outward its production-possibility frontier.

Given the potential difficulty of the material, the teacher planned the following procedures in light of his instructional objectives:

# Prereading

*Objectives:*

A. Students will become aware of the key economic concepts of Chapter 1, Section 3: "Trade Offs" (pp. 12–18).

B. Students will understand the graphic representation of economic concepts.

*Procedures:*

A. Have students preview this section by skimming; have them pay particular attention to the definitions of key concepts given in the page margins.

B. Have students examine and read the captions explaining a budget line (Figure 1.2, p. 14) and a production-possibility frontier (Figure 1.3, p. 15).

As an entire class, have them suggest the relationship of the concepts of trade offs and opportunity cost to these graphs.

# During Reading

*Objective:*

A. Students will interact with the text at the literal, interpretive, and applied levels of comprehension.

*Procedures:*

A. Distribute to each student a mimeographed handout of a three-level reading guide (see Box 7.2); have them preview this guide to set their purpose for reading this section of the textbook.

B. Have students read pp. 12–18 and then individually complete the reading guide.

---

**BOX 7.2    Three-Level Reading Guide for "Trade Offs"**

I. *Literal level*
   *Directions*: Check the items you believe are *true*, given your reading of Section 3.
   _____ 1. Since individuals cannot have everything they want, they must make trade offs.
   _____ 2. In answering the basic economic questions, all countries must consider the question of value.
   _____ 3. It is always simple for a nation to determine the relative value of different products.
   _____ 4. The trade offs a consumer must make when buying different quantities of two items can be shown graphically by a budget line.
   _____ 5. A production-possibility frontier shows graphically the relationship between a nation's existing resources and its level of technology.
   _____ 6. A curved production-possibility frontier means varying opportunity costs.

II. *Interpretive level*
    *Directions*: Check the items that are logical inferences that can be drawn from Section 3.
    _____ 1. Trade offs are necessary because productive resources are limited.
    _____ 2. The opportunity cost of using steel to produce buses is the number of cars that could not be produced from the same steel.
    _____ 3. The opportunity cost of working part time on school nights is the number of hours worked that cannot be used for other activities, such as studying or recreating.
    _____ 4. The concept of a budget line implies that a person's income is never constant.
    _____ 5. If the price of Item A is always twice the price of Item B, the budget line for these two items will be a straight line.
    _____ 6. If a person's weekly income is $20, a combination of two rock albums (@ $7) and one cassette tape (@ $8) would lie either on or within the budget line.

III. *Applied level*
     *Directions*: Check the items which are logical applications of the economic concepts discussed in Section 3.
     _____ 1. A nation's production-possibility frontier can be moved outward by discoveries of additional resources.
     _____ 2. Increasing a nation's level of technology will move its production-possibility frontier inward.
     _____ 3. In the long term, the increased use of robots in manufacturing would push a nation's production-possibility frontier outward.

---

# Postreading

*Objective:*

A. Students will understand and extend the meaning of the economic concepts.

*Procedures:*

A. In pairs, have students take about five minutes to compare and discuss their marking of the items on the three-level reading guide. Then, in a class-sized group, answer any questions over the guide that students still have.

B. In groups of four or five, give students about five minutes to list several specific examples from the news today of the following factors which could push the U.S. production-possibility frontier outward:

1. discoveries of additional resources;

2. advances which have raised our level of technology.

Then, have two students list these specific examples on the chalkboard during a whole-class discussion of them.

Finally, as a homework assignment, have students propose two or three of their own suggestions to:

1. increase the amount of productive resources in the U.S.; and

2. raise our level of technology.

(These will be discussed for seven to ten minutes in small groups to begin the next day's lesson; then they will be shared with the entire class.)

As you can observe from the social studies teacher's lesson, three-level reading guides don't run by themselves, nor do they represent busy work—something for the students to do—for homework or to occupy class time. Instead, teachers work reading guides into the structure of carefully planned classroom activity to support students' learning of text that may have been too difficult for them to attempt on their own. Let's take a closer look at how three-level guides can be adapted in various academic fields.

## Using and Constructing Three-Level Guides

Don't be misled by the apparent discreteness of comprehension levels. Don't, as Dale (1969) pronounced, suffer from "hardening of the categories." The term *levels* implies a cognitive hierarchy that may be more apocryphal than real. A reader doesn't necessarily read first for literal recognition, then interpretation, and finally application—although that may appear to be a logical sequence. Many readers, for instance, read text for overarching concepts and generalizations first and then search for evidence to support their inferences.

Most important is that you recognize that in reading, levels are probably interactive and inseparable. Nevertheless, the classroom teacher attempts to have students experience each aspect of the comprehension process as they read content material. In doing so, students adapt strategies as they interact with the material. They get a feel for the component processes within reading comprehension. They come to sense in an instructional setting what it means to make inferences, what it means to use information as the basis for those inferences, and what it means to rearrange or transform acquired understandings into what they know already in order to construct knowledge.

The reading guide is not meant to be used with every text assignment every day. If it were to be, it would soon be counterproductive. One math teacher's evaluation of a three-level guide crystallizes this point: "The students said the guide actually helped them organize in their minds the author's ideas and helped them to understand the material. I think the guide was successful but I would not use it all the time because many of the assignments don't lend themselves to this type of activity." The three-level reading guide is but one instructional aid that helps students grow toward mature reading and independent learning.

Merlin the magician doesn't wave his magic wand to ensure the effectiveness of three-level guides. They can be facilitative only when students know how to work in groups and know how to apply techniques that have been taught clearly. The heart of the matter is what the teacher does to make guided reading work.

Finally, we urge you also to consider guides as tools, not tests. Their real value ultimately lies in providing for the adaptation and application of skills to subject material. But we hasten to emphasize one more time that individual skills and levels are likely to be interactive and inseparable from one another. Think of each statement in a reading guide as a prompt that will initiate that interaction and reinforce the quality of the reader's response to meaning in text material.

There are no set of procedures for constructing three-level reading guides. Before constructing a guide, however, the teacher has to decide: What are the important ideas that should be emphasized? What are the students' competencies? The depth of understanding that you expect them to achieve? The difficulty of the material?

Having made these decisions, you may wish to consider these guidelines:

1. Begin construction of the guide at level II, the interpretive level. Analyze the text selection, asking yourself: "What does the author mean?" Write down in your own words those inferences that make sense to you and fit your content objectives. Make sure your statements are written simply and clearly. (After all, you don't want to construct a guide to read the guide.)

2. Next, search the text for propositions, explicit pieces of information, needed to support the inferences you have chosen for level II. Put these into statement form. You now have level I, the literal level.

3. Decide whether you want to add a distractor or two to levels I and II. We have found that a distractor can maintain an active response to the information search, mainly because students sense that they cannot indiscriminately check every item and therefore focus the information search more carefully.

4. Develop statements for level III, the applied level. Such statements represent additional insights or principles that can be drawn when relationships established by the author are combined with other ideas outside the text selection itself but inside the heads of your students. In other words, help students connect what they know already to what they have read.

5. Be flexible and adaptive. Develop a format that will appeal to you and your students. Try to avoid crowding too much print on the reading guide.

## Three-Level Guides: Illustrations

The format of the three-level guide should vary. The classroom examples that follow serve only as models. As you study these illustrations, think of ways that you will be able to adapt and apply the three-level construct to your content materials.

English. Reading guides are extremely useful adjuncts in the study of literature. A three-level guide can easily be adapted to dramatic, narrative, and poetic forms of literature. For example, note in Box 7.3 how a ninth-grade English teacher used a three-level guide for Shakespeare's *Romeo and Juliet*. The class was at the tail-end of its study of the play, and the guide helped students to pull together some of the important points related to the climactic action of the final act. Moreover, the statements in levels II and III of the guide helped students reflect on possible inferences and themes that emerge from the action.

Poems often present a problem at the interpretive and applied levels. Is it possible, or even desirable, to separate the poet's intended meaning from a reader's personal response to that meaning? In some reading situations you may wish to consider combining levels II and III when developing a reading guide. The guide will then prompt two levels of thinking—explicit and implicit responses to meaning.

Read the poem "They Were Rong," by Richard Niece. Then complete the guide in Box 7.4. Refer back to the poem as you work through the statements in the reading guide.

Math. Consider how mathematics teachers might adapt the reading guide to suit their purposes. The nature of the mathematical content should determine the form of the guide. Word problems in particular illustrate this point. For example, Riley and Pachtman (1978) explain: "Mathematical word problems

BOX 7.3    **Three-Level Guide for** *Romeo and Juliet*

I. *Literal Level:* Check the items that explicitly represent some of the important details and actions in the last part of the play.

_____ 1. The reason Friar Laurence married Romeo and Juliet was to bring the families of Montague and Capulet together

_____ 2. Friar Laurence believed words of wisdom would help Romeo deal with his banishment.

_____ 3. Juliet gave the ring to the Nurse to give to Romeo as a sign of her love.

_____ 4. Lady Capulet believed marriage to Paris would take care of all of Juliet's sorrows.

_____ 5. Paris was going to Juliet's grave nightly to place flowers.

_____ 6. Prince Escalus said that he was the one to blame for the deaths because he had not acted decisively enough.

II. *Interpretive Level:* Several statements are listed below which may represent what the playwright means. If you think any of the statements are reasonable inferences and conclusions, put a check on the line provided. Be prepared to support your answers using parts of the play.

_____ 1. Romeo would be alive if the apothecary had obeyed the law.

_____ 2. Lord and Lady Capulet are to blame for Juliet's death because they forced her into marriage.

_____ 3. If Prince Escalus had punished the Montagues and Capulets earlier, the entire tragedy would not have happened.

_____ 4. Romeo's impulsiveness, rashness, immaturity, and emotionalism caused him problems.

_____ 5. A fourteen-year-old is not capable of true love.

_____ 6. Romeo did not want to kill Paris.

III. *Applied Level:* To apply what you read means to take information and ideas from what you have read and connect it to what you already know. If you think the statements below are supported by state ments in Section II and by previous experience or study, place a check in the blank provided. Be sure you have good reasons to justify your answers if called upon to do so.

_____ 1. Those who live by the sword, die by the sword.

_____ 2. Those in positions of power must take responsibility for the actions of those under them.

_____ 3. A person cannot change the role that fate has ordained for him.

_____ 4. The most important thing in life is love. It is even worth dying for.

_____ 5. No person has the right to take his/her own life.

_____ 6. Nothing is worth dying for.

_____ 7. Our own personalities shape our lives, and we can shape our personalities by the choices we make.

_____ 8. Events outside our control shape our lives.

constitute a new area of difficulty for the student. Unlike the language of narrative material, the language of word problems is compact. Mathematical concepts and relationships are often 'hidden' or assumed and therefore not readily apparent to the student" (p. 531). Riley and Pachtman suggest how the three-level guide can be adapted to meet the reading demands implicit in solving word problems. The procedure is as follows: (1) level I = the facts of the problem, (2) level II = the mathematical ideas or concepts underlying the problem, and (3) level III = the numerical depictions related to the problem. Study Box 7.5, which illustrates the adaptations which can be made when reading word problems in math.

BOX 7.4    **Three-Level Guide for "They Were Rong"**

**They Were Rong**

by Richard Niece

They were rong
my teachers were.
Said if I quit sckool.
droped out.
Id never make it in the "real" world.
Im dum I no,
cant spell or read to good.
I tryed but gess I was just cut out
to be a yellow bird forever.
And I never could figger out
how it felt to be a daffadil in spring
or why they cared each fall
how I spent last summer.
And grammer, well my comas
just never seemed to fit to good.
And run ons.
But I did good in math
and I can count good.
At least Mr. Harris thinks so
thats why he hired me here at the station.
I make change ok

so I gess Im doin alright.
And I told Mrs. Wayne my old english teacher
so when she stoped here the other day for gas.
I just told her how this here at the station
made more cents then all that other stuff.
And I think she believed me to
cause she didn't laff or nothin,
she just shook her head
and sort of cleared her throte.

**Three-Level Guide**

*Level I.* In this poem, a school dropout expresses certain feelings and thoughts. What did the dropout say?
Check those statements you believe say what the dropout says.

_____ 1. I was just cut out to be a yellow bird forever.
_____ 2. Im dum . . .
_____ 3. I did good in school.
_____ 4. Mr. Harris thinks I can count good.
_____ 5. Im doin alright.
_____ 6. . . . My old english teacher liked my poems.

*Level II.* What does the poem mean to you? Check those statements that you can support from the poem.

_____ 1. The dropout is kidding himself in saying, "Im doin alright."
_____ 2. Mr. Harris took a risk when he hired the dropout.
_____ 3. A good education is essential for success.
_____ 4. The dropout's teachers were right, not wrong.
_____ 5. One's worth is not measured in grades or income.
_____ 6. If you were to write a letter to the dropout, what would you tell him?

## BOX 7.5    Word Problem Reading Guides

*Problem:* Tom has collected 239 empty cans for recycling. He puts 107 into a big box. How many must he put in each of two smaller boxes if he uses the rest of the cans and puts the same number in each box?

I. Facts of the Problem

*Directions:* Read the word problem above. Then under column A check those statements that contain the important facts of the problem. Look back at the problem to check your answers. Under column B check those statements you think will help you solve the problem.

| A<br>(Facts) | B<br>(Will help) | |
|---|---|---|
| _____ | _____ | 107 cans went into the big box. |
| _____ | _____ | The cans were for recycling. |
| _____ | _____ | Tom had collected 239 empty cans. |
| _____ | _____ | Tom had one big box and two smaller ones. |
| _____ | _____ | Tom put the cans into three boxes. |
| _____ | _____ | The cans were empty. |
| _____ | _____ | 107 cans had to be put into two smaller boxes. |

II. Math Ideas

*Directions:* Check the statements that contain math ideas about this problem. Look back to column B of part I to prove your answers. (You may change your answers in part I if you wish to.)

_____ Division is putting an amount into equal groups.

_____ To find the total amount of a group we add the parts.

_____ When we take an amount away we subtract to find the amount left.

_____ Adding groups with the same amount in each group is multiplying.

_____ Subtracting is separating a group into two parts.

_____ When we put an amount into groups of the same size we divide the amount by the number of groups.

III. Numbers

*Directions:* Below are possible ways of getting an answer. Check those that will work in this problem. Look back to column B of part I and to part II to prove your answers. (You may change some of your answers in parts I and II if you wish to.)

_____ $(239 \div 2) + 107$

_____ $(239 - 107) \div 2$

_____ $107 \div 2$

_____ $239 \div 2$

_____ $239 - 107$

_____ $107 + 239$

Now that you have responded to each part of the guide, you may compute the answer to the problem.

Social Studies. A ninth grade teacher developed the three-level guide in Box 7.6 to show students how to read a textbook section entitled "Building the First Cities." He directed the students to complete the three-level guide *as* they read the assignment. Examine the variation at the literal level. Completing the guide as you read helps you read selectively and focus on essential information.

---

### BOX 7.6    Three-Level Guide: Building First Cities

I. *Directions:* For the statements below, tell which of the four cities listed is being described exactly by the author. Use this letter code:

B = Boston
C = Charleston
N = New York
P = Philadelphia

_____  1. the first seaport to be settled
_____  2. rice the main crop
_____  3. many settlers businessmen
_____  4. a busy and beautiful city
_____  5. planned streets
_____  6. theaters here
_____  7. much fishing here
_____  8. a library here built by Ben Franklin
_____  9. the first public schools here
_____ 10. planters as leaders here
_____ 11. the University of Pennsylvania and religious freedom here
_____ 12. many dinners and dances for rich people
_____ 13. the largest city for 150 years
_____ 14. a hot, humid city

II. *Directions:* On the basis of what you've read, check each of the statements below about our first four major cities with which the author would agree:

_____ 1. Early American cities had some paved streets.
_____ 2. Cities were places where news and ideas were exchanged.
_____ 3. Minorities were rarely seen in the cities.
_____ 4. People of all religions were welcomed everywhere.
_____ 5. The common people were allowed a voice in controlling all of the earliest cities.
_____ 6. Trade was necessary for the survival of the cities.
_____ 7. Entertainment was available in some cities.
_____ 8. The early cities were inhabited by different national groups.

III. *Directions:* Check the statements below that you agree with:

_____ 1. The early cities were like people: To be healthy they had to be busy with work to do.
_____ 2. The early city could be pictured as "a strong young man wearing work clothes."
_____ 3. The early city could be pictured as "A middle-aged man wearing a clean, pressed suit."
_____ 4. Transportation + money = city problems.

**Health.** The simplicity of Box 7.7 speaks for itself. A fifth-grade teacher constructed it as part of a health unit. Notice how she uses QARs as cues to direct students' responses. Students completed the guide individually and then discussed their responses in small groups.

As we have shown, one important way to guide comprehension is through three-level reading guides, which a teacher constructs to bridge the gap between students' competencies and the difficulty of text material. As you consider adapting three-level reading guides to content area materials, keep these summarizing points in mind. First, the three-level guide stimulates an active response to meaning at the literal, interpretive, and applied levels. It helps readers to acquire and construct knowledge from content material that might otherwise be too difficult for them to read. Second, levels of comprehension interact with one another during reading; in all probability levels are inseparable among mature readers. Nevertheless, for instructional purposes, it is beneficial to have students experience each level in order to get a feel for the component processes involved in comprehending. And third, three-level guides will help students develop a good sense of the conceptual complexity of text material.

In the next section, another type of reading guide is considered: *text pattern guides.*

---

**BOX 7.7    Health and Growth: "How Do You Grow Up?"**

I. Right there! What did the author say?
*Directions:* Place a check on the line in front of the number if you think a statement can be found in the pages you read.
_____ 1. Every human being has feelings or emotions.
_____ 2. Research workers are studying the effects of repeated use of marijuana on the body.
_____ 3. You should try hard to hide your strong emotions such as fear or anger.
_____ 4. Your feelings affect the way the body works.
_____ 5. You are likely to get angry at your parents or brothers or sisters more often than at other people.

II. Think and search! What did the author mean?
*Directions:* Check the statements below that state what the author was trying to say in the pages you read.
_____ 1. Sometimes you act in a different way because of the mood you are in.
_____ 2. Emotional growth has been a continuing process since the day you were born.
_____ 3. The fact that marijuana hasn't been proven to be harmful means that it is safe to use.
_____ 4. Each time you successfully control angry or upset feelings you grow a little.

III. On Your Own! Do you agree with these statements?
*Directions:* Check those statements that you can defend.
_____ 1. Escaping from problems does not solve them.
_____ 2. Decisions should be made on facts, not fantasies.
_____ 3. Getting drunk is a good way to have fun.

# TEXT PATTERN GUIDES

In Chapter 2, we examined how authors organize information in text. An expository text may be organized according to several major patterns or organizational structures: *cause-effect, comparison-contrast, description, sequence,* and *problem-solution*. These patterns are difficult for maturing readers to discern, but once students become aware of the importance of text organization and learn how to search for relationships in text, they are in a better position to retain information more efficiently and effectively and to comprehend material more thoroughly.

The text pattern guide creates an experience for students similar to that of the three-level guide. A pattern guide helps students perceive and use the major text relationships that predominate in the reading material. Although the three-level guide focuses on a recognition of the relevant information in the material, text organization is implicit.

---

**BOX 7.8　　Today's Stone Age Elephant Hunters**

I. Recognizing the Sequence
*Directions:* The pigmy hunter follows ten steps in hunting and killing an elephant. Some of the steps are given to you. Decide which steps are missing and write them in the spaces provided. The pigmy hunter:
 1. takes the trail of an elephant herd.
 2. _____
 3. selects the elephant he will kill.
 4. _____
 5. moves in for the kill.
 6. _____
 7. _____
 8. pulls out the spear.
 9. _____
10. cuts off _____

II. What Did the Author Mean?
Directions: Check the statements you think suggest what the author is trying to say.
_____ 1. The pigmy hunter is smart.
_____ 2. The pigmy hunter uses instinct much as an animal does.
_____ 3. The pigmy hunter is a coward.

III. How Can We Use Meanings?
*Directions:* Based on what you read and what you know, check the statements you agree with.
_____ 1. A person's ingenuity ensures survival.
_____ 2. Where there's a will there's a way.
_____ 3. There are few differences between primitive and civilized people.

For example, an eighth-grade social studies class read a text assignment, "Today's Stone Age Elephant Hunters," as part of a unit on primitive cultures in the modern world. The text explains how pigmy hunters from the Western Congo hunt and kill elephants in response to a need for food as well as cultural rituals associated with young hunters' rights of passage into manhood. To get a feel for how a text pattern guide scaffolds the reader's recognition of text relationships, read an excerpt from "Today's Stone Age Elephant Hunters," and then complete the text pattern guide in Box 7.8.

Notice how part I of the guide helps you to recognize the temporal sequence of events associated with the elephant hunt. The sequence then forms the basis for the interpretive and applied levels of comprehension. Not only does the guide help the reader focus on explicit text relationships, but it also helps you to focus on important ideas implicit in the text.

How, then, might you scaffold the search for text patterns in reading materials as you teach your content? First, you should try to keep to a minimum the number of patterns that students identify and use. Second,

---

### Today's Stone Age Elephant Hunters
### B. F. Beebe

Some pigmies of the western Congo use a system of concealing their scent when hunting elephants. Few of these little jungle dwellers hunt elephants but those that do have chosen about the most dangerous way to secure food in today's world.

Hunting is done by a single man using a spear with a large metal spearhead and thick shaft. After taking the trail behind an elephant herd the hunter pauses frequently to coat his skin with fresh elephant droppings for several days until he has lost all human scent.

Closing on the herd the pigmy selects his prey, usually a young adult. He watches this animal until he is aware of its distinctive habits—how often it dozes, eats, turns, wanders out of the herd, and other individual behavior.

Then he moves toward his prey, usually at midday when the herd is dozing while standing. The little hunter moves silently between the elephant's legs, braces himself and drives the spear up into the stomach area for several feet. The elephant snaps to alertness, screaming and trying to reach his diminutive attacker. Many pigmy hunters have lost their lives at this moment, but if the little hunter is fast enough he pulls out the spear to facilitate bleeding and ducks for safety.

Death does not come for several days and the hunter must follow his wounded prey until it stops. When the elephant falls the pigmy cuts off the tail as proof of his kill and sets off for his village, which may be several days away by now.

your goal should be to guide students to recognize a single pattern that predominates over long stretches of print, even though you recognize that individual paragraphs and sentences are apt to reflect different thought relationships within the text selection.

## Using and Constructing Text Pattern Guides

A pattern guide is a variation of the three-level guide. The difference between the two lies in the literal level: rather than have students respond to relevant information per se, you can create guide material which allows them to experience how the information fits together. Research and experience (Vacca 1975, 1977; Herber 1978) indicate that the following teaching sequence works well in content classes:

1. Examine a reading selection and decide upon the predominant pattern used by the author.

2. Make students aware of the pattern and how to interpret the author's meaning as part of the total lesson.

3. Provide guidance in the process of perceiving organization through a pattern guide followed by small-group or whole-class discussion.

4. Provide assistance in cases where students have unresolved problems concerning the process and/or the content under discussion.

This sequence is deductive. Once you decide that a particular text selection has a predominant pattern, share your insights with the class. Perceiving text organization is undoubtedly one of the most sophisticated activities that a reader engages in. Chances are that most readers will have trouble recognizing text organization independently. By discussing the pattern before they read, students will develop a frame of reference which they can apply during reading. From a metacognitive point of view, discussing the pattern and why the reader should search for relationships is a crucial part of the lesson.

The pattern guide itself tears the text organization apart. The students' task, then, is really that of piecing together the relationships that exist within the predominant pattern. Interaction among class members as they discuss the guide heightens their awareness of the pattern and how the author uses it to structure information. Students learn from one another as they share their perceptions of the relationships in the reading selection.

The final step in the teaching sequence should not be neglected. As students work on or discuss a pattern guide, provide feedback that will keep them going, that will clarify and aid in rethinking the structure of the material, that will get students back into the material. Combining information is an important intellectual act requiring analysis followed by synthesis. It isn't enough, in most cases, to exhort students to "read for cause-effect" or "study the sequence." You must show them how to perceive organization over long stretches of print. Pattern guides will help you do this.

As you consider developing a pattern guide you may find it useful to follow these three steps:

1. Read through the text selection, identifying a predominant pattern.

2. Develop an exercise in which students can react to the structure of the relationships represented by the pattern.

3. Decide on how much guidance you want to provide in the pattern guide. If it suits your purposes you may develop sections of the guide for the interpretive and applied levels. Or you may decide that these levels can be handled adequately through questioning and discussion once students have sensed the author's organization through the guided reading activity.

Pattern guides help students to follow relationships among ideas. They are most suitable for expository materials, where a predominant pattern of organization is likely to be apparent.

## Text Pattern Guides: Illustrations

Note the variations in the first two classroom examples of pattern guides. Each was developed by a teacher to help students recognize the cause-effect pattern. In presenting the guides to their classes, the teachers followed the four-step teaching sequence just outlined. Study each illustration as a model for preparing your own guides based on causes and effects.

**Auto Mechanics.** The students in an auto mechanics class—part of a high school vocational arts program—were described by the teacher as "nonreaders." Most activities in the course are hands on, as you might expect, and although the students have a textbook, it's seldom used.

But the auto mechanics teacher felt that the textbook section on transmissions warranted reading because of the relevance of the material. To help the students follow the author's ideas about causes and effects, the teacher constructed the pattern guide in Box 7.9.

The students worked in pairs to complete the guide. When some had trouble locating certain effects in the assignment, the teacher told them what page to study. As a result of the guided recognition of cause-effect, the teacher felt that students would better be able to handle interpretation and application through class discussion followed by a hands-on activity.

**Social Studies.** A junior high school teacher prepared a matching activity to illustrate the cause-effect pattern for students who were studying a unit entitled "The American Indian: A Search for Identity." One reading selection from the unit material dealt with Jenny, an adolescent member of the Blackfoot tribe, who commits suicide.

---

**BOX 7.9     Power Mechanics**

*Directions:* In your reading assignment on transmissions, find the causes that led to the effects listed. Write each cause in the space provided.

1. Cause: _____
   Effect: Grinding occurs when shifting gears.
2. Cause: _____
   Effect: Car speed increases but engine speed remains constant while torque is decreasing.
3. Cause: _____
   Effect: Car makers changed over to synchronizing mechanisms.
4. Cause: _____
   Effect: Helical gears are superior to spur gears.
5. Cause: _____
   Effect: Some cars cannot operate correctly with three-speed transmissions and require extra speeds.
6. Cause: _____
   Effect: Most manuals have an idler gear.
7. Cause: _____
   Effect: All cars require some type of transmission.

---

The teacher asked, "Why did Jenny take her life?" The question led to prereading discussion. The students offered several predictions. The teacher then suggested that the reading assignment was written in a predominantly cause-effect pattern. He discussed this type of pattern, and students contributed several examples. Then he gave them the pattern guide to complete as they read the selection—Box 7.10.

The class read for two purposes: to see whether their predictions were accurate and to follow the cause-and-effect relationships in the material. Notice that the social studies teacher included page numbers after most of the causes listed on the guide. This helped students focus their attention on the relevant portions of the text. First the students read the selection silently, then they worked in groups of four to complete the pattern guide.

**English.** A final example, the comparison-contrast pattern guide in Box 7.11, shows how the format of a guide will differ with the nature of the material (in this case, narrative) and the teacher's objectives. In Box 7.11 juniors in an English class use the pattern guide to discuss changes in character from the story "A Split Cherry Tree."

Adapt pattern guide formats to match the major organizational structures in your content materials. If you do so, students will begin to develop the habit of searching for organization in everything they read.

Traditionally, questions have been used widely by teachers to develop study worksheets for students. These often focus on the product or the results of reading and studying (*what* the students have learned), but fail to guide readers in the processes needed to acquire content. Therein lies the

## BOX 7.10     Jenny

*Directions:* Select from the causes column at the left the cause which led to each effect in the effects column at the right. Put the letter of each effect next to its cause in the space provided.

| Cause | Effects |
|---|---|
| ____ 1. Jenny took an overdose of pills (p. 9). | a. Unemployment rate for the Blackfeet is about 50 percent. |
| ____ 2. The buffalo herds were destroyed and hunger threatened (p. 10). | b. The first victim of this life is pride. |
| ____ 3. Indians remained untrained for skilled jobs (p. 10). | c. Blackfeet became dependent on the white man's help for survival. |
| ____ 4. The temperature reaches 50 degrees below zero (p. 10). | d. Blackfeet turn to liquor. |
| ____ 5. There are terrible living conditions (no jobs, poor homes, and so on) (p. 10). | e. The Indian is robbed of his self-confidence. |
| ____ 6. Pride and hope vanish from the Blackfeet (p. 11). | f. They are always downgraded. |
| ____ 7. Because we're Indians (p. 12). | g. Eighty percent of the Blackfeet must have government help. |
| ____ 8. The old world of the Indians is crumbling, and the new world of the white rejects them. | h. Hope is a word that has little meaning. |
| ____ 9. The attitude of the Bureau of Indian Affairs (p. 13). | i. She killed herself. |

## BOX 7.11     "Split Cherry Tree": Character Change

*Directions:* Consider Pa's attitude (how he feels) toward the following characters and concepts. Note that the columns ask you to consider his attitudes to these things twice—the way he is at the beginning of the story (pp. 147–152) and the way you think he is at the end of the story. Whenever possible, note the page numbers where this attitude is described or hinted at.

| At the beginning of the story what is Pa's attitude toward: | | At the end of the story what is Pa's attitude toward: |
|---|---|---|
| | Punishment | |
| | Dave | |
| | Professor Herbert | |
| | School | |
| | His own work | |
| | His son's future | |
| | Himself | |

difference between traditional study questions and the reading guides suggested in this chapter. To make this point clear, one more type of scaffold, the *selective reading guide,* is explained below.

## SELECTIVE READING GUIDES

Selective reading guides show students how to think with print. The effective use of questions combined with signaling techniques helps to model the way readers interact with text when reading and studying.

Cunningham and Shablak (1975) were among the first to discuss the importance of guiding students to respond selectively to text. They indicate that content area teachers can impart tremendous insight into *how* to acquire text information through a selective reading guide:

> The teacher begins . . . by determining the overall purpose for a particular reading assignment. Second, he selects those sections of the reading which are necessary to achieve this purpose.
>
> Most important . . . he eliminates from the assignment any and all sections that are irrelevant to the purpose. Third, for those relevant sections that remain, the teacher determines, *based on his own model reading behaviors,* what a student must operationally do to achieve the purpose—step by step, section by section. (p. 318, italics ours)

The premise behind the selective reading guide rests with the notion that teachers best understand how to process information from their own subject matter areas.

Box 7.12 illustrates how an English teacher developed a selective reading guide which mixes written questions with appropriate signals for processing the material.

In elementary and middle school situations, selective reading guides have been called "reading roadmaps" (Wood, 1988). For maturing readers, teachers add a visual dimension to the guide. Study the reading roadmap in Box 7.13 on page 222, developed by a middle school science teacher. Notice how he guides students through the life functions of bacteria using various kinds of cues, signals, and statements. The guide provides location cues to focus students' attention to relevant segments of text, speed signals to model flexibility in reading, and mission statements that initiate tasks to help students think and learn with texts.

Space limitations prohibit us from including additional examples of the different reading and study guides for each content area. However, enough examples have been presented to model how guides might be used and developed for different instructional purposes across a wide range of texts. The ball is now in your court. We encourage you to develop and experiment with several reading and study guides for potentially difficult text assignments in your content area.

---

**BOX 7.12    Selective Reading Guide for "Advertising: The Permissible Lie"**

*Page 128.* Read the title. Write a definition of a permissible lie. Give an example of this type of lie.

*Page 128, par. 1.* Do you agree with this quotation? Why or why not?

*Pages 128–129.* Read paragraphs 2–6 slowly and carefully. What aspects of TV were borrowed from radio? Write them down. From personal experience, do you think TV reflects reality? Jot an answer down, then continue reading.

*Pages 129–130.* Read paragraphs 7–15 quickly. What specific types of commercials are being discussed?

*Pages 130–131.* Read paragraphs 16–26 to find out the author's opinion of this type of commercial.

*Page 131.* Read paragraph 7. The author gives an opinion here. Do you agree?

*Pages 131–133.* Read to page 133, paragraph 45. You can skim this section, slowing down to read parts that are especially interesting to you. What are some current popular phrases or ideas in modern advertising? Think of some commercials you've seen on TV. List another word or idea or fad that's used in a lot of advertising.

*Pages 133–134.* Read paragraphs 45–50 quickly. Give your own example of a sex-based advertisement.

*Page 134, par. 51.* According to the author, what is a good test for an advertisement? Do you agree? Would most advertisements pass or fail the test? Try out a few.

*Page 134, par. 52.* Restate Comant's quote in your own words.

After reading the assignment, summarize what you read in 100 words or less.

---

# LOOKING BACK, LOOKING FORWARD

When readers are not able to handle difficult texts on their own, a teacher supports their efforts to make meaning by *scaffolding* their interactions with texts. With the use of reading guides, teachers provide instructional support to allow students to interact with and respond to difficult text in meaningful ways. In this chapter, we explored and illustrated several types of guides: three-level reading guides, text pattern guides, and selective reading guides.

Three-level reading guides allow readers to interact with text, constructing meaning at different levels of abstraction and conceptual complexity: literal, interpretive, and applied levels. Text pattern guides help students to become aware of the importance of text organization and to learn how to search for relationships in text. The text pattern guide creates an experience for students similar to that of the three level guide. Teachers may adapt text pattern guide formats to match major organizational structures in their content materials. Selective reading guides show students how to think with print by modeling the reading behaviors necessary to read texts effectively.

## BOX 7.13    Reading Road Map

### Life Functions of Bacteria

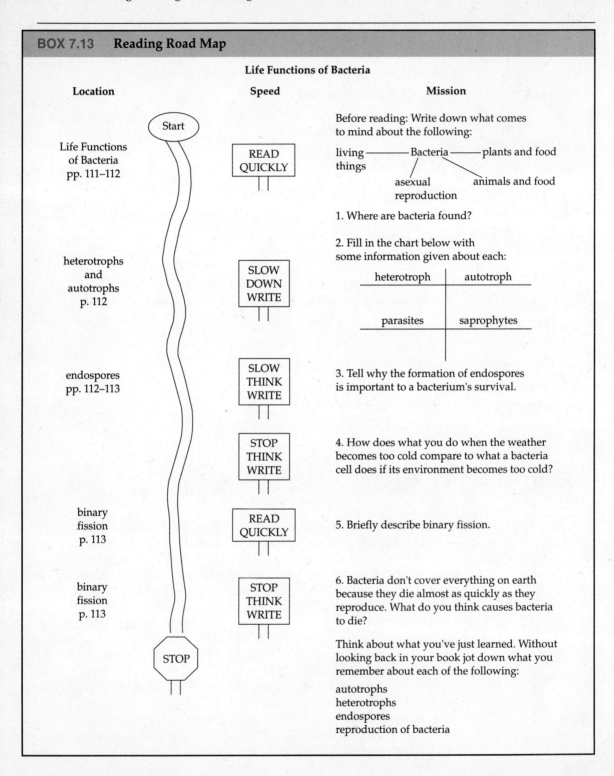

| Location | Speed | Mission |
|---|---|---|
| | Start | Before reading: Write down what comes to mind about the following: |
| Life Functions of Bacteria pp. 111–112 | READ QUICKLY | living — Bacteria — plants and food things / asexual reproduction  animals and food |
| | | 1. Where are bacteria found? |
| heterotrophs and autotrophs p. 112 | SLOW DOWN WRITE | 2. Fill in the chart below with some information given about each: |
| endospores pp. 112–113 | SLOW THINK WRITE | 3. Tell why the formation of endospores is important to a bacterium's survival. |
| | STOP THINK WRITE | 4. How does what you do when the weather becomes too cold compare to what a bacteria cell does if its environment becomes too cold? |
| binary fission p. 113 | READ QUICKLY | 5. Briefly describe binary fission. |
| binary fission p. 113 | STOP THINK WRITE | 6. Bacteria don't cover everything on earth because they die almost as quickly as they reproduce. What do you think causes bacteria to die? |
| | STOP | Think about what you've just learned. Without looking back in your book jot down what you remember about each of the following: autotrophs heterotrophs endospores reproduction of bacteria |

Chart for question 2:

| heterotroph | autotroph |
|---|---|
| parasites | saprophytes |

In the next chapter, "Writing to Learn," we focus on how, from a content area perspective, writing about ideas and concepts will improve students' acquisition of content more than just reading without writing. We underscore the interrelationships among reading, thinking, and writing processes as we explore the role of writing in content area learning.

## SUGGESTED READINGS

Alvermann, D. E., Moore, D. W., & Conley, M. C. (eds.). Research within reach secondary school reading. Newark, DE: International Reading Association.

Armstrong, D. P., Patberg, J., & Dewitz, P. (1988). Reading guides—helping students understand. *Journal of Reading, 31,* 532–541.

Bean, T. W., & Ericson, B. O. (1989). Text previews and three level study guides for content area critical reading. *Journal of Reading. 32,* 337–341.

Davey, B. (1986). Using textbook activity guides to help students learn from textbooks. *Journal of Reading. 29,* 489–494.

Herber, H. (1978). Levels of comprehension (Chapter 3). *Teaching reading in content areas.* Englewood Cliffs, NJ: Prentice-Hall.

Herber, H. L. (1985). Levels of comprehension: An instructional strategy for guiding students' reading. In T. Harris & E. Cooper (eds.), *Reading, thinking, and concept development: Strategies for the classroom.* New York: College Entrance Examination Board.

Olson, M., & Longnion, B. (1982). Pattern guides: A workable alternative for content teachers. *Journal of Reading, 25,* 736–741.

Slater, W. H. (1985). Teaching expository text structure with structural organizers. *Journal of Reading, 28,* 712–718.

# 8

# Writing to Learn

We do not write in order to be understood; we write in order to understand.

—*C. Day Lewis*

## ORGANIZING PRINCIPLE

Writing is not without its rewards or surprises. The surprises are discovering what you want to say about a subject; the rewards lie in knowing that you crafted to satisfaction that which you wanted to say. C. Day Lewis didn't sit down at his desk to write about things that were already clear in his mind. If he did, there would have been little incentive to write. Lewis used writing first to discover and clarify meaning—*to understand*—and second, to communicate meaning to others—*to be understood*.

Some may find it surprising to find a separate chapter in this book on the role that writing plays in content reading and learning. In other chapters, we have recommended various kinds of writing activities to scaffold students' interactions with texts. In this chapter, however, our intent is to highlight and reaffirm the powerful learning opportunities that arise whenever teachers link together reading and writing within the instructional frameworks that they create. Content acquisition and learning are within students' reach when writing and reading are integrated throughout the curriculum.

A classroom environment that supports reading and writing provides an instructional framework in which students can explore ideas, clarify meaning, and construct knowledge. Why connect reading and writing in the content area classroom? When reading and writing are taught in tandem, the union influences content acquisition and learning in ways not possible than if students were to read without writing or write without reading.

When reading and writing are brought together, the union fosters communication, enhances problem-solving, and makes thinking and learning with texts more powerful. When teachers invite a class to write before or after reading, they help students to use writing to think about what they will read and to explore and think more deeply about the ideas they have read about. Unfortunately, the merger of reading and writing in content area classrooms has been more the exception than the rule.

Reading and writing have been taught in most classrooms as if they bear little relationship to one another. The result has often been to sever the powerful bonds for meaning-making that exist between reading and writing. From our vantage point, there's little to be gained from teaching reading apart from writing. The organizing principle reflects this notion: *Writing facilitates learning with text by helping students to explore, clarify, and think deeply about ideas and concepts encountered in reading.*

## CHAPTER OVERVIEW

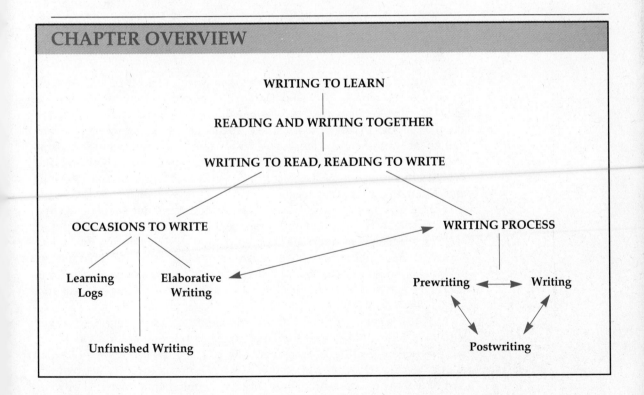

WRITING TO LEARN

READING AND WRITING TOGETHER

WRITING TO READ, READING TO WRITE

OCCASIONS TO WRITE

WRITING PROCESS

Learning Logs

Elaborative Writing

Prewriting ⟷ Writing

Unfinished Writing

Postwriting

## FRAME OF MIND

1. Why emphasize writing to learn in content areas?

2. Why teach writing and reading together?

3. How might teachers create occasions for students to write to read and read to write?

4. How can teachers use learning logs to connect writing and reading?

5. How can teachers use unfinished writing activities to connect reading and writing?

6. How can teachers develop elaborative writing assignments such as essays?

7. Why and how should teachers guide the writing process?

Sinclair Lewis, the first American author to win a Nobel prize for literature, said that writing is just work. It doesn't matter if "you dictate or use a pen or type or write with your toes—it is still just work." Microcomputers and word processors notwithstanding, writing isn't easy for most people. Yet for those who are successful, the process of writing—sweat and all—is enormously challenging and rewarding.

Perhaps for this reason Allyse's mother was a little bit perplexed with her daughter's writing. Allyse is thirteen years old and, by all accounts, a bright student. Yet her mother was bewildered by her daughter's writing activities *in* and *out* of school. "She'll spend hours slaving over pages to mail to an out-of-state friend, but writes skimpy, simple-minded paragraphs for school assignments." When she was questioned about the discrepancy in her writing, Allyse's gut-level reply was all the more confusing. "But, Mom, that's what my teachers want."

Allyse may never win a Nobel prize for literature. But she does have a need to write. Most children and adolescents do. Often, just out of sight of teachers, students will write continually to other students during the course of a school day—about boys, girls, teachers, intrigues, problems, parents, or on just about anything that happens to be on their mind at a particular time. The topics may not be academically oriented, but they are all quite real and immediate to students.

In Allyse's case, writing to an out-of-state friend is so important to her that she is willing to struggle with a blank page to keep in touch. However, as far as school writing is concerned, she probably has psyched out what teachers expect from her. She knows what she needs to do to get by and, most likely, to be successful. Allyse intuitively understands the role of writing in her classes and operates within that context.

Although students are often observed engaging in some form of writing in content area classrooms, few teachers use writing to its fullest potential as a tool for learning. Allyse's response to her mother's question reflects what researchers such as Judith Langer and Arthur Applebee (1987) have consistently observed to be the role of writing in content classrooms: namely, that it is mainly restricted to short responses to study questions or to taking notes in class. While the purposes behind these uses of writing may be legitimate, students need varied and frequent experiences with writing as a tool for learning. According to Langer and Applebee (1987), "Put simply, in the whole range of academic course work, American children do not write frequently enough, and the reading and writing tasks they are given do not require them to think deeply enough" (p. 4). At least three good reasons compel teachers to take a second look at the role of writing in their classrooms. First, writing improves thinking. Second, it facilitates learning. Third, writing is intimately related to reading.

Why include a separate chapter on writing to learn in a content area reading textbook? Although we have suggested writing activity in conjunction with reading in previous chapters, our reason is straightforward enough: In this chapter we focus on writing to emphasize the powerful bonds that exist between reading and writing. In the process of doing so, we underscore the constructive, meaning-making nature of writing and show that content area learning is more productive when writing and reading are integrated throughout the curriculum.

# READING AND WRITING TOGETHER

There is no better way to think about a subject than to have the occasion to read and write about it. However, the mere act of reading and writing doesn't necessarily guarantee improved thinking or learning. Students can more or less go through the motions of reading and writing, lacking purpose and commitment. Or they can work thoughtfully to construct meaning, make discoveries, and think deeply about a subject. A classroom environment for reading and writing is one that lends encouragement to students who are maturing as readers and writers and provides instructional support so that readers and writers can play with ideas, explore concepts, clarify meaning, and elaborate on what they are learning.

Reading and writing are acts of composing insomuch as readers and writers are always involved in an ongoing, dynamic process of constructing meaning (Tierney and Pearson 1983). In writing, composing processes are more obvious than in reading: The writer, initially faced with blank paper, constructs a text. The text is a visible entity and reflects the writer's thinking on paper. Less obvious is the "text"—the configuration of meanings—that students compose or construct in their own minds as they read.

A good way to think about reading and writing is that they are two sides of the same coin. While the writer works to make a text sensible, the reader works to make sense out of a text. As a result, the two processes, rooted in language, are intertwined with one another and share common cognitive and sociocultural characteristics. Reading and writing, for example, both involve purpose, commitment, schema activation, planning, working with ideas, revision and rethinking, and monitoring. Both processes occur within a social, communicative context. Skilled writers are mindful of their content (the subject about which they are writing), but also their audiences (the readers for whom they write); and skilled readers are mindful of text content, but also are aware that they engage in transactions with authors.

The relationships between reading and writing have been a source of inquiry for language researchers for the past two decades (Tierney and Shanahan 1991). Several broad conclusions about the links between reading and writing can be drawn: Good readers are often good writers and vice versa; students who write well tend to read more than those who do not write well; wide reading improves writing; students who are good readers and writers perceive themselves as such and are more likely to engage in reading and writing on their own.

Why connect reading and writing in instructional contexts? According to Shanahan (1990), reading and writing together in a classroom improves achievement and instructional efficiency. From a content area perspective, writing about ideas and concepts encountered in texts will improve students' acquisition of content more than just reading without writing. When reading and writing are taught in concert, the union fosters communication, enhances problem solving, and makes learning more powerful than if reading or writing is engaged in separately.

## WRITING TO READ, READING TO WRITE

When teachers integrate writing and reading, they help students to use writing to *think about what they will read* and to *understand what they have read*. Writing may be used to catapult students into reading. It is also one of the most effective ways for students to understand something they have read about. Teachers can put students into writing-to-read or reading-to-write situations because the writing process is a powerful tool for exploring and clarifying meaning.

Donald Murray (1980) explains that writers engage in a process of exploration and clarification as they go about the task of discovering meaning. In Figure 8.1, Murray suggests that writers progress from exploring meaning to clarifying it as they continue to draft and shape a piece of writing. A writer's first draft is an initial attempt to think on paper. The more writers work with ideas put on paper, the more they are able to revise, rethink, and clarify what they have to say about a subject.

**Figure 8.1    EXPLORATION AND CLARIFICATION**

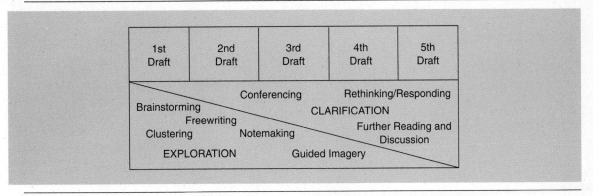

Exploratory writing is first draft writing. Often, it is messy, tentative, and unfinished. Exploration of ideas and concepts may be pursued before or after reading. Writing activities that help students tap into their store-house of memories—their prior knowledge—make excellent springboards into reading. Exploratory writing helps students to collect what they know and connect it to what they will be reading. For example, some teachers combine brainstorming a topic to be studied with five or so minutes of spontaneous freewriting in which students tell what they know about the subject to be studied.

Santa and Havens (1991) illustrate the power of writing before and after reading with an example from a biology class. Before reading a textbook assignment on flower reproduction, students write a before-reading entry in *learning logs* (a student resource we explain just ahead in this section), telling what they know about the subject they will be reading and studying. Here's an example of a student's entry:

> In this chapter I am going to learn about flower reproduction. I know that flowers have male and female parts. I think that these parts are in the inside of the flower. To see them you have to pull aside the petals. I think petals probably protect the reproductive parts, but I am not sure. I remember something about separate flowers for male and females, but I think many flowers have both parts on the same flower. I'm pretty sure you need to have at least two plants before they can reproduce (p. 124).

In the biology class, students also had an occasion to write about flower reproduction after reading. In an after-reading entry, writing helps the students to continue to explore and clarify meaning by focusing on what they learned and noting their misconceptions in their before-reading entries. Study the after-reading entry written by the student above:

> I learned that stamens are the male parts of the flower. The stamen pro-duces the pollen. The female part is the pistil. At the bottom of the pistil is the ovary. Plants have eggs just like humans. The eggs are kept in the ovary. I still am not sure how pollen gets to the female part. Do bees do all

this work, or are there other ways to pollinate? I was right, sometimes male and female parts are on separate flowers. These are called incomplete flowers. Complete flowers have both male and female parts on the same flower. I also learned that with complete flowers just one plant can reproduce itself. So, I was partially wrong thinking it always took two plants to reproduce (p. 124).

Occasions to write in content subjects, such as the before-reading and after-reading entries you just read, create powerful opportunities to learn content in concert with reading. Students who experience the integration of writing and reading are likely to learn more content, understand it better, and remember it longer. This is the case because writing, before or after reading, promotes thinking, but in different ways. Writing a summary after reading (see Chapter 9), for example, is likely to result in greater understanding and retention of important information. However, another type of writing—let's say an essay—may trigger an analysis, synthesis, and elaboration of ideas encountered in reading and class discussion.

Because writing promotes different types of learning, many different occasions to write should be present for students. Let's look at some ways that teachers can create occasions for students to think and learn with paper and pen.

## Learning Logs

Learning logs add a new dimension to personal learning in content area classrooms. Learning logs are probably one of the most versatile writing-to-learn strategies available to students and teachers in any subject area. And one of the most productive.

The strategy is simple to implement but must be used regularly to be effective. Students keep an ongoing record of learning *as* it happens in a notebook or looseleaf binder. They write in their own language, not necessarily for others to read but to themselves, about what they are learning. Entries in logs influence learning by revealing problems, clarifying thinking, and generating ideas and questions.

There is no one way to use learning logs, although teachers often prefer allowing five or ten minutes at the end of a period for students to respond to process questions such as the following: "What did I understand about the work we did in class today? What didn't I understand? At what point in the lesson did I get confused? What did I like or dislike about class today?" The logs can be kept in a box and stored in the classroom. The teacher then reviews them during or after school to see what students are learning and to better understand their concerns and problems. Let's take a look at how several teachers integrate logs into their instructional contexts.

Two math teachers report using learning logs with much success in their classrooms. Mr. Kennedy, a middle school teacher, has designed what he calls a "writing in math" program where learning logs are a key feature (Kennedy 1985). In addition to the preceding process questions, he likes to ask students what they're wondering about. What specific questions do they have about material being studied? He also finds that logs are effective for "making notes." According to Kennedy, the distinction between taking and making notes is central to the use of learning logs: "Taking notes is copying someone else's information; *making* notes is writing interpretive comments and personal reminders such as 'Ask about this' or just 'Why?'" (p. 61)

And then there's Ms. Church, a high school Algebra teacher. She introduces learning logs to her class this way:

> From time to time, I'll be asking you to write down in your logs how you went about learning a particular topic in this class. In other words, can you capture that moment when things finally made sense to you and how you felt? And can you express the frustration that might have preceded this moment? (Pradl and Mayher 1985, p. 5)

Students at first might be tentative about writing and unsure of what to say or reveal—after all, this type of writing is reflective and personal. It takes a trusting atmosphere to open up to the teacher. However, to win the trust of students, teachers like Ms. Church refrain from making judgmental or evaluative comments when students admit a lack of understanding about what's happening in class. If a trusting relationship exists, students will soon recognize the value of logs, although perhaps not as enthusiastically as one high school student:

> This journal has got to be the best thing that's hit this chemistry class. For once the teacher has direct communication with every member of the class. No matter how shy the student is they can get their lack of understanding across to the teacher. . . . These journals act as a "hot line" to and from the teacher. I feel this journal has helped me and everyone that I know in class. The only thing wrong is we should have started these on the first day of school!! In every class! (Pradl and Mayher 1985, p. 8).

Ms. Church's students probably feel the same way about their Algebra class. Here are some of the things that they do in their logs. For starters, Ms. Church likes to start a new topic by asking students to jot down their predictions and expectations of what the topic might involve. She also has her students write down their understanding of any new theorem that is introduced. After students feel that they have learned a theorem well, they use their logs to imagine how they might explain the theorem to another person, less well informed, like a younger sister or brother.

Both Ms. Church and Mr. Kennedy use logs to have students create word problems that are then used to challenge other members of the class. Kennedy likes to have students write different kinds of word problems in their learning logs: "Sometimes I have them supply the data (for example, 'Write a problem involving the use of percent'); other times I supply the data (for example, 'Write a problem using the numbers 200, 400, and 600')" (Kennedy 1985, p. 51).

Most learning log activities require thinking but do not demand a finished product. Students soon learn to write without the fear of making errors involving spelling, punctuation, capitalization, or grammar. Emphasis is on communicating content ideas or problems with content, not with the surface level of the writing.

However, there are times when students should know in advance that learning log entries will be read aloud in class. According to Levine (1985), this is when students often produce their best writing, because they are composing for an audience of peers. Josh, for example, an eighth grader, wrote about a lab experiment this way:

> Today in class we did a demo to try and find effective ways of recovering the solute from a solution.
>
> Several people came up with ideas as to how we could do this. A few people suggested filtering the solution, and others thought heating the solution so it evaporated would bring the solute back.
>
> First we tried filtering a copper sulfate solution but found that process didn't work. Evidently the crystals had dissolved to such an extent, that they were too small to be gathered by the filter paper.
>
> We then heated the solution and found we were far more successful than in our first try. Approximately thirteen minutes after we began heating the solution, a ring of copper sulfate crystals appeared in the bowl where the solution was. Eventually all the liquid evaporated leaving only the crystals. Quite obviously I learned that to recover the solute from a solution you can heat the solution. I also learned not to bother trying to filter the solution (Levine 1985, p. 45).

Learning log writing is often called free writing because students like Josh are able to express what's on their minds honestly—without pretense.

## Unfinished Writing

"Unfinished" writing is first draft writing. Gere (1985) describes unfinished writing as "writing that evinces thought but does not merit the careful scrutiny which a finished piece of writing deserves" (p. 4). There is much value in planning unfinished writing activity in the content classroom. The excellent monograph edited by Anne Gere, *Roots in the Sawdust*, shows how teachers from various disciplines use and adapt unfinished writing activities in their classrooms. Many of the activities described in *Roots in the Sawdust* make appropriate learning log assignments. However, these activities may also be introduced to students as separate learning tasks apart from a log format. We have found the following to be quite useful in elementary or secondary classes.

**Unsent Letters.**  This writing-to-learn activity, as its name implies, establishes a role-play situation in which students are asked to write letters in response to material being studied. The activity requires the use of imagination and often demands that students engage in interpretive and evaluative thinking. Jeremy's unsent letter to the President of the United States, written after he studied the effects of nuclear war in his social studies text, reflects both personal and informative writing.

> Dear Mr. President,
>
> How is life in the White House? In school we have been studying the horrible effects of a nuclear war. The United States alone has enough nuclear weapons to wipe out 1 million Hiroshimas. The earth doesn't even have that many cities that big.
>
> In a nuclear war 1.1 billion people would be killed outright, and they are the lucky ones. Another 1.1 billion would suffer from burns and radiation sickness.
>
> 1 nuclear warhead or 2 megatons is 2 million tons of TNT, imagine 15 megatons . . .
>
> During a nuclear war buildings and people would be instantly vaporized. The remaining people would starve to death. The radiation would be 250 rads or 1,000 medical x-rays which is enough to kill you.
>
> After all this I hope you have learned some of the terrible facts about nuclear war. (Levine 1985, p. 44)

Unsent letters direct students' thinking with particular audiences in mind. *Biopoems*, on the other hand, require students to play with ideas using precise language in a poetic framework.

**Biopoems.** A biopoem allows students to reflect on large amounts of material within the context of a poetic form. The biopoem follows a pattern which enables writers to synthesize what they have learned about a person, place, thing, concept, or event under study. For example, study the pattern suggested by Gere (1985) for a person or character.

Line 1.  First name

Line 2.  Four traits that describe character

Line 3.  Relative ("brother," "sister," "daughter," etc.) of _____

Line 4.  Lover of _____ (list three things or people)

Line 5.  Who feels _____ (three items)

Line 6.  Who needs _____ (three items)

Line 7.  Who fears _____ (three items)

Line 8.  Who gives _____ (three items)

Line 9.  Who would like to see _____ (three items)

Line 10. Resident of _____

Line 11. Last name

Notice how a science teacher adapted the preceding pattern for a writing activity synthesizing learning connected to the study of horseshoe crabs. Here's one of the student's poems:

**Horseshoe Crab**

Limulus,

Armored, a spine for a sword, gentle yet misunderstood, a living fossil.

The spider, your nearest living relative. You have survived the odds.

Unchanged by time, feeling forgotten, and savaged on unfriendly beaches

You need a better image, environmental protection, and a little understanding.

You fear the frightened reactions of unknowing bathers, being stranded on sunwashed sands, and extinction.

You give life during spring mating rites, clues to a prehistoric past, hope for all living species.

Washed ashore, you would like to see the next high tide, another day, and the safety of the deep.

Resident of the sea.

Polyhemus

**Dialogues.** In this activity, students are asked to create an exchange between two or more persons, historical figures, or characters being studied. Beaman (1985), a high school social studies teacher, illustrated the use of dialogue as a writing-to-learn assignment. His students were asked to write a dialogue between themselves and a "friend" who wanted them to do something they were opposed to but were unsure of how to respond to because of peer pressure. Beaman suggests to students that they write about awkward teenage situations of peer pressure. Here's an example dialogue between Mary and Betty:

**Mary:** Let's skip class and go out on the parking lot. I have some awesome dope and a new tape by the Scorpions.

**Betty:** I can't. I've skipped second period one too many times, and I really want to graduate. Contemporary Problems is required, and I'm afraid I may fail.

**Mary:** Get serious, one class missed is not going to get you an F. You need the relaxation and besides the Scorpions. . . .

**Betty:** I wish I could say "yes" to you.

**Mary:** Say "yes" then, or are you turning into a real "school" girl?

**Betty:** You are pressuring me, Mary!

**Mary:** No pressure, just fun, come on. . . .

**Betty:** No, I'm going to class, I do want to graduate. You can go, but I'm going to class. (Beaman 1985, p. 63)

A dialogue like this permits writers to think about situations and conflicts and possible solutions. As an unfinished writing activity, a dialogue also provides an opportunity for students to react upon ideas and extend thinking about material being studied.

**Admit Slips/Exit Slips.**  These activities should be introduced as a separate assignment and not as part of a learning log entry. Admit slips and exit slips involve anonymous writing and therefore, shouldn't be part of the permanent record of learning that builds over time in students' learning logs.

Admit slips are brief comments written by students on index cards or half sheets of paper at the very beginning of class. Gere (1985) recommends that these written responses be collected as tickets of admission to class. The purpose of the admit slip is to have students react to what they are studying or to what's happening in class. Students are asked to respond to a question such as:

What's confusing you about . . . ?

What problems did you have with your text assignment?

What would you like to get off your chest?

What do you like (dislike) about . . . ?

The admit slips are collected by the teacher and read aloud (with no indication of authorship of individual comments) as a way of beginning class discussion. Admit slips build a trusting relationship between teacher and students and contribute to a sense of community in the classroom.

An exit slip, as you might anticipate, is a variation on the admit slip. Toward the end of class, the teacher will ask students for exit slips as a way of bringing closure to what was learned. An exit slip question might require students to summarize, synthesize, evaluate, or project. The several minutes devoted to exit-slip writing often are quite revealing of the day's lesson and establish direction for the next class.

## Elaborative Writing Activities

As useful as learning logs and unfinished writing activities are, they represent informal tools to help students explore content that they will be or are reading and studying about in class. Elaborative writing activities, on the other hand, are more formal and finished in nature. When students engage in an elaborative writing assignment, they become immersed in the content and are able to think more deeply about the subject they are exploring and clarifying. The purpose, then, of elaborative writing is to create a context in which students discover, analyze, and synthesize ideas through the process of writing.

Whereas learning log and unfinished writing activities represent expressive, loosely written explorations of a subject, elaborative writing activities engage students in longer, more considered pieces of writing such as those associated with essays and reports. Essays and reports are conventional vehicles for writing in schools. Essays, for example, often represent the type of writing students might perform on a unit test or a final exam. Traditionally, essays have been the province of English teachers whose students sometimes become more preoccupied with the form and organization of the essay—learning how to write a three-paragraph or five-paragraph paper—than with the exploration of content and the analysis and synthesis of ideas. Times, however, are changing.

Essays and other types of elaborative writing assignments have been shown to be powerful writing-to-learn tools (1) when content exploration and synthesis, not form and organization, become the primary motives for the writing assignment, (2) when writing involves reading more than a single text source, and (3) when students engage in the writing process. Important research conducted in the past decade shows that when students combine reading and writing, they think more deeply about the subject they are studying.

Spivy (1984), for example, found that when writers read more than a single text source in order to write their own texts (a process she calls *discourse synthesis*), they are immersed in organizing, selecting, and connecting content. Newell (1984) discovered that students who engage in essay-type writing acquire more content knowledge than students who take notes or answer study questions. Langer and Applebee (1987) concluded that when reading is combined with analytical writing, students are able to think more deeply about key ideas and concepts encountered during reading.

What the research on writing to learn demonstrates is that students who read to write engage in a range of reasoning processes. Elaborative writing activities create occasions for students to discover, analyze, and synthesize ideas from multiple sources of information. The key to thoughtful student writing is to design good writing assignments. The teacher's primary concern should be with how to make an assignment *explicit* without stifling interest or the spirit of inquiry. An assignment should provide more than a subject to write on.

Suppose you were assigned one of the topics below to write on, based on text readings and class discussion:

- the arms race,
- batiking,
- the role of the laser beam in the future,
- victims of crime.

No doubt, some of you would probably begin writing on one of the topics without hesitation. Perhaps you already know a great deal about the subject, have strong feelings about it, and can change the direction of the discourse without much of a problem. Others, however, might resist or even resent the activity. Your questions might echo the following concerns: "Why do I want to write about any of these topics in the first place? For whom am I writing? Will I write a paragraph? a book?" The most experienced writer must come to grips with questions such as these, and even more complicated ones: "How will I treat my subject? What stance will I take?" If anything, the questions raise to a level of awareness the *rhetorical context—the purpose, audience, form* of the writing, and the writer's *stance*—that most writing assignments should provide. A rhetorical context for writing allows students to assess the writer's relationship to the subject of the writing (the topic) and the reader (the audience for whom the writing is intended). Lindemann (1982) suggests a *communications triangle* to show how the context can be defined. Some of the questions raised by the relationships among writer-subject-reader within the communications triangle are depicted in Figure 8.2. The writer plans a response to the assignment by asking questions such as: "Who am I writing this for? What do I know about my subject? How do I feel about it? What stance can I take in treating the topic?" A good assignment, then, *situates* students in the writing task by giving them a purpose for writing and an intended audience. It may also allude to the form of the writing and the stance the writer will take toward his or her topic.

**Creating Lifelike Contexts for Writing.** Students need to know why they are composing and for whom. One of the ways to characterize discourse, oral or written, is through its aims or purposes. As students approach a writing assignment, let them know its purpose. Is the writing aiming at personal expression? Is it to persuade? describe? explain? Or is it to create a text which can be appreciated in its own right for its literary or imaginative quality? These purposes are broad, to be sure, but each underscores an important aim of discourse (Kinneavy 1971).

Some essays will stimulate inquiry when they create lifelike situations in which the purpose for writing is directly tied to the audience. Instead of assigning an essay on how to batik, give students a situation to ponder:

> To show that you understand how batiking works, imagine that you are giving a demonstration at an arts and crafts show. Describe the steps and procedures involved in the process of batiking to a group of onlookers, recognizing that they know little about the process, but are curious enough to find out more.

**Figure 8.2    COMMUNICATIONS TRIANGLE: DEFINING A RHETORICAL PROBLEM IN WRITING**

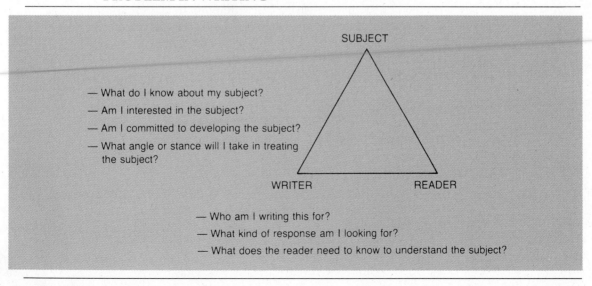

Or take, as another example, the arms race topic:

> The debate over the arms race has people taking different sides of the argument. There are some who argue that the arms race will lead to a nuclear holocaust. There are others who contend the arms race is the only way to maintain peace in the world.
>
> You have been selected to write a position paper for the class in which you debate your side of the argument. Another student has been selected to defend an opposing position. The class will then vote on the most persuasive of the two positions.
>
> Once you have investigated the issue thoroughly, convince as many classmates as possible that your position is the best one. Your paper should be long enough to persuade the class effectively.

As you can see from the two examples, each creates a lifelike context, identifies a purpose, an audience, and suggests the writer's stance and a form of discourse, i.e., a position paper or demonstration. In each case, students will not necessarily make the assumption that the teacher is the audience, even though ultimately the teacher will evaluate the written product. McAndrew (1983) portrayed the reality of classroom audiences this way:

> The real audience in the classroom is the teacher. Let's admit that up front. The teacher in his/her role as teacher-as-grader—is always and inescapably the audience for class assignments. But if we are to improve our students' writing skills, we must . . . try to create situations that allow students to experience writing to a variety of audiences even though we know, and the students know, that somewhere down the line the teacher will be the audience (p. 49).

Elaborative writing assignments contrive situations and audiences in the context of what is being read or studied. However, they are far from trivial, nonacademic, or inconsequential. Instead, when students "become" someone else they must look at situations in a nontraditional way. After writing, they can compare different stances on the same issue and examine the validity of the viewpoints that were taken.

Although some writing assignments may contrive situations and audiences, others should reflect real situations and audiences outside the classroom. For example, letters to the editor of the local newspaper, and to political leaders, authors, and scientists can be an important part of classroom study. We will have more to say on audience identification later in this chapter when we examine the role of publication in the writing process.

**Discourse Forms.**   Ideas can be expressed through a variety of writing forms. These discourse forms can be easily incorporated into the context of writing assignments. In Figure 8.3, Tchudi and Yates (1983) provide a representative listing of some of these forms for content area writing. When students write in a particular discourse form, the work bears a stamp of authenticity.

# Figure 8.3 SOME DISCOURSE FORMS FOR CONTENT AREA WRITING

Journals and diaries
(real or imaginary)
Biographical sketches
Anecdotes and stories:
from experience
as told by others
Thumbnail sketches:
of famous people
of places
of content ideas
of historical events
Guess who/what descriptions

Letters:
personal reactions
observations
public/informational
persuasive:
to the editor
to public officials
to imaginary people
from imaginary places
Requests
Applications
Memos
Resumés and summaries
Poems
Plays
Stories
Fantasy
Adventure
Science fiction
Historical stories
Dialogues and conversations
Children's books
Telegrams
Editorials
Commentaries
Responses and rebuttals
Newspaper "fillers"
Fact books or fact sheets
School newspaper stories
Stories or essays for local papers
Proposals

Case studies:
school problems
local issues
national concerns
historical problems
scientific issues
Songs and ballads
Demonstrations
Poster displays

Reviews:
books (including textbooks)
films
outside reading
television programs
documentaries
Historical "you are there" scenes

Science notes:
observations
science notebook
reading reports
lab reports

Math:
story problems
solutions to problems
record books
notes and observations
Responses to literature
Utopian proposals
Practical proposals
Interviews:
actual
imaginary

Directions:
how-to
school or neighborhood
guide
survival manual
Dictionaries and lexicons
Technical reports
Future options, notes on:
careers, employment
school and training
military/public service

Written debates
Taking a stand:
school issues
family problems
state or national issues
moral questions
Books and booklets
Informational monographs
Radio scripts
TV scenarios and scripts
Dramatic scripts
Notes for improvised drama
Cartoons and cartoon strips
Slide show scripts
Puzzles and word searches
Prophecy and predictions
Photos and captions
Collage, montage, mobile, sculpture

**Source:** From *Teaching Writing in the Content Areas: Senior High School* by Stephen Tchudi and JoAnne Yates. Copyright © 1983, National Education Association. Reprinted with permission.

Although a good assignment doesn't fully prepare students to engage in writing, it does give them a framework for planning and drafting. How teachers guide students through stages of the writing process ensures that students construct meaning by exploring and clarifying ideas.

# GUIDING THE WRITING PROCESS

Blank paper is the writer's call to battle. Getting started can be difficult, even terrifying. However, a good writer recognizes the difficulty of the undertaking and finds it stimulating. Writing is motivating.

Some writers come to grips with the blank page by performing one or more starting rituals. Pencils are sharpened, the desk top cleared of clutter. Eventually, the first words are put on paper and everything which has occurred to this point—all of the mental and physical gymnastics a writer goes through—and everything that will happen toward completion of the writing task—can best be described as a process.

One of the teacher's first tasks is to make students aware that the writing process occurs in stages (Kirby and Liner 1981). It's the exceptional student who leaps in a single bound from a finished product in his or her head to a finished product on paper. In this book, the stages of writing are defined broadly as *prewriting, writing, rewriting,* and *postwriting.* Figure 8.4 overviews these stages.

By no means are the stages in the writing process neat and orderly. Few writers proceed from stage to stage in a linear sequence of events. Instead, writing is a back-and-forth activity. Exploring and generating ideas before writing may lead to plans for a piece of writing; but once engaged in the physical act of composing, writers often discover new ideas, reformulate plans, write, and revise.

## Exploring, Planning, and Organizing

What students do before writing is as important as what they do before reading. Prewriting activity, like the prereading strategies discussed in Chapter 5, involves planning, building and activating prior knowledge, setting goals, and getting ready for the task at hand. In other words, prewriting refers to everything that students do before the physical act of putting words on paper for a first draft. Actually, the term *prewriting* is somewhat misleading because students often engage in some form of writing before working on a draft. As we have shown, freewriting in learning logs is a good strategy for the student writer.

The time and energy spent before writing might best be described as rehearsing (Graves 1978). Rehearsal is what the writer consciously or

**Figure 8.4    STAGES IN THE WRITING PROCESS**

| | |
|---|---|
| *Prewriting*<br>"getting it out" | Exploring and generating ideas<br>Finding a topic<br>Making plans<br>   audience?<br>   form?<br>   voice?<br>Getting started |
| *Writing*<br>"getting it down" | Drafting<br>Sticking to the task<br>Developing fluency and coherence |
| *Rewriting*<br>"getting it right" | Revising for meaning<br>Responding to the writing<br>Organizing for clarity<br>Editing and proofreading for the conventions of writing, word choice, syntax<br>Polishing |
| *Postwriting*<br>"going public" | Publishing and displaying finished products<br>Evaluating and grading |

**Source:** Adapted from D. Kirby and T. Liner, *Inside Out: Developmental Strategies for Teaching.* Montclair, NJ: Boynton/Cook, 1981.

unconsciously does to get energized—to get ideas out in the open, to explore what to say and how to say it. What will I include? What's a good way to start? Who is my audience? What form should my writing take? Prewriting instruction involves any activity or experience that motivates a student to write, generates ideas for writing, or focuses attention on a particular subject. Through prewriting preparation, students can be guided to think about a topic in relation to a perceived audience and the form that a piece of writing will take. A teacher who recognizes that the writing process must slow down at the beginning will help students to discover that they have something to say and that they want to say it.

Getting started on the right foot is what prewriting is all about. Generating discussion about an assignment before writing buys time for students to gather ideas and organize them for writing. Discussion prior to writing is as crucial to success as discussion prior to reading. In preparing seniors to write letters to the editor concerning the legal age for drinking in Ohio, a "Problems in Democracy" teacher asked students for their opinions: "At what age do you think people in Ohio should be permitted to drink alcoholic beverages?" The discussion among the senior students, as you might anticipate, was animated. The teacher followed the discussion by assigning a newspaper article on the legal age issue. Further discussion generated more ideas and helped students formulate a stand on the issue.

Prereading strategies, with some modification, can be used effectively for writing situations. Several strategies in particular will help students to rehearse for writing by gathering and organizing ideas: *brainstorming*, *clustering*, and *concept-charting*.

**Brainstorming.** Brainstorming permits students to examine ideas from content area lessons as rehearsal for reading or writing. In doing so, it helps them to set purposes for reading or writing because it gives students problems to solve. Examine how the following two variations on brainstorming can easily be adapted to writing situations:

1. Present a concept or problem to students based on some aspect of what they have been studying. Set a time limit for brainstorming ideas or solutions. The teacher calls "Stop" but allows *one more minute* for thinking to continue. Creative ideas are often produced under time pressure.

   In a high school special education class for students with learning problems, several weeks had been spent on a unit dealing with the Civil War era. As part of their study of the Reconstruction period, students explored issues such as the rebuilding of the South and the dilemma presented by freed slaves. One of the culminating learning experiences for the chapter on freed slaves concerned a writing activity designed to help students synthesize some of the important ideas that they had studied. As part of her introduction to the writing assignment, the teacher began the prewriting phase of the lesson with the lead-in: "Using any information that you can recall from your text or class discussion, what might have been some of the problems or concerns of a freed slave immediately following the Civil War? Let's do some brainstorming." As students offered ideas related to prejudice and lack of money, homes, and food, the teacher listed them on the board. Getting ideas out in the open in this manner was the first step in her prewriting strategy. In the next subsection, on *clustering*, we'll discuss how the teacher used brainstorming as a stepping stone for students to organize ideas and make decisions about the writing assignment.

2. Engage students in "brainwriting" (Rodrigues 1983). Here's how it works. Divide the class into cooperative groups of four or five students. Each group member is directed to jot down ideas about the writing assignment's topic on a sheet of paper. Each student then places his or her paper in the center of the group, chooses another's list of ideas, and adds to it. The group compiles the best ideas into a single list and shares them with the class. The advantages of brainwriting include: (1) the contribution of every student, and (2) the time to consider ideas.

   Brainstorming techniques allow students to become familiar with a topic, and therefore, to approach writing with purpose and confidence. Often teachers combine brainstorming with another prewriting strategy—*clustering*.

**Clustering.**  To introduce the concept of clustering, the teacher should write a key word on the chalkboard and then surround it with other associated words that are offered by the students. In this way students not only gather ideas for writing but also connect the ideas within categories of information. Teacher-led clustering provides students with an awareness of how to use the prewriting strategy independently. Once they are aware of how to cluster their ideas around a topic, students should be encouraged to create their own clusters for writing.

A cluster can take many different forms, but essentially student writers must connect supporting ideas to a key concept word by drawing lines and arrows to show the relationships that exist, as in Figure 8.5.

For each supporting idea, students can generate additional ideas (examples, details) which are connected by lines to extend the cluster, as in Figure 8.6.

In one of the earlier brainstorming examples, we described how a special education teacher used the list of ideas generated by her students to

**Figure 8.5    RELATIONSHIP BETWEEN KEY CONCEPT AND SUPPORTING IDEAS IN A CLUSTER**

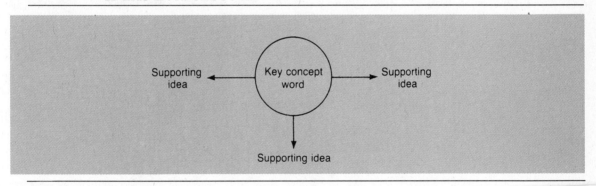

**Figure 8.6    EXPANDING A CLUSTER WITH EXAMPLES AND DETAILS**

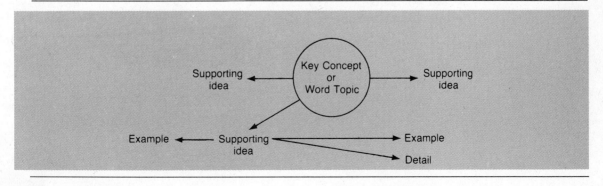

explore the concerns of freed slaves during the post-Civil War period. This was a first step in the pre-writing phase of the writing activity. The second step was to cluster the words into meaningful associations based on student suggestions. The teacher modeled the activity by choosing as the key word the concept of "Freed Slaves." She then drew a line to the upper right-hand corner of the chalkboard and connected the key word to the word *problems*. She connected some of the words generated by students during brainstorming to the cluster. The teacher then asked what some of the results of the freed slaves' problems would be. One student volunteered the word *suffering*. The teacher wrote *suffering* in the upper left-hand corner of the cluster and asked students to brainstorm some examples. These examples were then connected to the cluster.

The remainder of the prewriting experience centered on discussion related to the *aid* freed slaves received and the *opportunities* that resulted from the Reconstruction years. Examine Box 8.1, which depicts the completed cluster that the teacher and students produced on the chalkboard.

**BOX 8.1     Free Slaves Immediately After Civil War**

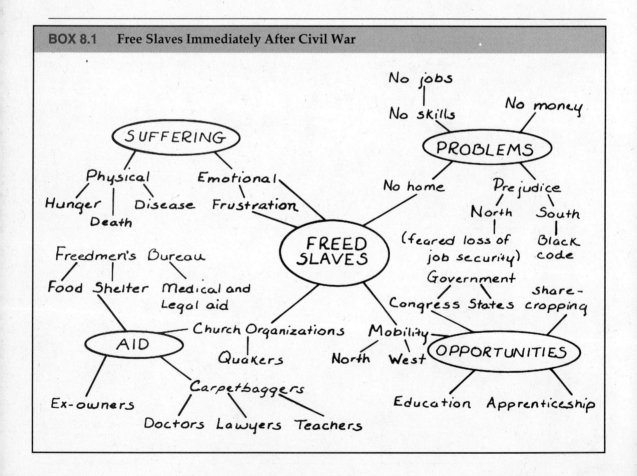

With the cluster as a frame of reference, students were assigned to write what it would have been like to be a freed slave in the 1860s and 1870s. They were asked to consider what the form of the writing should be. Since the textbook presented a variety of primary sources (diary entries, newspaper clippings, death notices), the students could, if they decided, write in one of those forms. Or they could approach the writing activity as a historian would and write an account that might be read by other students as a secondary source of information. One member of the class became so involved in the activity that he wanted his historical document to appear authentic by aging the paper. This he did by burning the edges so that it would like "historic." (See Figure 8.7.)

Students should begin to develop their own clusters for writing as soon as they understand how to use the strategy effectively. They should feel comfortable enough to start with a basic concept or topic—written in the center of a sheet of paper—and then to let go by making as many connections as possible on the paper. Connections should develop rapidly, "radiating outward from the center in any direction they want to go" (Rico 1983, p. 35). Since there is no right or wrong way to develop a cluster, students should be encouraged to play with ideas based on what they are studying and learning in class.

The value of clustering in writing shouldn't be sold short. Gabriele Rico (1983), a leading proponent of this prewriting strategy, maintained that it not only "unblocks and releases" information stored in the student writer's mind, but it also generates inspiration for writing. Moreover, clustering becomes a self-organizing process. According to Rico (1983), "As you spill out seemingly random words and phrases around a center, you will be surprised to see patterns forming until a moment comes—characterized by an 'Aha!' feeling—when you suddenly sense a focus for writing" (p. 35). Students can discuss their clusters in small groups and share their plans for writing. Or, as Rico recommended, they can begin to write immediately after clustering.

**Concept Matrix.** Like clustering, a concept matrix provides a way for students to organize information. However, it doesn't rely on freely associating ideas to a key concept word. Instead, students collect and connect ideas by outlining them on a matrix. The strategy is especially appropriate for writing that relies on explanation and description of ideas, people, events, characters, or processes.

Across the top of the matrix, list some of the main ideas that are to be analyzed or described in the writing assignment. Along the side of the matrix, list some of the areas by which these ideas are to be considered. As part of the prewriting preparation, students complete the chart by jotting notes and ideas from course material, class lectures, etc., in the spaces created by the matrix.

A language arts teacher used a concept matrix as a planning tool for a writing activity that compared famous heroes from the stories that the class had read. The activity directed students to write about how the heroes

**Figure 8.7     STUDENT'S WRITING SAMPLE ON WHAT IT WOULD BE LIKE TO BE A FREED SLAVE**

May 3, 1866

My mane is Toby and I had been a slave for eight years before we were freed. It was good at fist But them we realizied there were problems.

We had great prolblems. Prejudice kept us from doing what we wanted to do. Black Codes which were suppose to help Dudnt help us at all. we werent allowed to be out after dark. We werent allowed to Carry a gun. We werent allowed to go out without a pass.

We had mo food. my famly had mo food. my kids were all sick and there was mothing I could do nothing to help them. We had mo money to buy any medicine to help them.

But there was some mice people. They were The army and Quakers helpd my kids get better and they helpd us get some land and food for my famly. then we started a farm we graw crops and got money.

We had some opertumites. We could move to anther state for a Job. We could also get an Education. Some Blacks even gained Gooerment positions.

(David, Hercules, Beowulf) approached and handled challenges. The chart in Box 8.2 helped students to reread selectively and to take notes in preparation for the writing assignment.

Students in the language arts class discussed their concept matrices before engaging in writing. Charting can be an effective outlining tool for writing and also has value as a study strategy in that it provides a framework

| BOX 8.2    Chart for "Stories About Heroes" | | | |
|---|---|---|---|
| | David | Hercules | Beowulf |
| Each hero's feelings when confronted with his challenge. | | | |
| How did each hero handle his challenge? | | | |
| How did each hero react after conquering his challenge? | | | |

upon which students can organize and relate information. In the next chapter, additional outlining procedures will be introduced to show how you can help students organize information through graphic representations. These student-generated graphic representations are excellent springboards into writing.

## Guiding the First Draft

The writing stage involves getting ideas down on paper in a fluent and coherent fashion. The writer drafts a text with an audience (readers) in mind. If students are well rehearsed for writing, first drafts should develop without undue struggle. The use of in-class time for first-draft writing is as important as alotting in-class time for reading. In both cases, teachers can regulate and monitor the process much more effectively. For example, while students are writing, a teacher's time shouldn't be occupied grading papers or attending to other unrelated chores. As Tchudi and Yates (1983) explain in *Writing in the Content Areas*, teachers can do much to influence the quality of writing and learning *as* students are writing:

> When students are writing during class time, the teacher can take an active role. For example, monitor facial expressions—they often tell when a student is starting to get in a jam and needs help. Float around the class during a writing assignment, glancing at first paragraphs and rough beginnings, offering advice if it seems needed—In other words, help students get it right *while* they are writing and encourage them to solve problems the first time around (pp. 12–17).

The writing stage, then, should be a time to confer individually with students who are having trouble using what they know to tackle the writing task. Serve as a sounding board or play devil's advocate: "How does what we studied in class for the past few days relate to your topic?" or "I don't quite understand what you're getting at. Let's talk about what you're trying to say." Students should also have the opportunity to confer with one another: "There are great benefits from such forms of peer collaboration as encouraging writers to bounce ideas off one another, reading draft paragraphs aloud to seek advice, pumping their friends for new advice" (Tchudi and Yates 1983, p. 17). Teacher feedback and peer collaboration underscore the importance of *response* in the writing process.

## Responding and Revising

Rewriting helps students to take another look—to rethink a paper. This is why good writing often reflects good rewriting. From a content area learning perspective, rewriting is the catalyst for clarifying and extending concepts under study. Rewriting text hinges on the feedback students receive between first and second drafts.

Teacher feedback is always important, but it's often too demanding and time consuming to be the sole vehicle for response. It may also lack the *immediacy* that student writers need to try out their ideas on an audience—especially if teachers are accustomed to taking home a stack of papers and writing comments on each one. The paper load soon becomes unmanageable and self-defeating. An alternative is to have students respond to the writing of other students. By working together in response groups, students can give reactions, ask questions, and make suggestions to their peers. These responses to writing-in-progress lead to revision and refinement during rewriting.

**Student Response Groups.**  The purpose of peer response groups is to provide a testing ground for students to see how their writing influences a group of readers. Writers need response to sense the kinds of changes they need to make.

Healy (1982) makes an important distinction between *response* and *evaluation*. Response involves an initial reaction to a first draft. The reaction is usually in the form of questions to the writer about the content and organization of the writing. Both teacher and student share responsibility for responding. Evaluation, on the other hand, involves a final assessment of a piece of writing that has progressed through drafts. The teacher has primary responsibility for evaluating a finished product.

Learning to respond to writing in peer groups requires demonstrations and modeling. Response groups must be phased in gradually—students can't be expected to handle response tasks in groups without extensive modeling and coaching. Moreover, response groups shouldn't be initiated too early in the school year. After a month or two of regular writing activity, students will be more confident in their writing ability and will, in all probability, have developed some fluency in their writing. It is at this point that they are ready to be introduced to responding and rewriting situations.

The following steps, adapted from Healy (1982) and Camp (1982), provide enough structure to shift the burden of feedback from teacher to students:

**Step 1.** Discuss students' attitudes toward school writing and attempt "to shape new ones if existing attitudes are constricting or counterproductive" (Healy 1982, p. 268). For example, talk about writing as a process that occurs in stages. When students are engaged in an important writing task that will be presented to others ("published"), they shouldn't expect a finished product in one sitting. A first draft is often rough around the edges. It usually needs focus and clarity. Let students know what you value in their writing. Moreover, emphasize the importance of trying out writing on an audience before tackling a final draft. Tryouts are a time to react as readers to writing, not nitpick over errors or correct writing as evaluators.

**Step 2.** Use the whole class as a response group to demonstrate how to give feedback to a writer. On an overhead transparency, show a paper that was written by an anonymous student from a different class. Read the paper aloud and talk about it. The goal is to practice talking about writing without posing a threat to any of the students. Camp (1982) suggested kicking off discussion with the question: "If you were the teacher of this student, and you received this paper, what would you decide to teach the student *next*, so that the next paper he or she writes will be better than this one?" (p. 21). Let the class brainstorm responses. List their suggestions on the chalkboard, and then ask the students to reach a consensus as to the most important points for improvement. Conclude the discussion by acknowledging that responses to content and organization have a higher priority than to mechanics. Writers-in-progress need feedback on how to set their content and organize it before attending to concerns related to spelling, capitalization, punctuation, and grammar.

**Step 3.** On an overhead transparency, project another paper from a different class and ask students to respond to the writing by making comments or raising questions. Write these on the transparency next to the appropriate section of the paper. You may find that students have difficulty with this task, so demonstrate several responses that tell what is positive about the paper. What do you as a reader like about it? What is done well?

Note the differences between *useful* and *useless* feedback. The response "This section is confusing" is of little help to the writer because it isn't specific enough. A useful response, however, is one in which the writers learn what information a reader needs: "I was confused about the Bay of Pigs invasion. Did Kennedy fail to give backup support to the commandos?" Students will soon catch on to the idea that a response gives information which helps the writer to better understand the needs of an audience.

**Step 4.** Form cooperative groups of three or four students. Distribute dittoes of a paper that was written in a different class. Also pass out a response sheet to guide the group discussions. The response sheet contains several questions which pattern what to look for in the writing. In Figure 8.8 Camp (1982) used a response sheet to guide response to a paper based on a personal experience.

Tchudi and Yates (1983) provide categories of questions to ask in response groups. The questions relate to *purpose, content, organization, audience, language,* and *style* and are presented in Figure 8.9. Note that students shouldn't respond to more than three or four questions in any one response group session. Choose or devise questions that are the most appropriate to the writing assignment.

**Step 5.** Form response groups to discuss first drafts that the students have written. Healy (1982, p. 274) recommends the following conditions for working in small groups:

- Keep the groups small—two to five at first.
- Sit as far away as possible from other groups for noise control.
- Write the names of your response partners on the top of your original draft.

**Figure 8.8    EXAMPLE OF A RESPONSE SHEET**

Response sheet: personal experience writing
Writer _____
Responder _____
 A. What did you like best about this paper? What worked really well?
 _____
 _____
 _____

 B. What questions would you ask the writer about things in this paper that were confusing or unclear to you?
 _____
 _____
 _____

 C. Where in the paper would you like more detail? Where could the writer show instead of tell?
 _____
 _____

D. Rate each of the following on a scale from 1 to 4. 4 is tops.
   1. Beginning _____          3. Ending _____
   2. Use of conversation _____    4. Title _____

**Source:**  Adapted from Gerald Camp, *A Success Curriculum for Remedial Writers.* Berkeley, Calif.: The National Writing Project, University of California, Berkeley, 1982, p. 28.

**Figure 8.9    QUESTIONS FOR RESPONSE GROUPS**

*Note:* Do not have students ask *all* these questions (or similar ones) at every revising session. Rather, pick some questions that seem most appropriate to your assignment and have the students work on two or three each time.

Purpose

- Where is this writing headed? Can readers clearly tell?
- Is it on one track, or does it shoot off in new directions?
- Is the writer trying to do too much? Too little?
- Does the author seem to *care* about his/her writing?

Content

- When you're through, can you easily summarize this piece or retell it in your own words?
- Can a reader understand it easily?
- Are there parts that you found confusing?
- Are there places where the writer said too much, or overexplained the subject?
- Can the reader visualize the subject?
- Does it hold your interest all the way through?
- Did you learn something new from this paper?

Organization

- Do the main points seem to be in the right order?
- Does the writer give you enough information so that you know what he/she is trying to accomplish?
- Does the writing begin smoothly? Does the writer take too long to get started?
- What about the ending? Does it end crisply and excitingly?

Audience

- Who are the readers for this writing? Does the writer seem to have them clearly in mind? Will they understand him/her?
- What changes does the writer need to make to better communicate with the audience?

Language and style

- Is the paper interesting and readable? Does it get stuffy or dull?
- Can you hear the writer's voice and personality in it?
- Are all difficult words explained or defined?
- Does the writer use natural, lively language throughout?
- Are the grammar, spelling, and punctuation OK?

**Source:**    From *Teaching Writing in the Content Areas: Senior High School,* by Stephen Tchudi and JoAnne Yates. Copyright © 1983, National Education Association. Reprinted with permission.

- After hearing a paper read, ask the writer any comments or questions which occur to you. The writer will note the questions on the paper.
- Encourage the writer to ask for help with different sections of his/her paper.
- Make all revisions on your original draft before doing the final. Staple both copies together.

A variation on these conditions is to use response sheets to guide the group discussions. They are particularlyl useful in the beginning when the task of responding is still new to students. However, with enough modeling and practice, response sheets will probably not be necessary.

One additional point: During the revision of the original draft, encourage students to be messy. For example, show them how to use carets to make insertions, and allow them to cross out or to cut and paste sections of text, if necessary. The use of arrows will help students show changes in the position of words, phrases, or sentences within the text.

Once feedback is given on the content and organization of a draft, response group members should work together to edit and proofread their texts for spelling, punctuation, capitalization, word choice, and syntax. Accuracy counts. Cleaning up a text shouldn't be neglected, but students must recognize that concern for proofreading and editing comes toward the end of the process.

Revising a text is hard work. Some students even think that *rewriting* is a dirty word. They mistake it for recopying—emphasizing neatness as they painstakingly transcribe from pencil to ink. They need a good rationale for going the extra mile. One solid reason is the recognition that their work will be presented to others. Publishing is an incentive for revising. As Camp explained, "... the final drafts of all major writing assignments are published in some way. This final step is ... just as essential as any of the others" (p. 41). If writing is for reading—and indeed it is—then teachers must find ways to value students' finished products.

## Publishing

Kirby and Liner (1981, p. 215) give four good reasons for publishing students' written products:

1. Publishing gives the writer an audience, and the writing task becomes a real effort at communication—not just writing to please the teacher.

2. Publishing is the only reason for the writing to be important enough for the hard work of editing and proofreading.

3. Publishing involves the ego, which is the strongest incentive for the student writer to keep writing.

4. Publishing is fun.

Most students realize early in their school experience that the teacher is their only audience for writing. When the audience is not described in a writing assignment, students typically assume that the teacher will be the sole reader. Topic-only assignments reinforce this assumption:

- How does the Cuban government squelch dissidents?
- Argue for or against smoking in public places.
- What causes acid rain?

We do not deny or denigrate the importance of the teacher as an audience. Neither do students. We agree with Purves (1983) that "... schools, real institutions that they are ... should teach writing for general audiences represented by the real teacher" (p. 44).

However, when the classroom context for writing encourages a range of possible audiences for assignments (including the teacher), the purposes for and the quality of writing often change for the better. This is why we called for audience-specific writing assignments early in the chapter.

When students know that their written products will be presented publicly for others to read, they develop a heightened awareness of audience. Teachers need to mine the audience resources that exist in and out of the classroom. As we just showed, response groups are one way to share writing-in-progress. Following are some ways to share finished products.

**Oral Presentations to the Class.**  Reading finished papers aloud is a natural extension of peer responding for work-in-progress. When the writing is tied directly to content objectives, students not only have fun sharing their products, but they also learn a great deal from their colleagues. We recommend the frequent use of read-aloud sessions as a way of publishing so that all students will at one time or another have an opportunity to present.

Teachers should establish a tone of acceptance during oral presentations of original writing. The writer reads; the listeners react and respond. One variation is to establish a professional conference atmosphere wherein student scientists, historians, literary critics, mathematicians, business executives, etc., convene to share knowledge with one another. Several students who have written on a related topic might even present a symposium—in which case one or two of their classmates should serve as discussants. Opportunities for learning abound when the focal point for class reaction and discussion centers on student-developed texts.

**Class Publications.**  Class-produced newspapers, magazines, anthologies, and class books are excellent ways to publish student writing. These vehicles for publication fit in effectively with the culmination of a unit of study. Identify a title for a class publication that reflects the theme or objective of the unit. For example, *The Civil War Chronicle,* a magazine produced by an eleventh-grade American history class, was patterned after the formats found in *Time* and *Newsweek.* A ninth-grade English class studying *To Kill a Mockingbird* put together *The Maycomb Register.* The students researched events associated with the time period (1936) set in the novel and wrote a variety of local (related to the story), national, and international news items. The teacher had students involved in all phases of the newspaper's production, including typesetting and layout. She even had the paper professionally printed. To pay for the printing, the students sold the newspaper to schoolmates, parents, and neighbors.

Producing a newspaper or a magazine requires teamwork and task differentiation. We suggest that students not only participate as writers, but also work in groups to assume responsibility for editing, proofreading, design, and production. Production of a class publication need not be as elaborate or expensive an activity as *The Maycomb Register.* Dittoed publications have the same effect on student writers when they see their work in print.

**Room Displays.** Display student writing. As Kirby and Liner (1981) find, ". . . a display of finished products attracts attention and stimulates talk and thinking about writing" (p. 217). Establish a reading fair in which students circulate quietly around the room reading as many papers as they can. Judy and Judy (1981) suggested that student writers provide blank sheets of paper to accompany their finished products so that readers can comment. They also recommended one-of-a-kind publications for display. These publications preserve the writing in a variety of forms (folding books, leaflets, scrolls, quartos, and folios). In their book, *Gifts of Writing* (1980), the Judys have outlined numerous formats for one-of-a-kind publications.

**Publishing for Real World Audiences.** Letters, community publications, commercial magazines, and national and state contests are all vehicles for real world publishing outside of the classroom and school. Letters, in particular, are valuable because there are so many audience possibilities:

> Students can write everyone from school officials to administrators of policies in education, industry, and business. They can write to artists, musicians, poets and actors to offer adulation or criticism. They can write on issues of immediate concern or long range interest (Judy and Judy 1980, p. 119).

In addition to letters, the local newspaper, PTA bulletin, or school district newsletter sometimes provide an outlet for class-related writing activity. Commercial magazines (see Appendix B for a list of addresses compiled by Teachers and Writers Collaborative) and national and state writing contests also offer opportunities for publication. Commercial magazines and writing contests, of course, are highly competitive. However, the real value of writing for commercial publication lies in the authenticity of the task and the audience specification it provides.

Guiding the writing process leads to products which eventually must be evaluated. How do teachers assign grades to writing that has progressed through drafts?

## Evaluating and Grading

The paperload in classrooms where writing happens regularly is a persistent matter of concern for teachers. They often blanch at the prospect of grading 125 or more papers. A science teacher reacted to us in a workshop this way: "The quickest way to squelch my interest in writing to learn is to sock me with six sets of papers to correct at once." We couldn't agree more—weekends weren't made for drowning in a sea of red ink.

Yet the notion of what it means to evaluate written work must be examined. Evaluating to correct papers is an inappropriate concept in a process approach to writing. It suggests that the teacher's role is primarily one of detecting errors and making corrections or revisions in papers. Overemphasis on error detection often telegraphs to students that correctness rather than the discovery and communication of meaning is what writing is all about. Content area teachers who view their job as an error hunt soon become, and understandably so, reluctant to devote hours to reading and correcting papers.

The types of errors that often take the most time to detect and correct are those which involve various elements of language such as punctuation, spelling, and grammar. These elements, sometimes referred to as the *mechanics* or *form* of writing, must take a back seat to other features of writing, mainly *content* and *organization.* It's not that linguistic elements should be ignored or left unattended. However, they must be put into perspective. As Pearce (1983) explains, "If writing is to serve as a catalyst for gaining insight into course material, then content—not form—needs to be emphasized. . . . If a paper has poor content, then no amount of correcting elements of form will transform it into a good piece of writing" (p. 214). Ideas, and how they are logically and coherently developed in a paper, must receive top priority when one is evaluating and grading writing in content area classrooms.

Once writing is thought of and taught as a process, teachers can begin to deal effectively with the paperload. While the volume of papers will inevitably increase, it is likely to become more manageable. For one thing, when provisions are made for active student response to writing, much of the feedback that a student writer needs will come *while* writing is still going on. Guiding and channeling feedback as students progress with their drafts is a type of *formative* evaluation. In contrast, a *summative* evaluation takes place during the postwriting stage, usually after students have shared their finished products with one another.

Summative evaluations are often *holistic* so that a teacher can quickly and accurately judge a piece of writing based on an impression of its overall effectiveness. Thus, a holistic evaluation permits teachers to sort, rank, and grade written pieces rather efficiently and effectively. Holistic scoring is organized around the principle that a written composition is judged on how successfully it communicates a message, rather than on the strengths and weaknesses of its individual features. The whole of a composition, if you will, is greater than the sum of its parts. In other words, teachers don't have to spend inordinate amounts of time enumerating and counting errors in a paper. Instead, the paper is judged for its total effect on a rater.

One type of holistic measure, *primary trait scoring*, is of particular value in content area writing situations. Primary trait scoring is tied directly to a specific writing assignment. An effective assignment, as you recall, provides a rhetorical context. The student writer's task is to respond to the special blend of purpose, audience, subject, and role specified in the assignment. Primary trait scoring helps the teacher to decide how well students completed the writing task.

As a result, primary trait scoring focuses on those characteristics in a paper which are crucial for task completion. How successfully did students handle the assignment in relation to purpose, audience, subject, or role? For example, reread the arms race assignment in this chapter. Given the rhetorical context of that assignment, papers should be evaluated for these primary traits or characteristics: (1) accurate content in support of a position, (2) a logical and coherent set of ideas in support of a position, and (3) a position statement that is convincing and persuasive when aimed at an audience of fellow students.

Pearce (1983) recommends that teachers develop a *rubric* based on the primary traits exhibited in student papers. A rubric is a scoring guide. It provides a summary listing of the characteristics that distinguish high-quality from low-quality compositions. Study the rubric in Box 8.3 that Pearce developed for the following assignment.

---

**BOX 8.3     A Rubric for Grading**

Paper topic: 1960s approaches to civil rights in the United States

High-quality papers contain:
An overview of civil rights or their lack during the 1960s, with three specific examples.
A statement defining civil disobedience, with three examples of how it was used and Martin Luther King's role.
At least one other approach to civil rights, with specific examples, and a comparison of this approach with King's civil disobedience that illustrates differences or similarities in at least two ways.
Good organization, well-developed arguments, few mechanical errors (sentence fragments, grammatical errors, spelling errors).

Medium-quality papers contain:
An overview of Black civil rights during the 1960s, with two specific examples.
A statement defining civil disobedience, with two examples of its use and Martin Luther King's involvement.
One other approach to civil rights, with examples, and a comparison of it with King's civil disobedience by their differences.
Good organization, few mechanical errors, moderately developed arguments.

Lower-quality papers contain:
A general statement defining civil disobedience with reference to Martin Luther King's involvement and at least one example.
One other approach to civil rights and how it differed from civil disobedience.
Fair organization, some mechanical errors.

Lowest-quality papers contain:
A general statement on who Martin Luther King was or a general statement on civil disobedience.
A general statement that not all Blacks agreed with civil disobedience.
A list of points, poor organization, many mechanical errors.

**Source:**  From "Guidelines for the use and evaluation of writing in content classrooms" by Daniel L. Pearce, *Journal of Reading*, December 1983. Reprinted with permission of Daniel L. Pearce and the International Reading Association.

> Write a time capsule document analyzing Martin Luther King's approach to civil rights during the 1960's. Compare this approach to one taken by other Black leaders (p. 214).

For this assignment, papers were evaluated for the following traits: (1) accurate and adequate content about civil disobedience, (2) a comparison of King's approach to civil disobedience with at least one black leader's approach, and (3) a logical and organized presentation which provides evidence for any generalization made.

There are other types of holistic scoring procedures that can be used to evaluate and grade papers. For example, *analytical scales* and *checklists* can be developed to judge the quality of a piece of writing. These are explained in detail in an excellent monograph, *Evaluating Writing*, published by the National Council of Teachers of English (Cooper and Odell 1977).

# LOOKING BACK, LOOKING FORWARD

In this chapter we focused on writing to emphasize the powerful bonds that exist between reading and writing. Content area learning, in fact, is more productive when writing and reading are integrated throughout the curriculum. The two processes, both rooted in language, are intertwined with one another and share common cognitive and sociocultural characteristics. Reading and writing together in a classroom improves achievement and instructional efficiency. When students write to learn in content area classrooms, they are involved in a process of manipulating, clarifying, discovering, and synthesizing ideas. The writing process can be a powerful strategy for helping students gain insight into course material. Once more, students who write more read more.

The uses of writing have been noticeably limited in content area classrooms. Writing has often been restricted to noncomposing activities such as filling in the blanks on worksheets and practice exercises, writing one-paragraph-or-less responses to study questions, or taking notes. The role of writing in content areas should be broadened because of its potentially powerful effect on thinking and learning.

Because writing promotes different types of learning, many different occasions to write should be present for students. These occasions include the use of learning logs, unfinished writing activities, and essays. Learning logs, one of the most versatile writing-to-learn strategies, entails students keeping an ongoing record of learning as it happens in a notebook or looseleaf binder. When students use learning logs, they soon learn to write without the fear of making errors of a mechanical nature. Unfinished writing activities such as the unsent letter place students in a role-playing situation in which they are asked to write letters in response to material being studied. Additional activities include biopoems, dialogues, and admit and exit slips. Students can also be assigned essays for inquiry-centered writing. Essay topics should be introduced in assignments that make the writing task explicit. An explicit assignment helps students to assess the purpose, audience, and form of the writing as well as the writer's role.

Writing should be thought of and taught as a process. When students are guided through a process for writing, they will be in a better position to generate ideas, set goals, organize, draft, and revise. The writing process occurs in steps or stages, not necessarily in a linear sequence of events but more as a back-and-forth activity. The stages of writing presented in this chapter included prewriting, writing, rewriting, and postwriting. Prewriting activitites such as brainstorming, clustering, concept matrices, and discussion help students to explore ideas, set purposes, and organize for writing. Prewriting situations get students ready to write—to transcribe ideas into words onto paper. This step—writing—leads to an initial draft. Rewriting activities include a response by students or teachers to drafts. Feedback while writing is in progress is essential for revision to occur. Postwriting activities involve sharing a finished product and a summative evaluation. Holistic scoring was recommended as a means of evaluating completed drafts.

The chapter that follows examines what it means to study. Studying texts requires students to engage in purposeful independent learning activities. Organizing text information, summarizing large chunks of information, taking and making notes, and conducting and reporting inquiry-centered research are examples of learner-directed strategies.

## SUGGESTED READINGS

Applebee, A. N. (1981). *Writing in the secondary school: English and the content areas.* Urbana, IL: Council of Teachers of English.

Camp, G. (1982). *A success curriculum for remedial writers.* Berkeley, CA: The National Writing Project, University of California.

Fulwiler, T. (1987). *Teaching with writing.* Portsmouth, NH: Boynton/Cook.

Gere, A. (1985). *Roots in sawdust: Writing to learn across the curriculum.* Urbana, IL: National Council of Teachers of English.

Jensen, J. (ed). (1984). *Composing and comprehending.* Urbana, IL: National Council of Teachers of English.

Kirby, D., & Liner, T. (1981). *Inside out: Developmental strategies for teaching writing.* Montclair, NJ: Boyton/Cook.

Langer, J. A. (1986). Learning through writing: Study skills in the content areas. *Journal of Reading, 29,* 400–406.

Lindemann, E. (1982). *A rhetoric for writing teachers.* New York: Oxford University Press.

Macrorie, K. (1980). *Searching writing*. Rochelle Park, NJ: Hayden.

Martin, N., D'Arcy, P., Newton, B., & Parker, R. (1976). *Writing and learning across the curriculum*. Montclair, NJ: Boyton/Cook.

Murray, D. (1982). *Learning by teaching*. Montclair, NJ: Boyton/Cook.

Myers, J. (1984). *Writing to learn across the curriculum*. Bloomington, IN: Phi Delta Kappa.

Tchudi, S., & Huerta, M. (1983). *Teaching writing in the content areas: Middle school/junior high*. Washington, D.C.: National Education Association.

Tchudi, S., & Tschudi, S. (1983). *Teaching writing in the content areas: Elementary school*. Washington, D.C.: National Education Association.

Tchudi, S., & Yates, J. (1983). *Teaching writing in the content areas: Senior high school*. Washington, D.C.: National Education Association.

# 9

# Studying Texts

Minds, like bodies, will often fall into a pimpled, ill-conditioned state from mere excess of comfort.

*—Charles Dickens*

## ORGANIZING PRINCIPLE

Studying texts is hard work. It takes deliberate effort. Concentration. Discipline. Stick-to-itiveness. Patience with print. Good readers know how to study texts and why. They have reasons for studying, whether their purposes involve acquiring, organizing, summarizing, or using information and ideas. To study effectively, students need to learn not only how to work hard but also how to work smart. They can't be content, to use Dickens' words, with the "mere excess of comfort" that comes from having read a text assignment mindlessly.

Many students, we argue, lack discipline and patience with texts because they are products of a society in which electronic media have been a primary source of information and pleasure for them. Television, for example, with its rapid-fire images increasingly dominates the lives of today's students. Little wonder that studying texts is hard work. Learning how to work with a text—to read and reread and, perhaps, to reread again—is an acquired skill. It's difficult for students today to develop a commitment and a positive attitude toward studying texts, let alone strategies for effective studying. Yet it is in these areas that content area teachers have an important role to play.

The use of learning strategies is directly related to students' knowledge and awareness of what it means to study. As they become more aware, not only of the nature of the texts they read, but also of themselves as learners and the tasks they are required to engage in, students become more strategic.

Skilled readers develop more strategies for studying than unskilled readers. Although these strategies will invariably differ from learner to learner, they are often put to effective use when needed for specific reading tasks. Students who know how to study, for example, know how to approach texts, raise questions, and make plans for reading. They also know how to "do something" with texts in order to think more deeply about the ideas they encounter during reading. Unskilled readers, on the other hand, often flounder with tasks that require studying  These students lack knowledge of and control over the strategies necessary for effectively learning with texts. In a nutshell, the unskilled reader lacks independence as a learner.

The common denominator among skilled readers is that they use learning strategies spontaneously and independently as they are working with texts. What is the content area teacher's role in helping students to use learning strategies independently? Shifting the burden of learning from the teacher's shoulders to students' is at the heart of the organizing principle of this chapter: *A content area teacher is in a strategic position to show students how to use study strategies independently as they interact and learn with texts.*

## CHAPTER OVERVIEW

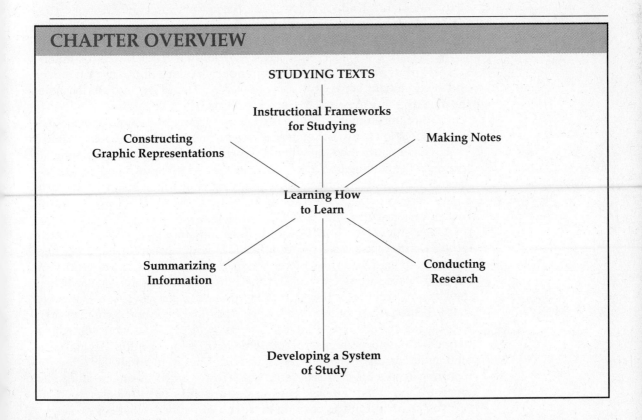

## FRAME OF MIND

1. How can you frame instruction in the use of study strategies?

2. How can you show students how to construct graphic representations?

3. How can you show students how to summarize information?

4. How can you show students how to annotate texts?

5. How can you support students' efforts to conduct and report research?

6. How do students learn to develop a system of study?

The poster caught our attention immediately. It had just gone up on the bulletin board in Julie Meyer's classroom. "School Daze: From A to Z" defined significant school activities in the lives of students, each beginning with a letter of the alphabet. The entry for the letter *S* just happened to be the subject of this chapter. It read, "STUDY: *Those precious moments between soap operas, movies, sports, video games, food, personal grooming, and general lollygagging when one opens one's school books—and falls asleep*" (Hallmark Cards 1982).

While some students might agree that study is a quick cure for insomnia, few of us would deny that studying texts is one of the most frequent and predominant activities in schools today. The older students become, the more they are expected to learn with texts.

It's not uncommon to find a teacher prefacing text assignments by urging students to "study the material." And some do. They are able to study effectively because they know what it means to *approach* a text assignment: to *analyze* the reading task at hand, to *make plans* for reading, and then to *use* strategies to suit their purposes for studying. Students who approach texts in this manner achieve a level of independence because they are in charge of their own learning.

Other students, less skilled in reading and studying, wage a continual struggle with texts. Some probably wonder why teachers make a big fuss out of studying in the first place. For them, the exhortation to "study the material" goes in one ear and out the other. Others try to cope with the demands of study. Yet they are prone to equate studying texts with rote memorization—cramming "meaningless" material into short-term memory.

Whenever you urge students to study, you probably have something definite in mind. Whatever that something is, it shouldn't remain an ambiguous or unattainable classroom goal. The problem all too often for maturing readers is that they aren't *aware* of what it means to study, let alone use and orchestrate various learning activities and strategies.

You are in a strategic position to make a difference. What better context than the content area classroom to teach learners what it means to be a *student*. The term *student*, derived from Latin, means "one who studies; one who pursues knowledge."

The extrinsic reason that most students give for studying is to cover the material or do well in a course. Students will tell you that they study to pass tests. Fair enough. They are quick to associate studying with memorizing information. A concept of study which includes retention has merit. But students run the risk of committing a reductionist fallacy by believing that one part equals the whole, or simply that memorizing is study. Too many students spend too much time using up too much energy on what often becomes their only means of study—rote memorization. Rote memorizing leads to short-lived recall of unrelated bits and pieces of information. Alternatives to rote memorization should be taught and reinforced when and where they count the most—in a content classroom.

Reading and studying are closely knit processes, but reading can be performed without studying, and good readers are not necessarily good studiers. Studying frequently involves reading that is text driven in the sense that the questions that guide the reading are not necessarily the ones the reader would have chosen to pursue. In academic contexts, studying is the vehicle by which students achieve academic standards that frequently are set by others. Meeting standards may involve memorizing facts, but it may also involve developing a sophisticated understanding of concepts and issues.

The lack of discipline and patience with print is probably one reason why so few adolescents and young adults study effectively on their own in secondary school or in college. A sociology instructor once met with students who were doing poorly in his class during their first semester in college. The purpose of the meeting was to discuss ways to study sociology. The students, however, soon turned the meeting into a battleground, venting their own frustrations with the course. The sociologist finally reached his own boiling point: "Listen, the bottom line is this: Studying is hard work. You can't read sociological material once and expect to 'get it' through osmosis. You should 'work' the material. Read it. And reread it. First, get the facts straight in your head. And eventually you will make them a part of you."

We find ourselves agreeing with the college instructor's analysis of the "bottom line." Studying texts is hard work. Cultivating the right habits and attitudes toward studying is essential. And this is where teachers can help the most.

# FRAMING INSTRUCTION IN THE USE OF STUDY STRATEGIES

A teacher has the right to expect students to study a subject—and a responsibility to show them how to do this. We read once that *effective* means doing the right thing and *efficient* means doing the thing right. When it comes to studying, it's easy to do the wrong things well. In order for students to use study strategies effectively and efficiently, a content area teacher must help them connect what they know already about their own reading strategies to the act of studying.

Explicit instruction helps students become aware of, use, and develop control over study strategies (Brown and Palincsar 1982). Explicit methods provide an alternative to blind instruction. In blind instructional situations, students are taught what to do, but this is where instruction usually ends. Although directed to make use of a set of procedures which will improve studying, students seldom grasp the rationale or payoff underlying a particular study strategy. As a result, they attempt to use the strategy with little basis for evaluating its success or monitoring its effectiveness. Explicit instruction, however, attempts not only to show students *what* to do, but also *why, how,* and *when.* Pearson (1982b) concludes that such instruction helps "students develop independent strategies for coping with the kinds of comprehension problems they are asked to solve in their lives in schools" (p. 22).

The instructional framework that follows combines explicit teaching of study strategies with content area texts. The framework has four components: *assessment, awareness, modeling and demonstration,* and *application.*

By way of analogy, the instructional framework provides experiences similar to those needed by athletes and other performers who are in training. To perform well with texts, students must understand the rules, rehearse, work on technique, practice. A coach (the teacher) is needed to provide feedback, guide, inspire, and share the knowledge and experiences that she or he possesses.

## Assessing What Students Know How to Do

The assessment component of the instructional model is tryout time. It gives the teacher an opportunity to determine the degree of knowledge the students have about a study strategy under discussion. Moreover, assessment yields insight into how well the students use a strategy to handle a reading task. For these reasons, assessing the use of a strategy should occur in as natural a context as possible.

Assessment usually can be accomplished within a single class period, following the steps outlined here:

1. Assign students a text passage of approximately 1000–1500 words. The selection should take most students 10 to 15 minutes to read.

2. Direct students to use a particular study strategy. For example, suppose that the strategy students are to develop involves summarizing a text selection. Simply ask students to do the things they normally do to read a passage and then develop a summary of it. Allow adequate time to complete the task.

3. Observe the use of the strategy. Note what students do. Do they underline or mark important ideas as they read? Do they appear to skim the material first to get a general idea of what to expect? In the case of summarizing, what do they do when actually constructing the summary?

4. Ask students to respond in writing to several key questions about the use of the study strategy. For example, What did you do to summarize the passage? What did you do to find the main ideas? Did you find summarizing easy or difficult? Why?

## Creating Strategy Awareness

Assessment is a springboard to making students aware of the *why* and *how* of a study strategy. During the awareness step, a give-and-take exchange of ideas takes place between teacher and students. As a result, students should recognize the *rationale* and *process* behind the use of a study strategy. To make students more aware of a study strategy, consider the following activities:

1. Discuss the assessment. Use your observations and students' reflective responses to the written questions.

2. Set the stage by leading a discussion of *why* the strategy is useful. What is the payoff for students? How does it improve learning?

3. Engage in activities that define the rules or procedures necessary to be successful with the study strategy.

4. Have students experience the use of the study strategy by practicing the rules or procedures on a short selection from the textbook.

   Awareness provides students with a clear picture of the study strategy: The *why* and *how* are solidly introduced. The road has been paved for more intensive modeling and demonstration of the strategy.

## Modeling and Demonstrating Strategies

Once the why and a beginning sense of how are established, the students should receive careful follow-up in the use of the study strategy. Follow-up sessions are characterized by demonstration through teacher modeling, explanations, practice, reinforcement of the rules or procedures, and more practice. The students progress from easy to harder practice situations, and from shorter to longer text selections. The following activities are recommended:

1. Use an overhead transparency to review the rules or steps that students should follow.

2. Have students keep a learning log. Learning logs help students keep an ongoing record, in a notebook or looseleaf binder, of learning as it happens.
   Consider this specific application: Each section of the log might reflect a study strategy that students are learning to control. Direct the students to the section of the learning log that deals with the study strategy under development. Each student should have a copy of the rules and/or steps in the log to review. The log is also used by students to make entries toward the end of a demonstration session. The entries may include their progress and struggles as well as their thoughts and reflections on the use

of the strategy. As Hoffman (1983) explains, "They can write about their participation or lack of it; their difficulty in paying attention, or in understanding the teacher; what they learn . . ." (p. 345). Collect the logs periodically and respond to entries accordingly. The entries are also quite useful in planning additional sessions to help reinforce the use of the strategy.

3. Demonstrate the study strategy. Walk students through the steps. Provide explanations. Raise questions about the procedures.

4. As part of a demonstration, initiate the think-aloud procedure to model how to use the study strategy. By thinking aloud, the teacher shares with students the thinking processes he or she uses in applying the study strategy. Thinking aloud is often accomplished by reading a passage out loud, stopping at key points in the text to ask questions and/or provide prompts. The questions and prompts mirror the critical thinking required to apply the study strategy. Once students are familiar with the think-aloud procedure, encourage them to demonstrate and use it during practice sessions.

5. Reinforce and practice the study strategy with trial runs using short selections from the textbook. Debrief with questions after each trial run. Did the students follow the steps? How successful were they? What caused them difficulty? Have them make learning log entries. Often a short quiz following a trial run shows students how much they learned and remembered as a result of using the study strategy.

The demonstration sessions are designed to provide experience with the study strategy. Students should reach a point where they have internalized the steps and feel in control of the strategy.

## Applying Strategies

The preceding components of the instructional framework should provide enough practice for students to know *why*, *how*, and *when* to use study strategies that have been targeted by the teacher for emphasis. Once students have made generalizations about strategy use, regular class assignments should encourage application. Rather than assign for homework a text selection accompanied by questions to be answered, frame the assignment so that students will have to apply certain study strategies.

## LEARNING TO LEARN WITH TEXTS

Students who study effectively and efficiently know how to learn on their own. They have a strong expectation for success. They have confidence in themselves, despite the challenge and difficulty often inherent in specific study tasks across the curriculum. They are not only able but also willing to engage in study because they know that their efforts will pay off.

In addition, independent learners know themselves as students. They know when, where, and under what conditions they study most effectively. They are aware of their strengths as students and know how to compensate for their weaknesses. As a result, they set goals for studying and choose strategies that allow them to experience the success and satisfaction that comes from working smart as well as working hard.

In the next several sections, we explore how to help students develop several important study strategies. It is not possible to list all the study strategies that students may find effective, let alone to describe all of the instructional activities that teachers might use to develop these strategies. Instead, our intent is to present models for the ways in which teachers, students, and texts might interact to produce growth in students' ability to learn independently.

## Learning to Use and Construct Graphic Representations

Graphic or visual representations help learners to comprehend and retain *textually important information*. When students learn how to use and construct graphic representations, they are in control of a study strategy that allows them to identify what parts of a text are important, how ideas and concepts encountered in text are related, and where they can find specific information to support more important ideas.

To make information accessible, authors organize ideas in text. Some ideas, of course, are more important than others. Suppose you were reading a magazine article and came across the passage in Box 9.1. First read the passage and then write what you think is the most important idea and why in the space provided.

No doubt, if you were to compare your response to the passage with others' responses, there would be variation in what each of you had written as the most important idea. You may have written something to the effect that "Standards guide the decisions we make," while someone else may have responded, "One should try not to lose one's head in an emergency." Why is this the case? Why not a single main idea?

In their research, Moore and Cunningham (1986) classify the main ideas produced by readers according to the similarity in their responses. As a result, the researchers were able to identify nine types of main-idea response. They concluded that the term *main idea* serves as an umbrella for *a wide range of tasks* that readers engage in when they search for and produce main ideas from text. No wonder Pearson (1981) characterizes the concept of main idea as an abstraction, "a polyglot of tasks and relations among ideas" (p. 124).

So what are important ideas? At least one thing is certain. What a reader thinks the main idea is *may not be* what the author intended the main idea of the text to be. The reader's purpose and the perspective that he or she brings to the text often determines the relative importance attached to what the author is saying. In this respect, the important ideas in text may vary from reader to reader and text situation to text situation (Winograd and Bridge 1986).

---

### BOX 9.1    What's the Most Important Idea in This Passage?

Standards are essential as reference points. Wise living depends upon finding a standard against which values may be measured. Consider, for example, the story about a fellow who was riding his motorcycle on a cold day. The zipper on his jacket was broken, so the rider stopped and put the jacket on backwards to shield him from the wind. A bit later, the rider had an accident and was knocked unconscious. He stayed in the hospital for weeks. The doctors said the boy wasn't hurt much in the wreck, but he was severely injured when the policeman tried to turn his head around to match his jacket. You see, a coat is supposed to zip up the front and the policeman made his judgment against that standard, which just goes to show you: If the standard is wrong, then the resulting decision will be wrong.

What is the most important idea in the passage?

_____

_____

_____

Why do you think so?    _____

_____

_____

_____

**Source:**  *From "Things Worth Keeping" by Bishop Ernest A. Fitzgerald, *Pace* Magazine, December 1987. Reprinted by permission of *Pace* Magazine, the Piedmont Airlines in flight magazine, *Pace* Communications, Inc., Greensboro, N.C., and the author.

The distinction between *contextually* important information and *textually* important information helps the teacher to understand where students are coming from when they respond to main-idea questions during discussion or writing activity. Van Dijk (1979) explains that textually important information is considered central to the text by the author. As a result, authors will often showcase textually important ideas in the text patterns they use, as we explained in Chapter 2.

Contextually important information, on the other hand, is that which is considered important by the reader. In Chapters 4, 5, and 6 we explored strategies that encourage students to use what they know to respond to text; in effect, to construct meaning that is personally or contextually important. But throughout this book we also underscore the importance of grasping an author's intended meaning. On the road to reading maturity, students must develop flexibility in distinguishing what is textually important from what is contextually important in the texts that they read.

An entire family of teacher-directed and learner-directed techniques and strategies is associated with the use of graphic representations to depict relationships in text: word maps, semantic maps, semantic webs, graphic organizers, flowcharts, concept matrices, and tree diagrams, to name a few. Although it is easy to get confused by the plethora of labels, a rose by any other name is still a rose.

What these techniques and strategies have in common is that they help students to interact with and outline textually important information. For example, when students read a text with an appropriate graphic organizer in mind, they focus on important ideas and relationships. And when they construct their own graphic organizers, they become actively involved in outlining those ideas and relationships.

Outlining helps students to clarify relationships. Developing an outline is analogous to fitting together pieces in a puzzle. Think of a puzzle piece as a separate idea and a text as the whole. A completed puzzle shows the separate identity of each idea as well as the part each idea plays in the total picture (Hansell 1978). Outlining strategies can be used effectively to facilitate a careful analysis and synthesis of relationships in text. They can form the basis for critical discussion and evaluation of the author's main points.

Problems arise when students are restricted by the means in which they must depict relationships spatially on paper. The word *outlining* for most of us immediately conjures up an image of the "correct" or "classic" format that we have all learned at one time or another but have probably failed to use regularly in real-life study situations. The classic form of outlining has the student represent the relatedness of information in linear form:

I. Main Idea
  A. Idea supporting I
    1. detail supporting A
    2. detail supporting A
      a. detail supporting 2
      b. detail supporting 2
  B. Idea supporting I
    1. detail supporting B
    2. detail supporting B
II. Main Idea

This conventional format represents a hierarchical ordering of ideas at different levels of subordination. Roman numerals signal the major or superordinate concepts in a text section, upper-case letters the supporting or coordinate concepts, Arabic numbers the supporting or subordinate details, and lower-case letters sub-subordinate details.

Maturing readers have trouble using a restricted form of outlining. Initially, at least, they need a more visual display than the one offered by the conventional format. And this is where graphic representations can play a critical role in the development of independent learners.

To show students how to use and construct graphic representations, use the instructional framework alluded to earlier. Begin by assessing how students normally outline text material. Do they have a sense of subordination among ideas? Do they have strategies for connecting major and minor concepts? Do they use alternatives to the conventional format? Make them aware of the rationale for organizing information through outlining. The jigsaw puzzle analogy—fitting pieces of information together into a coherent whole—works well for this purpose. With assessment and awareness building thoroughly accomplished, the stage is set for illustrating, modeling, and applying the strategies.

Semantic Mapping. A popular graphic representation, often called a semantic map or a semantic web, helps students to identify important ideas and show how they fit together. Teachers are not faced with the problem of teaching a restricted, conventional outline format but instead, of helping students understand what is read. The students are responsible for creating a logical arrangement among key words or phrases that connect main ideas to subordinate information. When maps are used, instruction should proceed from teacher-guided modeling and illustration to student-generated productions.

A semantic map or web has four components (Freedman and Reynolds 1980):

1. *A core question or concept.* The question or concept (stated as a key word or phrase) establishes the main focus of the map. All the ideas generated for the map by the students are related in some way to the core question/concept.

2. *Strands.* The subordinate ideas generated by the students that help to clarify the question or explain the concept.

3. *Strand supports.* The details, inferences, and generalizations that are related to each strand. These supports help to clarify and distinguish one strand from another.

4. *Strand ties.* The connections that students make between or among the strands; in other words, strand ties depict the relationships strands have with one another.

Students use the semantic map as an organizational tool to visually illustrate categories and relationships associated with a core question or concept under study. To model and illustrate the use of a semantic map, a junior high school social studies teacher walked students through the process. The class began a unit on Ohio's early settlements. As part of pre-reading discussion four questions were raised for the class to ponder: What do you think were the three most important early settlements in Ohio? What do you think these settlements had in common? How were they different? In what ways might the location of a settlement be important to the survival of the settlers? Predictions were made and discussed and led naturally to the text assignment.

The teacher assigned the material, directing students to read with the purpose of confirming or modifying their predictions and remembering everything they could about the early settlements.

After reading, the students formed small groups. Each group listed everything they could remember about the settlements on index cards—with one piece of information per card.

In the center of the chalkboard, the teacher wrote "The First Ohio Settlements" and circled the phrase. She then asked students to provide the main strands that helped answer the question and clarify the concept, "What were Ohio's most important early settlements?" The students responded by contrasting their predictions to the explanations in the text assignment. The teacher began to build the semantic map on the board by explaining how strands help students answer the questions and understand the main concept.

Next, she asked the students to work in their groups to sort the cards that were compiled according to each of the settlements depicted in the map. Through discussion, questioning, and think-aloud probes, the class completed the semantic map depicted in Figure 9.1.

Some teachers prefer to distinguish strands from strand supports through the use of lines. Notice that in Figure 9.1, a double line connects the strands to the core concept. Strand supports are linked to each web strand by single lines. With younger students, some teachers also recommend using different colored chalk to distinguish one strand from another. Finally, notice that strands are tied together by lines with arrows. In Figure 9.1, the strand ties were initiated by such teacher probes as "What did Marietta and Gallipolis have in common?"

**Figure 9.1    SEMANTIC MAP: THE FIRST OHIO SETTLEMENTS**

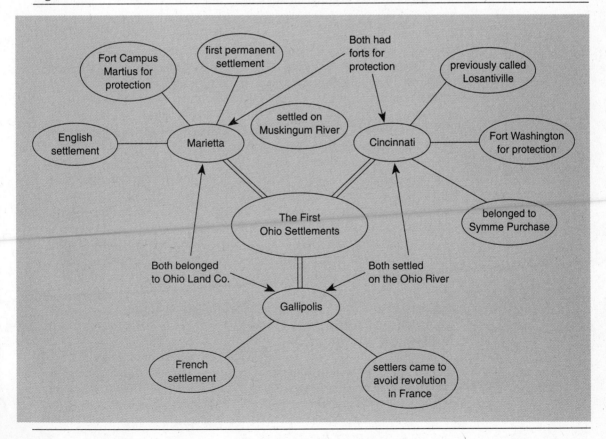

With appropriate modeling, explanation, and experience, students soon understand the why, what, and how of semantic maps and can begin to develop individual maps. We suggest that the teacher begin by providing the core question or concept. Students can then compare and contrast their individual productions in follow-up discussion. Of course, text assignments should also be given in which students identify the core concept on their own and then generate the structures that support and explain it.

**Text Frames.** Students can be shown how to construct maps and other types of graphic representations to reflect the text patterns used by authors to organize ideas. According to Jones, Pierce, and Hunter (1988), "A fundamental rule in constructing graphic representations is that the structure of the graphic should reflect the structure of the text it represents" (p. 21). For example, the map of the first Ohio settlements in Figure 9.1 reflects a comparison-contrast pattern. Notice how the strand ties make explicit what certain towns had in common with one another. Without the strand ties, however, the comparisons among the towns are implied.

Graphic representations are closely associated with *text frames.* Text frames are the key questions and categories of information that parallel text patterns used by authors (Armbruster and Anderson 1985). Skilled readers are aware of these key questions and categories and study text with the expectation that authors have organized content within texts patterns that are associated with a content area.

For example, a reading selection from an American history textbook on the Civil War may have been organized around a cause-effect frame. Thus readers expect answers to such key questions as: What caused the Civil War to happen? How do the causes of the Civil War interrelate? How might the Civil War have been prevented, if events had been different? What were the immediate and long-term results of the Civil War? As Beuhl (1991) explains, a frame *frames* the most important events, propositions, relationships, arguments, or ideas in a piece of writing so that the "reader 'gets the point' and can make some sense out of it all" (p. 4).

Text frames provide models that can be used with students to show them how to represent text patterns and categories of information visually. One such frame is known as a *compare-contrast matrix* (Jones, Pierce, and Hunter 1988). The matrix frame is used to show similarities and differences between two or more things (people, places, events, ideas, etc.). Study the matrix frame in Figure 9.2, which was used by students in a biology class to outline likenesses and differences between algae and fungi.

In modeling the frame, the teacher showed students how they might organize textually important information about algae and fungi according to the attributes listed in the left-hand column of the matrix. As students gained experience with the use of compare-contrast frames in the biology class, the teacher encouraged them to construct their own matrices as they studied text assignments that reflected a comparison-contrast pattern.

A generic map format can be used to depict a problem-solution frame, as shown in Figure 9.3.

**Figure 9.2  A COMPARISON-CONTRAST CHART IN BIOLOGY**

|  | Fungi | Algae |
|---|---|---|
| Body Structure |  |  |
| Food Source |  |  |
| Method of Reproduction |  |  |
| Living Environment |  |  |

**Figure 9.3    PROBLEM WITH MORE THAN ONE SOLUTION**

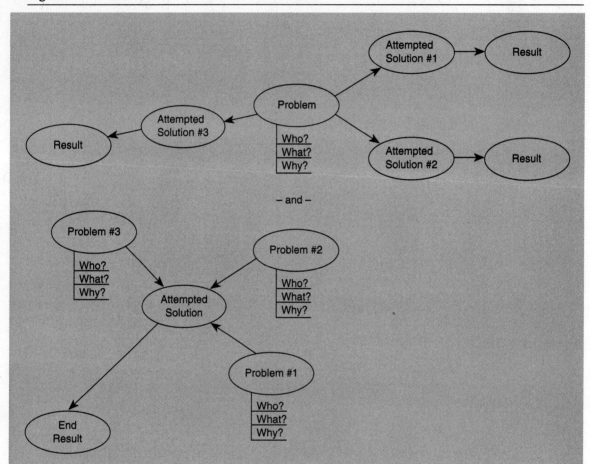

Cause-effect relationships may be shown visually on a generic map through the networks seen in Figure 9.4. Note that lines and arrows are used in the problem-solution and cause-effect semantic maps to show the direction of the relationships.

Along with the generic graphic structures, introduce students to the key questions associated with each of the frames. Beuhl (1991), for example, lists the types of questions associated with the comparison-contrast, problem-solution, and cause-effect frames just illustrated:

**Problem/Solution Frame**

1. What is the problem?

2. Who has the problem?

3. What is causing the problem?

**Figure 9.4     TEXT FRAMES ASSOCIATED WITH CAUSE-EFFECT TEXT PATTERNS**

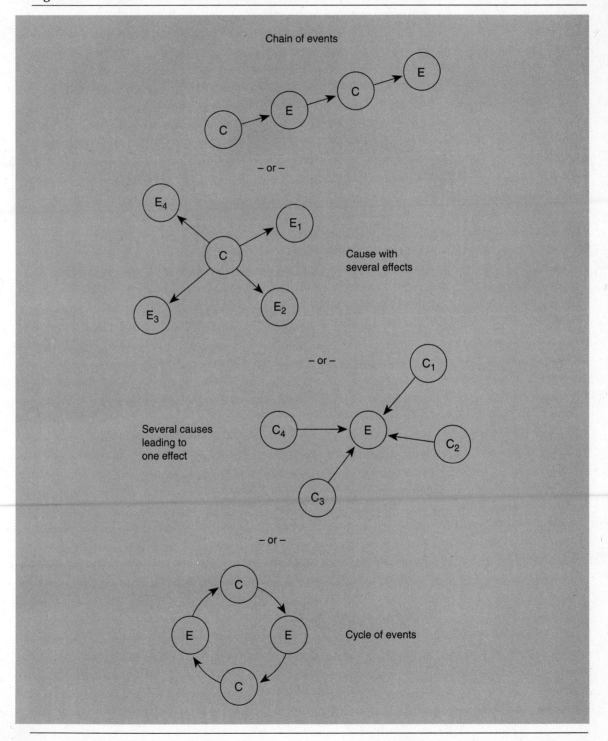

4. What are the effects of the problem?

5. Who is trying to solve the problem?

6. What solutions are attempted?

7. What are the results of these solutions?

8. Is the problem solved? Do any new problems develop because of the solutions?

### Cause/Effect Frame

1. What is it that happens?

2. What causes it to happen?

3. What are the important elements or factors that cause this effect?

4. How do these factors or elements interrelate to each other?

5. Will this result always happen from these causes? Why or why not?

6. How would the result change if the elements or factors are different?

### Compare/Contrast Frame

1. What are the items that are being compared and contrasted?

2. What are the categories of attributes that can be used to compare and contrast the items?

3. How are the items alike or similar?

4. How are the items not alike or different?

5. What are the most important qualities or attributes that make the items similar?

6. What are the most important qualities or attributes that make the items different?

7. In terms of the qualities that are most important, are the items more alike, or more different?

There are many benefits to learning how to use and construct graphic representations, not the least of which is that they make it easier for students to summarize large chunks of information. Why is summarizing a potentially powerful learner-directed strategy? Let's take a closer look.

## Learning to Summarize Information

Summarizing involves reducing a text to its gist—to its main points. To become adept at summary writing, students must be able to discern and analyze text structure. If they are insensitive to the organization of ideas and events in expository or narrative writing, students will find it difficult to distinguish important from less important information. Good summarizers, therefore, guard against including information that is not important to the text passage being condensed. Immature text learners, on the other hand, tend to *retell* rather than condense information, often including interesting but inessential tidbits from the passage in their summaries. Good summarizers write in their own words but are careful to maintain the author's point of view and stick closely to the sequence of ideas or events as presented in the reading selection. When important ideas are not explicitly stated in the material, good summary writers create their own topic sentences to reflect textually implicit main ideas.

Kintsch and van Dijk (1978) were among the first to formulate a set of basic rules for summarization based on analyses of how people summarize effectively. Others have modified and adapted these rules, but generally students must become cognizant of the following procedures:

1. *Include no unnecessary detail.* In preparing a summary, students must learn to delete trivial and repetitious information from a text passage.

2. *Collapse lists.* When a text passage includes examples, details, actions, or traits, students must learn how to compact these into broader categories of information. With frequent exposure to instructional activities such as graphic organizers, vocabulary categorization exercises and outlining strategies, students will soon become aware that similar items of information can be subsumed within more inclusive concepts. They must learn to summarize information by collapsing a list of details and thinking of a key word or phrase that names its concept. Study the examples that Hare and Borchardt (1984) gave: ". . . if you saw a list like eyes, ears, neck, arms, and legs, you could say 'body parts.' Or, if you saw a list like ice skating, skiing or sledding, you could say 'winter sports'" (p. 66).

3. *Use topic sentences.* Expository text sometimes contains explicit topic sentences which tell what a paragraph is about. However, if a paragraph doesn't have a topic sentence, students must learn to create their own for a summary. This is probably the most difficult task demand placed on maturing learners.

4. *Integrate information.* Summarizers must learn how to use key words, phrases, and explicit and invented topic sentences to compose a summary. The first three rules help students to do the leg work for summarizing. In other words, the rules *prepare* students for writing the summary. Yet when they actually put ideas into words on paper, they must integrate the information into a coherent piece of writing.

5. *Polish the summary.* Because writing often follows a composing process, students must learn to revise a *draft* of a summary into a more organized, natural-sounding piece of writing. While rethinking a summary, students will get a firmer grasp on the main points of the material and state them clearly.

**Using the GRP to Write a Summary.** Teachers can show students how to summarize information through the Guided Reading Procedure (GRP). The GRP has already been explained in Chapter 6. As you may recall, after students have read a text passage, they turn the books face down and try to remember everything that was important in the passage. Their recalls are recorded by the teacher on the chalkboard. Seize this opportune moment to show students how to delete trivial and repetitious information from the list of ideas on the board. As part of the procedure, the students are given a second chance to return to the passage, review it, and make sure that the list contains all of the information germane to the text.

When this step is completed, the teacher then guides students to organize the information in outline form using a graphic organizer format. Here is where students can be shown how to collapse individual pieces of information from a list into conceptual categories. These categories can be the bases for identifying or creating topic sentences. The students can then integrate the main points into a summary.

Hayes (1989) shows how to adapt the GRP for summarizing information. As part of his instructional framework, he modeled the development and writing of an effective summary by guiding students through a procedure he labeled *GRASP* (Guided Reading and Summarizing Procedure). After following the initial steps of the GRP, Hayes illustrates in Figure 9.5 the information that his students remembered based on their first recollections after reading an article on the Rosetta Stone and their additions and corrections after rereading.

The students then organized the information into the following categories: importance of the Rosetta Stone, its discovery, its description, its decipherment, and the result of having made the discovery. These categories, along with the subordinate information associated with each, became the basis for writing the summary. Hayes walked the students through the summary-writing process as a whole class. First he asked students to contribute sentences to the summary based on the outline of information that was organized on the chalkboard. Then he invited their suggestions for revising the summary into a coherent message. Figure 9.6 displays the completed summary, as revised by the class.

**Polishing a Summary.** As you can see from the summary in Figure 9.7, a good summary often reflects a process of writing *and* rewriting. Teaching students how to write a polished summary is often a neglected aspect of instruction. When students reduce large segments of text, the condensation often is stilted. It sounds unnatural. We are convinced that students will learn and understand the main points better and retain them longer when they attempt to create a more natural-sounding summary that communicates the selection's main ideas to an audience, for example, a reader such as the teacher and/or other students. Rewriting in a classroom situation is often preceded by *response* to a draft—by peers and the teacher. We deal in much more detail with responding and revising situations in a later section of this chapter. For now, however, let us suggest the following:

**Figure 9.5    DETAILS REMEMBERED FROM ROSETTA STONE ARTICLE**

| Students' first recollections | Additions and corrections |
|---|---|
| found by an officer in Napoleon's (Army) | engineering corps |
| 1799 | taken to British Museum, where it is today |
| key to language of Egypt | ancient |
| forgotten language of Egypt | Champollion published a pamphlet |
| found in mud near Rosetta | the pamphlet a tool scholars use to translate ancient Egyptian literature |
| black basalt | ancient language of Egypt had been a riddle for hundreds of years |
| 3' 9" tall | the stone half buried in mud |
| inscription in hieroglyphics and Greek | Demotic, the popular Egyptian language at the time |
|  | written with Greek letters |
| Jean Champollion deciphered the inscription | Champollion knew Coptic |
| compared Greek (words) with Egyptian words in same position | proper names |
| Coptic was the Egyptian language | Coptic was last stage of Egyptian language |
| decree to commemorate (birth) of an Egyptian king | crowning |
| 2' 4½" wide | carved by Egyptian priests |
| he knew Greek | Ptolemy V Epiphanes 203–181 B.C. |

- Compare a well-developed summary that the teacher has written with the summaries written by the students. Contrasting the teacher's version with the student productions leads to valuable process discussions such as the use of introductory and concluding statements, the value of connectives like *and* and *because* to show how ideas can be linked, and the need to paraphrase, that is, putting ideas into your own words to convey the author's main points.
- Present the class with three summaries: One is good in that it contains all the main points and flows smoothly. The second is OK: it contains most of the main points but is somewhat stilted in its writ-

**Figure 9.6    THE COMPLETED SUMMARY, AS REVISED**

The Rosetta stone provided the key for reading the ancient ~~language of Egypt. The~~

,which
~~ancient~~ Egyptian language‸had been a riddle for hundreds of years. (An officer in

was found in 1799
Napoleon's engineering corps,) ~~found~~ ⌐he Rosetta stone ~~half buried in the~~

the Egyptian city of ⌐ by ←
~~mud~~ near‸Rosetta ‸. The black basalt stone bore inscriptions in ancient Egyptian

in          in
hieroglyphics,‸Demotic, and‸Greek. The inscriptions were deciphered by Jean

Champollion, who with knowledge of Greek and Coptic (the last stage of the Egyptian

in the Greek text     in the Egyptian texts         had been
language) compared ~~Greek~~ words‸ with ~~Egyptian~~ words‸. The inscriptions ~~were~~ carved

by Egyptian priests to commemorate the crowning of Egyptian king Ptolemy Epiphanes,

203–181 B.C. In 1822 Champollion described the decipherment in a pamphlet which has

since been used as a tool for translating ancient Egyptian literature. The Rosetta stone

preserved
~~kept~~
is‸ in the British Museum.

---

ing. The third is poor in content and form. Let the class rate and discuss the three summaries.

- Team students in pairs or triads and let them read their summaries to one another. Student response groups are one of the most effective ways to create feedback for writing in progress.
- In lieu of response groups, use the whole class for responding. With prior permission from several students, discuss their summaries. What were the merits of each one and how could they be improved for content and form?

The real learning potential for summary writing lies in students using their own language to convey the author's main ideas.

## Learning to Make Notes

An effective study activity for acting upon and remembering material is to annotate what is read in the form of reading notes. Reading notes can be put on study cards (index cards), in a learning log, or in a thought book that is kept expressly for the purpose of compiling written reactions, reflections, and annotations on text readings.

Reading notes should avoid verbatim text reproductions. Instead, notes can be used to paraphrase, summarize, react critically, question, or respond personally to what is read. Whatever the form reading notes take, students need to become aware of the different types of notes that can be written and then be shown how to write them.

Eanet and Manzo (1976) underscore the importance of writing notes as a means of helping students learn what they read. They describe the different kinds of annotations that students can write. Several of the annotations are particularly appropriate for middle grade and secondary school students. For example, read the passage on "Wild Cargo: The Business of Smuggling Animals" in Box 9.2. Then study each of the annotations made by a high school student.

The *summary annotation,* as you might surmise, condenses the main ideas of a text selection into a concise statement as discussed in the previous section. Summary notes are characterized by their brevity, clarity, and conciseness. When a note summarizes expository material, it should clearly distinguish the important ideas in the author's presentation from supporting information and detail. When the summary note involves narrative material such as a story, it should include a synopsis containing the major story elements. Examine the example of a summary notation from a student's notecard in Figure 9.7.

---

**BOX 9.2    Wild Cargo: The Business of Smuggling Animals**

Unpleasantness for those trading illegally in wild animals and their products is escalating around the world. Within the past decade government after government has passed laws to restrict or prohibit the sale of wildlife seriously depleted by hunting and habitat destruction. With legal channels pinched, animal dealers have resorted to nefarious schemes to continue the flow.

Wildlife is big business. Exotic-bird collectors will pay $10,000 for a hyacinth macaw . . . in New York I tried on a pair of trendy western boots trimmed in lizard skin. The price? "Two hundred thirty five," the clerk said, with an archness suggesting that most of his customers didn't bother to ask. . . .

These items are being sold legally. But somewhere in the dim beginnings of their trail through commerce, they may have been acquired illegally. . . .

This fascination with wildlife within the affluent nations of the world adds to the disappearance of animals in the less developed countries. In between stand the illegal traders willing to circumvent the wildlife-protection laws to satisfy the demand and their own pocketbooks. . . .

Wildlife smuggling is costing the U.S. millions of dollars to control and is denying income to the treasury of any nation that would otherwise receive duty from legal imports. It has spread diseases that would have been detected in legal quarantine periods . . . an irreversible effect of illegal trade could be the extinction of animal species that are finding fewer and fewer places to hide. (pp. 290–294)

**Figure 9.7    SUMMARY NOTE**

Summary Notes

The illegal trading of wildlife and their products is a profitable business in affluent countries around the world. The continuation of such trade threatens both developed and undeveloped nations economically and ecologically. More recent laws are making this illegal trade much more difficult to carry out.

The *thesis annotation* answers the question, "What is the main point the author has tried to get across to the reader?" The thesis annotation has a telegramlike character. It is incisively stated yet unambiguous in its identification of the author's main proposition. The thesis note for a story identifies its theme. Study the example in Figure 9.8.

The *critical annotation* captures the reader's reaction or response to the author's thesis. It answers the question, "So what?" In writing critical notes, the reader should first state the author's thesis, then state his or her position in relation to the thesis, and finally defend or expand upon the position taken. See Figure 9.9.

The *question annotation* raises a significant issue in the form of a question. The question is the result of what the reader thinks is the most germane or significant aspect of what he or she has read. See Figure 9.10.

**An Instructional Framework for Reading Notes.** Showing students how to write different types of notes begins with assessment, leads to awareness and knowledge building, modeling and practice, and culminates with application. First, assign a text selection and ask students to write whatever reading notes they wish on a separate sheet of paper. Then have the class analyze the assessment, share student notes, and discuss difficulties in taking notes. Use the assessment analysis to orient students to the importance of reading notes as a strategy for learning and retention.

**Figure 9.8    THESIS NOTE**

Thesis Note

Illegal wild animal trade is a very profitable business. Illegal wildlife trade is a threat to man and his environment. More laws throughout the world can restrict this activity.

**Figure 9.9    CRITICAL NOTE**

Critical Note

The trading of wildlife for high profits is something all men will pay for ultimately. Countries are being cheated out of needed revenues. But more importantly, the future of species of animals is being threatened. The money-minded traders also give little thought to the spread of disease that could be avoided by legal quarantines. All nations need to cooperate to pass stricter laws to control or prohibit the trade of life and survival for temporary luxury.

**Figure 9.10    QUESTION NOTE**

Question Note

(Should illegal wildlife trade be allowed to continue or, at least, be ignored, after unsuccessful attempts to stop it?)

The author says that it is becoming more unpleasant for illegal traders of wildlife and their products due to more laws instituted by governments around the world. He also cites serious economic and ecological reasons not to give up the fight.

Teaching students how to actually write different types of notes from their readings begins first with awareness and knowledge building. They should be able to recognize and define the various kinds of reading notes that can be written. Eanet and Manzo recommend the following strategy: first, assign a short selection to be read in class, then write a certain type of annotation on the board. Ask students how what they read on the board relates to the passage that was just assigned. Through discussion, formulate the definition and concept for the annotation under discussion.

As part of a growing understanding of the different annotations, students should be able to tell a well-written note from a poorly written one. Have the class read a short passage, followed by several examples of a certain type of annotation. One is well written; the others are flawed in some way. For example, a discussion of critical annotations may include one illustration of a good critical note, one that lacks the annotator's position, another that fails to defend or develop the position taken.

Modeling and practice should follow naturally from awareness and knowledge building. The teacher should walk students through the process of writing different types of notes by sharing his or her thought processes. Show how a note is written and revised to satisfaction through think-aloud procedures. Then have students practice writing notes individually and in peer groups of two or three. Eanet and Manzo suggested that peer-group interaction is nonthreatening and leads to productions that can be duplicated or put on the board, compared, and evaluated by the class with teacher direction.

To facilitate application to real classroom reading tasks, we suggest that students write regularly in a thought book or compile study cards.

As part of taking reading notes on a regular basis, students should keep a learning log to share with others. The students should be directed to write certain types of notes in the learning log depending on the teacher's objectives. For example, they may be directed to summarize, react critically, pose questions based on what they have read, or state the author's thesis.

It may be wise to save note writing in the learning log for the latter half of a class period. The next class period then begins with a review or a sharing of notes, followed by discussion and clarification of the text material based on the annotations.

Notes written on index cards are an alternative to the learning log. Require students to compile study cards based on text readings. One tactic is to write question annotations formulated during previewing on one side of the cards and responses to the questions on the other side. For example, ask students to convert the major subheadings of a text selection to questions, writing one question per card. The responses probably will lend themselves to summary or critical annotations depending on the questions posed. Later, students can use the study cards to prepare for a test. As part of test preparation a student can read the question, recite out loud the response, and then review the written annotation that was previously compiled.

Lester (1984) offers the following tips for recording note card information:

1. *Use ink.* Penciled notes blur easily with repeated shuffling of the cards.

2. *Use index cards.* Index cards for taking notes are more durable and can be rearranged and organized more easily than large sheets of paper.

3. *Jot down only one item per card.* Don't overload a card with more than one type of annotation or one piece of information.

4. *Write on one side of card.* Material on the back of a card may be overlooked when studying.

**Recording Listening Notes.** Walter Pauk's response to the question, "Why take notes?" is profound in its simplicity—because we forget (Pauk 1978). Over 50 percent of the material read or heard in class is forgotten in a matter of a few minutes. A system for making listening notes triggers recall and overcomes forgetting.

A popular note-taking procedure, suggested by Palmatier (1973), involves the following steps: First, have students use only one side of an

8¹/₂-by-11-inch sheet of looseleaf paper with a legal-width margin (if necessary, the student should add a margin line three inches from the left side of
the paper). Second, the students take lecture notes to the right of the margin.
Although no specific format for recording notes is required, students should
develop a format which uses subordination and space to illustrate the organization of the material; for example, they can indent to show continuation
of ideas or enumerate to show series of details. Third, have the students put
labels in the left-hand margin that correspond with units of information
recorded in the notes. The labels help to organize the welter of information
in the right-hand column and give students the chance to fill in gaps in the
notes. The labeling process should be completed as quickly as possible following the original taking of notes. (See Figure 9.11.)

Once notes are taken and the labeling task is completed, students can
use their notes to study for exams. For example, in preparing for a test, the
student can spread out the note pages for review. One excellent strategy is
to show students how to spread the pages, in order, in such a way that the
lecture notes are hidden by succeeding pages and only the left-margin
labels show. The labels can then be used as question stems to recall information—for example, "What do I need to know about *(label)*?" Accuracy of
recall, of course, can be checked by referring to the original notes, which
were concealed by overlapping the pages.

## Learning to Conduct and Report Research

Library research projects are probably the most commonly used activity in
content area classrooms involving nontextbook reading. Such projects
would seem to be a timely vehicle for students to develop information-gath-
ering and reporting strategies. Yet many students fail to grasp what it
means to be a researcher in the true sense of the word. They must learn useful strategies for each stage of the research process so that they are equipped
to transfer their abilities to new research situations.

Research strategies are not learned in a few short lessons. They are
acquired through the guidance of teachers as students actively engage in the
process of searching out information to share with others.

Rycik (1992) conducted an in-depth study of seventh-grade library
research projects which showed that such projects do, in fact, provide many
opportunities for teachers to demonstrate strategies through planned
lessons and through scores of responses to individual students' questions
and concerns. The outline below shows some of the reading and writing
tasks that were observed during the projects:

**Prereading**
- Preliminary exploring of topic and resources
- Choosing a topic
- Writing research questions
- Seeking background knowledge

**Figure 9.11    AN EXAMPLE OF A NOTETAKING PROCEDURE THAT USES LABELS AND NOTES**

| Labels | Notes |
|---|---|
| Neurons are detectors which signal messages to brain | Our eyes, ears, nose, tongue, and skin pick up messages and send them to the brain<br>1. The lens of the eye focuses light on the retina and neurons change it into a message that's carried by the optic nerves<br>2. The tongue and nose work together to detect chemicals and send a message to the brain<br>- tongue has areas for sweet, salty, sour<br>- each area has neurons<br>3. The skin has neurons that detect pain, pressure, touch |

### Locating Source Materials

- Using the card catalogue
- Using the periodical index
- Requesting materials from the school library
- Searching other libraries
- Making photocopies of materials
- Using preselected books

### Extracting Information from Source Materials

- Using indexes in source materials
- Judging the usefulness of sources
- Skimming and searching texts
- Highlighting photocopied material
- Using the dictionary to clarify meaning

### Recording Information

- Preparing source cards
- Putting questions/headings on notecards
- Writing notes
- Judging when sufficient information has been collected

### Prewriting: Organizing Information

- Sorting notecards
- Making outlines

### Writing Drafts

- Planning text
- Generating text
- Counting words

### Making Final Drafts

The research process opens the shelf for the reading of many different kinds of materials. Developing inquiry-centered projects helps students to understand and synthesize what they're learning.

Inquiry-centered projects must be carefully planned, giving just the right amount of direction to allow students to explore and discover ideas on their own. The research process isn't a do-your-own-thing proposition, for budding researchers need structure. Many a project has been wrecked on the shoals of nondirection. The trick is to strike a balance between teacher guidance and student self-reliance. A research project must have just enough structure to give students (1) a problem focus, (2) physical and intellectual freedom, (3) an environment in which they can obtain data, and (4) feedback situations to report the results of their research.

Box 9.3 on pp. 290–291 outlines various aspects of the procedures for guiding an inquiry-centered project.

**Finding and Investigating Problems.** Ideally, an inquiry arises out of the questions students raise about the subject under study. A puzzling situation may arouse curiosity and interest. Or perhaps the teacher will provoke puzzlement through a discussion of differences in opinion, a reaction to inconsistencies in information in content material, or a response to an emotional issue. We recommend using such questions as the following to initiate research:

How is _____ different from _____? How are they alike?

What has changed from the way it used to be?

What can we learn from the past?

What caused _____ to happen? Why did it turn out that way?

What will happen next? How will it end?

How can we find out?

Which way is best?

What does this mean to you? How does this idea apply to other situations?

As a result of questioning, students should become aware of their present level of knowledge and the gaps that exist in what they know. They can use the questioning session to identify a problem. You might ask, "What do you want to find out?" During the planning stage of a research project the emphasis should be on further analysis of each individual or group problem, breaking it down into a sequence of manageable parts and activities. The teacher facilitates by helping students to clarify problems. As students progress in their research, data collection and interpretation become integral stages of the inquiry. Students will need the physical and intellectual freedom to investigate their problems. They will also need an environment—a library or media center—where they will have access to a variety of information sources including printed material (books and encyclopedias; magazines, catalogues, directories; newspapers), nonprinted materials (audiotapes; records; films, filmstrips, slides; videotapes, television programs), and human resources (interviews; letters; on-site visitations).

The teacher's role during data collection and interpretation is that of a resource. Your questions will help the student interpret data or perhaps raise new questions, reorganize ideas, or modify plans. "How are you doing?" "How can I help?" "Are you finding it difficult to obtain materials?" "Which ideas are giving you trouble?"

**Using the Library and Reference Materials.** In addition to textbooks, three sources of information are basic learning and instruction in content area subjects. They are (1) reference sources which contain specialized information, (2) books and pamphlets pertinent to the content area, and (3) periodical sources of information dealing with a specific subject. Gaining access to these sources means that students need a working knowledge of *where to go and how to use information* not usually housed in their classrooms.

For this reason we endorse in principle the need for systematic, organized instruction in the use of the library.

---

### BOX 9.3    Procedures for Guiding Research Projects

I. Raise Questions, Identify Interests, Organize Information
  A. Discuss interest areas related to the unit of study
  B. Engage in goal setting
    1. arouse curiosities
    2. create awareness of present level of knowledge
  C. Pose questions relating to each area and/or subarea
    1. "what do you want to find out?"
    2. "what do you want to know about _____?"
    3. record the questions or topics
    4. "what do you already know about _____?"
  D. Organize information; have students make predictions about likely answers to gaps in knowledge
    1. accept all predictions as possible answers
    2. encourage thoughtful speculations in a nonthreatening way
II. Select Materials
  A. Use visual materials
    1. books and encyclopedias
    2. magazines, catalogues, directories
    3. newspapers and comics
    4. indexes, atlases, almanacs, dictionaries, readers' guides, card catalogue
    5. films, filmstrips, slides
    6. videotapes, television programs
  B. Use nonvisual materials
    1. audiotapes
    2. records
    3. radio programs
    4. field trips
  C. Use human resources
    1. interviews
    2. letters
    3. on-site visitations
  D. Encourage self-selection of materials
    1. "what can I understand?"
    2. "what gives me the best answers?"

---

Knowing what the sources of information are and how to use those sources become the main goals for instruction. To put these goals into practice, teachers should provide preliminary or review activities such as the following:

1. *Introduce students to the ways libraries work.* Plan an informal tour to take a class to the library. Locate the loan desk, reference desk, and magazines; point out posted regulations and physical arrangements. The students will get a look at others using the library; later have a discussion about

III. Guide the Information Search
- A. Encourage active research through
  1. reading
  2. listening
  3. observing
  4. talking
  5. writing
- B. Facilitate with questions
  1. "how are you doing?"
  2. "can I help you?"
  3. "do you have all the materials you need?"
  4. "can I help you with ideas you don't understand?"

IV. Have Students Keep Records
- A. Keep a learning log that includes plans, procedures, notes, rough drafts, etc.
- B. Keep book-record cards
- C. Keep a record of conferences with the teacher

V. Consider Different Forms of Writing
- A. Initiate a discussion of sharing techniques
- B. Encourage a variety of writing forms:
  1. an essay or paper
  2. a lecture to a specific audience
  3. a case study
  4. story, adventure, science fiction, etc.
  5. dialogue, conversation, interview
  6. dramatization through scripts
  7. commentary or editorial
  8. thumbnail sketch

VI. Guide the Writing Process
- A. Help students organize information
- B. Guide first-draft writing
- C. Encourage responding, revising, and rewriting
- D. "Publish" finished products
  1. individual presentations
  2. classroom arrangement
  3. allow for class interaction

their observations. Also, invite a librarian to speak to the class (in the library if possible) about his or her job responsibilities. Encourage students to ask the librarian about procedures. Have them guess what kinds of questions are usually asked of librarians.

2. *Provide brief "search encounters" in the library.* Ask students to think of questions they personally want answered about the subject they are studying. Subsequent introductory instruction on library use can then be

built naturally around helping students answer their own questions. Act as a resource person while the students learn to use reference books, periodical indexes, and card catalogs. After two or three individual, personal "search encounters," students should be ready to use the library for larger inquiry tests.

3. *Reinforce library strategies that are truly basic.* Once students acquire the basic concepts behind the library as a learning resource, it's time for some direct advice on how to become library-wise. The basic approach to "intelligent library use at all levels" centers on how to locate (1) general information through general reference books, (2) specific information through periodical indexes, and (3) ideas and information in greater depth through books from card catalogues (Devine 1981). Locate and explain encyclopedias, dictionaries, almanacs, periodical indexes, and the card catalog.

Strategy instruction in using the library and reference materials pays off. This becomes apparent when you observe students in the library who have had this instruction. Instead of simply going to the same shelves continually, they are now able to locate sources of information for specific purposes.

## WHAT ABOUT LEARNING A SYSTEM OF STUDY?

When students know how, why, and when to study, they will use and orchestrate strategies into a system of learning. Students will approach a text assignment differently, choosing the study strategies best suited to themselves and the subject they're studying (Moore 1981).

In the past, systems for study have been readily taught to students with the expectation that once a formula is learned it will be applied in independent learning situations. Numerous study systems, often identified by acronyms, have presented a complex set of steps for students to follow. Perhaps the most widely recommended study system is SQ3R (Robinson 1961).

SQ3R stands for:

*Survey.* The reader previews the material to develop a general outline for organizing information.

*Question.* The reader raises questions with the expectation of finding answers in the material to be studied.

*Read.* The reader next attempts to answer the questions formulated in the previous step.

*Recite.* The reader then deliberately attempts to answer aloud or in writing the questions formulated in the second step.

*Review.* The reader finally reviews the material by rereading portions of the assignment in order to verify the answers given during the previous step.

There is little doubt that SQ3R and other study systems incorporate many of the accepted principles of reading and learning with texts, including the activation of prior knowledge, the setting of purposes, and the construction of meaning. Why is it, then, that learners who are exposed to SQ3R find it difficult to use on their own? Often, they are easily frustrated, if not overwhelmed, by strict adherence to the steps in the procedure.

We suspect that a study system such as SQ3R is not used by most students because it is taught as a formula. Memorize the steps. Practice the procedures several times. Now use it for life. In other words, students are often taught what to do without enough explicit instruction to lead to self-control. The key to any system's effectiveness may very well lie in how students learn to control it through selective and flexible use. A system for studying evolves gradually within each learner. Maturing readers need to make the transition from teacher-centered guidance to self-control and regulation of their own reading and studying.

In the final analysis students need to learn how to become text-smart. Being text-smart is comparable to being street-smart. It's knowing how to stay out of trouble; it's knowing when to and when not to take shortcuts; it's knowing how to survive the everyday cognitive demands that are a natural part of classroom life.

Becoming a student requires time and patience. A personal system of studying gradually evolves in each learner. Studying, after all, is a process that is learned inductively through trial and error and the repeated use of different strategies in different learning situations. And this is where teachers have a role to play. Through the instructional support you provide, students learn that some learning strategies work better for them than others in different learning situations. As they experience what it means to study in a content area, they gain confidence with and competence in the use of learning strategies.

# LOOKING BACK, LOOKING FORWARD

Teaching students how to study texts involves showing them how to become independent learners. To be successful at studying, students must develop knowledge and awareness of the use of learning strategies. An explicit instructional framework for teaching learning strategies includes the following components: assessment, strategy awareness, modeling and demonstration, and application. In this chapter, we used the instructional framework to illustrate how you can teach students to use learner-directed strategies that involve constructing graphic representations of textually important information, writing summaries, making text annotations, and conducting research.

Graphic representations help students to outline important information that is reflected in the text patterns that authors use to organize ideas. The construction of graphic representations allows students to map the relationships that exist among ideas presented in text. This strategy is a valuable tool for comprehending and retaining information. Another study tool involves summarizing information. When students engage in summarizing what they have read, it often results in greater understanding and retention of main ideas in text. Students need to become aware of summarization rules and receive instruction in how to use these rules to write and polish a summary. Making and taking notes is another useful strategy for studying text. Making reading notes through various kinds of annotations allows students to reflect and react to important ideas in text. Learning how to learn also means learning how to conduct research and investigate problems associated with content area studies. To this end, we explored how to help students raise questions for research and engage in an inquiry process.

In the next chapter, our focus is on the uses of literature to teach concepts in content areas. Literature is an alternative to textbook study. We argue that literature should be used interchangeably with content area textbooks to give students an intense involvement with subject matter. We explore not only the rationale for literature across the curriculum, but also the wide array of text possibilities, the role that critical perspectives play in learning with literature, and the use of thematic units to weave literature into content area studies.

## SUGGESTED READINGS

Anderson, T. H., & Armbruster, B. B. (1984). Studying. In Pearson, P. D. (ed.). *Handbook of reading research.* New York: Longman.

Armbruster, B. B., & Anderson, R. C. (1981). Research synthesis on study skills. *Educational Leadership. 19,* 154–156.

Hoffman, S. (1983). Using student journals to teach study skills. *Journal of Reading. 26,* 344–347.

Heimlich, J. E., & Pittleman, S. D. (1986). *Semantic mapping: Classroom applications.* Newark, DE: International Reading Association.

Jones, B. F., Palincsar, A. S., Ogle, D. S., & Carr, E. G. (1987). *Strategic teaching and learning: Cognitive instruction in content areas.* Alexandria, VA: Association of Supervision and Curriculum Development.

McAndrew, D. A. (1983). Underlining and notetaking: Some suggestions from research. *Journal of Reading. 27,* 103–108.

Peresich, M. L., Meadows, J. D., & Sinatra, R. (1990). Content area cognitive mapping for reading and writing proficiency. *Journal of Reading. 34,* 424–432.

Simpson, M. L. (1984). The status of study strategy instruction: Implications for classroom teachers. *Journal of Reading. 28,* 136–142.

Sinatra, R., Stahl-Gemake, J., & Morgan, N.W. (1986). Using semantic mapping after reading to organize and write original discourse. *Journal of Reading. 30,* 4–13.

Winograd, P. (1984). Strategic difficulties in summarizing text. *Reading Research Quarterly. 19,* 404–425.

# 10

# Learning with Literature

Literature is no one's private ground, literature is common ground; let us trespass freely and fearlessly and find our own way for ourselves.

—*Virginia Woolf*

## ORGANIZING PRINCIPLE

Literature isn't the sole province of the English teacher. Nor is it the private ground of a select few—the *literati*—of a culture. Literature is for anyone who delights in a story and searches for meaning in the human condition. In schools, literature belongs to all teachers who embrace the common-ground belief that imaginative texts have the potential to capture students' interest and extend their knowledge of people, places, processes, events, and ideas.

Yet most content area teachers stick close to familiar ground—the text-book. Textbooks, however, cannot treat subject matter with the breadth and depth necessary to fully develop ideas and concepts. Textbooks, particularly the way they are written today, are "dumbed down" to such an extent that they are more apt to mention ideas and concepts than to provide a rich basis for understanding the content being presented. As a result, textbooks are likely to serve as a compendium of facts, taking a subject and reducing it to its minimum essentials. The poor quality of textbooks often restricts their use in content area classrooms. More teachers and students than we would like to admit find that textbooks are inconsequential to learning in content areas classrooms. Some students are likely to avoid the use of textbooks altogether while most probably read only to answer questions in order to satisfy the requirements of a homework assignment. Some teachers, no doubt, circumvent the use of textbooks, giving up on reading a vehicle for learning, in favor of lecture notes and various forms of instructional media. What is the alternative? More and more teachers are turning to the use of literature in tandem with textbooks to help students learn subject matter. Why literature? The promise of literature is that it has the potential to provide students with intense involvement in a subject and the power to develop in-depth understandings in ways that textbooks aren't designed to do.

The use of literature across the curriculum extends and enriches information provided in textbooks. Literature is a powerful means of learning because it has the potential to capture students' curiosity, interest, and imagination in people, places, events, and ideas. When readers are intensely involved in a subject through literature, the literary event itself serves to generate background knowledge and vicarious experience, that will make textbook concepts easier to grasp and understand. One of the most compelling reasons to use literature is as a schema builder for subjects under study in the curriculum.

For many teachers, putting literature to good use in their classrooms means breaking new ground. Virginia Woolf's words apply to adventuresome teachers as well as adventuresome readers: ". . . let us trespass freely and fearlessly and find our own way for ourselves." The organizing principle of this chapter underscores the value of literature across the curriculum: *When teachers combine the use of textbooks with literature, they extend and enrich the curriculum.*

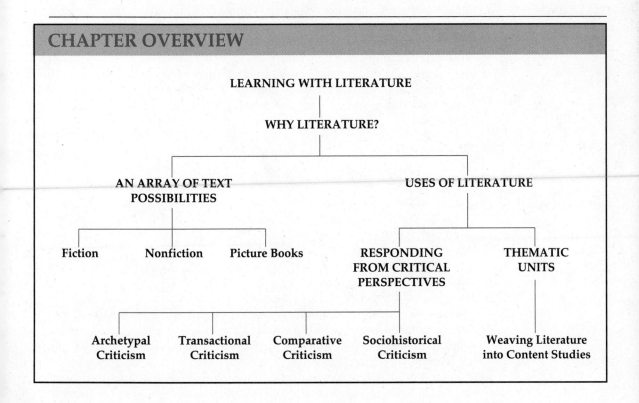

## CHAPTER OVERVIEW

**LEARNING WITH LITERATURE**

**WHY LITERATURE?**

**AN ARRAY OF TEXT POSSIBILITIES**                    **USES OF LITERATURE**

Fiction        Nonfiction        Picture Books        **RESPONDING FROM CRITICAL PERSPECTIVES**        **THEMATIC UNITS**

Archetypal Criticism        Transactional Criticism        Comparative Criticism        Sociohistorical Criticism        Weaving Literature into Content Studies

## FRAME OF MIND

1. Why use literature to study academic content?

2. How does reading strengthen the reading process?

3. What kinds of literature can content area teachers use in their classrooms?

4. How can content teachers put literature to use in their classrooms?

5. How can literature be woven into the fabric of content area study?

Textbooks, by their very nature, are often bland and lifeless. They aren't designed to entertain or to tell a story, but rather to inform. For some students, the very size, appearance, and writing style of a textbook make it a formidable adversary, not a partner, in the learning process. Because they do serve to inform, textbooks play an important role in schools. A textbook synthesizes a body of knowledge and functions as a compendium of facts, generalizations, and principles that defines and gives shape to an academic discipline.

One way of thinking about a textbook is that it takes a subject and distills it to its minimum essentials. In doing so, a textbook runs the risk of taking world-shaking events, monumental discoveries, profound insights, intriguing and far-away places, colorful and influential people, and life's mysteries and processes and compressing them into a series of matter-of-fact statements.

Perhaps this is why many learners don't view a textbook as a significant event in their academic lives. Anyone who has been in schools for a period of time will tell you that students generally engage in textbook study to take tests and then proceed to forget some, if not all, of the information they have studied as soon as the test is over. Yet these same learners can tell you with vivid detail and description what their favorite book, movie, or television characters did and said. This is the case, in part, because that which they remember revolves around a story.

A good narrative—a story—is imbued with all of the elements that make life interesting and memorable. A story has an importance much deeper and greater than most people might expect. Stories are part of the human psyche and are as old as humankind itself. A well-told narrative illuminates the human condition and shapes a reader's insights. No wonder Harold Rosen (1986) describes narrative as a primary and irreducible form of human comprehension.

Literature, rich in narrative and informational content, provides a vehicle by which learners may interact with people, places, and ideas. Learning with literature involves exposure to many different genres, all of which are potential sources of information for the active learner. While textbooks contain the minimum essentials, literature is the magnifying glass that enlarges and enhances the reader's personal interaction with a subject. When teachers use textbooks and literature in tandem, they help learners to think deeply and broadly about content.

Our definition of literature includes any kind of imaginative text whose content informs and illuminates the human experience. Literature, then, is the imaginative shaping of life and thought into the forms and structures of language (Huck, Hepler, and Hickman 1987). The content of literature across the curriculum serves a dual purpose: to educate and to entertain.

The literature of children and young adults relates to their personal needs and interests. It is written from the *viewpoint* of children and adolescents. Editors delineate trade books as children's or young adults' based on criteria that include the type of book (i.e., picture book, concept book, novel, etc.), the age of the protagonist(s), and the perceived interest level of the story. Literature selection for different age groups is often arbitrary and based on subjective criteria. But one thing is for sure: People of all ages tend to be attracted to books that speak to them in some kind of personal way.

## WHY USE LITERATURE ACROSS THE CURRICULUM?

There are several compelling reasons to use a combination of textbook and literature in content area classrooms. Trade books are filled with good stories that are well written and documented with a particular audience in mind. The authors of these books are conscious not only of relaying information, but also of telling a good tale—and that makes all the difference between a piece of literature and a textbook chapter on the same topic. The combination of storytelling and informing is an ancient concept that can be traced to the beginnings of the oral tradition, when storytellers were the newscasters, entertainers, and teachers who kept society intact and growing. The ancient storyteller knew that "if lore can be encoded into stories, it can be made more memorable than by any other technique" (Egan 1989, p. 282). A student can learn the dates and the names of important battles for a test covering World War II, but it takes reading books such as Aranka Siegal's *Upon the Head of the Goat: A Childhood in Hungary, 1939–1944* (1983) to begin to understand the real stories of that time period.

No wonder Brown and Abel (1982) propose revitalizing American history through literature. They recommend the use of biography, historical fiction, and fiction with applicability to historical content. Biographies, for example, present insights into a particular period of time and often spotlight conflicts the subject of the biography had to deal with and overcome. Historical fiction, likewise, deals with conflicts which characters must resolve in a particular period. Actual historical figures can give authenticity to a piece of historical fiction; consider, for example, Michener's *Chesapeake* and *Centennial* for a high school American history class.

Historical stories provide a fine vehicle for gathering a wide range of knowledge. As a result, readers acquire a *framework for remembering and understanding* historical content. The same holds for science content as well as content from other subject areas. As Dole and Johnson (1981) indicate, popular science books—either fact or fiction—can provide background knowledge for science concepts covered in class and can help students relate these concepts to their everyday lives.

Stories go beyond facts to get to the heart of a matter. They consider the human side of things by focusing on people and how they react to an infinite number of ideas and experiences in this world. Stories personalize ideas for readers by allowing the audience to experience a situation vicariously; that is to say, to share the thoughts of another person. People of all ages encounter aspects of human dilemmas in literature in ways that are not always possible between the pages of a textbook. Readers who are invited to participate in a tale of a chimney sweep of the nineteenth century are likely to find themselves caught in the act of experiencing the information, instead of merely memorizing it for a test.

This is not to say that textbooks are somehow inherently useless, but rather that textbooks are not the be-all and end-all of learning. Students need diversity in the material they read so they can compare information and make informed judgments. While textbooks provide students with a broad base of information, they lack the ability to convey the information that lies below the tip of the iceberg. Often, topics are given only minor exposure so that a great deal of information is left out—information that is crucial to real learning. Levstik (1990), for example, describes young learners who were willing to delve into historical novels and other literature in order to find answers to the questions they raised after reading their textbooks. These students expressed their interest in historical topics in terms of "needing to know" about a topic, of wanting to learn "the truth," or "what really happened." The logical alternative for them to find answers to their questions and concerns was a good book.

When students are given opportunities to interact with quality literature, a number of things happen. Perhaps the most important is that they have a better chance of becoming lifelong learners. Textbooks alone cannot meet the need to motivate students to continue their learning, particularly in the case of reluctant or at-risk readers who often are frustrated and defeated by textbooks in the first place. The difficulties inherent in comprehending unfamiliar, difficult material in content textbooks hinder many maturing readers to the point that they quit trying altogether. Students need to be able to read trade books that capture their imaginations and that appeal to their affective and cognitive needs.

The use of literature in the content area classroom provides a variety of perspectives for students to examine a topic. By comparing expository and narrative texts on a related subject, students learn to read more critically. In other words, *reading literature strengthens the reading process.* Reading about a topic can dramatically improve comprehension of related readings on the same topic. Crafton (1983) found that this was indeed the case when high school students read two different texts on the same subject. Not only did comprehension of the second text improve, but students read more actively. Thus, the act of reading in itself can be an important strategy for generating prior knowledge and building a frame of reference. Reading experiences allow readers to construct background knowledge which can be used to comprehend other kinds of related texts.

There is a vast array of literature to speak to the needs of every student in every academic discipline. Box 10.1 provides a list of references to help both elementary and secondary teachers in selecting good books for their classrooms.

## AN ARRAY OF TEXT POSSIBILITIES

When students are given opportunities to learn with literature, they are in a position to explore and interact with many kinds of books, both fictional and nonfictional. Let's explore some of the text possibilities for content area learning.

### Fiction in the Content Area Classroom

Fiction entices readers to interact with texts from a number of perspectives that are impossible to achieve in nonfiction alone. Fantasy, traditional (e.g., folktales and myths), historical, and realistic fiction, for example, help readers to step outside of their actual worlds for a while to consider a subject from a different point of view. And by doing so, they learn something about what it means to be a human being on this planet of ours.

Ray Bradbury (1989), an acclaimed contemporary author, likens the ability to fantasize to the ability to survive. While fantasy seems an unlikely addition to the required reading list in a content area classroom, consider the possibilities for a moment. Robert C. O'Brien's *Z for Zachariah* (1974), Figure 10.1 on p. 303, and Louise Lawrence's *Children of the Dust* (1985) contemplate the aftermath of a nuclear holocaust and the fate of the people who are left alive. Can students really know enough about nuclear issues without considering the crises raised in these books? Probably not. The facts concerning the effects of nuclear war are too large, and too disconnected from

## BOX 10.1    A Book Selection Guide for Children's and Young Adults' Literature

*Adventuring with Books: A Booklist for Pre-K–Grade 6,* ed. Mary Lou White. National Council of Teachers of English, 1981.

*ALAN Review.* Assembly on Literature for Adolescents, National Council of Teachers of English. Published three times per year.

*Appraisal: Science Books for Young People.* Children's Science Book Review Committee. Published three times per year.

*The Best Science Books for Children: A Selected and Annotated List of Science Books for Children Ages Five through Twelve,* compiled by Bonnie Baron. Association for Childhood Educational International, 1977.

*The Bookfinder: A Guide to Children's Literature About the Needs and Problems of Youth Aged 2–15,* ed. Sharon Dreyer. American Guidance Service, 1977.

*Booklist.* American Library Association. Published 22 times per year.

*Books for You: A Reading List for Senior High School Students.* National Council of Teachers of English. Available editions from 1971, 1976, 1982, and 1985.

*Bulletin of the Center for Children's Books.* The University of Chicago, Graduate Library School, University of Chicago Press. Published each month except August.

*Children's Books: Awards and Prizes,* compiled and edited by the Children's Book Council, 1985.

*Children's Books of International Interest,* ed. Barbara Elleman. 3rd ed. American Library Association, 1984.

*Children's Literature Association Quarterly.* Children's Literature Association. Published four times per year.

*Children's Literature in Education: An International Quarterly.* Agathon Press. Published four times per year.

*English Journal.* National Council of Teachers of English. Published eight times per year.

*Folklore: An Annotated Bibliography and Index to Single Editions,* compiled by Elsie Ziegler. Faxon, 1973.

*Girls are People Too! A Bibliography of Nontraditional Female Roles in Children's Books,* Joan E. Newman. Scarecrow, 1982.

*A Guide to Historical Reading: Non-fiction,* compiled by Fred R. Czarra. 11th rev. ed. Heldref, 1983.

*Health, Illness, and Disability: A Guide to Books for Children and Young Adults,* compiled by Pat Azarnoff. Bowker, 1983.

*The Horn Book Magazine.* Horn Book. Published six times per year.

*An Index to Children's Collective Biographies,* compiled by Judith Silverman. 3rd ed. Bowker, 1979.

*Interracial Books for Children Bulletin.* Council of Interracial Books for Children. Published eight times per year.

*Journal of Reading.* International Reading Association. Published eight times per year.

*Journal of Youth Services in Libraries.* Association of Library Service for Children and the Young Adult Services Division of the American Library Association. Published four times per year.

*Junior High School Library Catalog,* ed. Gary L. Bogart and Richard H. Isaacson. 4th ed. Wilson, 1980.

*Kirkus Reviews.* Kirkus Service. Published four times per year.

*Language Arts.* National Council of Teachers of English. Published nine times per year.

*New York Times Book Review.* New York Times Company. Published weekly.

*The Reading Teacher.* International Reading Association. Published eight times per year.

*School Library Journal.* R. R. Bowker Company.

*Senior High School Library Catalog,* eds. Ferne Hillegas and Juliette Yakkov. 13th ed. Wilson.

*Voice of Youth Advocates (VOYA).* Scarecrow Press. Published six times per year.

**Figure 10.1**    COVER ILLUSTRATION FOR *Z FOR ZACHARIAH*

our present reality to understand. It's only by focusing in on the possible experiences of a small group of people that readers begin to take in the depth of the ramifications of such an event.

Perhaps even more unlikely in a secondary content curriculum would be the inclusion of traditional or folk literature because of its associations with younger children; however, the protagonists of most folk tales are adolescents who have much to say to today's young adults. Robin McKinley's *Beauty* (1978) and Robert Nye's *Beowulf* (1968) continue to teach readers that strength of character is the crucial ingredient in changing the world. The human dimension of

**Figure 10.2    ILLUSTRATION, "TURTLE AND EARTH"**

**Source:** Reprinted with permission from Virginia Hamilton. *In the Beginning: Creation Stories from Around the World*, page 61. Fort Worth, TX: Harcourt Brace Jovanovich, 1988.

slavery is powerfully told in *The People Could Fly* (1985) by Virginia Hamilton, and true multicultural understanding is enhanced in her compilation of creation myths, *In the Beginning* (1988). Also, John Langstaff's *Climbing Jacob's Ladder* (1991), richly illustrated by Ashley Bryan, provides a musical compendium of African-American spirituals. This is an important offering toward young people's understanding of African-American history. A host of folk tale collections from around the world is also readily available to add insight to the study of history, social studies, and geography. Folk literature is the "cement" or "mirror" of society (Sutherland and Arbuthnot 1986, p. 163), and as such, gives readers an insider's view of a culture's beliefs and attitudes that is not found in the study of population density and manufacturing trends.

Poetry and drama also provide fascinating insight into a myriad of topics. From poetry about the rather mundane world of work in *Saturday's Children in Poems of Work* (1982) to that written about more lofty ideas as in *Poetry of the First World War* (1988), this genre provides students with personal glimpses into the human experience of everyday life and unanswerable questions. And while the reading of drama takes a special kind of skill, it is possible to handle it well so that students can read Fugard's *"Master Harold". . . and the Boys* (1984) to more fully and actively comprehend the racial tensions of South Africa. For teachers who feel uncomfortable with group plays, Murray's *Modern Monologues for Young People* (1982) provides a forum for single character sketches that cover a broad range of concepts.

Even cartoons have their place in the classroom, particularly when they are as well written as Art Spiegelman's *Maus: A Survivor's Tale* (1986). In this book, the story of the Nazi Holocaust is vividly told with the Nazis depicted as cats and the Jewish people as mice. Rather than detracting from the seriousness of the subject, the cartoon format lends force to the plight of the Nazis' victims.

The variety of fiction books runs the gamut of problem realism, animal realism, sports stories, mysteries, adventure stories, historical fiction, regional realism, and romance books. While the books in each of these categories run the risk of formulized plots, stereotypical characters, and overly sentimental themes, there remains a large body of quality literature available. Many of these are found on the annual *Young Adults' Choices List*, established by research sponsored by the International Reading Association and the International Reading Foundation. This list represents the diversity of young adult literature with titles dealing with social and political issues, such as drunk driving, women's rights, death, and war. From the 1990 Young Adults' Choices List, Walter Dean Myers' *Fallen Angels* (1988) is a stark portrayal of a young soldier's experiences in Vietnam, and *A Different Season* (1988) by David Klass focuses on the issues of women's equality in athletics.

The host of realistic fiction books available can do much to enhance and clarify the content curriculum. An author's ability to bring lifelike characters into sharp focus against a setting that smacks of real places makes for compelling reading.

## Nonfiction in the Content Area Classroom

Informational literature has blossomed in recent years to attain the level of art. It is evident in recent historical writing, for example, that really good historical writers do not invent the past, but instead give it artistic shape to connect with the reader (Meltzer 1989). No longer is nonfiction strictly objective in tone and literal in content; it often contains elements of fiction that flesh out the details and provide a component of entertainment in what Donelson and Nilsen (1989) call "the new journalism." This is the kind of reading that students can sink their teeth into and become involved in, while learning something about the content area at the same time.

The range of nonfiction books is enormous, spanning all types of topics and book designs. There are biographies and autobiographies about all sorts of people, including rock stars, writers (*Louisa May: The World and Works of Louisa May Alcott*, 1991, and *Sorrow's Kitchen: The Life and Folklore of Zora Neale Hurston*, 1990), scientists (*Carl Sagan: Superstar Scientist*, 1987), or classical music composers (*Mozart Tonight*, 1991). Many of these are found in series which focus on thematic concepts or in collections which offer shorter pieces with fewer details. There are books about careers, about drugs and alcohol (*On the Mend*, 1991), about AIDS (*Fighting Back*, 1991) and other health issues, and books about manners. There are even collections of essays written with young readers in mind, such as *Busted Lives: Dialogues with Kids in Jail* (1982) by Ann Zane Shanks, which offers first-person perspectives of prison life.

Perhaps the greatest difficulty faced by teachers when selecting nonfiction books for the classroom is in deciding which to use from the large number offered. An important thing to keep in mind is that variety is truly the spice of life where reading and learning are concerned. No one book will satisfy all readers. The point of using nonfiction trade books in the classroom is to expose students to more than one point of view and to do it in a way that is at once informational and readable. While a great number of nonfiction books tend to sound like textbooks packaged in pretty covers, teachers can choose quality books that adhere to the qualifications suggested in Table 10.1.

## Picture Books in the Content Area Classroom

Some of the most interesting, but often overlooked, books that can be used at all grade levels are picture books. Piero Ventura's *Venice: Birth of a City* (1987), for example, offers a wealth of information that can be gleaned both from the text and from the detailed and whimsical illustrations. This is a book for all ages, as are David Macaulay's scholarly, picture books. The practical question becomes, "What role do picture books play in secondary classrooms?"

Picture books aren't just for kids anymore. Advanced technology and high-quality artistry have led to the production of unique and aesthetically pleasing books that appeal to all age groups. These books cover a wide range of subject matter and can be used to enhance any content area. Not

**Figure 10.3**   **COVER ILLUSTRATION FROM *MOZART TONIGHT***

**Source:**  Reprinted with permission from Julie Downing. *Mozart Tonight*. NY: Bradury Press, 1991.

**Table 10.1**   QUALIFICATIONS FOR CHOOSING QUALITY NONFICTION BOOKS

**NONFICTION**

| Genre | Essential Qualities | Organization and Scope |
|---|---|---|
| Informational books | Gives information and facts; relates facts to concepts; stimulates curiosity; "starter," not "stopper" | From simplest to most complex; from known to unknown; from familiar to unfamiliar; from early developments to later; chronological; slight narrative for younger reader |
| Biography | Gives accurate, verifiable facts, and authentic picture of period; subject worthy of attention | Assumes no omniscience; shows individual, not stereotype; does not ignore negative qualities of subject; focuses not only on events, but on nature of person |

only do the books invite students to mull over the illustrations, but they also teach lessons through the integration of pictures and texts. Neal and Moore (1991) offer the following points underlying the principles of using picture books with secondary students:

1. Themes of many picture books have universal value and appeal for all age levels.

2. Some of the best picture books may have been missed when students were younger or may have been published since that time.

3. Many issues demand a maturity level that young children do not possess.

4. The short format of these books facilitates incorporating picture books into lessons.

5. Our visually oriented society has conditioned students to employ pictures as comprehension aids. (pp. 290–291)

The meaning readers construct from a picture book occurs in much the same way as with other types of texts, in that the reader's purposes for reading, prior knowledge, attitudes, and conceptual abilities determine in large part what and how the reader comprehends. In this way, the author's intent and the reader's purpose interact to produce an interpretation. Picture books inspire a variety of meanings because the illustrations function to enhance the story, to clarify and define concepts, and to set a tone for the words.

| Style | Tone | Illustration |
|---|---|---|
| Imagery, figurative language, all devices; comparisons extremely useful; flawed if style is monotonous, repetitious, fragmented in statements | Wonder, not mystery; respect; objectivity, occasional humor; fostering scientific attitude of inquiry; flawed condescension, anthropomorphism, oversimplification; facts not separated from opinions | Diagrams and drawings often clearer than photographs |
| Storytelling permissible for youngest reader; too much destroys credibility | Interest enthusiasm; objectivity; didacticism and preaching to be avoided | Authentic |

**Source:** Reprinted with permission from Rebecca J. Lukins (1986). *A Critical Handbook of Children's Literature.* Glenview, IL: Scott, Foresman.

There are several types of picture books to consider:

- *Wordless books:* books in which the illustrations completely carry the story; no text is involved. Example: *Vagabul Escapes* (1983) by Marol.
- *Picture books with minimal text:* the illustrations continue to carry the story with a few words used to enhance the pictures. Example: *Bored—Nothing to Do!* (1978) by Peter Spier.
- *Picture story books:* more print is involved; the illustrations are integral to the text in that the pictures and text are interdependent. Example: *The Moonbow of Mr. B. Bones* (1992) by J. Patrick Lewis, illustrated by Dirk Zimmer.
- *Books with illustrations:* books in which there are more words than pictures; however, the illustrations remain important to the text. Example: *Kashtanka* (1991) by Anton Chekov, illustrated by Barry Moser.

A number of picture books lend themselves to use in science and math classes. Several of Mitsumasa Anno's books can only be used with older students who have a firm grasp of mathematical concepts. His *Anno's Counting House* (1982), *Anno's Math Games II* (1989), and *Topsy-Turvies: Pictures to Stretch the Imagination* (1970) inspire critical analysis of the notion of sets and logical possibilities presented in the detailed illustrations. *Moja Means One: Swahili Counting Book* (1971) by Muriel and Tom Feelings is an excellent introduction to African traditions in addition to learning to count in Swahili. And Macaulay's *Pyramid* (1982) is an historically accurate look at the mathematical genius of the ancient Egyptians.

Environmental issues can be explored in books such as Rylant's *When I Was Young in the Mountains* (1982), Lowe's *Walden* (1990), Van Allsburg's *Just a Dream* (1990), and Baker's wordless *Window* (1991). Each of these books provides a thought-provoking story concerning human beings and their relationships to the earth. *The Story of the Seashore* (1990) by John Goodall and *Oceans* (1990) by Simon offer fascinating scientific information about the sea. Goodall's book is a wordless historic overview, while Simon's book is an exquisite collection of photographs and color drawings combined with an informative yet poetic text.

A book that can be used well in math, science, and art classes is Molly Bang's *Picture This* (1991). Gerard Piel, in *Scientific American*, said that this book is "a disarming and dazzling insight into visual perception" (back cover of book). Bang has succeeded in explaining how the artistic mind works while composing an illustration, and in the process she has taught a great deal about geometry, color, and size. Bang uses the familiar story of Little Red Riding Hood to make her point to audiences of all ages.

For history classes, David Macauley's *Castle* (1978) and *Cathedral* (1973) are rich in detail, in both the texts and the illustrations. Both books focus on the medieval world, and they nicely complement Aliki's *A Medieval Feast* (1986) and Goodall's *Story of a Main Street* (1987) and *The Story of an English Village* (1979). Aliki's book follows the preparations of a wealthy landowner's dinner for the king, and Goodall's books give wordless historical overviews from medieval times to the present. All of these offer a plethora of information that is impossible to find in history textbooks.

Many picture books focus on the events surrounding World War II. Maruki's *Hiroshima No Pika* (1982) is a moving book about a family's experiences with the atomic bombs dropped on Japan in 1945. Innocenti's *Rose Blanche* (1991) offers a look at a young girl's discovery of a Nazi concentration camp near her home and her attempts to comfort the inmates there until she is killed by a Nazi soldier. In *The Butter Battle Book* (1984), Dr. Seuss explores the illogical nature of war and poses the timeless question that all contemporary students are concerned about: which country will "push the button" first. Finally, Brent and Jennifer Ashabranner's book, *Always to Remember: The Story of the Vietnam Veterans Memorial* (1988) reminds readers that we must never forget the men and women who have died fighting for peace.

For language study, bilingual picture books offer enticing ways to teach. Simple alphabet books, such as Edwards's *Alef-bet: A Hebrew Alphabet Book* (1982), provide entertaining illustrations with cultural information along with easy-to-learn letters in the foreign language with English translations provided. Longer texts are also available, as in Volkmer's *Song of the Chirimia* (1990), a Guatemalan folktale told in both English and Spanish with colorful Mayan illustrations.

All of these picture books, and those suggested in Box 10.2 on page 312, can be used with older students to provide interesting schema builders, anticipatory sets to begin lessons, motivators for learning, and springboards into discussion and writing.

**Figure 10.4**   **COVER ILLUSTRATION FROM DAVID MACAULAY'S** *CATHEDRAL*

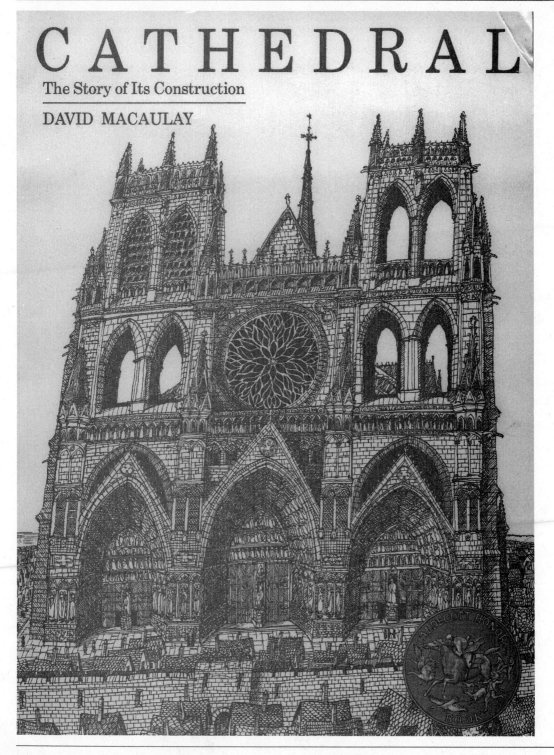

**Source:**  Reprinted with permission from David Macaulay. *Cathedral*. NY:Trumpet Club, 1973.

## BOX 10.2  Picture Books for Secondary Students

Aliki. (1986). *A Medieval Feast*. New York: Harper Collins.

Anno, M. (1982). *Anno's Counting House*. New York: Philomel.

Anno, M. (1989). *Anno's Math Games*. New York: Philomel.

Anno, M. (1970). *Topsy-Turvies: Pictures to Stretch the Imagination*. New York: Weatherhill.

Ashabranner, B. (1988). *Always to Remember: The Story of the Vietnam Veterans Memorial*. Ill. J. Ashabranner. New York: Putnam's.

Baker, J. (1991). *Widow*. New York: Greenwillow.

Barg, M. (1991). *Picture This: Perception and Composition*. New York: Bullfinch Press.

Chekov, A. (1991). *Kashtanka*. Trans. R. Pevear. Ill. B. Moser. New York: Putnam's.

Edwards, M. (1982). *Alef-bet: A Hebrew Alphabet Book*. New York: Lothrop, Lee & Shepard.

Feeling, M. (1971). *Moja Means One: Swahili Counting Book*. Ill. J. Feelings. New York: Dial.

Goodall, J. (1979). *The Story of an English Village*. New York: Atheneum.

Goodall, J. (1987). *Story of a Main Street*. New York: Macmillan.

Goodall, J. (1990). *The Story of the Seashore*. New York: Macmillan.

Innocenti, Roberto. (1991). *Rose Blanche*. New York: Stewart, Tiboria Chang.

Lewis, J. P. (1992). *The Moonbow of Mr. B. Bones*. New York: Knopf.

Lobel, A. (1981). *On Market Street*. New York: Greenwillow.

Lowe, S. (1990). *Walden*. New York: Philomel.

Macauley, D. (1978). *Castle*. New York: Houghton Mifflin.

—. (1973). *Cathedral*. New York: Houghton Mifflin.

—. (1982). *Pyramid*. Boston: Houghton Mifflin.

—. (1988). *The Way Things Work*. New York: Houghton Mifflin.

Marol, J. (1983). *Vagabul Escapes*. Mankato, Minnesota: Creative Education.

Maruki, T. (1982). *Hiroshima No Pika*. New York: Lothrop, Lee & Shepard.

—. (1985). *The Relatives Came*. Ill. Stephen Gammell. New York: Bradbury.

Rylant, C. (1984). *Waiting to Waltz: A Childhood*. Ill. Stephen Gammell. New York: Bradbury.

Rylant, C. (1982). *When I Was Young in the Mountains*. New York: Dutton.

Seuss, Dr. (1984). *The Butter Battle Book*. New York: Random House.

Simon. R. (1990). *Ocenas*. New York: Morrow Junior Books.

Spier, P. (1978). *Bored—Nothing to Do!* New York: Doubleday.

Van Allsburg, C. (1990). *Just a Dream*. New York: Houghton Mifflin.

Van Allsburg, C. (1987). *The Z Was Zapped*. New York: Houghton Mifflin.

Volkmer, J.A. (1990). *Song of the Chirimia: A Guatemalan Folktale*. Minneapolis: Carolrhoda.

**Figure 10.5    COVER ILLUSTRATION FROM *ROSE BLANCHE***

**Source:** Reprinted with permission from Roberto Innocenti. *Rose Blanche*. NY: Stewart, Tabori and Chang, 1985.

## PUTTING LITERATURE TO USE

There is so much more to do with a good book than to write a report about it! Literature can be used both as the focal point in a lesson and as a companion to the textbook. There are at least two avenues that you can take to incorporate literature into content area study. One involves the critical perspectives that students assume as they interact with different types of literature. Another involves weaving textbooks and literature together within the context of thematic explorations.

## Responding to Literature from Different Critical Perspectives

Literature demands response from its readers. Creating an active learning environment in which students respond personally and critically to what they are reading is an important outcome of literature use in content area classrooms. Often in text learning situations, a teacher's tack is to focus on what students have learned and how much. There's value in having what Rosenblatt (1982) calls an *efferent stance* as a reader. When readers assume an efferent stance, they focus attention on the ideas and information they interact with and carry away from reading.

Reader response to a story, however, is also likely to involve feelings, personal associations, and insights. When students assume an *aesthetic stance*, they shift their attention inward on what is being created as part of the literary experience itself (Rosenblatt, 1982). An aesthetic response to literature is driven by personal feelings, insights, and attitudes that are stirred up by the reader's interactions and transactions with the text.

One way to organize literature in the content classroom is to take advantage of both efferent and aesthetic stances that readers take in their transactions with texts. This works well when students assume the role of literary critic. In this role, they assume various critical perspectives as they learn with literature.

Four critical perspectives in particular allow students to get inside themselves *and* a text to explore and construct meaning. Literary critics, for example, examine works of literature within the framework of *comparative criticism*, in which comparisons are made of literature across genres, cultures, or literary elements; *archetypal criticism*, in which patterns, motifs, and themes are explored and analyzed as they occur and recur in literary works; *sociohistorical criticism*, in which the literary work is studied in terms of how it reflects social and historical trends concerning the time period about which and/or in which it is written; and *transactional criticism*, in which a literary work is explored and analyzed in terms of how it impacts the life, attitudes, and thinking of the reader. Showing students how to become critics works well in conjunction with some of the instructional activities presented in previous chapters.

**Comparative Criticism.**   Booktalks provide a forum for students to share the books they have read. Book sharing is a crucial part of the reading process, if students are to grow as readers and as learners. Chambers (1985) calls booktalking a powerful strategy in which students pool their powers of thought in ways that far exceed what any one member of the group could possibly achieve alone. Booktalks thus serve as a way for students to compare books on similar topics or books from different cultures.

For example, a history teacher divides the class into two groups, and has one group read *Bearstone* (1989) by Will Hobbs and the other read *The Cage* (1986) by Ruth Sender. Each of these books involves protagonists who are being held against their wills in situations that are beyond their control.

As the students read the books, they keep response logs, in which they react to questions such as how the protagonists feel as captives of societies that discriminate against their race. When the class meets to discuss the books, students offer ideas from their response logs to generate a comparison concerning the ways in which the Jewish woman's captivity in *The Cage* during World War II differed from the contemporary American Indian boy's sense of belonging in *Bearstone*. From this, students go on to explore the concept of slavery and how it changes across circumstances, societies, and historical periods.

Another way to compare and contrast literary concepts in several stories is through the use of a semantic feature analysis (SFA) chart. Using a grid as depicted in Figure 10.6, the SFA provides a visualization of the stories' pertinent characteristics and develops students' explorations of critical concepts.

In the same vein, students can develop Venn diagrams, such as the one illustrated in Figure 10.7. The Venn allows the student to make comparisons and contrasts between two or more people, places, things, or ideas. For example, in the Venn depicted in Figure 10.7, students were invited to compare and contrast two picture books dealing with the Vietnam War. How were the two books alike and different? The similarities between the two books are reflected in the area where the two circles intersect. Their individual features are captured in the nonintersecting space within each circle. The students completed the Venn on their own and then used their productions

**Figure 10.6    SEMANTIC FEATURE ANALYSIS USED TO COMPARE SEVERAL STORIES**

| Features / Stories | Evil to Good | Good to Evil | Animal to Human | Human to Animal | Animate to Inanimate | Inanimate to Animate |
|---|---|---|---|---|---|---|
| Frog Princess | | | | | | |
| Paper Crane | | | | | | |
| Crane Wife | | | | | | |
| Mufaro's Beautiful Daughters | | | | | | |
| Cinderella | | | | | | |

+ = Characteristic of the story
− = Not a characteristic of the story
? = Not sure

**Figure 10.7**    VENN DIAGRAM OF TWO STORIES

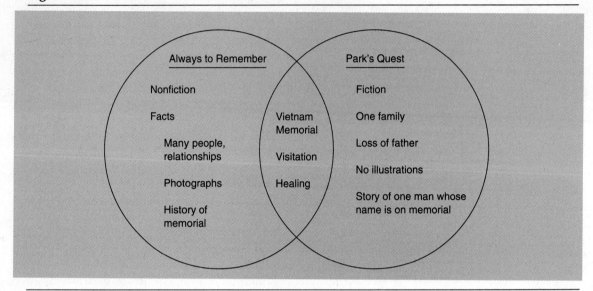

to discuss the two stories in cooperative groups, adding to and revising their diagrams based upon the discussion. Afterwards, the teacher asked students to synthesize what they had learned by writing a comparison-contrast essay about the two books.

Comparisons can also be made between what students already know and what they learn in the process of studying a particular unit. Students, for instance, might brainstorm to discover what they know about how the brain works and how memory functions. They could use these ideas to explore reasons for differences in memory abilities among people and for differences in the kinds of information that are retained within any one person's short-term and long-term memory. A textbook might be used to provide a foundation for the learning that would follow such a discussion. As a capstone experience, the class could read Roy Gallant's *Memory: How It Works and How to Improve It* (1980) and keep a chart with new knowledge gained from the book. Not only would comparisons be made between personal existing knowledge and the book, but also between the textbook information that was available and the trade book. Follow-up discussions could then address purposes for using the textbook and the trade book (i.e., which type of book would be most appropriate in which learning situations).

Archetypal Criticism. Exploring and analyzing patterns, motifs, and themes can open up new worlds for readers who might otherwise overlook such things, particularly if they are reading strictly for plot. Patterns provide ways of seeing. If we realize that wolves are presented as nurturing beings in Eskimo folk tales, and as evil predators in Western folklore, we understand

something important about those cultures. When we know about the significance of specific story patterns and prototypes, we see more deeply into a
culture's or a particular author's belief systems and expectations.

Semantic mapping is an excellent way to help students visualize patterns. In Figure 10.8, the creation myth motifs of the Guinea and Huron
Indians are used to show how ancient archetypes offer a perspective of
these cultures. As the figure shows, the importance of nurturing in the
Huron Indian culture and the prominence of death in the Guinea way of
thinking are contrasting elements between these two peoples. However, it is
also clear that both civilizations appreciate the presence of good and evil as
forces that move the world.

In *The Terrorists* (1983), Milton Meltzer explores cultural archetypes
involving the dark world of terrorist activity. Here, the reader is led to
understand that the original concept, or prototype, for murder is completely
redefined by those who use terrorist tactics to make change. This particular
kind of violence is depicted in terms of political, religious, and personal
belief systems that are part of a society's way of seeing the world, which has
everything to do with the archetypal images that become so evident in the
literature of a people. Concept circles, such as those depicted in Figure 10.9,

**Figure 10.8    SEMANTIC MAPPING OF CREATION MYTHS
OF TWO INDIAN TRIBES**

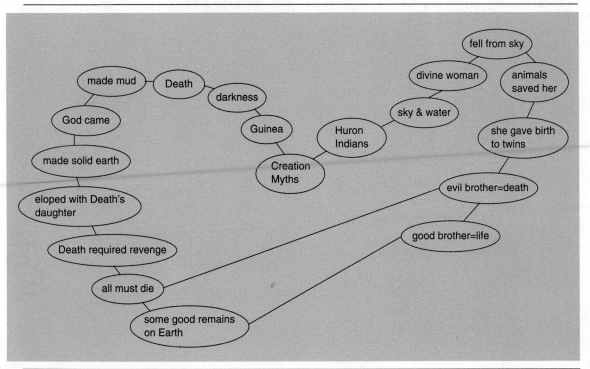

**Figure 10.9    CONCEPT CIRCLES FOR THE TERRORISTS**

Directions: In each of the concept circles below, work with a partner, fill in sections of each concept circle with pertinent ideas and information that help to describe the terrorist group named.

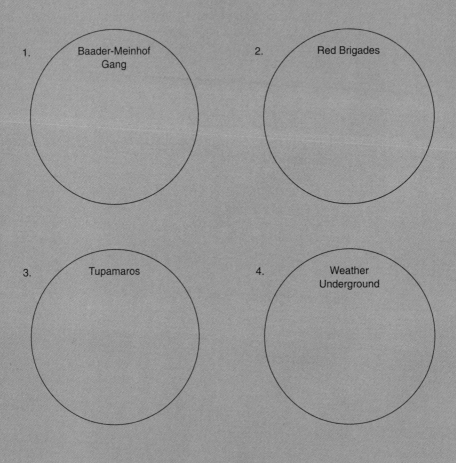

1.   Baader-Meinhof Gang

2.   Red Brigades

3.   Tupamaros

4.   Weather Underground

Information items that students identified as they constructed concept circles:

| | |
|---|---|
| antiwar beliefs | fire bombs |
| student protestors | kidnapped people |
| "troublemaker" | United States of America |
| fought against unemployment | guerilla warfare |
| Germany | "revolutionary love" |
| violence vs. violence | Italy |
| held in steel cages | against the government |
| Uruguay | modern Robin Hoods |
| destroyed democracy | |

help students to define and redefine the images that Meltzer uses and can serve as excellent discussion starters concerning the issues—ethical, political, and otherwise—surrounding terrorism. Newspaper and magazine articles would be very useful additions to classroom, small group, and/or individual inquiries into this topic, given the plethora of such violent activities on local and more global levels.

**Sociohistorical Criticism.** While the study of patterns is one way to focus on cultural belief systems, there are other portholes to look through in order to more completely understand how a text reflects the world about which or in which it was written. Sociohistorical criticism seeks to explore social and historical concepts from the perspectives that are presented in books. It is clear from the lessons of historians that historical fiction has the ability to pull readers into the time period ("Booksearch," p. 84). This is certainly reason enough to use trade literature in the social studies curriculum, either alone as the basis for instruction or in conjunction with the designated textbook.

A book such as *Shabanu, Daughter of the Wind* (1989) by Suzanne Fisher Staples is a provocative story to stir discussion about the state of the Arab world. Students are drawn into an alien desert civilization through the eyes of the main character, a young girl who is experiencing the changing roles of Arabian women, and trying to find where she fits. Shabanu's need for independence and her fears about entering adulthood are universal characteristics all adolescents can identify with. However, her particular life as an Arab poses problems for Western students that can lead to interesting entries in learning logs and responses to statements in an anticipation/reaction guide such as that presented in Figure 10.10.

**Figure 10.10**    ANTICIPATION/REACTION GUIDE FOR *SHABANU: DAUGHTER OF THE WIND* by Suzanne Fisher Staples

Before you read the book, think about your feelings concerning the items below. Do you believe that they are true or not? Mark your "before" answers "true" or "false" in the spaces provided. After you have completed the book, rethink your "before" answers and mark your answers now that you have read *Shabanu*. Have you changed your mind? Why?

| Before | After | |
|--------|-------|---|
| _____ | _____ | 1. Living in a desert would be so difficult that it would be impossible to be happy. |
| _____ | _____ | 2. Arranged marriages are cruel and are better left in the history books. |
| _____ | _____ | 3. Women should have rights equal to those of the men in every society in the world. |
| _____ | _____ | 4. Arab societies are not as advanced as Western cultures. |
| _____ | _____ | 5. Change in society is a good thing. Old habits were meant to give way to the new. |

**Transactional Criticism.**   Of all the critical perspectives for a student to take, transactional criticism is the most subjective and diverse in its scope. It is also perhaps the most important because it is so basic to all of the others. Transactional criticism explores the communication that occurs between the reader and the text, and places heavy emphasis on the personal aesthetic response of the reader that tends to influence how the reader perceives the content. David Bleich (1978) suggests that reading response involves both the author and the reader taking active parts in the making of meaning. Thus, the initial response of "I like this" or "I hate this" becomes the springboard for other, more complex reactions. *Why* a student likes or does not like a text becomes the genesis for discussions, drama, art, and compositions that probe the readers' intentions.

A *reader response heuristic* allows students to explore their personal responses and to take those initial reactions into more analytical realms. According to Brozo (1989), the rationale behind a reader response heuristic is this: "It is through a personal connection that a text becomes meaningful and memorable" (p. 141). Questions that guide student response to informational texts are:

1.  What aspect of the text excited or interested you the most? (The reader identifies an idea, issue, event, character, place, or any other aspect of the content that aroused strong feelings.)

2.  What are your feelings and attitudes about this aspect of the text? (The reader describes and explains feelings and attitudes.)

3.  What experiences have you had that help others understand why you feel the way you do? (The reader supports feelings and attitudes with personal experiences.) (Brozo 1989, p. 142)

The answers to these questions will help readers to consciously connect their own experiences and the content of the text, and the questions can be used well in both small group and individual instructional settings.

Study a student's response to a book entitled *Atoms, Molecules and Quarks* (1986) by Melvin Berger, presented in Figure 10.11. From his transactions with the text, it is evident that meaningful and personal response is not limited to fiction books. Students can and do become interested and excited about scientific information when it is presented in a motivational format.

## Weaving Literature into Thematic Units

The whole language movement in elementary schools serves as a prototype for literature use in middle and high school classrooms. Authentic texts, sometimes called real books, are a mainstay of whole language classrooms in the elementary grades. Children approach content area studies within the framework of thematic units that make use of a wide array of literature. Although textbooks are used to provide an information base, the foundation

**Figure 10.11    STUDENT RESPONSE TO BROZO'S RESPONSE HEURISTIC FOR**
*ATOMS, MOLECULES AND QUARKS*

*The Student's Most Interesting Part of Text*

The information about quarks was good. It was something that I didn't know before. I really thought that the names of the different types of quarks (up, down, truth, beauty, strange, and charm) were kind of weird, but these names made them easier to remember because they are so different.

*The Student's Feelings and Attitudes toward Subject*

The author did a good job in making all of this interesting and pretty easy to read. Quarks and their flavors and colors are kind of hard to understand when you read about them in the textbook, but I could follow this book. I think it's amazing what scientists have been able to find out about atomic particles. I especially wonder about why the universe hasn't blown up already, since the book said that it should have because of the way particles and antiparticles react. Scientists don't have the answer, either. But it makes you feel a little uneasy, not knowing what holds all of this together.

*The Student's Personal Associations*

I suppose that all of us have wondered about what keeps the universe going at some time or other. I guess what started me thinking about this was a science fiction movie that I saw that showed the world exploding into outer space. A lot of people see these kinds of shows and start to think about if that could really happen. Then when you read about quarks, it makes you think.

for individual and group investigation of a theme or topic is the use of both fiction and nonfiction books geared to the students' interests and inquiry needs.

Suppose, for example, that in an intermediate grade classroom students are engaged in a thematic unit on the environment. What might you observe over several weeks? For starters, the teacher might be conducting several whole class lessons at the beginning of the unit using the textbook as a basis for developing a conceptual framework for individual and group investigation. As the weeks progress, however, whole class activity appears less prevalent. Instead, small groups might be seen working on research projects or in discussion teams using Gary Paulsen's *Woodsong* (1990) and *Hatchet* (1987), as well as Roy Gallant's *Earth's Vanishing Forests* (1991). Individual students might also be working on inquiries with books such as Paul Goble's *I Sing for the Animals* (1991), and Peter Parnall's *Marsh Cat* (1991) and *The Daywatchers* (1984). Toward the end of the unit, the class can be observed completing culminating activities, which may involve panel discussions, report writing, and oral presentations that would call on individuals or groups to share knowledge gleaned from the various activities and texts. In this class, what you would observe is that everyone has something to contribute. Learning with literature is a significant event in the lives of the students.

Thematic units, as you recall from Chapter 3, organize instruction around concepts to be studied and multiple sources of informational and imaginative texts within the context of meaningful and relevant classroom activity. In the elementary grades, teachers use units to integrate various content areas around the study of a theme. In middle and secondary classrooms, the unit theme usually has a strong topical focus that relates to a set of major concepts prescribed within the course of study. Textbook and literature are used interchangeably to explore the topic and then develop the concepts under study.

Units are titled according to the topic or the theme. A title with a bit of pizzazz arouses students' curiosity and piques interest in the topic under study. The title often is a springboard into the introduction and initial discussion of the unit. Most teachers use a graphic organizer to help conceptualize, plan, and introduce the unit. In the elementary grades, the organizer takes the form of a *literature web*. These webs outline the relationships among major components of the unit. Usually the web displays the content areas to be integrated and the literature and/or activities to be used. Secondary teachers often prefer to develop a graphic organizer that outlines the relationships among the major concepts to be studied. In either case, multiple literature sources are woven into the unit.

Brozo and Tomlinson (1986) define several steps that facilitate the uses of literature in thematic units:

1. Identify salient concepts that become the content objectives for the unit.

    a. What are the driving human forces behind the events?
    b. What patterns of behavior need to be studied?
    c. What phenomena have affected or may affect ordinary people in the future?

2. Identify appropriate trade books to help teach concepts.

    a. Read and become familiar with a variety of books.
    b. Use literature textbooks and subject guide reference indices such as those suggested in Box 10.1.

3. Teach the unit.

    a. Use textbook and trade books interchangeably.
    b. Use strategies such a read-aloud in which a trade book becomes a schema builder before reading the textbook.
    c. Use trade books to elaborate and extend content and concepts related to the unit.

4. Follow up.

    a. Engage students in strategies and activities that involve collaboration, inquiry, and various forms of expression and meaning construction.
    b. Evaluate students' learning by observing how they interpret and personalize new knowledge.

Here's how several teachers put literature to work as they follow the steps outlined above.

**First Grade: Myths and Legends of American Indians.** This unit is an ambitious attempt by Susan Hovan, the teacher, to develop insight with first graders into the myths and legends of American Indians. Susan designed the unit to integrate content from several areas of study, including plants and seeds from the science curriculum, nutritious foods from health education curriculum, and the Pilgrims from the social studies curriculum. As a result, she identified the following concepts for thematic exploration:

### Major Concepts

1. Indians have a rich cultural heritage.

2. Indians have contributed a rich culture to the American heritage.

3. The Indians helped the Pilgrims by teaching them how to plant crops.

4. American Indians were the first Americans.

5. Indian art consists of drawings, masks, blankets, baskets, jewelry, etc. It is varied and beautiful.

6. Much of Indian culture is derived from the Indians' interaction with the Earth and nature.

7. The Indians had a sacred respect for the Earth.

8. The Indians' rich culture has led to much art and literature.

9. Corn was a mainstay for Indians; it became the same for Pilgrims, as well.

10. The Indians developed a relationship of cooperation with Pilgrims, based on need.

11. Corn grows from a seed. A seed grows into a plant.

12. Corn is a vegetable. Vegetables make up part of the Four Food Groups.

13. We use our knowledge about the Four Food Groups to keep healthy.

To help conceptualize the various components of the unit, Susan developed the literature web in Box 10.3.

The literature sources available to the children in Susan's class included picture books for read-alouds and individual/group study. A partial list of the literature appears in Box 10.4.

**Eighth Grade Life Science: Birds—The Feathered Ones.** Rod Rush, a life science teacher in a middle school, uses a textbook and literature interchangeably for a unit on birds. In his classes, students have already mastered the concept of warm-blooded animals. Birds are the first group of warm-blooded animals that the students will study. Because the students possess varying degrees of prior knowledge about birds, the unit is focused around a wide variety of species and the economic and aesthetic value of birds.

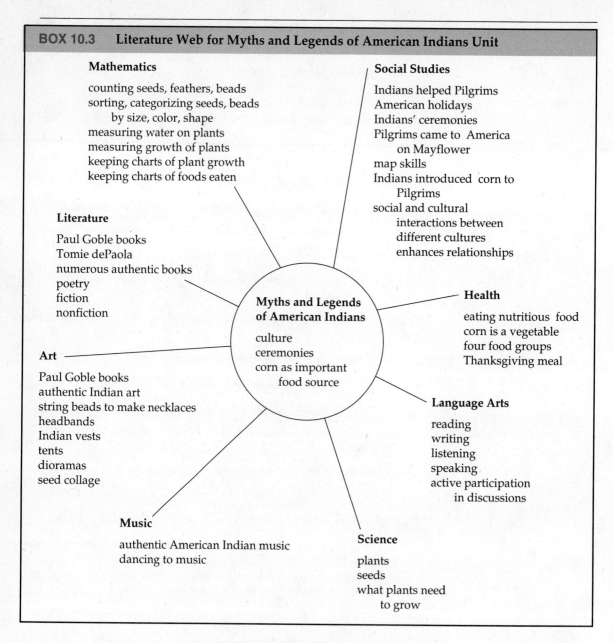

BOX 10.3    Literature Web for Myths and Legends of American Indians Unit

**Mathematics**

counting seeds, feathers, beads
sorting, categorizing seeds, beads
    by size, color, shape
measuring water on plants
measuring growth of plants
keeping charts of plant growth
keeping charts of foods eaten

**Literature**

Paul Goble books
Tomie dePaola
numerous authentic books
poetry
fiction
nonfiction

**Art**

Paul Goble books
authentic Indian art
string beads to make necklaces
headbands
Indian vests
tents
dioramas
seed collage

**Music**

authentic American Indian music
dancing to music

**Myths and Legends of American Indians**

culture
ceremonies
corn as important
    food source

**Social Studies**

Indians helped Pilgrims
American holidays
Indians' ceremonies
Pilgrims came to America
    on Mayflower
map skills
Indians introduced corn to
    Pilgrims
social and cultural
    interactions between
    different cultures
    enhances relationships

**Health**

eating nutritious food
corn is a vegetable
four food groups
Thanksgiving meal

**Language Arts**

reading
writing
listening
speaking
active participation
    in discussions

**Science**

plants
seeds
what plants need
    to grow

Several major concepts are taught in the unit:

Major Concepts

1.  General characteristics of the class, Aves (birds).

2.  A comparison to find the relationship between reptiles and birds.

3.  Adaptations of various species of birds to their environment.

4. Adaptations of birds for flight.

5. Migration.

6. Importance of birds as an indicator of the health of the environment.

7. Economic importance of birds.

8. The aesthetic value of birds.

9. Identification of various families and species.

---

**BOX 10.4   Partial List of Literature Resources for Myths and Legends of American Indians Unit**

**Books**

*The Legend of the Indian Paintbrush* by Tomie de Paola
*The Legend of the Bluebonnet* by Tomie de Paola
*Arrow to the Sun* by Gerald McDermott
*Beyond the Ridge* by Paul Goble
*Three Little Indians* by Gene S. Stuart
*Iktomi and the Boulder* by Paul Goble
*Dream Wolf* by Paul Goble
*Iktomi and the Berries* by Paul Goble
*Geronimo* by John Keely
*The Girl Who Loved Wild Horses* by Paul Goble
*The Mud Pony* by Caron Lee Cohen
*Pocahontas* by Ingri and Edgar Parin d'Aulaire
*The Gift of the Sacred Dog* by Paul Goble
*Rainbow Crow* by Nancy Van Laan
*Whale in the Sky* by Anne Siberell
*The Great Race of the Birds and Animals* by Paul Goble
*Her Seven Brothers* by Paul Goble
*Buffalo Woman* by Paul Goble
*Ceremony in the Circle of Life* by White Deer of Autumn
*Desert Voices* by Byrd Baylor and Peter Parnell
*The Other Way to Listen* by Baylor and Parnell

**Poetry**

*Our Fathers Had Powerful Songs* by Natalia Betting
*Dancing Tepees, Poems of American Indian Youth* by Virginia Driving Hawk Sneve
*The Turquoise Horse, Prose and Poetry of the American Indians* by Flora Hood

The students engage, first of all, in a study of the relationship between birds and reptiles. Then they explore the characteristics of birds as a class of animals and explore the many and varied adaptations birds have made to their environment, including adaptations for flight and migration. The students also examine the importance of birds as an indicator of the health of the environment. The final phase of the unit centers on the value of birds from an economic and aesthetic perspective. Box 10.5 displays the relationships among the key concepts that students will master as a result of their studies.

Rod weaves literature into the unit through the use of informational books, popular literature, and poetry. Students engage in a variety of activities that incorporate the textbook and literature. For example, Rod supplements textbook study with outside readings. He also requires the use of a science notebook in which students set aside a section of the notebook to respond to literature they are reading as part of the unit. The centerpiece of the unit, however, revolves around a jigsaw group investigation of birds as we described in Chapter 3. As you may recall, the students participate in jigsaw groups to investigate several of the main concepts of the unit. Each group member investigates a different concept and then reports his or her findings to the group. As preparation for the report, students temporarily meet in expert groups (all of the students in an expert group are responsible for teaching the same concept to their jigsaw teammates) to share and discuss what they are reading and studying about. Box 10.6 contains a list of literature resources available to the students during their investigations.

In addition to inquiry as a springboard into literature, Rod uses different types of literature as part of direct instruction in the teaching of specific concepts. This often results in an opportunity to combine reading, literature,

---

**BOX 10.5    Graphic Organizer for Unit on Birds**

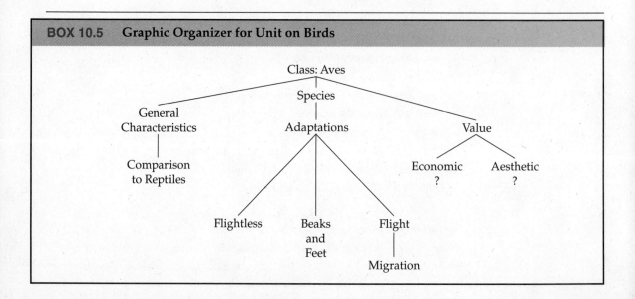

---

**BOX 10.6    Literature Resources for Unit on Birds**

**Textbook**

Bierer, Loretta M., & Lein, Violetta F. *Heath Life Science.* Lexington, MA.: D. C. Heath and Co., 1985, pp. 290–295.

**Nonfiction**

Brooks, Bruce. *On the Wing.* New York: Macmillan, 1989.

Bull, John, & Ferrand, John Jr. *The Audubon Society Field Guide to North American Birds.* New York: Alfred A. Knopf, Inc., 1977.

Collins, Henry H. Jr. *Complete Field Guide to American Wildlife.* New York: Harper and Row, 1959.

Fichter, George S. *The Changing World of Wildlife.* New York: Golden Press, 1977.

*Gift of Birds.* Washington, D.C.: National Wildlife Federation, 1979.

Harrison, Kit & George. *The Birds of Winter.* New York: Random House, 1990.

*Life Histories: Notes on Ohio's Fish and Wildlife Species.* Ohio Dept. of Natural Resources, Division of Wildlife, 1985.

*Project Wild: Elementary Activity Guide.* Boulder, CO: Western Regional Environmental Council, 1985, pp. 97–97.

Robbins, Chandler S., Bruun, Bertel & Zim, Herbert. *A Guide to Field Identification: Birds of North America.* New York: Golden Press, 1966.

Schutz, Walter E. *How to Attract, House, and Feed Birds.* New York: Collier Books, 1970.

Stokes, Donald and Lillian. *The Bird Feeder Book.* Little, Brown, and Co., 1987.

Whitfield, Phillip. *The Macmillan Illustrated Encyclopedia of Birds.* New York: Collier Books, 1988.

Wood, Richard H. *Wood Notes: A Companion and Guide for Birdwatchers.* Englewood Cliffs, NJ: Prentice–Hall, 1984.

**Fiction**

*Gift of Birds.* Washington, D.C.: National Wildlife Federation, 1979, pp. 94–118.

---

and writing to learn. For example, he will read to the class poems about birds such as Randall Jarrell's "The Bird of Night," Robert Francis's "Seagulls," and Ogden Nash's "Up from the Egg: The Confessions of a Nuthatch Avoider." After each poem, the students write in their notebooks for three minutes on how the poem made them feel. They then share their responses with others in the class. Next, the students are asked to write for another three minutes on a memory they may have associated with the poem which influenced their initial response. Also as part of their response to the poem, the students choose one word they feel summarizes the poem and write about the reasons for their choice. As a follow-up activity, the students engage in the writing of haiku poems using birds as the basic theme.

**Eleventh-Grade American History: The Revolutionary War.** Beth Dawson, an American history teacher, designed this unit to draw upon students' prior knowledge of the American Revolution to better understand the interrelatedness of the events of the Revolutionary period and its effects upon later American history. She combined textbook study, in which she used many of the instructional alternatives presented in this book, with literature exploration. The students in Beth's classes approached the unit with a wide range of reading and writing ability. As a result, Beth relied heavily on collaborative learning techniques in which she combined whole class, cooperative small groups, dyads, and individual inquiry patterns to engage the students in study.

Beth's content analysis for the unit yield the following concepts:

### Major Concepts

1. The thirteen colonies became an independent country, the United States of America.

2. There was no single cause of the Revolution but rather an interrelated web of causes.

3. The Declaration of Independence was important for its immediate propaganda effect.

4. The Declaration of Independence remains important for its influence on later political thought.

5. The Revolution was a civil war as well as a revolt.

6. The colonies achieved their independence through a variety of factors.

7. Washington developed the concept of the war of attrition.

8. The concept of a war of attrition has been used in virtually every insurrection since the Revolution.

9. Not all groups in America benefited from independence.

10. There is considerable debate among historians whether the American Revolution was a revolution at all.

In planning the unit, Beth constructed a graphic organizer of the major concepts and then identified literature for group and individual investigation. Notice in Box 10.7 that Beth positions key fiction and non-fiction books on the organizer in relationship to the concepts to be taught.

The literature list for the unit included the annotated bibliography in Box 10.8 on page 330.

Beth weaved literature into the unit in two ways. First she had students self-select a fiction or nonfiction book related to the American Revolution, and then set up an ongoing response journal activity. She explained to the students:

**BOX 10.7     Graphic Organizer for Revolutionary War Unit**

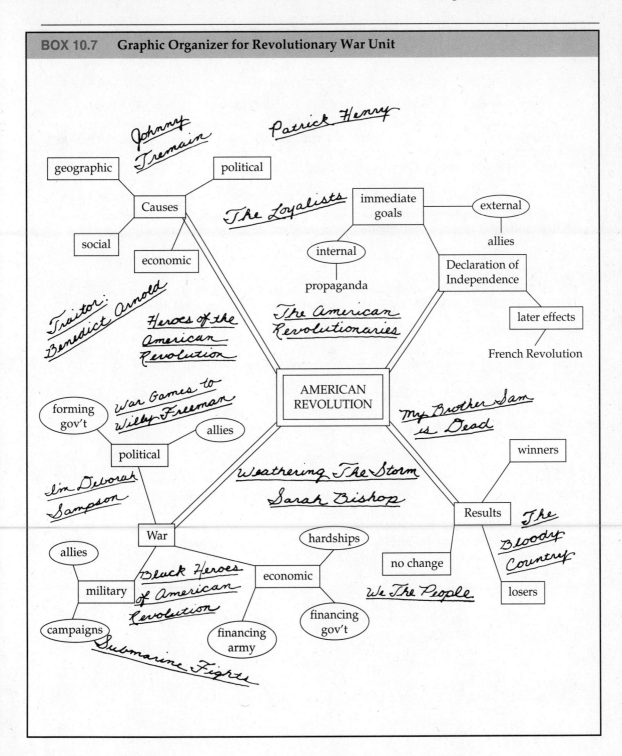

**BOX 10.8    Annotated Bibliography for Revolutionary War Unit**

**Fiction**

Collier, James Lincoln and Collier, Christopher. (1976). *The bloody country*. New York: Four Winds.

Ben Buck, his family, and Joe Mountain, the family slave, while living on the western Pennsylvanian frontier during the Revolution, struggle with British soldiers, loyalists, and Indians, and with Joe's growing desire for the equality proclaimed in the Declaration of Independence. Appropriate for average and developing readers.

Collier, James Lincoln and Collier, Christopher. (1974). *My brother Sam is dead*. New York: Four Winds.

Tragedy strikes the Meeker family when one son joins the rebels while the rest of the family tries to stay neutral in a Tory town. Appropriate for average and developing readers.

Collier, James Lincoln and Collier, Christopher. (1983). *War comes to Willy Freeman*. New York: Delacorte.

Free thirteen-year-old Willy Freeman risks a return to slavery as she searches for her mother in British-held New York during the Revolution. Appropriate for average and developing readers.

Forbes, Esther. (1971). *Johnny Tremain*. New York: Dell.

Johnny Tremain, an apprentice silversmith, becomes involved in the events leading up to the Boston Tea Party and the Battle of Lexington. Appropriate for developing readers.

O'Dell, Scott. (1980). *Sarah Bishop*. Boston: Houghton Mifflin.

After the deaths of her Tory father and rebel brother, Sarah flees her Long Island home to create a new life for herself in the wilderness. Appropriate for average readers.

**Nonfiction**

Campion, Nardi Reeder. (1961). *Patrick Henry: Firebrand of the Revolution*. Boston: Little.
Biography. Appropriate for developing readers.

Chidsey, Donald Barr. (1973). *The Loyalists: The story of those Americans who fought against independence*. New York: Crown Publishers.

Using letters, diaries, and speeches the motivations, actions and final treatment of the loyalists is recounted. Appropriate for advanced readers.

Clapp, Patricia. (1977). *I'm Deborah Sampson: A soldier in the War of the Revolution*. New York: Lothrop.
Biography. Appropriate for developing readers.

Davis, Burke. (1976). *Black Heroes of the American Revolution*. New York: Harcourt, Brace, Jovanovich.

More than just Crispus Attucks, Davis writes about the African-American revolutionaries who are seldom mentioned in the standard text. Appropriate for the developing reader.

Davis, Burke. (1971). *Heroes of the American Revolution.* New York: Random House.

Eleven concise biographies of Revolutinary War heroes, some well known—Paul Revere, Benjamin Franklin, and George Washington, and some lesser known men—Henry Knox, Friedrich von Steuben, and George Rogers Clark. Appropriate for developing readers.

Evans, Elizabeth. (1975). *Weathering the storm: Women of the American Revolution.* New York: Charles Scribner's Sons.

Accounts of the Revolution drawn from the journals and diaries of eleven women. Especially interesting is the account of Deborah Sampson Gannett who, dressed as a man, became a decorated soldier.

Evans, R. E. (1977). *The American War of Independence.* Cambridge, England: Cambridge University Press.

Evans, R. E. (1976). *The War of American Independence.* Cambridge, England: Cambridge University Press.

The same book despite the title change. The spelling was Americanized for the 1977 edition. A short 50-page history of the Revolution. Chapter Four: A world war looks at the war from the perspective of world politics and economics, a view usually slighted in American history texts.

Fritz, Jean. (1981). *Traitor: The case of Benedict Arnold.* New York: Putnam.

Biography. Appropriate for developing readers.

Hilton, Suzanne. (1981). *We the people: The way we were 1783–1793.* Philadephia: Westminster Press.

Describes the life, customs and controversies of the new country created in 1783. This new nation had no official capital, currency, or navy. Its borders had not been decided and no one was even sure if United States was singular or plural. Appropriate for the developing reader.

Meltzer, Milton. (1987). *The American revolutionaries: A history in their own words, 1750–1800.* New York: Thomas V. Crowell.

Using letter, diaries, journals, memoirs, newspapers, and speeches, Meltzer describes the experience of Revolution from a variety of viewpoints—soldiers, Quakers, wives, politicians, and preachers.

Quarles, Benjamin. (1961). *The Negro in the American Revolution.* New York: W. W. Norton.

Meant for the serious historian, this book probably is too much for the average high school student. However, the first four pages of the preface are an excellent brief history of the interrelated military and political realities that led to the recruitment of blacks, generally slaves, by both sides. Appropriate for advanced readers or teacher resource.

Wagner, Frederick. (1963). *Submarine fighter of the American Revolution: The story of David Bushnell.* Binghamton, New York: Vail-Ballou Press.

The biography of David Bushnell, the inventor of the first practical submarine, the Turtle, and of the contact underwater mine.

You will keep a response log of the book that you are reading. A response log records your feelings, reactions, and personal insights about the book. Decide how many pages you will read at a time. After reading each section of the book, make an entry in your log: What moved you the most in the section? How did the section make you feel? Why do you think you felt that way? What did you learn from the reading? Be sure to include details or quotations from the book, so someone who hasn't read it would understand why you were moved by the reading.

Beth and the students decided on three due dates, each covering about one third of the book, for turning in the log. In class, Beth would periodically put the students into booktalk groups to discuss their reactions to what they were reading.

In addition to the response log activity, the students engaged in literature study through an inquiry-centered project (see Box 10.9). The inquiry provided class members the opportunity to work in pairs to investigate an historical figure from the Revolutionary period. The inquiry resulted in a written interview that each pair of students role-played for the class.

## LOOKING BACK, LOOKING FORWARD

The use of literature in content area classrooms extends and enriches information provided in textbooks. Often, textbooks are not equipped to treat subject matter with the depth and breadth necessary to fully develop ideas and concepts. Literature, however, has the potential to capture students' interest and imagination in people, places, events, and ideas.

Whereas textbooks compress information, literature provides readers with intense involvement in a subject. As a result, students are likely to develop interest in and emotional commitment to the subject. Moreover, books are schema builders. Reading books helps students to generate background knowledge and provides them with vicarious experiences. There are many types of literature, both fiction and nonfiction, that can be used in tandem with textbooks.

Putting literature to use in content area classrooms occurs within the context of critical analysis and thematic units. Students need to approach books as literary critics, focusing attention on comparative study, sociohistorical reflections, archetypal patterns and motifs, and personal response. In addition, units provide a framework in which textbooks and literature can be used interchangeably to develop concepts under study.

In the third part of this book, we shift our attention from instructional matters to assessment. Concern for assessment is one of the major issues in American education today. What role do standardized assessments play in the life of a content area teacher? How do naturalistic assessment methods

| BOX 10.9 | Inquiry Project for Revolutionary War Unit |
|---|---|

**Directions:**

Congratulations! You have been chosen to anchor the new series *Time-Line*. This show features the same type of in-depth interview as *Night Line*, except you have a TIME MACHINE. You can go back in time and interview someone from the Revolution. In order to prevent changing the future, here are the rules.

1. Work in pairs. Both will do research and write the interview. Decide who will be the interviewer and who the interviewee. Decide on an historical interview date.

2. Your interviewee may be either an actual historical figure (e.g., Paul Revere), or you may create a fictional eyewitness to an historical event (e.g., Boston Tea Party).

3. Your research must be based on at least two sources, only one of which may be the encyclopedia. A bibliography must be included in the written interview turned in after presentation.

4. Presentation

   a. Introduce the interviewee and briefly tell why he or she is important or interesting.

   b. Your questions must stay within your time frame. You can't ask George Washington if he wants to be president; the office doesn't exist yet. You may ask him if he would like a political office in the future.

   c. The interviewee's answers must be reasonable based on historical facts from your research.

   d. You are encouraged to include visual aids; pictures, cartoons, maps, props and costumes.

   e. The interview should last a minimum of four minutes and no more than 10 minutes.

Below is a list of possible subjects, or you may choose your own.

| | | |
|---|---|---|
| George Washington | Haym Solomon (financier) | Peter Zenger |
| Samuel Adams | George Rogers Clark | David Bushnell (submarine |
| Crispus Attucks | John Dickinson | inventor) |
| Thomas Jefferson | Thomas Paine | Boston Massacre |
| John Adams | John Locke | Boston Tea Party |
| Benjamin Franklin | Jean Jacques Rousseau | Reading and responding to the |
| Benedict Arnold | Abigail Adams | Declaration of |
| Francis Marion, "the Swamp | James Arnistead (spy) | Independence as a wealthy |
| Fox" | Deborah Sampson Gannet | merchant or planter, a poor |
| Marquis de Lafayette | (soldier) | craftsman or farmer, a slave |
| General Cornwallis | Patrick Henry | Revolutionary battle or |
| Lord North (Prime Minister) | John Hancock | campaign of your choice |
| King George III | Ethan Allen | Treaty of Paris |

inform instructional decisions? How can teachers use portfolios and make decisions about the texts they use? The key to assessment in content areas, as we contend in the next chapter, is to make it as authentic as possible. Let's find out how and why this is the case.

## SUGGESTED READINGS

Bleich, D. (1978). *Subjective criticism*. Baltimore: The Johns Hopkins UP.

Bohning, G. & Radencich, M. (1989). Informational action books: a curriculum resource for science and social studies. *Journal of Reading, 32,* 434–439.

Booksearch: Recommended historical fiction. (1989). *English Journal,* 84–86.

Borasi, R., Sheedy, J. R., & Siegel, M. (1990). The power of stories in learning mathematics. *Language Arts, 67,* 174–189.

Bromley, K. D. (1991). *Webbing with literature: Creating story maps with children's books.* Boston: Allyn and Bacon.

Brozo, W. G. (1989). Applying a reader response heuristic to expository text. *Journal of Reading, 32,* 140–145.

Carnes, E. J. (1988). Teaching content area reading through nonfiction book writing. *Journal of Reading, 31,* 354–360.

Donelson, K. L. & Nilson, A. P. (1989). *Literature for today's young adults.* 3rd. ed. Glenview, IL: Scott, Foresman.

Egan, K. (1989). Layers of historical understanding. *Theory and Research in Social Education, 17,* 280–294.

Johnson-Weber, M. (1989). Picture books for junior high. *Journal of Reading, 32,* 219–220.

Levstik, L. S. (1990). Research directions: Mediating content through literary texts. *Language Arts, 67,* 848–853.

Miletta, M. (1992). Picture books for older children: Reading and writing Connections. *The Reading Teacher, 45,* 555–556.

Neal, J. C. & Morre, K. (1991). *The Very Hungry Caterpillar* meets *Beowulf* in secondary classrooms. *Journal of Reading, 35,* 290–296.

Rosen, H. (1986). The importance of story. *Language Arts, 63,* 226–237.

San Jose, C. (1988). Story drama in the content areas. *Language Arts, 65,* 26–33.

# PART III

# Assessment

# 11

# Making Authentic Assessments

Be not deceived with the first appearance of things, for show is
not substance.

—*English proverb*

## ORGANIZING PRINCIPLE

Authentic assessments in content area classrooms require that both teachers
and students are engaged actively in an ongoing process of evaluation and
self-evaluation. While it's relatively easy for a teacher to latch onto a standardized test score, you may be getting appearance, not substance, as the
English proverb we quote reminds us. Just as readers are active participants
in the reading process, you must become actively involved in developing
and scoring assessments, overseeing the development of student work for
portfolios, and in examining your own students. This kind of assessment,
which has come to be known as authentic assessment, is characterized by a
direct connection to teaching and to the improvement of practice.

Teachers who venture into authentic assessment will be making decisions about instruction for which they will need to gather and interpret several different kinds of information. Understanding assessment requires that
you distinguish between two major yet different approaches: a formal, standardized approach and an informal, naturalistic approach. As depicted in
the Chapter Overview, these major views of assessment form the base from
which more balanced practices, such as the use of portfolios, have emerged.
Tests, observations, checklists, interviews, and inventories are some of the
methods and techniques that make authentic assessments possible. Authentic assessments cut across students, texts, and teachers. That is to say,
they help you to better understand student performance and provide a basis
for making instructional decisions; they also provide a framework for tuning

into the text difficulty of the materials you use to teach subject matter; and they provide a context in which you can self-evaluate your teaching performance in relation to a particular group of students and the texts that you use.

Assessing for instruction, first and foremost, should provide the opportunity to gather and interpret useful information about students: their prior knowledge, their attitudes toward reading, writing, and subject matter, and their ability to use reading and writing to learn with texts. Through the use of portfolios—a collection of student work and information—both students and teachers gather information to better understand those factors that affect literacy and learning and characterize an individual student's performance. The organizing principle of this chapter supports the view that assessment should be authentic and responsive to teacher decision-making: *Instructional assessment is a continuous process that makes use of multiple methods of gathering relevant data for instructional purposes.*

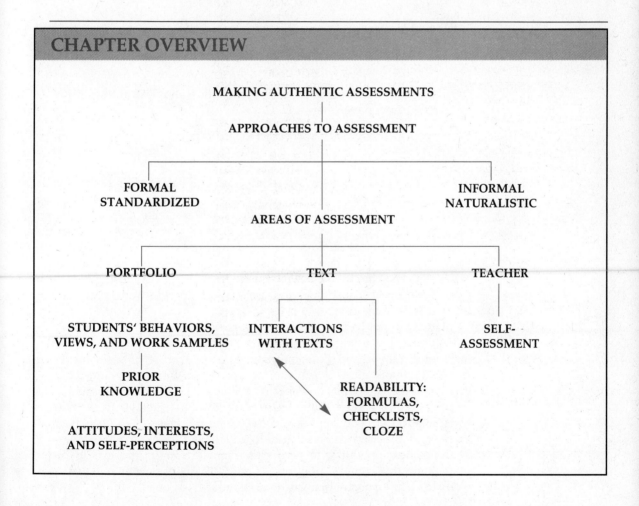

## CHAPTER OVERVIEW

MAKING AUTHENTIC ASSESSMENTS

APPROACHES TO ASSESSMENT

FORMAL STANDARDIZED

INFORMAL NATURALISTIC

AREAS OF ASSESSMENT

PORTFOLIO

TEXT

TEACHER

STUDENTS' BEHAVIORS, VIEWS, AND WORK SAMPLES

INTERACTIONS WITH TEXTS

SELF-ASSESSMENT

PRIOR KNOWLEDGE

READABILITY: FORMULAS, CHECKLISTS, CLOZE

ATTITUDES, INTERESTS, AND SELF-PERCEPTIONS

## FRAME OF MIND

1. How does assessment aid in setting instructional goals?

2. How does a formal, standardized approach differ from an informal, naturalistic approach?

3. What are advantages of ongoing assessment occurring in the natural context of the classroom?

4. What are portfolios and how are they constructed in the content classroom?

5. How can teachers assess students' background knowledge?

6. Why and how should teachers assess students' attitudes and interests toward reading?

7. How does the teacher assess students' interactions with text?

8. When and how might teachers use professional judgment in analyzing the difficulty of textbooks?

9. What are predictive measures of readability and how do they differ from performance measures?

You are in a good position to identify and emphasize the strengths your students bring to learning situations whenever you engage in an ongoing process of assessment. This is why efforts at assessment should center on the classroom context, where the focus of assessment is not only on students but also on texts and on teacher-student-text interaction. In this sense, *diagnostic teaching* is one of the most worthwhile activities content area teachers participate in. Nevertheless, the prospect of diagnosing is often a formidable one because it evokes images of expertise and specialization beyond your domain.

This need not be the case. What, then, do you need to know about students and texts to better plan classroom activities? As you go about the tasks of planning and decision-making, several areas of assessment are essential. First of all, you will want to assess students' prior knowledge in relation to thematic units and specific text lessons. Moreover, you will want to assess student knowledge and use of reading strategies to learn with texts. In addition, you should consider assessing the texts you use. Each of these areas of assessment is integral to understanding some of the dynamics of the context operating in your classroom. If your purpose is to better understand that context, an informal, naturalistic approach to evaluation is likely to be more useful than a formal, standardized one.

# STANDARDIZED AND NATURALISTIC APPROACHES TO ASSESSMENT

Teachers sometimes intuitively know that what they do in class is working. More often, however, information for making decisions is best obtained through careful observation of students. Their strengths and weaknesses as they interact with one another and with texts can be assessed as students participate in small groups, contribute to class discussions, respond to questions, and complete written assignments. This approach to assessment is informal and naturalistic.

A naturalistic approach to assessment has two main elements. First, it is based on the responses of those directly involved. Second, it uses methods within the natural context of the classroom. The presence of these two criteria ensures that assessment begins with classroom-centered concerns.

Naturalistic methods may include personal observation, interviews, and anecdotal records and student-selected products. The information gained from a naturalistic evaluation can be organized into a rich description or portrait of your content area classroom or into student *portfolios*. Concerns that emerge, whether about individual students or the delivery of instructional strategies, are likely to make sense because they came directly from the classroom context and often result from teacher-student or student-student interaction.

Consider how a naturalistic approach differs from a more formal, standardized one. In Table 11.1, the two approaches are compared in several categories. Certainly there are many gray areas in an assessment where the standardized and naturalistic approaches overlap. In this table, however, differences between the two approaches are emphasized. Traditional, formal assessments are product oriented. They are more tangible and can be obtained at specific points in time. Naturalistic assessment is informal and process-oriented. When informal assessment is stressed, the process is ongoing and provides as much information about the reader as about the product. Together, they permit a more balanced approach that uses a combination of traditional, formal and naturalistic, informal practices. The end result is an understanding of *why* particular results are obtained in formal evaluation, which informs the *how* of the teacher decision-making process.

## The Role of Standardized Tests

An assessment based on standardized test information is different from an assessment that evolves from naturalistic methods. A standardized reading test is more formal, may be administered at the beginning or end of the school year, and uses test methods that are considered to be objective. Moreover, schools may purchase a computer printout or report of students' strengths and weaknesses in reading subskills along with the test results.

**Table 11.1    COMPARISONS OF TWO APPROACHES TO ASSESSMENT**

|  | Standardized | Naturalistic |
|---|---|---|
| Orientation | Formal; developed by test publishers | Informal; developed by teachers |
| Administration | Testing at the beginning/end of school year; paper and pencil, multiple-choice; to groups at one seating | Continuously evolving/intermittent throughout an instructional unit; small group, one on one |
| Methods | Objective; standardized reading achievement tests designed to measure levels of current attainment | Classroom tests, checklists, observations, interviews, etc., designed to evaluate understanding of course content |
| Uses | Compare performance of one group with students in other schools, classrooms; estimate range of reading ability in a class; select appropriate materials for reading; identify students who need further diagnosis | Make qualitative judgments about students' strengths and instructional needs in reading and learning content subjects. Select appropriate materials; adjust instruction when necessary |
| Feedback Format | Reports, printouts of subtest scores; summaries of high and low areas of performance; percentiles, norms, stanines | Notes, profiles, portfolios, recommendations that evolve throughout instructional units; expansive (relate to interests, strategies, purpose for reading) |

Today, pressures for outcomes assessment have forced many school districts to use standardized tests as a means of assessment. For example, Ohio and many other states mandate statewide proficiency exams in math and reading for all ninth graders. According to Moore (1983), standardized tests help to satisfy the public's demand that assessment be objective, exact, and convenient. As a result, school officials often want "hard" data that are statistically validated and reliable. Enter the standardized test! Standardized reading tests are formal, usually machine-scorable instruments in which scores for the tested group are compared with standards established by an original normative population. The purpose of a standardized reading test is to show where students stand in relation to other students based on a single performance.

Reading researchers have studied the relationships between standardized tests of reading and student performance on reading tasks in specific content areas (Artley 1975; Peters 1975). They have generally concluded that specific factors not accounted for on a test of general achievement influence the reading of subject matter materials. In fact, Peters (1975) said a standardized reading test may not provide the information that content teachers desire.

Performance on standardized reading tests can yield only rough estimates at best of how students will apply reading to textbooks in a particular subject. Static assessment, in which the teacher derives performance levels with scoring keys and norming tables, persists (Brozo 1990). Yet a student who is a good reader of social studies may be a poor or mediocre reader of math or science. It's safe to say that teachers who consult standardized reading tests should do so judiciously and with reasonable expectations.

Standardized tests often are not intended to be used to make decisions about individual students. They have been developed with a prescribed content, directions to adhere to, and a scoring arrangement by test publishers to maintain a standardized analysis of the responses answered. Above all, standardized tests measure performance on a test. Hence, you need to proceed with caution: Make doubly sure to understand what performance on a particular reading test means before using test results to judge the ability of a reader. A single test result, in other words, can't possibly provide a whole picture of a student's ability to interact with text.

**What Teachers Need to Know About Standardized Tests.** To make sense out of test information and to determine how relevant or useful it may be, you need to be thoroughly familiar with the language, purposes, and legitimate uses of standardized tests. For example, as a test user, it's your responsibility to be knowledgeable about the norming and standardization of the reading test employed by your school district. Consult a test manual for an explanation of what the test is about, the rationale behind its development, and a clear description of what the test purports to measure. Not only should test instructions for administering and scoring be clearly spelled out, but also information related to *norms, reliability,* and *validity* should be easily defined and made available.

Norms represent average scores of a sampling of students selected for testing according to factors such as age, sex, race, grade, or socioeconomic status. Once a test maker determines norm scores, those scores become the basis for comparing the test performance of individuals or groups to the performance of those who were included in the norming sample. *Representativeness,* therefore, is a key concept in understanding student scores. It's crucial to make sure that the norming sample used in devising the reading test resembles the characteristics of students you teach.

Norms are extrapolated from raw scores. A *raw score* is the number of items a student answers correctly on a test. Raw scores are converted to other kinds of scores so that comparisons among individuals or groups of students can be made. Three such conversions—percentile scores, stanine scores, and grade equivalent scores—are often represented by test makers as they report scores.

*Percentile scores* describe the relative standing of a student at a particular grade level. For example, a percentile score of 85 by a student in the fifth grade means that his or her score is equal to or higher than the scores of 85 percent of comparable fifth graders.

*Stanine scores* are raw scores that have been transformed to a common standard to permit comparison. In this respect, stanines represent one of several types of standard scores. Because standard scores have the same mean and standard deviation, they permit direct comparison of student performance across tests and subtests. The term *stanine* refers to *sta*ndard *nine*-point scale, in which the distribution of scores on a test is divided into nine parts. Each stanine indicates a single digit ranging from 1 to 9 in numerical value. Thus, a stanine of 5 is at midpoint on the scale and represents average performance. Stanines 6, 7, 8, and 9 indicate increasingly better performance; stanines 4, 3, 2, and 1 represent decreasing performance. As teachers, we can use stanines effectively to view a student's approximate place above or below the average in the norming group.

*Grade equivalent scores* provide information about reading test performance as it relates to students at various grade levels. A grade equivalent score is a questionable abstraction. It suggests that growth in reading progresses throughout a school year at a constant rate, for example, a student with a grade equivalent score of 7.4 is supposedly performing at a level that is average for students who have completed four months of the seventh grade. At best, this is a silly and spurious interpretation: "Based on what is known about human development generally and language growth specifically, such an assumption (underlying grade equivalent scores) makes little sense when applied to a human process as complex as learning to read" (Vacca, Vacca, and Gove 1991, p. 432).

*Reliability* refers to the consistency or stability of a student's test scores. A teacher must raise the question: Can similar test results be achieved under different conditions? Suppose your students were to take a reading test on Monday, their first day back from vacation, and then take an equivalent form of the same test on Thursday. Would their scores be about the same? If so, the test may indeed be reliable.

*Validity,* on the other hand, tells the teacher whether the test is measuring what it purports to measure. Validity, without question, is one of the most important characteristics of a test. If the test purports to measure reading comprehension, what is the test maker's concept of reading comprehension? Answers to this question provide insight into the *construct validity* of a test. Other aspects of validity include *content validity* (does the test reflect the domain or content area being examined?) and *predictive validity* (does the test predict future performance?).

Standardized test results are probably more useful at the building or district, not the classroom, level. A school, for example, may wish to compare itself for reading performance against a state or national norm. Or local district-wide norms may be compared with national norms, which is sometimes necessary when applying for federal or state funds. In general, information from standardized tests may help to screen for students who might have major difficulties in reading, to compare general reading achievement levels or different classes or grades of students, to assess group reading achievement, and to assess reading growth of groups of students (Allington and Strange 1980).

However, you need useful information about students' text-related behavior and background knowledge. You would be guilty of misusing standardized test results if you were to extrapolate about students' background knowledge or ability to comprehend course materials on the basis of standardized reading test performance.

Alternatives to standardized reading assessment are found in an informal, naturalistic approach to assessment. One of the most useful tools for naturalistic inquiry is observation.

## The Role of Teachers as Observers

In a standardized approach to assessment, the *test* is the major tool; in a naturalistic approach, the *teacher* is the major tool. Who is better equipped to observe students, provide feedback, and serve as a key informant about the meaning of classroom events? You epitomize the process of assessing students in an ongoing, natural way because you are in a position to observe and collect information continuously (Valencia 1990). Consequently, you become an observer of the relevant interactive and independent behavior of students as they learn in the content classroom.

Observation is one unobtrusive measure that ranges from occasional notice of unusual student behavior, to frequent anecdotal jottings, to regular and detailed written field notes. Besides the obvious opportunity to observe students' oral and silent reading behaviors, there are other advantages to observation. Observing students' appearance, posture, mannerisms, enthusiasm, or apathy may reveal information about self-image. However, unless you make a systematic effort to tune in to student performance, you may lose valuable insights. You have to be a good listener and a good watcher of students. Observation should be a natural outgrowth of teaching; it increases teaching efficiency and effectiveness. Instructional decisions based on accurate observation help you zero in on what and how to teach in relation to reading tasks.

However, before this can happen, you must view yourself as a participant observer and action researcher/problem solver. You need to systematically collect information about and samples of students' work in relation to instructional goals with an eye toward what you think best represents students' capabilities (Resnick and Resnick 1991).

For example, a science teacher is beginning a unit on plants and plant life. She probably approaches the unit with certain preconceptions about the difficulty of the reading material, the work and study habits of the students, and the students' ability to use reading as a vehicle for learning. But she suspends these preconceptions; she purposely tries not to let presuppositions interfere with class presentations until classroom events and experiences during the unit suggest that her preconceptions are relevant.

The science teacher responds to the happenings that unfold before her. She guides daily observations by asking herself questions that reflect her objectives: How did students react to the class presentation? Which students had trouble with the reading assignment? How did students respond to instructional procedures and materials? Were students bored with the lesson? Did they grasp the concept related to man's dependence on green plants? What adjustments should I make in class presentations for the remainder of the unit?

According to Croll (1986), teachers are often in the role of observer, whether seeking "to monitor some aspect of their own" or their students' "classroom activities for very particular and specific purposes concerned with a problem or concern . . ." (p. 2). In other words, you search for meaning in the actions and words of your students and in doing so, sometimes blur the boundary between the researcher and the practitioner models of classroom observation.

To record observations done systematically, to note significant teaching-learning events, or to simply make note of classroom happenings, you need to keep a notebook or index cards on hand. Information collected in a purposeful manner is called field notes. They aid in classifying information, inferring patterns of behavior, and making predictions about the effectiveness of innovative instructional procedures. As they accumulate, field notes may serve as anecdotal records that provide documentary evidence of students' interactions over periods of time. To illustrate, an eighth-grade math teacher has been using vocabulary activities in two of her morning classes once a week for a month. Her intention is to increase the level of students' engagement in a cooperative activity, especially several of the more reticent students. Consequently, in addition to some general descriptive field notes, she devised a time sample format such as the one outlined in Figure 11.1. This provides an efficient way to collect data about what individuals or groups of students are doing in the classroom. For example, she selected a two-minute time interval and described behavior she observed at three successive intervals.

Listening and discussing are two other assessment tools that go hand in hand with observing students. Many students want to establish a personal rapport with their teachers. They may talk of myriad subjects, seemingly unrelated to the unit. It is often during this informal chatter, however, that you find out about the students' background, problems, and interests. This type of conversation, in which you assume the role of active listener, can provide suggestions about topics for future lessons and materials.

Discussion, both casual and directed, is also an integral part of evaluation. You need to make yourself available, both before and after class, for discussion about general topics, lessons, and assignments. For an assessment of reading comprehension, nothing replaces one-to-one discussion of the material, whether before, during, or after the actual reading. Finally, you may even

**Figure 11.1    TIME SAMPLE**

Date:  10/12/92      Time:  Start:  11:05   Stop:  11:10

School:  Notre Dame    Grade:  8

Class:  Pre-Algebra    Period:  3

Other pertinent information

Time Intervals Used:  2 min.

Time  10:05   Behavior:  Emily listens  to directions as Magic
                              Squares are distributed.

Time  10:07   Behavior:  She seems confused and is looking at
                              the others in her group.

Time  10:09   Behavior:  Matt gets up, goes over to Emily with
                              his Magic Square and points to the first
                              term while talking quietly.

encourage students to verbalize their positive and negative feelings about the class itself as well as about topics, reading, and content area activities.

Teachers who observe with any sort of regularity soon discover they are able to acquire enough information to process "in a meaningful and useful manner" (Fetterman 1989, p. 88). You can then make reliable decisions about instruction with observation and other techniques used in portfolio assessment.

## PORTFOLIO ASSESSMENT

*WANTED: A means to:*

- *provide information about the nature of students' work and achievements;*
- *involve students themselves in reflecting on their capabilities and making decisions about their work;*
- *take into account the holistic nature of instruction as a base from which to consider attitudes, strategies, and responses;*
- *assist in the planning of appropriate instruction to follow;*
- *serve as a showcase of student and teacher mutually-selected work;*
- *reveal special needs of students as well as special talents;*
- *display multiple student-produced artifacts collected over time;*
- *integrate assessment into the daily instruction as a natural, vital part of teaching and learning;*
- *expand both the quantity and quality of evidence with a variety of indicators.*

The term *portfolio assessment* has come to collectively define the use of global, alternative, balanced practices in gathering information about students. Tierney et al. (1991) define portfolios as *vehicles for on-going assessment. They are composed of purposeful collections that examine achievement, effort, improvement, and most importantly processes (selecting, comparing, sharing, self-evaluation, and goal setting).* As such, they lend themselves beautifully to instruction in content areas ranging from math and science to English, history, health education, and so on.

Significant pieces that go into student portfolios are *collaboratively* chosen by teachers and students. Selections represent processes and activities more than products. A distinct value underlying the use of portfolios is a commitment to students' self-evaluation of their understanding and personal development.

Contrasting portfolios with traditional assessment procedures, Walker (1991) submits that instead of a contrived task representing knowledge of a subject, portfolios are an "authentic" assessment that measure the process of the construction of meaning. *Students* make choices about what to include; this in turn encourages self-reflection on their own development, evaluation of learning, and personal goal setting. Advantages of portfolios are more easily visualized when compared with traditional assessment practices as displayed in Table 11.2, adapted from Tierney et al. (1991, p. 44).

**Table 11.2    PORTFOLIOS VERSUS TESTING: DIFFERENT PROCESSES AND OUTCOMES**

| Portfolio | Testing |
|---|---|
| Represents the range of learning activities students are engaged in | Assesses students across a limited range of assignments which may not match what students do |
| Engages students in assessing their progress and/or accomplishments and establishing ongoing learning goals | Mechanically scored or scored by teachers who have little input |
| Measures each student's achievement while allowing for individual differences between students | Assesses all students on the same dimensions |
| Represents a collaborative approach to assessment | Assessment process is not collaborative |
| Has a goal of student self-assessment | Student assessment is not a goal |
| Addresses improvement, effort, and chievement | Addresses achievement only |
| Links assessment and teaching to learning | Separates learning, testing, and teaching |

**Source:**    From *Portfolio Assessment in the Reading-Writing Classroom* by Tierney, Carter and Desai. Reprinted by permission of Christopher-Gordon Publishers, Inc.

## Adapting Portfolios to Content Area Classes

You can, by making some individual adjustments, adapt portfolios to meet your needs. Techniques such as interviewing, observing, and using checklists and inventories provide good sources of information about students in the classroom. The use of portfolios is in many ways a more practical method of organizing this type of information. Linek (1991) suggests that many kinds of data be collected for thorough documentation of attitudes, behaviors, achievements, improvement, thinking, and reflective self-evaluation. For example, students may begin a math course with poor attitudes and constantly challenge the validity of the content by saying things like, "What are we learning this for anyway? It's got nothing to do with me and my life." If you provide opportunities for functional application in realistic situations, comments may change over time to, "Boy, I never realized how important this was going to be for getting a job in real life!"

Noting behaviors of students is a way of documenting their maturing approach to content area subjects. For example, at the beginning of a general science course that includes hands-on laboratory experience, students may be confused about the scientific method, which in turn results in a great deal of off-task behavior. The teacher at this point in the semester then decides to spoon-feed students one small step at a time when conducting an experiment. Yet as the semester progresses and students internalize the construct—scientific method—they can proceed to experiment with less direct teacher involvement. An illustration of individual growth during a semester occurred with Chip, a student in a ninth-grade vocational workshop class, who improved in his ability to use a jigsaw between September and November. Early on when using the tool Chip was erratic; his products needed a lot of planing, filing, and sanding. Later in the semester as Chip gained in precision, less time was spent in planing, filing, and sanding. A grade on only the final product may not have taken into account elapsed production time and increased precision from the initial stages. Through documentation, then, it is possible to note thinking and reflective self-evaluation, which in essence increase students' metacognitive knowledge about their own performance.

Much more than a folder for housing daily work, a record file or a grab-bag, a portfolio is a comprehensive profile of each student's progress and growth. In math class, whether it's arithmetic, algebra, or trig, teachers would decide with students what types of samples of student-produced work would be included. According to Stenmark (1991), a *math portfolio* might include samples of student-produced written descriptions of the results of practical or mathematical investigations; pictures and dictated reports from younger students; extended analyses of problem situations and investigations; descriptions and diagrams of problem-solving processes; statistical studies and graphic presentations. Still other "likely candidates for inclusion in a math portfolio are: coordinate graphs of arithmetic, algebra, and geometry; responses to open-ended questions or homework problems; group reports and photographs of student projects; copies of awards or prizes; video, audio, and computer-generated examples of student work . . . " (p. 63). In addition to these suggestions, a math portfolio might also in one sense be considered a mathematical biography because it may contain important information about a student's attitude toward math.

**Implementing Portfolios in the Classroom.**  In order to get started in the implementation of the portfolio assessment process, there are some logical steps to take and certain decisions that need to be made:

- *Discuss with your students the notion of portfolios as an interactive vehicle for assessment.* Explain the concept and show some examples of items that might be considered good candidates for the portfolio. Provide some examples from other fields such as art and business, where portfolios have historically recorded performance and provided updates.
- *Specify your assessment model.* That is, what is the purpose for the portfolio? Who is the audience for the portfolio? How much involvement will be entailed for students? Purposes, for example, may be to showcase students' best work, to document or describe an aspect of their work over time (to show growth), to evaluate by making judgments using either certain standards agreed upon in advance or relative growth and development of each individual, to document the process that goes into the development of a single product such as a unit of work on the Vietnam Era or the Middle East or nutrition, and so on.
- *Decide what types of requirements will be used, approximately how many items, and what format will be appropriate for the portfolio.* Furthermore, will students be designing their own portfolios, will they include videos or computer disks, or will they have a uniform look? Plan an explanation of portfolios for your colleagues and the principal; also, decide on the date that this process will begin.

■ *Consider which of the following possibilities for contributions are appropriate for your content area.* For example, writing samples, video records, conference notes, interviews, inventories, tests and quizzes, standardized tests, pupil performance objectives, self-evaluation, peer evaluations, daily work samples, a collection of written work from teaching-learning strategies such as three-level guides, vocabulary matching exercises, structured overviews, semantic maps, Your Own Questions, free writing, group projects . . . along with checklists, inventories, and interviews are the main techniques for assessing students' behaviors, background knowledge, attitudes, interests and perceptions.

## Assessing Students' Behavior and Views

Informal assessment techniques such as checklists, interviews, and content area reading inventories, discussed later in this chapter, are different from natural, open-ended observation. They often consist of categories or questions that have already been determined; they impose an a priori classification scheme on the observation process. A checklist is designed to reveal categories of information the teacher has preselected. When constructing a checklist you should know beforehand which reading and study tasks or attitudes you plan to observe. Individual items on the checklist then serve to guide your observations in a selective manner.

The selectivity that a checklist offers is both its strength and its weakness as an observational tool. Checklists are obviously efficient because they guide your observations and allow you to zero in on certain kinds of behavior. But a checklist can also restrict observation by limiting the breadth of information recorded—excluding potentially valuable raw data.

Box 11.1 presents sample checklist items that may be adapted to specific instructional objectives in various content areas.

In addition to checklists, observations, and inventories, interviews should also be considered part of the portfolio assessment repertoire. There are several advantages of using interviews, "be they *formal,* with a preplanned set of questions, or *informal,* such as a conversation about a book . . ." (Valencia, McGinley, and Pearson 1990, p. 14). First, students and teachers interact in collaborative settings. Second, an open-ended question format is conducive to the sharing of students' own views. Third, it reveals to what extent students are in touch with their internal dispositions toward reading subject matter material.

In general, there are several *types of interviews:* structured, semistructured, informal, and retrospective. As described by Fetterman (1989), these types blend and overlap in actual practice:

*Formally structured and semistructured*

Verbal approximations of a questionnaire; allow for comparison of responses put in the context of common group characteristics; useful in securing baseline data about students' background experiences.

## BOX 11.1 Sample Checklist Items for Observing Reading and Study Behavior

| Reading and Study Behavior | Fred | Pat | Frank | JoAnne | Jerry | Courtney | Mike | Mary |
|---|---|---|---|---|---|---|---|---|
| **Comprehension** | | | | | | | | |
| 1. Follows the author's message | A | B | B | A | D | C | F | C |
| 2. Evaluates the relevancy of facts | | | | | | | | |
| 3. Questions the accuracy of statements | | | | | | | | |
| 4. Critical of an author's bias | | | | | | | | |
| 5. Comprehends what the author means | | | | | | | | |
| 6. Follows text organization | | | | | | | | |
| 7. Can solve problems through reading | | | | | | | | |
| 8. Develops purposes for reading | | | | | | | | |
| 9. Makes predictions and takes risks | | | | | | | | |
| 10. Applies information to come up with new ideas | | | | | | | | |
| **Vocabulary** | | | | | | | | |
| 1. Has a good grasp of technical terms in the subject under study | | | | | | | | |
| 2. Works out the meaning of an unknown word through context or structural analysis | | | | | | | | |
| 3. Knows how to use a dictionary effectively | | | | | | | | |
| 4. Sees relationships among key terms | | | | | | | | |
| 5. Becomes interested in the derivation of technical terms | | | | | | | | |
| **Study Habits** | | | | | | | | |
| 1. Concentrates while reading | | | | | | | | |
| 2. Understands better by reading orally than silently | | | | | | | | |
| 3. Has a well-defined purpose in mind when studying | | | | | | | | |
| 4. Knows how to take notes during lecture and discussion | | | | | | | | |
| 5. Can organize material through outlining | | | | | | | | |
| 6. Skims to find the answer to a specific question | | | | | | | | |
| 7. Reads everything slowly and carefully | | | | | | | | |
| 8. Makes use of book parts | | | | | | | | |
| 9. Understands charts, maps, tables in the text | | | | | | | | |
| 10. Summarizes information | | | | | | | | |

**Grading Key:** A = always (excellent)
B = usually (good)
C = sometimes (average)
D = seldom (poor)
F = never (unacceptable)

*Informal*

More like conversations; useful in discovering what students think and how one student's perceptions compare with another's; help identify shared values; useful in establishing and maintaining a healthy rapport.

*Retrospective interviews*

Can be structured, semistructured, or informal; used to reconstruct the past, asking students to recall personal historical information; may highlight their values and reveal information about their worldviews (pp. 48–50).

One technique developed to interview students about the comprehension process is the Reading Comprehension Interview (Wixson et al. 1984). Designed for grades three through eight, it takes about 30 minutes per student to administer in its entirety. The RCI explores students' perceptions of (1) the purpose of reading in different instructional contexts and content areas, (2) reading task requirements, and (3) strategies the student uses in different contexts.

The RCI's main uses are to help identify patterns of responses (for the whole group and individuals) that could then serve as guides to instruction and to analyze an individual's flexibility with different reading activities.

Several questions on the RCI are particularly appropriate for content area reading. Although the RCI was developed for grades three through eight, high school teachers can make good diagnostic use of some of the questions.

Rather than interview each student individually, we suggest the following adaptation. Have students keep a learning log. In these logs, students write to themselves about what they are learning. For example, they can choose to focus on problems they are having with a particular reading assignment or activity. A variation on this general purpose would be to ask students to respond to some of the more pertinent questions on the RCI— perhaps one or two at any one time over several weeks.

In relation to a particular content area textbook, examine the kinds of questions students can write about from the RCI*:

1. What is the most important reason for reading this kind of material? Why does your teacher want you to read this book?

2. Who's the best reader you know in *(content area)*? What does he/she do that makes him/her such a good reader?

3. How good are *you* at reading this kind of material? How do you know?

4. What do you have to do to get a good grade in *(content area)* in your class?

*From "An interview for assessing students' perceptions of classroom reading tasks" by K. K. Wixson, A. B. Bosky, M. M. Yochum, and D. E. Alverman, The Reading Teacher, January 1984. Reprinted with permission of the authors and the International Reading Association.

5.  If the teacher told you to remember the information in this story/chapter, what would be the best way to do this?
    Have you ever tried (*name a strategy, e.g., outlining*)?

6.  If your teacher told you to find the answers to the questions in this book what would be the best way to do this? Why?
    Have you ever tried (*name a strategy, e.g., previewing*)?

7.  What is the hardest part about answering questions like the ones in this book?
    Does that make you do anything differently?

Having students respond to these questions in writing does not deny the importance of interviewing individuals. However, it does save an enormous amount of time while providing a teacher with a record of students' perceptions of important reading tasks related to comprehension.

Another way to get at some of the same perceptions students hold about reading activities is through a questionnaire. Hahn (1984) developed a ten-item questionnaire based on modifications of a research instrument used by Paris and Meyers (1981). Five items on the questionnaire represent positive reading strategies (procedures students should use to comprehend effectively), and five items depict negative strategies (those that are ineffective and should be avoided). See Box 11.2.

Students who rate positive strategies as not very helpful can easily be identified upon scoring the questionnaire. These students may benefit from some explicit instruction in the strategies. Also, a good point of discussion would be why the negative strategies are not helpful for effective *studying*.

## Assessing Students' Prior Knowledge

As we discussed in Chapter 2, one of the reasons for the recent increase in attention given to prior knowledge is the popularization of a schema-theoretic view of reading. Understanding the role of schema in reading comprehension provides insights into why students may fail to comprehend text material. Pearson and Spiro (1982) argue that "schema inadequacies" are responsible for a great many roadblocks to reading comprehension.

Three kinds of schema-related problems can interfere with understanding. The first deals with *schema availability*. Students may lack the relevant background knowledge and information needed to comprehend a text assignment. A teacher might ask, "Does my student have the schema necessary to make sense of a particular text selection?"

A second schema inadequacy is *schema selection*. Students who have sufficient background knowledge may fail to bring it to bear as they read. For example, students may be unaware that what they already know about the selection is of any importance in the reading process. How a teacher evaluates and activates available schema is essential to effective reading instruction in content areas.

---

**BOX 11.2    Questionnaire on Reading Strategies**

Does it help to understand a text selection (or a story) if you . . .

1. Think about something else while you are reading?
   _____ always        _____ almost always     _____ almost never     _____ never

2. Write it down in your own words?
   _____ always        _____ almost always     _____ almost never     _____ never

3. Underline important parts of the selection?
   _____ always        _____ almost always     _____ almost never     _____ never

4. Ask yourself questions about the ideas in the selection?
   _____ always        _____ almost always     _____ almost never     _____ never

5. Write down every single word in the selection?
   _____ always        _____ almost always     _____ almost never     _____ never

6. Check through the selection to see if you remember all of it?
   _____ always        _____ almost always     _____ almost never     _____ never

7. Skip the parts you don't undertand in the selection?
   _____ always        _____ almost always     _____ almost never     _____ never

8. Read the selection as fast as you can?
   _____ always        _____ almost always     _____ almost never     _____ never

9. Say every word over and over?
   _____ always        _____ almost always     _____ almost never     _____ never

10. Ask questions about parts of the selection that you don't understand?
   _____ always        _____ almost always     _____ almost never     _____ never

Positive Strategies: Questions 2, 3, 4, 6, 10
Negative Strategies: Questions 1, 5, 7, 8, 9

**Source:** Amos Hahn, "Assessing and Extending Comprehension: Monitoring Strategies in the Classroom." *Reading Horizons,* 1984, 24, 225–230. By permission of *Reading Horizons.*

A third type of schema inadequacy involves *schema maintenance.* Students may not be aware or skilled enough at recognizing when shifts in schema occur during reading. They may not know how or when to adapt and change schema as a particular reading situation demands. In other words, how does a teacher help students to maintain reader-text interactions during reading? The question implies that readers may have a schema available for a text selection and that it has been activated for reading. But somewhere during reading, the reading process breaks down. Students may get lost in a welter of details or bogged down in the conceptual complexity of the selection. Or they may be unable to interact with the text because of the way it is written— the author's language is too complex, convoluted, or stylized. As a result, readers only process bits and pieces of the text and fail to grasp in any coherent way the author's broad message or intent.

Determining whether students possess, select, or maintain schema helps the teacher to make decisions about content area reading instruction. For example, one critical decision involves how much prereading preparation students will need for a text assignment. Another might be to decide how much background building and skill direction will be necessary. Seeking information to help make decisions such as these requires that teachers adapt and use the informal, naturalistic procedures that we have already outlined.

One assessment strategy might be to informally test students' knowledge of the material to be learned. The teacher should construct a background knowledge inventory according to the content objectives, that is, the major ideas and concepts, to be covered in a unit of study. The inventory or pretest can be a short-answered assessment or a set of open-ended essay questions. Many teachers combine short-answer questions with open-ended ones.

The pretest should not be graded, but it should be discussed with the class. In fact, use the pretest to introduce students to the major concepts that will be developed in the unit. Explain why you chose to ask certain questions. Share your content objectives with the class. Students will get a sense of what they already know as a result of the discussion. But the discussion should also underscore *what students need to know* in relation to the new material to be studied.

Alternatives to background knowledge pretesting include assessment procedures that are instructionally based. For example, the Prereading Plan (PreP), developed by Langer (1981), may be used to estimate background knowledge that students bring to text assignments. It is presented in Chapter 5 as a prereading activity. PreP provides the teacher with practical evaluative information about the extent to which students' language and concepts match up with the text and promote comprehension.

## Assessing Students' Attitudes, Interests, and Self-Perceptions

When students learn to analyze a reading assignment by questioning what they know and don't know about the subject matter, they are taking a giant step toward self-awareness. Knowledge of *self* in relation to *texts* and reading *tasks* puts students in a strategic position to learn. Although knowledge about one's own knowledge plays an important role in this respect, a teacher needs to help students to be in touch with another aspect of *self*—attitude toward reading. Do students value reading as a source of pleasure? a tool for acquiring knowledge? Do they believe that reading can help them solve problems? Do they read text assignments with confidence? Or do they feel helpless when faced with a textbook assignment?

Attitude is a primary determination of whether students will approach or avoid textbooks. On one hand, attitude can be defined globally as the internal position one takes for or against something or someone (Quandt 1977). However, reading attitude is a much more complicated issue than simply knowing how one feels about reading.

In an age of interactive video, with students who are as used to compact discs and personal computers as they are to worksheets, attitude toward reading is a more complex construct than may have been previously realized. In fact, Lewis and Teale (1980) proposed a multidimensional view of reading attitude, which included such factors as (1) the value placed on reading as a means of gaining insight into self, others and/or life in general; (2) the value placed on the role of reading for attaining educational or vocational success; and (3) the pleasure derived from reading. Reading attitude, based on these factors, consists of three components; a *cognitive component* (one's beliefs or opinions about reading), an *affective component* (one's evaluations of or feeling about reading), and a *behavioral component* (one's intentions to read and actual reading behavior).

Students' interests and self-concepts are interwoven into the fabric of reading attitude. What students *like* to read—their interests—impacts on when they read, why they read, and how often they read. Moreover, how students *view* their prior experiences with reading and reading instruction also affects reading attitude. The perceptions they hold about themselves as readers can make or break a positive attitude toward reading. McNeil (1987) put it this way: "Learners have perceptions and feelings about themselves as readers that affect their performance. 'Learned helplessness'—the perceived inability to overcome failure—is particularly self-defeating" (p. 92). Depending on whether students view a reading task as within reach or out of their control, they will probably approach it in a positive or negative fashion.

In this book, we show how students can achieve success with textbooks. Developing a positive reading attitude is one of the keys to that success. You can influence positive attitudes toward reading through effective planning, instructional strategies that bridge the gap between students and textbooks, enthusiastic teaching, and a classroom context that supports reading and writing activity. Students may not learn to love reading in some generic sense, but they will learn to (1) value reading as a source of information and knowledge, (2) believe that it can help them do well in school and everyday life, and (3) use reading to solve problems and develop insights.

**Identifying Attitudes.** Reading attitudes are never easy to identify. However, as you accumulate information about students' strengths and instructional needs in relation to content area texts, it would be difficult to *ignore* their attitudes, interests, or self-concepts.

Observational techniques and attitude scales are the two major ways to assess reading attitude. Indeed, observation is the method most widely used by teachers to assess reading attitudes (Heathington and Alexander 1984). Focused teacher observations in which anecdotal notes or checklists are used can be valuable in identifying and recording attitude, interests, and students' self-perception. So too can individual conferences with students. Any of these methods will elicit data about typical attitude-related behavior, including the following:

- willingness to receive instruction,
- class participation,
- quality of work performed,
- library habits,
- independent reading,

- amount and kind of free reading,
- personal goals related to learning. (Readence, Bean, and Baldwin 1981)

Unfortunately, time constraints often impede continuous informal observation, especially for content area teachers who see five or six different classes each day.

An alternative or partner to observational techniques is a paper-and-pencil attitude survey. An attitude survey, according to Heathington (1975), should meet certain requirements such as reliability and validity and take minimal time for administering and scoring. Certainly one use of an attitude survey is to document changes in student attitude through pre- and post-test scores. The survey should be given early in the school year. Data from the assessment should give teachers a better sense of how students in a particular class approach reading in different situations. This is particularly the case when specific survey items cluster around different areas of reading activity in and out of school. By paying attention to students' *cluster scores*, teachers can begin to make plans related to their classroom reading environment. Posttesting later in the year may show that positive changes in attitude occurred for some students in conjunction with the creation of a reading environment and the application of content area reading strategies.

Awareness of the complexity of reading attitudes can be enlightening for some students. Begin a class discussion of a survey's results by explaining how feelings toward reading may vary from situation to situation. Use the case of two students that is presented by Lewis and Teale (1980). One doesn't enjoy reading and never reads in her spare time, but she sees that reading is valuable to her in achieving success in school. The other student reads for pleasure outside of school but doesn't consider reading to be valuable in school or for career success.

The discussion can lead to an awareness that negative attitude is situation specific. With whom did the class members identify in the above example? How can the teacher help? The teacher may even want to profile the class results without indicating individual scores. What can be done in this class to make reading a more positive experience?

**Exploring Interests and Self-Perceptions.** A textbook that appeals to students is probably high in *interestability,* a topic we'll discuss later in connection with evaluating the difficulty of text to determine its readability. A textbook low in interestability almost always complicates instruction because students make known their lack of interest.

This does not mean that textbooks should be banished to student lockers for the entire school year. Nor does it necessarily mean that a teacher must seek out high interest/low vocabulary material to serve as a vitamin supplement for the textbook. Some high interest/low vocabulary texts have been watered down to a point where key concepts are merely mentioned rather than developed to a substantive degree.

An alternative is to help students realize that interest is not inherent in the material, but instead is a state of mind (Ortiz 1983). When they express little interest in the material or say that it is boring, it may represent a masking of what students would really like to say, that "this textbook is difficult, and I'm having trouble making sense out of what I'm reading." If this is the case, adjustments can be made within the context of instruction to help students approach the material more positively.

Ortiz (1983) recommends that students need to reflect on how they become involved or interested in reading material. The teacher might begin the discussion with an exaggerated circumstance: "You're locked in a telephone booth with a disconnected phone for two hours and only the telephone book to read. How would you make it interesting?" After several minutes of suggestions on making the telephone book interesting, switch the topic to textbooks. "Which part of the chapter do you usually find most interesting? Have you ever been bored by one part of a textbook and later become interested in another part? What are some things you can do to make the textbook more interesting?"

The discussion should provide valuable insights for the teacher. It can lead to additional activities that will build and reinforce students' awareness of their own interest-generating capability:*

- Have students analyze their present reading habits. How do they decide what to read? Where does interest come from? Who controls interest?
- Have students select a passage that interests them from several available. Ask them to analyze why they selected a particular passage over the others. Have them read and reflect on what they found themselves doing as they read the passage that was of interest.
- Have students scan a table of contents and select items of interest. Analyze why they found them interesting.
- Have students lightly dot a passage with a pencil as they read whenever they begin to lose interest. Why?
- Have students read a passage they are not interested in and have them find one item they understand. Then have them find another, and so on. Evaluate how understanding relates to interest. (Ortiz 1983)

Although students must learn to generate interest in materials that are required for course study, the power of choice should also play a major role in content area reading. Students must have the leeway to read course-related texts of their own choosing.

## ASSESSING TEXT DIFFICULTY

Evaluating text and assessing students' interactions with texts are critical tasks for content area teachers and students—which call for sound judgment and decision making. One of the best reasons we know for making

*From "Generating interest in reading" by Rose Katz Ortiz. *Journal of Reading*, November 1983. Reprinted with permission of Rose Katz Ortiz and the International Reading Association.

decisions about the quality of texts is that the assessment process puts you and students in touch with their textbooks. To judge well, you must approach text assessment in much the same manner as you make decisions about other aspects of content area instruction. Any assessment suffers to the extent that it relies on a single source or perspective on information rather than on multiple sources or perspectives. Therefore, in order to make effective decisions based on professional judgment, you need to take into account different types of information, including student input.

One perspective or source of information to consider is publisher-provided descriptions of the design, format, and organizational structure of the textbook along with grade-level readability designations. Another perspective is your acquired knowledge of and interactions with the students in the class. A third perspective or source of information is your own sense of what makes the textbook a useful tool. A fourth source is the student perspective, so that instructional decisions are not made from an isolated teacher perception of the student perspective. To complement professional judgment there are several procedures that can provide you with useful information: readability formulas, close procedure, readability checklists, and a content area framework for student analysis of reading assignments. The first order of business then, if content area reading strategies are to involve students in taking control of their own learning, is to find out how students are interacting with text.

## Assessing Students' Interactions with Text

Teacher-made tests provide another important indicator of how students interact with text materials in content areas. A teacher-made *content area reading inventory* (CARI) is an alternative to the standardized reading test. The CARI is informal. As opposed to the standard of success on a norm-referenced test, which is a comparison between the performance of the tested group and the original normative population, success on the CARI test is measured by performance on the task itself. The CARI measures performance on reading materials actually used in a course. The results of the CARI can give a teacher some good insights into *how* students read course material.

Administering a CARI involves several general steps. First, explain to students the purpose of the test. Mention that it will be used for evaluation only, to help you plan instruction, and that grades will not be assigned. Second, briefly introduce the selected portion of the test to be read and give students an idea direction to guide silent reading. Third, if you want to find out how the class uses the textbook, consider an open book evaluation; but if you want to determine students' ability to retain information, have them answer test questions without referring back to the selection. And, finally, discuss the results of the evaluation individually in conferences or collectively with the entire class.

A CARI can be administered piecemeal over several class sessions so that large chunks of instructional time will not be sacrificed. The bane of many content instructors is spending an inordinate amount of time away from actual teaching.

A CARI elicits the information you need to adjust instruction and meet student needs. It should focus on students' ability to (1) comprehend text, and (2) read at an appropriate rate of comprehension. Some authorities suggest that teachers should also evaluate additional competency areas such as study skills—skimming, scanning, outlining, taking notes, and so forth. We believe, however, that the best use of reading inventories in content areas is on a much smaller scale. A CARI should seek information related to basic reading tasks. For this reason, we recommend that outlining, note taking, and other useful study techniques be assessed through observation and analysis of student work samples. Chapter 9 presents a lesson plan organization for teaching study strategies in which assessment through observation is an internal component.

**Levels of Comprehension.** Teachers should gauge their students' ability to comprehend text material at different levels of comprehension as a science teacher did with the inventory in Box 11.3. The science teacher assessed whether students were able to respond at literal (getting the facts), inferential (making some interpretations), and applied (going beyond the material) levels of comprehension. At this time you can also determine a measure of reading rate in relation to comprehension.

You can construct a comprehension inventory using these steps:

1. Select an appropriate reading selection from within the second fifty pages of the book. The selection need not include the entire unit or story but should be complete within itself as to overall content. In most cases two or three pages will provide a sufficient sample.

2. Count the total number of words in the excerpt.

3. Read the excerpt and formulate ten to twelve comprehension questions. The first part of the test should ask an open-ended question like "What was the passage you read about?" Then develop three or more questions at each level of comprehension.

4. Prepare a student response sheet.

5. Answer the questions and include specific page references for discussion purposes after the testing is completed.

While students read the material and take the test, the teacher observes, noting work habits and student behavior, especially of those students who appear frustrated by the test. The science teacher of Box 11.3 allowed students to check their own work as the class discussed each question. Other teachers prefer to evaluate individual students' responses to questions first and then discuss them with students either individually or during the next class session.

**Rates of Comprehension.** To get an estimate of students' rates of comprehension, follow these steps:

## BOX 11.3    An Example of a Comprehension Inventory in Science

*General Directions:* Read pages 228–233. Then look up at the board and note the time it took you to complete the selection. Record this time in the space provided on the response sheet. Close your book and answer the first question. You may then open your textbook to answer the remaining questions.

### STUDENT RESPONSE FORM

*Reading Time:*_____ min _____ sec

I. *Directions:* Close your book and answer the following question. In your own words, what was this selection about? Use as much space as you need on this page. Continue on the opposite side if you should need more room to complete your answer.

II. A. *Directions:* Open your book and answer the following questions.
   1. An insect has six legs and a three-part body.
      a. true
      b. false
      c. can't tell
   2. Insects go through changes called metamorphosis.
      a. true
      b. false
      c. can't tell
   3. Most insects are harmful.
      a. true
      b. false
      c. can't tell
   4. Bees help flowers by moving pollen from flower to flower.
      a. true
      b. false
      c. can't tell

   B. *Directions:* Answers to these questions are not directly stated by the author. You must "read between the lines" to answer them.
   1. How is a baby cecropia moth different from a full-grown moth?

      _____
   2. Why does a caterpillar molt?

      _____
   3. What are the four stages of a complete metamorphosis?

      _____

   C. *Directions:* Answers to these questions are not directly stated by the author. You must read "beyond the lines" to answer them.
   1. Why do you suppose the caterpillar spins a long thread of silk around itself?

      _____
   2. During which season would the full-grown cecropia moth leave the cocoon? Why?

      _____
   3. Why do you think they leave in that season rather than another?

      _____

1. Have students note the time it takes to read the selection. This can be accomplished in an efficient manner by recording the time in five-second intervals by using a "stopwatch" that is drawn on the board.

2. As students complete the reading, they look up at the board to check the stopwatch. The number within the oval represents the minutes that have elapsed. The number that the teacher is pointing to along the perimeter of the oval represents the number of seconds.

3. Later on, students or the teacher can figure rate of reading in words per minute.
   *Example:*
   Words in selection: 1500
   > Reading time: 4 minutes, 30 seconds
   > Convert seconds into a decimal fraction. Then divide time into words.

   $$\frac{1500}{4.5} = 333 \text{ words per minute}$$

4. Determine the percentage of correct or reasonable answers on the comprehension test. Always evaluate and discuss rate of reading in terms of students' comprehension performance.

In summary, information you glean from a CARI will help you organize specific lessons and activities. You can decide the background preparation needed, the length of reading assignments, and the reading activities when you apply your best judgment to the information you have learned from the assessment.

## Readability

There are many readability formulas that can be used by classroom teachers to estimate textbook difficulty. Most popular formulas today are quick and easy to calculate. They typically involve a measure of sentence length and word difficulty to determine a grade-level score for text materials. This score supposedly indicates the reading achievement level that students need to comprehend the material. Because of their ease, readability formulas are used to make judgments about materials. These judgments are global and are not intended to be precise indicators of text difficulty.

A readability formula can best be described as a "rubber ruler" because the scores that it yields are estimates of text difficulty, not absolute levels. These estimates are often determined along a single dimension of an author's writing style: sentence complexity (as measured by length) and vocabulary difficulty (also measured by length). These two variables are used to predict text difficulty. But even though they have been shown to be persistent correlates of readability, they only indirectly assess sentence complexity and vocabulary difficulty. Are long sentences always more difficult to comprehend than short ones? Are long words necessarily harder to understand than short ones? When a readability formula is used to rewrite materials by breaking long sentences into short ones, the inferential burden of the reader actually increases (Pearson 1974–1975).

And while we're examining inferential burden, keep in mind that a readability formula doesn't account for the experience and knowledge that readers bring to content material. Hittleman (1973) characterized readability as a moment in time. He maintains that readability estimates should include the reader's emotional, cognitive, and linguistic backgrounds. A person's human makeup interacts at the moment with the topic, the proposed purposes for reading, and the semantic and syntactic structures in the material. Formulas are not designed to tap the variables operating in the reader. Our purpose, interest, motivation, and emotional state as well as the environment that we're in during reading contribute to our ability to comprehend text.

The danger, according to Nelson (1978), is not in the use of readability formulas: "The danger is in promoting the faulty assumptions that matching the readability score of materials to the reading achievement scores of students will automatically yield comprehension" (p. 622). She made these suggestions to content teachers:

1. Learn to use a simple readability formula as an aid in evaluating text.

2. Whenever possible, provide materials containing the essential facts, concepts, and values of the subject at varying levels of readability within the reading range of your students.

3. Don't assume that matching readability level of material to reading achievement level of students results in automatic comprehension. Remember there are many factors that affect reading difficulty besides those measured by readability formulas.

4. Don't assume that rewriting text materials according to readability criteria results in automatic reading ease. Leave rewriting of text material to the linguists, researchers, and editors who have time to analyze and validate their manipulations.

5. Recognize that using a readability formula is no substitute for instruction. Assigning is not teaching. Subject area textbooks are not designed for independent reading. To enhance reading comprehension in your subject area, provide instruction which prepares students for the assignment, guides them in their reading, and reinforces new ideas through rereading and discussion (pp. 624–625).

Within the spirit of these suggestions, let's examine a popular readability formula and an alternative, the *cloze* procedure.

**The Fry Graph.** The readability graph developed by Edward Fry (1977) is a quick and simple readability formula. The graph was designed to identify the grade-level score for materials from grade one through college. Two variables are used to predict the difficulty of the reading material: sentence length and word length. Sentence length is determined by the total number of sentences in a sample passage. Word length is determined by the total number of syllables in the passage. Fry recommended that three 100-word samples from the reading be used to calculate readability. The grade-level scores for each of the passages can then be averaged to determine overall readability. According to Fry, the readability graph predicts the difficulty of the material within one grade level. See Box 11.4 for the graph and expanded directions for the Fry formula.

**Cloze Procedure.** The cloze procedure does not make use of a formula to estimate the difficulty of reading material. Originated by Taylor in 1953, a cloze test determines how well students can read a particular text or reading selection as a result of their interaction with the material. Simply defined, then, the cloze procedure is a method by which you systematically delete words from a text passage and then evaluate students' ability to accurately supply the words that were deleted. An encounter with a cloze passage should reveal the interplay between the prior knowledge that students bring to the reading task and their language competence. Knowing the extent of this interplay will be helpful in selecting materials and planning instructional procedures. Box 11.5 presents part of a cloze test passage developed for a health education class studying sleep.

Here is how to construct, administer, score, and interpret a cloze test.

1. Construction
   a. Select a reading passage of approximately 275 words from material that students have not yet read, but that you plan to assign.
   b. Leave the first sentence intact. Starting with the second sentence, select at random one of the first five words. Delete every fifth word thereafter, until you have a total of 50 words for deletion. Retain the remaining sentence of the last deleted word. Type one more sentence intact. For children below grade four, deletion of every tenth word is often recommended.
   c. Leave an underlined blank fifteen spaces for each deleted word as you type the passage on a ditto master.

2. Administration
   a. Inform students that they are not to use their textbooks or work together in completing the cloze passage.
   b. Explain the task that students are to perform. Show how the cloze procedure works by providing several examples on the board.
   c. Allow students the time they need to complete the cloze passage.

3. Scoring
   a. Count as correct every *exact* word students apply. *Do not* count synonyms even though they may appear to be satisfactory. Counting synonyms will not change the scores appreciably, but it will cause unnecessary hassles and haggling with students. Accepting synonyms also affects the reliability of the performance criteria since they were established on exact word replacements.

## BOX 11.4    Fry Readability Graph

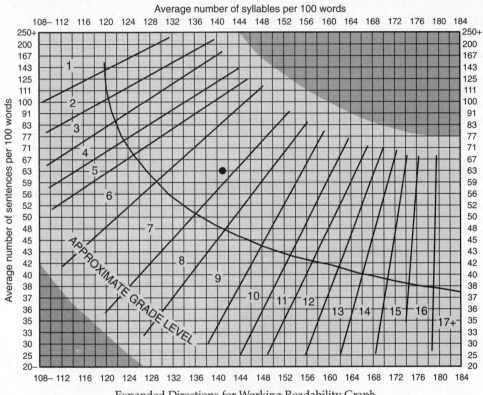

Average number of syllables per 100 words

Expanded Directions for Working Readability Graph

1. Randomly select three (3) sample passages and count out exactly 100 words each, beginning with the beginning of a sentence. Do count proper nouns, initializations, and numerals.

2. Count the number of sentences in the hundred words, estimating length of the fraction of the last sentence to the nearest one-tenth.

3. Count the total number of syllables in the 100-word passage. If you don't have a hand counter available, an easy way is to simply put a mark above every syllable over one in each word, then when you get to the end of the passage, count the number of marks and add 100. Small calculators can also be used as counters by pushing numeral 1 then push the + sign for each word or syllable.

4. Enter graph with *average* sentence length and *average* number of syllables; plot dot where the two lines intersect. Area where dot is plotted will give you the approximate grade level.

5. If a great deal of variability is found in syllable count or sentence count, putting more samples into the average is desirable.

6. A word is defined as a group of symbols with a space on either side; thus, *1945* is one word.

7. A syllable is defined as a phonetic syllable. Generally, there are as many syllables as vowel sounds. For example, *stopped* is one syllable and *wanted* is two syllables. When counting syllables for numerals and initializations, count one syllable for each symbol. For example, *1945* is four syllables.

**Source:**  Edward Fry, "Fry's readability graph: clarifications, validity, and extension to level 17." *Journal of Reading*, 21 (1977): 242–252. Reproduction permitted—no copyright.

---

**BOX 11.5     Sample Portion of Cloze Test**

Everybody sleeps—everybody, that is, except for an Italian and an Australian. These two men, according (1) twentieth-century medical literature, (2) slept at all. On (3) other hand, not long (4) *The New York Times* (5) on a professor who (6) to have fourteen hours (7) sleep a night. If (8) woke after even thirteen (9), he spent the day (10) foggy and tense. Apart (11) their sleeping patterns, though, (12) three men, according to (13) experts on such matters, (14) to be perfectly normal. (15) why, by inference, assume (16) their sleep habits were (17)? Indeed, when it comes (18) sleep, what is normal (19), by contrast, abnormal? Who's (20) say that what's perfectly natural for me might not be absurd for you?

**Answers:**

| | | | |
|---|---|---|---|
| 1. to | 6. had | 11. from | 16. that |
| 2. never | 7. of | 12. these | 17. abnormal |
| 3. the | 8. he | 13. the | 18. to |
| 4. ago | 9. hours | 14. appeared | 19. and |
| 5. reported | 10. feeling | 15. Yet | 20. to |

---

   **b.** Multiply the total number of exact word replacements by two in order to determine the student's cloze percentage score.

   **c.** Record the cloze scores on a sheet of paper for each class. For each class you now have one to three instructional groups that can form the basis for differentiated assignments. See Box 11.6.

4. Interpretation

   **a.** A score of 60 percent or above indicates that the passage can be read with a great deal of competence by students. They may be able to read the material on their own without reading guidance.

   **b.** A score of 40–60 percent indicates that the passage can be read with some competence by students. The material will challenge students if they are given some form of reading guidance.

   **c.** A score below 40 percent indicates that the passage will probably be too difficult for students. They will need either a great deal of reading guidance to benefit from the material or more suitable material.

---

**BOX 11.6     Cloze Performance Chart**

Subject _____

Period _____

Teacher _____

| Below 40% | Between 40% and 60% | Above 60% |
|---|---|---|
| | | |

The cloze procedure is an alternative to a readability formula because it gives an indication of how students will actually perform with course materials. But two potential problems may have a negative effect on the results of student performance on a cloze test. First, the nature of the test itself will probably be foreign to students. They will be staring at a sea of blank spaces in running text, and having to provide words for them can seem a formidable task. Don't expect a valid score the first time you administer the test. It's important to discuss the purpose of the cloze test and give students ample practice and exposure to it.

A second source of difficulty may be in students' reactions to the criteria for successful performance. An excellent score on a cloze test means that a student can respond incorrectly to twenty out of fifty test items—a mind-boggling standard of success that may cause unnecessary anxiety.

## Readability Checklist

Despite the many factors to consider in text evaluation, *teachers ultimately want texts that students will understand, be able to use, and want to use.* To help guide your assessment and keep it manageable, a checklist that focuses on *understandability, usability,* and *interestability* is useful. One such checklist is in Box 11.7, an adaptation of the Irwin and Davis (1980) Readability Checklist.

The domain of *understandability* provides information about how likely a given group of students is to understand, to comprehend adequately the text. It helps the teacher to assess relationships between students' own schema and conceptual knowledge and the text information. When teachers judge textbooks for possible difficulties, it is imperative to decide whether the author has taken into consideration the knowledge students will bring to the text. The match between what the reader knows and the text will have a strong influence on the understandability of the material.

Armbruster and Anderson (1981) indicate that one way to judge the author's assumptions about students' background knowledge and experiences is to decide if enough relevant ideas are presented in a text to satisfy the author's purpose. Often authors use headings to suggest their purposes for text passages. Convert the headings to questions. If the passage content answers the questions then the authors have achieved their purposes and the passage is *considerate.* If an author hasn't provided enough information to make a passage meaningful, the passage is *inconsiderate.*

The second major domain is *usability.* Is the text coherent, unified, and structured enough to be usable? Divided into two subsections on the Readability Checklist, this section provides information about the presentation and organization of content. It helps assess pertinent factors that contribute to the teacher's day-to-day use of the text in teaching and the students' use in learning. These items help pinpoint for a teacher exactly what needs supplementing or what might take additional preparation time or class time to compensate.

## BOX 11.7    General Textbook Readability Checklist

| Understandability | | Yes | To some extent | No (or does not apply) |
|---|---|---|---|---|
| Are the assumptions about students' vocabulary knowledge appropriate? | 1 | | | |
| Are the assumptions about students' prior knowledge of this content area appropriate? | 2 | | | |
| Are the assumptions about students' general experiential backgrounds appropriate? | 3 | | | |
| Does the teacher's manual provide the teacher with ways to develop and review the students' conceptual and experiential backgrounds? | 4 | | | |
| Are new concepts explicitly linked to the students' prior knowledge or to their experiential backgrounds? | 5 | | | |
| Does the text introduce abstract concepts by accompanying them with many concrete examples? | 6 | | | |
| Does the text introduce new concepts one at a time with a sufficient number of examples for each one? | 7 | | | |
| Are definitions understandable and at a lower level of abstraction than the concept being defined? | 8 | | | |
| Does the text avoid irrelevant details? | 9 | | | |
| Does the text explicitly state important complex relationships (e.g., causality, conditionality, etc.) rather than always expecting the reader to infer them from the context? | 10 | | | |
| Does the teacher's manual provide lists of accessible resources containing alternative readings for the very poor or very advanced readers? | 11 | | | |
| Is the readability level appropriate (according to a readability formula)? | 12 | | | |

## Usability

| | Yes | To some extent | No (or does not apply) |
|---|---|---|---|
| *External organizational aids* | | | |
| 1. Does table of contents provide a clear overview of the contents of the textbook? | | | |
| 2. Do chapter headings clearly define the content of the chapter? | | | |
| 3. Do chapter subheadings clearly break out the important concepts in the chapter? | | | |
| 4. Do topic headings provide assistance in breaking the chapter into relevant parts? | | | |
| 5. Does the glossary contain all the technical terms of the textbook? | | | |
| 6. Are graphs and charts clear and supportive of the textual material? | | | |
| 7. Are illustrations well done and appropriate to the level of the students? | | | |
| 8. Is print size of the text appropriate to the level of student readers? | | | |
| 9. Are lines of text an appropriate length for the level of the students who will use the textbook? | | | |
| 10. Is a teacher's manual available and adequate for guidance to the teachers? | | | |
| 11. Are important terms in italics or boldfaced type for easy identification by readers? | | | |
| 12. Are end-of-chapter questions on literal, interpretive, and applied levels of comprehension? | | | |
| *Internal organizational aids* | | | |
| 1. Are concepts spaced appropriately throughout the text, rather than being too many in too short a space or too few words? | | | |
| 2. Is an adequate context provided to allow students to determine meanings of technical terms? | | | |
| 3. Are the sentence lengths appropriate for the level of students who will be using the text? | | | |
| 4. Is the author's style (word length, sentence length, sentence complexity, paragraph length, numbers of examples) appropriate to the level of students who will be using the text? | | | |

*(Continued)*

| | Yes | To some extent | No (or does not apply) |
|---|---|---|---|
| Does the author use a predominant structure or pattern of organization (compare-contrast, cause-effect, time order, problem-solution) within the writing to assist students in interpreting the text?     5 | | | |

**Interestability**

| | Yes | To some extent | No (or does not apply) |
|---|---|---|---|
| Does the teacher's manual provide introductory activities that will capture students' interests?     1 | | | |
| Are chapter titles and subheadings concrete, meaningful, or interesting?     2 | | | |
| Is the writing style of the text appealing to the students?     3 | | | |
| Are the activities motivating? Will they make the student want to pursue the topic further?     4 | | | |
| Does the book clearly show how the knowledge being learned might be used by the learner in the future?     5 | | | |
| Are the cover, format, print size, and pictures appealing to the students?     6 | | | |
| Does the text provide positive and motivating models for both sexes as well as for other racial, ethnic, and socioeconomic groups?     7 | | | |
| Does the text help students generate interest as they relate experiences and develop visual and sensory images?     8 | | | |

**Summary Rating**

| | Understandability | Usability | Interestability |
|---|---|---|---|
| The text rates highest in............................. | | | |
| The text rates lowest in ............................... | | | |
| My teaching can best supplement.............. | | | |
| I would still need assistance with .............. | | | |

**Statement of Strengths:**

**Statement of Weaknesses:**

**Source:** Adapted from Judith W. Irwin and Carol A. Davis, "Assessing Readability: The Checklist Approach," *Journal of Reading,* November 1980, 124–130. By permission of Judith W. Irwin and Carol A. Davis and the International Reading Association.

Essentially, a teacher's response to these items is another way of deciding if a text is considerate or inconsiderate. A considerate text not only fits the reader's prior knowledge but also helps "the reader to gather appropriate information with minimal cognitive effort"; an inconsiderate text "requires the reader to put forth extra effort" in order to compensate for poorly organized material (Armbruster and Anderson 1981, p. 3).

The third domain, *interestability*, is intended to ascertain whether features of the text have appeal for a given group of students. Illustrations and photos may have instant appeal; students can relate to drawings and photographs depicting persons similar to themselves. The more relevant the textbook, the more interesting it may be to students.

Experiment with the Readability Checklist by trying it out on a textbook in your content area. Once you've completed the checklist, summarize your placement of checks on the brief rating chart at the end. Does the text rate high in understandability, usability, or interestability? Is a low rating in an area you can supplement well through your instruction, or is it in an area in which you could use more help? Also, summarize the strengths and weaknesses of the textbook. If you checked two areas in which you'd still need assistance, this text is less likely than another to meet your needs. Finally, decide how you can take advantage of the textbook's strengths and compensate for its weaknesses.

Recently, efforts to directly access student/reader-based judgment have resulted in a strategy to provide students with the guidelines they need to size up reading tasks (Schumm and Mangrum 1991). While checklists are designed for *teacher* use, a strategy such as "FLIP" is designed to engage the *reader* in helping to estimate the level of difficulty in a given material or textbook. With teacher guidance, perhaps using an overhead projector and think-aloud technique, students actually walk through the FLIP and consider these factors:

F    Friendliness
     How friendly is my reading assignment? *(Students look for text features such as index, graphs, pictures, summaries, study questions, etc.)*

L    Language
     How difficult is the language in my reading assignment? *(Students estimate the number of new terms.)*

I    Interest
     How interesting is my reading assignment? *(Students look over the title, headings, pictures, etc.)*

P    Prior knowledge
     What do I already know about the material covered in my reading assignment? *(Students think about the title, heading, summary . . .)* (Schumm and Mangrum pp. 121–122).

## TEACHER SELF-ASSESSMENT

If you are using a portfolio approach to assess students, it seems logical to extend the process and collect some useful information about yourself in the context of the classroom environment. It is a marvelous opportunity to ask that important question, "How am I doing?"

Teachers who want to deal with real concerns within their own classrooms can use several straightforward self-reporting techniques. You can do these individually or, after a while, get together and share with one another.

The first self-reporting technique is a systematic reflection about teaching behaviors. As illustrated in Box 11.8, you ask a series of questions about your behavior in relation to a specific class or even a particular topic or unit of study.

This may be done almost any time, but we suggest asking the questions before or within a week of beginning a new unit or semester. Jotting down the answers on a card or in a small notebook makes it even more useful because the answers will be easy to locate as time goes on. This keeps the process of self-evaluation going and takes a minimal amount of time.

Another systematic reflection is an effort to analyze whether our own attitudes and behaviors are conducive to forming positive attitudes in students. As you read each statement in Box 11.9 (adapted from Vacca, Vacca, and Gove 1991), think about the expectations you may be communicating

---

**BOX 11.8    Questions for Teacher Self-Evaluation**

1. *Focus on Present*
   What unit (or class, or part of the day) do I want to look at?

2. *Identify Behaviors*
   What do I usually do now?

3. *Analyze Behaviors*
   What results am I getting?

4. *Expose Alternatives*
   What additional possibilities exist?

5. *Set Goals*
   Where do I hope to go?

6. *Plan Change*
   How will I get there?

7. *Practice for Effectiveness*
   What can I do to assure getting there?

8. *Evaluate*
   Did I get there?

---

| BOX 11.9 | Teacher Self-Analysis |
|---|---|

1. I respect each student's efforts at becoming a better reader and value each one as a learner.
   Example: _____
   _____

2. I convince my students they don't have to be afraid of making mistakes.
   Example: _____
   _____

3. I believe each student can achieve some measure of success with reading.
   Example: _____
   _____

4. When my methods and materials are not resulting in student progress, I change the methods or materials.
   Example: _____
   _____

5. I am aware of verbal and nonverbal ways in which I communicate to my students my feelings about reading.
   Example: _____
   _____

---

**Source:** From *Reading and Learning to Read* by Jo Anne L. Vacca, Richard T. Vacca and Mary K. Gove. Copyright © 1987 by Jo Anne L. Vacca, Richard T. Vacca, and Mary K. Gove. Glenview, Illinois: Scott, Foresman and Company.

through verbal and nonverbal signals and classroom atmosphere. Try to provide at least one example from your past experiences or projected ones for each "yes" response.

A third self-reporting technique is not as systematic but is more personal: keeping a daily journal. Write down your thoughts about what happened in class that day. Regular notebook paper will suffice; what's important is that there is an entry for each school day. Setting a certain time aside each day, whether morning, afternoon, or evening, ensures that this becomes a habit.

In the beginning, a few questions may be needed just to get the writing flow started. Were you satisfied with the way you presented the strategies today? What did you do for the class that was most helpful to them? What did students do that helped you with your teaching? Is there anything you wish you could do over?

Initial entries will tend to be mundane, dealing with classroom management and describing what happened in the class. As time goes on and you become used to writing in this way, what you write about often changes (Holly 1984). You will write more personally, reacting with feelings to certain events and students and colleagues. You will be able to identify real issues and concerns about your own teaching. What could be more useful?

And, finally, to ascertain whether you are already implementing some instructional practices that positively affect students' attitudes by *combining* interests and needs, use the items in Box 11.10 (adapted from Vacca, Vacca, and Gove 1991). Check "yes" for those you are implementing; check "perhaps" if you are interested in exploring the suggestion; check "no" if you are neither using it nor interested in the suggestion.

---

**BOX 11.10     Instructional Practices Inventory**

|  | Yes | Perhaps | No |
|---|---|---|---|
| 1. I am aware of my students' attitudes toward reading and plan activities they tend to like. | | | |
| 2. I use reading materials in which my students can succeed. | | | |
| 3. I use materials related to the interests and needs of my students' norm group. | | | |
| 4. I read myself, orally or silently, so that my students can see that I value reading. | | | |
| 5. I create situations in which the usefulness of reading is apparent, such as reading essential to doing a certain project or activity. | | | |
| 6. I provide for recreational reading connected to subject areas. | | | |
| 7. I use reading material found in students' everyday world. | | | |
| 8. I avoid using reading as a punishment. | | | |

**Source:** From *Reading and Learning to Read* by Jo Anne L. Vacca, Richard T. Vacca and Mary K. Gove. Copyright © 1987 by Jo Anne L. Vacca, Richard T. Vacca and Mary K. Gove. 1991. New York: HarperCollins.

## LOOKING BACK, LOOKING FORWARD

Making authentic assessments is a continuous process in which teachers and students collect and analyze information about classroom interactions, text, and themselves. Multiple methods of gathering relevant data are taken from two distinct approaches to assessment: a formal, standardized one and an informal, naturalistic one. To develop goals and objectives for teaching, you need (1) to access information aboutp students' prior knowledge in relation to instructional units and text assignments, (2) to assess student knowledge and use of reading strategies to learn from texts, (3) to assess texts, and (4) to self-assess your own teaching.

An informal, naturalistic approach is a precursor to portfolio assessment. Through the use of portfolios a more balanced approach to collecting and organizing many kinds of information can inform decision making. Careful observation of students' strengths and weaknesses as they interact with one another and with content-specific material sheds light on the *why* as well as the *what* in teaching and learning.

In this chapter, key terms, major purposes, and legitimate uses of standardized tests were presented. Contrasts were drawn between portfolios and testing. Suggestions for assessing students' background knowledge included interviews, pretesting, or instructionally based strategies. Attitudes, interests, and self-perceptions rely on the interpretation of interviews, surveys, scales, and teacher observation. For insights into how students interact with text material and a measure of performance on reading materials used in a course, teacher-made content area reading inventories were suggested.

Assessing the difficulty of text material requires both professional judgment and quantitative analysis. Text assessment takes into account various factors within the reader and the text, with the exercise of professional judgment as useful as calculating a readability formula. Teachers, therefore, must be concerned with the quality of the content, format, organization, and appeal of the material. We supplied three types of procedures to assess text difficulty: readability formulas, cloze procedure, and readability checklists. Finally, some techniques to assist content area teachers reflect on their own attitudes and behaviors in the classroom/school environment were offered for teacher self-assessment.

Taking content literacy into the field will be the key to its impact in the 1990s. Professional staff development in schools is one of the vehicles by which the literacy practices in this book will become part of the instructional repertoire of content teachers. Appendix A, Guide to Staff Development, provides an overview for instructional leaders who want to plan and initiate collaborative staff development programs in content area reading.

## SUGGESTED READINGS

Croll, P. (1986). *Systematic classroom observation*. Philadelphia: The Falmer Press.

Guba, E. & Lincoln, Y. (1981). *Effective evaluation*. Washington, D.C.: Jossey-Bass.

Lyman, H. B. (1986). *Test scores and what they mean* (4th ed.). Englewood Cliffs, NJ: Prentice-Hall.

Stake, R., Shapson, S., & Russell, L. (1987). "Evaluation of staff development programs," in Wideen and Andrews (eds.). *Staff development for school improvement*, New York: The Falmer Press.

Tierney, R. J., Carter, M. A., & Desai, L. E. (1991). *Portfolio assessment in the reading-writing classroom*. Norwood, MA: Christopher Gordon.

Vacca, J. L., Vacca, R. T., & Gove, M. K. (1991). *Reading and learning to read*. New York: HarperCollins Publishers.

# A

# Guide for Staff Development

Teachers who want a successful content area reading program in their schools need more than knowledge and enthusiasm for this important aspect of instruction to become a reality. There are certain things that can be done to ensure success as colleagues engage in what can best be described as a process of change. When teachers work together to grow professionally, they can provide the support and essential reinforcement for change in the school context. Staff development can be the catalyst for providing professional opportunities for adults to act on. During staff development, experiences need to be provided by teachers and for teachers who want to grow in their ability to deliver content area reading strategies. As they do this, teachers are engaging in lifelong learning, becoming willing to try new practices in a collaborative relationship with other teachers at various grade levels, with teachers in other schools, and with teachers from colleges and universities.

Purposes and guidelines notwithstanding, staff development in content area reading may still at times appear to be a nebulous undertaking; there are no set prescriptions or prepackaged programs that will work for any one type of school in particular. An inservice program in content area reading is too individual a matter; it grows from within a school system depending on the individual needs of teachers and their students. One thing is for certain: going it alone has no place in staff development. Collaboration is the cornerstone of effective staff development today.

As veteran teachers know, staff development can be risky. Yet once we make up our minds to change, it is often necessary to take risks. When professionals begin to develop working partnerships with each other, when practicing teachers and administrators work with university faculty, collaboration begins to take shape. One type of collaboration is in professional development schools and centers, and one of the major ways that professionals in these centers work with each other is around the concept of inquiry into change. *The main goal of collaborative inquiry in content area reading is improved instructional practice.* Correspondingly, schools in which inquiry takes place are centers in which teachers become researchers inquiring into change.

Collaborative inquiry can lead to improvement in classroom practice. It can lead to an increase in reciprocity between schools and universities. It can begin to break down the unfortunate state of affairs described well by Marc Tucker (1988): "The University has learned how to talk to itself." We need instead a lot of contact between colleges/universities and practicing teachers. We must no longer accept the isolation of teaching; walls that have been built up over the years need to come down. Mutual inquiry about content area reading is one way to begin. Here is how one high school developed and implemented a model for change.

## COLLABORATIVE MODEL

First, the school's six-member planning committee met and decided to develop and distribute a survey to get at the needs, concerns, and interests of the teaching staff. Box A.1 is an example of an assessment survey for content area reading.

Next, the committee summarized the data, clarifying them with interviews of teachers. They needed to arrive at some agreement about the status quo and the content needs and delivery preferences of building-level personnel. Box A.2 illustrates how some very basic questions asked by the committee at this juncture helped it determine how to proceed.

The collaborative model that seemed to best fit the needs of the high school was an action planning model for staff development. The committee contacted members of the faculty from different subject areas and asked them to be on two problem-solving teams, each made up of four faculty members and an assistant principal. These teams then met once a week during the fall semester, following explicit procedures to develop an action plan. The results of one team's work are shown here:

1. *Define the Problem*

   a. We understand the problem to be:
      Large vocabulary and concept load in high school textbooks.
   b. The following people are involved in the problem:
      Teachers in selecting and teaching vocabulary terms and students who act uninterested.

---

**BOX A.1    Survey of Needs and Concerns**

*Directions:*    Please number in order of importance the areas in which you feel you need additional help to teach content through reading. Then answer each question as completely as possible.

_____ Determining the reading difficulty level of my content area materials.
_____ Guiding students to comprehend their reading assignments.
_____ Developing questions for a reading assignment.
_____ Reinforcing technical vocabulary by providing opportunities for repeated use.
_____ Developing vocabulary skills that will help students unlock the meaning of words independently.
_____ Planning instruction so that students know how to approach their reading assignments.
_____ Differentiating reading assignments in a single textbook to provide for a range of reading abilities.
_____ Guiding students to read graphs, charts, maps and illustrations.
_____ Teaching key vocabulary terms before students meet them in an assignment.
_____ Showing students how to read content materials critically.
_____ Teaching students how to outline text material.
_____ Developing a unit that coordinates instructional resources and materials.

1. What is your area of greatest concern about your delivery of instruction in content area reading?
2. What is your area of least concern?

---

    c. Other factors relevant to the problem:
      Pressures to get through the content and produce acceptable test scores.
    d. One aspect of the problem we need to change:
      Finding more effective ways of teaching vocabulary to students.

**2.** *Plan for Change*

    a. Exactly what are we trying to accomplish?
      Find better ways to use social studies and history subject matter as a natural context for the development of students' vocabularies.
    b. What behavior is implied?
      History and social studies teachers will identify key words, show students interrelationships, preteach, and guide students. Students will understand and use strategies they are shown.
    c. Who is going to do it?
      Each team member will meet with several other teachers to get their input, then come back to the team. Eventually most of the history and social studies staff and their students will be involved.
    d. Can it be done?
      Yes. There is every reason to expect support from the staff because the problem is a real one and we all expect improvement.

---

| BOX A.2 | Selecting a Collaborative Model | | |
|---|---|---|---|
| **Status Quo**<br>What is the current situation or climate in the building? | **Needs**<br>What is necessary to improve this? | **Delivery**<br>How can this be done? | **Model**<br>Which model can we follow or adapt? |
| There is little contact among faculty; problems are mentioned in the lounge, but there is no opportunity to share possible solutions. | The faculty need a more structured way of sharing; they need to find ways to collaborate about specific instructional problems. | Setting up problem-solving teams would give structure and mutual support. | Action planning |

 

    **e.** What tangible evidence will indicate change?
       Teachers will be meeting to share vocabulary strategies, and students will be observed improving their vocabularies in class and using this knowledge and skill in tests.

**3.** *Take Action Steps*

    **a.** Actions that need to be taken:
       1. Discussions with and memo to faculty.
       2. Selecting consultant.
       3. Arranging workshops for faculty with and without consultant.
       4. Formative evaluations of progress.
       5. Concerted effort in classroom vocabulary instruction.
       6. Post-assessment of teachers, consultant, and students; summative evaluation compiled.
    **b.** Persons responsible for each action:
       1. Team and principal
       2. Team and faculty
       3. Principal
       4. Team and principal
       5. Team and faculty
       6. Team, principal, and planning committee
    **c.** Timing of each action:
       1. January
       2. January
       3. February
       4. February, March
       5. April
       6. May

   **d.** Necessary human and financial resources:
   1. School office budget
   2. Team requesting money from district staff development committee
   3. Principal
   4. Released time for workshops budgeted; consultant
   5. Materials reproduced
   6. Principal; report disseminated

Effective staff development requires someone who is willing to take the lead. Leading is "influencing, guiding in direction, course, action, opinion," according to Bennis and Nanus (1985, p. 21). It is taking charge; and making change happen requires leadership. Whether you are content area teacher or reading consultant, supervisor or administrator, it's likely you'll one day find yourself in the role of staff developer. As you assume responsibility for staff development and initiate collaboration, the preceding chapters in this book may provide a good deal of the program substance. But staff development leaders must also have strategies: *How* we work with teachers is as important as the content we deliver.

## SELECTING CONSULTANTS

A staff development project in content area reading may make use of outside expertise such as that offered by a college- or university-based consultant. But staff development ultimately fails or succeeds because of the professional expertise of local talent—school-based personnel who work inside the system. The local staff developers for content area reading are often the reading consultants or reading teachers within a school or district. However, total responsibility need not and should not be exclusively theirs. The classroom teacher must play an integral role in content area reading staff development. An ideal situation, for example, may occur when a reading specialist teams up with a classroom teacher to lead an inservice program. The reading specialist may not feel comfortable with the content of a subject area but knows the reading process and how to apply it. The classroom teacher, on the other hand, knows the content but may not feel comfortable with the reading process. Each draws on the other's expertise and strengths to conduct the program.

Even greater time, attention, and deliberation are required when contracting with consultants outside the district because they are often unknown. Yet their behavior can "make or break staff development experiences" (Vacca 1981, p. 53). Whether the consultant is to conduct a single session or work with a district over an extended period of time, his or her selection can have long-term effects.

Choosing skillful presenters is a difficult process. Ascertaining participants' needs and program objectives will help determine the criteria for the selection of consultants. But the criteria must often be supplemented and corroborated through telephone calls and colleagues' impressions.

For example, some characteristics may be verified in an indirect way via telephone conversations with prospective consultants. Are they enthusiastic about the topic being negotiated? Do they have clear and pleasant voices? Do they have a sense of humor? More direct conversation about the topic should reveal whether or not the consultant's knowledge is current. Do they inquire about audio-visual materials or seating arrangements? Do they want to know the results of the needs assessments? What cannot be learned on the telephone should be discussed with people who have previously heard or worked with the prospective consultant.

Using these techniques and formulating criteria cannot guarantee that a content area staff developer will be successful, but at least the probability of success is increased. A checklist for selecting and assessing consultants, derived from the categories of staff developer behaviors previously discussed, is an efficient guide, which we include in Box A.3.

Realistically, staff developers have a complex leadership role. It's unlikely they will be perceived as effective 100 percent of the time in any situation. Yet when staff developers are aware of effective delivery strategies and show concern for the quality of their delivery, the implementation of any program is bound to improve. An effective staff development leader is sincerely trying to create an environment in which teachers are motivated to grow as fully as possible. Even in the best circumstances some teachers will be more ready than others to change.

When participants are ready to become actively involved, staff development leaders should use a range of instructional options and alternatives—the techniques, strategies, and materials developed throughout this book. The program leader may arrange a series of workshop sessions to demonstrate them. Involvement is the key to this continuing process. Teachers sense the process of content area reading by playing the role of student. Once the participants have had the opportunity to experience certain strategies and materials, the leader follows with explanations involving the how and why of them.

As they demonstrate strategies, presenters need to sustain the rapport that has been established. Although no single technique will be effective in all situations, there are process strategies that teachers consistently associate with the effective delivery of staff development. A sample of these strategies is contained in Table A.1 on p. 382.

We designed the chart as a way to cross-check several important variables in staff development delivery. Each of the 13 strategies can help accomplish certain objectives or meet typical staff development needs. Associated with each strategy are the necessary materials and facilities. Also indicated are the number of potential participants and the approximate time needed to complete the process. Elements such as time or numbers of teachers can be adjusted to accommodate specific situations.

Reflective questions should be encouraged on the part of teachers and staff developer. Teachers might ask, "Why should I do this?" "When should I use this approach rather than the other one?" "How can I construct these guide materials based on my content?" Staff developers might ask, "Is this delivery strategy producing the expected results?" "Is it increasing the willingness of

| BOX A.3 | A Checklist for Selecting and Assessing Consultants* |
|---|---|

The following checklist was compiled from a national survey of teachers' perceptions of successful presenters. The characteristics represent an ideal type of consultant.

1. *Content Delivery*

_____ Uses active involvement techniques.

_____ Avoids straight lecture method.

_____ Maintains balance between group participation and presentation of information.

_____ Demonstrates ideas and strategies with classroom examples.

_____ Demonstrates materials that have immediate use in classroom.

2. *Personal Influence*

_____ Is enthusiastic and interested in the topic itself.

_____ Is dynamic and stimulates excitement.

_____ Relates to group in an open, honest, and friendly way.

_____ Answers questions patiently.

_____ Avoids alienating participants by talking down to them.

_____ Possesses a sense of humor.

3. *Professional Competence*

_____ Is knowledgeable about the topic.

_____ Has clear objectives in mind.

_____ Is well organized.

_____ Keeps on schedule.

_____ Explains procedures and gives directions for all activities.

_____ Adheres to the topic.

_____ Uses audio-visual materials skillfully.

_____ Allows time for questions.

_____ Provides opportunity for practice.

4. *Arrangements*

_____ Assesses needs of group in advance of presentation.

_____ Uses seating arrangements appropriate for group size and type of activity.

_____ Attends to comfort of group.

_____ Gives breaks as needed.

_____ Adjusts noise levels as needed.

_____ Schedules sessions other than directly after school if possible.

**\*Source:** Jo Anne L. Vacca, "Program Implementation," in *Staff Development Leadership: A Resource Book*. Columbus, Ohio: Department of Education, 1983, pp. 51–58.

content area teachers to continue participating?" "Is the process improving their ability to incorporate functional reading into content area instruction?"

Many projects in content area reading screech to a halt at this point. Time, funding, or staff constraints are some of the reasons typically given for the lack of follow-through and support that are essential to professional

**Table A.1    PROCESS STRAGEGY IMPLEMENTATION CHART**

| Type of strategy | Materials | Facilities | Participants | Time |
|---|---|---|---|---|
| 1. Brainstorming. Identify a broad concept with large group; small groups generate word lists; compare in large group. | Notepaper, pencils, chalkboard, or overhead projector | Student desks or tables and chairs | 20–500 small groups of 5–8 | 10–20 minutes |
| 2. Open-ended discussions. Set up hypothetical situation(s) or create conceptual conflict(s). Work through alternative solutions in groups; compare. | Paper, pencils, worksheets | Movable furniture or auditorium and break-out rooms | 20–500; small groups of 5–8 | 15–30 minutes |
| 3. Lecture-feedback. Present information first, then stimulate questions, discussion(s). | Lectern, or table; overheads; agenda or outline | Auditorium or classroom with chairs in semicircle | 20–500 | 20 minutes each |
| 4. Role-playing. Simulate a teaching situation; call on volunteer, give test. Share feelings, responses of group, and relate to students. | Handouts, ditto; chalkboard; commercial tests; published books | Student desks; chairs and tables | 20–100 | 30–40 minutes |
| 5. Demonstration teaching. Bring in student or visit classroom. | Outline; introduction reactions forms; anecdotes or checklist | Open space or stage; classroom or resource room | 10–50; 5–10 depending on size of room | 30–60 minutes |
| 6. Videotapes. Preceded by introduction or by experiencing first the technique, then watching, then comparing. | Tapes, color playback machine; outline or brochure | Comfortable seating; adjustable lighting | 10–50 | 10–60 minutes |
| 7. Materials-producing. Design strategy for a specific content and group of students. Produce in form it will be used. | Oak tag, ditto, typing paper, transparencies, markers, rulers, scissors, stapler | Tables, chairs, nearby office, thermofax, ditto or copy machine, cutting board. | 10–50 | 1–2 hours |

growth. Teachers need time and shared expertise to actually produce classroom materials or design new strategies for their students. Few things are more frightening than trying out a new idea for the first time, especially when teachers attempt to incorporate content area reading strategies into their lessons. Teachers need three kinds of assistance to attain closure to implementation: positive support, constructive criticism, and help with redesign or modification of strategies and materials.

Both feedback and follow-up are necessary to ensure that initial changes in behaviors, attitudes, or knowledge are being supported. If changes dealing with instructional strategies are to be meaningful, they must be refined and incorporated into the teachers' repertoire daily.

| Type of strategy | Materials | Facilities | Participants | Time |
|---|---|---|---|---|
| 8. Feedback or gripe sessions. Allow time for "what's wrong with" or "why it won't work"; acknowledge problems so they won't dominate. | Feedback forms | | Everyone or optional attendance | 5–10 minutes |
| 9. Learning centers. Teachers follow a minischedule in which they work through centers, each with a different activity. | Sample teacher-made and commercial | Tables, plenty of space and light; large room or several class-rooms | 20–100 | 1–2 hours; 15 minutes per station |
| 10. Conferences. Individual teachers sign up to meet with instructor . . . only if they feel a need. | Sign-up sheet with dates, times | Private area with desk, two chairs | 1, possibly 2 (if paired) at a time | 15–30 minutes each |
| 11. Pairing. Have teachers work in pairs (or triads) according to grade level or interest area or count off to get new combinations. | Match information from informal assessment on 5-by-8 cards or discus-sion; or match by number, etc. | Movable chairs or student desks | 10–30 | 15–45 minutes |
| 12. Observations. Teachers observe behaviors of one or a group of children in a clinic or regular classroom. | Checklist or anecdotal narrative form or time-sample form | One-way glass/mir-ror; classroom or resource room | 2 or 3 in each | 30–45 minutes |
| 13. Interviewing. Interview one or two teachers in front of group or have teachers interview each other or students. | Schedule or open-ended, structured or unstructured questions | Two chairs in front; or regular seating | 1 at a time or everyone in pairs | 10–20 minutes |

# EVALUATING CHANGE

At times it seems as if some school districts have jumped the gun in handling evaluation of staff development programs. In their haste to show the results of staff development programs, they have tended to confuse process with product. For example, are the goals of staff development aimed at showing automatic gain in student achievement even before the teachers' growth and the program designed to influence that growth have been carefully evaluat-ed? One way of avoiding confusion between process and product of staff

**Figure A.1    LEVELS OF EVALUATION IN STAFF DEVELOPMENT**

| Level 1 | Teacher | | |
|---------|---------|---------|---------|
| Level 2 | Teacher | Classroom | |
| Level 3 | Teacher | Classroom | Student |

development is to plan for various levels of evaluation within the process itself. Figure A.1 shows three levels for evaluation of a staff development program.

Level 1 evaluates the process by which teacher skills are developed and fine-tuned, answering such questions as: What was the quality of individual workshops? Were the goals and objectives of the program achieved? Was the consultant or program leader effective?

Level 2 considers the effect of the staff development process on what teachers are actually doing in the classroom. Are teachers attempting to incorporate or implement content area reading activities into instruction? Have they modified their previous strategies and materials to fit their new purposes? Are their instructional units incorporating a wider range of instructional materials and resources?

Level 3 considers the effect of the staff development process on its ultimate product—improved student attitude toward and performance in content area reading.

Staff development programs sometimes move too quickly from teacher and classroom evaluation to student evaluation in a rush to prove their worth.

The push for visible returns is understandable; in the wake of the school improvement movement, it's probably inevitable. But programs that center predominantly on evaluation on levels 1 and 2 offer teachers the opportunity to grow professionally and improve the quality of their classroom instruction.

---

**BOX A.4    Rating Scale for Workshops**

*Directions:* To determine whether this particular workshop met your needs and the established objectives of the program, please provide your honest opinion on its design, presentation, and value. Circle the number which best expresses your reactions to each of the items below.

| | | | | | | | |
|---|---|---|---|---|---|---|---|
| 1. The organization of the workshop was | Excellent | 5 | 4 | 3 | 2 | 1 | Poor |
| 2. The objectives of the workshop were | Clear | 5 | 4 | 3 | 2 | 1 | Vague |
| 3. The contribution of the workshop leader(s) was | Excellent | 5 | 4 | 3 | 2 | 1 | Poor |
| 4. The ideas and activities presented were | Very Interesting | 5 | 4 | 3 | 2 | 1 | Dull |
| 5. My participation in this workshop should prove | Very Beneficial | 5 | 4 | 3 | 2 | 1 | Of No Benefit |
| 6. Overall this workshop was | Excellent | 5 | 4 | 3 | 2 | 1 | Poor |

7. The strongest feature of the workshop was _____

8. The weakest feature of the workshop was _____

9. Would you like further help on any of the topics presented at the workshop? If so, please list them. _____
_____
_____

A number of evaluative tools can be used to determine the extent of teachers' professional growth. Pre- and post-testing of teachers' knowledge of reading on tests specifically constructed for the staff development program can yield evaluative insights if it is agreed that knowledge of reading is a good indicator of teacher growth. Changes in teachers' attitudes toward content area reading can be interpreted from pre- and post-tests with an attitude scale. Systems for analyzing and classifying interactions between teachers and students and observation checklists can help evaluate the effect of the program on teachers' classroom activities.

We recommend using the same checklist developed for selecting consultants when you want to assess participants' perceptions of the staff developer's performance. For rating the quality and perceived effectiveness of individual workshop sessions, try a simple rating scale like the one in Box A.4.

# B

# Magazines That Print
# Work by Student Writers

Adapted from Teachers and Writers Collaborative
October 1984

This compilation is a listing and not an endorsement of magazines which print work by student writers (an asterisk indicates a purely literary magazine):

*Action.* Scholastic, Inc., 730 Broadway, New York, NY 10003. Publishes student writing based on writing assignments in its previous issues. For students 12–14

*Alive! for Young Teens.* Box 179, St. Louis, MO 63166. Christian education magazine. Ages 12–16.

*\*Chart Your Course.* P.O. Box 6448, Mobile, AL 36660. Material by gifted, creative, and talented children. Ages 6–18.

*Child Life.* The Children's Better Health Institute, 1100 Waterway Blvd., Indianapolis, IN 46206. Ages 7–9.

*Children's Digest.* The Children's Better Health Institute, 1100 Waterway Blvd., Indianapolis, IN 46206. Ages 8–10.

*City Kids.* 1545 Wilcox, Los Angeles, CA 90028. Ages 11–14.

*Cobblestone: The History Magazine for Young People.* 20 Grove St., Peterborough, NH 03458. Each issue devoted to a particular theme. Ages 8–14.

*Cricket.* Box 100, LaSalle, IL 61301. Note: considers *only* material that complies with current contest rules and descriptions (see each issue for current contest rules). Ages 5–13.

*District: Young Writers Journal.* 2500 Wisconsin Ave., N.W., #549, Washington, D.C. 20007. For District of Columbia students and residents only. Ages 9–14. Write for information.

*Ebony Jr.!* 820 S. Michigan Ave., Chicago, IL 60605. Specializes in material about Blacks. Ages 6–12.

*English Journal.* National Council of Teachers of English, 1111 Kenyon Rd., Urbana, IL 61801. Poetry, no fiction. Ages 12–17.

*\*Hanging Loose.* 231 Wyckoff St., Brooklyn, NY 11217. Since 1968 has included a special section of student poetry and fiction. Ages 14–18.

*Just About Me.* Ensio Industries, 247 Marlee Ave., Suite 206, Toronto, Ont., Canada M6B 4B8. For girls. Ages 12–19.

*Paw Prints.* National Zoo, Washington, D.C. 20008. Specializes in wild exotic animal conservation and other animal-related material. Ages 6–14.

*Purple Cow.* Suite 315, Lates Center, 110 E. Andrews Dr., N.W., Atlanta, GA 30305. Prefers nonfiction. Ages 12–18.

*Scholastic Scope.* 730 Broadway, New York, NY 10003. Uses student manuscripts in the "Mini Mystery" and "Student Writing" pages. Ages 15–18.

*Science World.* Scholastic Inc., 730 Broadway, New York, NY 10003. Uses material on life science, earth science, health, biology, etc. Ages 12–16.

*Seventeen.* 850 Third Avenue, New York, NY 10022. Ages 13–21.

*Sprint.* Scholastic, Inc., 730 Broadway, New York, NY 10003. Publishes student writing based on assignments in its previous issues. For students aged 9–11.

*\*Stone Soup.* P.O. Box 83, Santa Cruz, CA. 95063. Ages 6–12.

*The Sunshine News.* Canada Sunshine Publishing, Ltd., 465 King St., East, #14A, Toronto, Ont., Canada M5A 1L6. Ages 14–17.

*Teenage Magazine,* 217 Jackson St., P.O. Box 948, Lowell, MA 01853. Formerly *Highwire,* Ages 14–19.

*Voice.* Scholastic, Inc., 730 Broadway, New York, NY 10003. Ages 12–18.

*Wee Wisdom.* Unity Village, MO 64065. Ages 6–13.

# BIBLIOGRAPHY

Alexander, J. E. (ed.) (1983). *Teaching reading* (2nd ed.). Boston: Little, Brown and Company.

Aliki (1986). *A medieval feast.* New York. Harper Collins.

Allington, R. and Strange, M. 1980. *Learning through reading in the content areas.* Lexington, MA: D. C. Heath.

Alvermann, D. E. (1992). Educational reform initiatives and the move to more student-centered textbook instruction. In E. K. Dishner, T. W. Bean, J. E. Readence, & D. W. Moore (eds.), *Reading in the content areas: Improving classroom instruction* (3rd ed.) (pp. 142–154). Dubuque, IA: Kendall-Hunt.

Alvermann, D. E., Dillon, D. R. & O'Brien, D. G. (1988). *Using discussion to promote reading comprehension.* Newark, DE: International Reading Association.

Alvermann, D. E., & Moore, D. W. (1991). Secondary school reading. In P. D. Pearson, R. Barr, M. Kamil, & P. Mosenthal (eds.), *Handbook of reading research* (2nd ed.) (pp. 951–983). New York: Longman.

Anderson, R. C & Freebody, P. (1981). Vocabulary knowledge. In J. T. Guthrie (ed.). *Comprehension and teaching: Research perspectives.* Newark, DE: International Reading Association.

Anderson, R. C., Reynolds, R. E., Schallert, D. L. & Goetz, E. T. (1977). Frame works for comprehending discourse. *American Educational Research Journal, 14,* 367–382.

Anno, M. (1982). *Anno's counting house.* New York: Philomel.

Anno, M. (1989). *Anno's math games.* New York: Philomel.

Anno, M. (1970). *Topsy-turvies: Pictures to stretch the imagination.* New York: Weatherhill.

Applebee, A. N. (1984). *Contexts for learning to write: Studies of secondary school instruction.* Norwood, NJ: ABLEX.

Applebee, A. N. (1981). *Writing in the secondary school: English and the content areas.* Urbana, IL: National Council of Teachers of English.

Archer, A. (1979). Study skills. In D. Carnine and F. J. Silbert (eds.), *Direct instruction: Reading.* Columbus, OH: Merrill.

Armbruster, B. B. & Anderson T. H. (1981). *Content area textbooks.* Reading Education Report No. 23, Urbana, IL: University of Illinois Center for the Study of Reading.

Armbruster, B. B., & Anderson, T. H. (1985). Frames: Structure for informational texts. In D. H. Jonassen (ed.), *Technology of text.* Englewood Cliffs, NJ: Education Technology Publications.

Armbruster, B. B., Echols, C., & Brown, A. L. (1982). The role of metacognition in reading to learn: A developmental perspective. *Volta Review,* 1982, *84,* 45–56.

Artley, A. S. (1975). Words, words, words. *Language Arts, 52,* 1067–1072.

Ashabranner, B. (1988). *Always to remember: The story of the Vietnam Veterans Memorial.* New York: G. P. Putnam's Sons.

Ashabranner, B. (1988). *Always to remember: The story of the Vietnam Veterans Memorial.* Illus., J. Ashabranner. New York: Putnam's.

Baker, J. (1991). *Window.* New York: Greenwillow.

Baker, L., & Brown, A. (1984). Cognitive monitoring in reading. In J. Flood (ed.). *Understanding reading comprehension* (pp. 21–44). Newark, DE: International Reading Association.

Baker, L. (1991). Metacognition, reading, and science education. In C. M. Santa & D. E. Alvermann (eds.), *Science learning: Processes and applications.* Newark, DE: International Reading Association.

Barg, M. (1991). *Picture this: Perception and composition.* New York: Bullfinch Press.

Barron, R. (1969). The use of vocabulary as an advance organizer. In H. L. Herber and P. L. Sanders (eds.) *Research in reading in the content areas: First Report.* Syracuse, NY: Syracuse University Reading and Language Arts Center.

Barron, R., & Earle, R. (1973). An approach for vocabulary development. In H. L. Herber and R. F. Barron (eds.), *Research in reading in the content areas: Second report.* Syracuse, NY: Syracuse University Reading and Language Arts Center.

Barron, R., & Stone, F. (1973, December). *The effect of student constructed graphic post organizers upon learning of vocabulary relationships from a passage of social studies content.* Paper presented at the meeting of the National Reading Conference, Houston.

Bartlett, B. (1978). Top-level structure as an organizational strategy for recall of classroom text. Unpublished doctoral dissertation, Arizona State University.

Baylor, B. (1972). *When clay sings.* New York: Charles Scribner's Sons.

Beaman, B. (1985). Writing to learn social studies. In A. R. Gere (ed.), *Roots in sawdust: Writing to learn across the disciplines.* Urbana, IL: National Council of Teachers of English.

Beck, I., McKeown, M., McCaslin, E., & Burket, A. (1979). Instructional dimensions that may affect reading comprehension: Examples of two commercial reading programs. Pittsburgh: University of Pittsburgh, Language Research and Development Center Technical Report.

Beebe, B. F. (1968). *African elephants*. New York: McKay.

Berger, M. (1986). *Atoms, molecules and quarks*. New York: G. P. Putnam's Sons.

Berlyne, D. E. (1965). *Structure and direction of thinking*. New York: John Wiley & Sons.

Bernhardt, B. (1977). *Just writing*. New York: Teachers and Writers.

Betts, E. (1950). *Foundations of reading* (rev. ed.). New York: American Book Company.

Beuhl, D. (Spring, 1991). *Frames of mind*. The Exchange: Newsletter of the IRA Secondary Reading Interest Group. 4–5.

Blachowicz, C. (1986). Making connections: Alternatives to the vocabulary notebook. *Journal of Reading, 29,* 643–649.

Bleich, D. (1978). *Subjective criticism*. Baltimore: The Johns Hopkins University Press.

Bohning, G., & Radencich, M. (1989). Informational action books: A curriculum resource for science and social studies. *Journal of Reading, 32,* 434–439.

Booksearch: Recommended historical fiction. (1989). *English Journal,* 84–86.

Borasi, R., Sheedy, J. R., & Siegel, M. (1990). The power of stories in learning mathematics. *Language Arts, 67,* 174–189.

Bower, B. (February 29, 1992). Reading the code, reading the whole. *Science News, 141,* 138–140.

Bransford, J. D., & Stein, B. S. (1984). *The ideal problem solver: A guide for improving thinking, learning, and creativity*. New York: Freeman.

Bridgers, S. E. (1976). *Home before dark*. Toronto: Bantam.

Bromley, K. D. (1991). *Webbing with literature: Creating story maps with children's books*. Boston: Allyn & Bacon.

Brown, A. L. (1978). Knowing when, where, and how to remember: A problem of metacognition. In R. Glaser (ed.). *Advances in instructional psychology*. Hillsdale, NJ: Erlbaum.

Brown, A. L (1982). Learning to learn how to read. In J. Langer and M. T. Smith-Burke (eds.). *Reader meets author/bridging the gap*. Newark, DE: International Reading Association.

Brown, A. L., Bransford, J. W., Ferrara, R. F., & Campione, J. (1983). Learning, remembering, and understanding. In J. Flavell, & E. Markham (eds.), *Handbook of child psychology*. New York: John Wiley & Sons.

Brown, A. L., Campione, J., & Day, J. D. (1981). Learning to learn: On training students to learn from texts. *Educational Researcher, 10,* 14–24.

Brown, A. L., & Day, J. D. (1983). Macrorules for summarizing texts: The development of expertise. *Journal of Verbal Learning Behavior, 22,* 1–14.

Brown, A. L., Day, J. D., & Jones, R. (1983). The development of plans for summarizing texts. *Child Development, 54,* 968–979.

Brown, A. L., & Palincsar, A. A. (1982). Inducing strategic learning from texts by means of informed, self-control training. *Topics in Learning and Learning Disabilities, 2,* 1–17.

Brown, A. L., & Smiley, S. S. (1977). Rating the importance of structural units of prose passages: A problem of metacognitive development. *Child Development, 48,* 1–8.

Brown, J. E., & Abel, F. J. (1982). Revitalizing American history: Literature in the classroom. *The Social Studies, 73,* 279–282.

Brozo, W. G. (1989). Applying a reader response heuristic to expository text. *Journal of Reading, 32,* 140–145.

Brozo, W. G. (1990). Learning how at-risk readers learn best: A case for interactive assessment. *Journal of Reading, 33*(7), 522–527.

Brozo, W. G., & Simpson, M. L. (1991). *Readers, teachers, learners: Expanding literacy in secondary schools.* New York: Macmillan.

Brozo, W. G., & Tomlinson, C. M. (1986). Literature: The key to lively content courses. *The Reading Teacher, 40,* 288–293.

Bruner, J. (1961). The act of discovery. *Harvard Educational Review, 31,* 21–32.

Bruner, J. (1970). The skill of relevance or the relevance of skills. *Saturday Review, 53.*

Bruner, J. (1986). *Actual minds, possible worlds.* Cambridge, MA: Harvard University Press.

Bruner, J. (1990). *Acts of meaning.* Cambridge, MA: Harvard University Press.

Bruner, J., Goodnow, J., & Austin, G. (1977). *A study of thinking.* New York: Science Editions.

Camp, G. (1982). *A success curriculum for remedial writers,* Berkeley, CA: The National Writing Project, University of California, Berkeley.

Carnes, E. J. (1988). Teaching content area reading through nonfiction book writing. *Journal of Reading, 31,* 354–360.

Chambers, A. (1985). *Booktalk: Occasional writing on literature and children.* New York: Harper & Row.

Chekov, A. (1991). *Kashtanka.* Trans. R. Pevear. IL B. Moser. New York: Putnam's.

Cherry, L. (1990). *The great kapok tree: A talk of the Amazon Rain Forest.* San Diego: Gulliver Books.

Cianciolo, P. (1981). Yesterday comes alive for readers of historical fiction. *Language Arts, 58,* 452–462.

Cicchetti, G. (1990). *Cognitive modeling and reciprocal teaching of reading and study strategies.* Watertown, CT: Cicchetti Associates.

Cohen, D. (1987). *Carl Sagan: Superstar scientist.* New York: G. P. Putnam's Sons.

Collette, A. (1973). *Science teaching in the secondary school.* Boston: Allyn and Bacon.

Cooper, C. R., & Odell, L. (eds.) (1977). *Evaluating writing.* Urbana, IL: National Council of Teachers of English.

Crafton, L. (1983). Learning from reading: What happens when students generate their own background knowledge. *Journal of Reading, 26,* 586–593.

Croll, P. (1986). *Systematic classroom observation.* Philadelphia: The Falmer Press.

Cuban, L. (1986). Persistent instruction: Another look at constancy in the classroom. *Phi Delta Kappan, 68,* 7–11.

Cunningham, R. & Shablak, S. (1975). Selective reading guide-o-rama: The content teacher's best friend. *Journal of Reading, 18,* 380–382.

Dale, E. (1969). Things to come. *Newsletter, 34.*

Dale, E. (1975). *The word game: Improving communications.* Bloomington, IN: Phi Delta Kappa.

Davey, B. (1983). Think aloud—Modeling the cognitive processes of reading comprehension. *Journal of Reading, 27,* 44–47.

Davidson, J. L., & Wilkerson, B. C. (1988). *Directed reading-thinking activities.* Monroe, NY: Trillium Press.

DePaola, T. (1978). *The popcorn book.* New York: Scholastic.

DePaola, T. (1983). *The legend of the bluebonnet.* New York: Scholastic.

DePaola, T. (1988). *The legend of the Indian paintbrush.* New York: Scholastic.

Devine, T. (1981). *Teaching study skills.* Boston: Allyn & Bacon.

Dillon, J. T. (1983). *Teaching and the art of questioning.* Bloomington, IN: Phi Delta Kappa.

Dole, J. A., & Johnson, V. R. (1981). Beyond the textbook: Science literature for young people. *Journal of Reading, 24,* 579–582.

Donelson, K. L, & Nilson, A. P. (1989). *Literature for today's young adults* (3rd ed.). Glenview, Il: Scott, Foresman.

Drummond, H. (1978). *The western hemisphere.* Boston: Allyn and Bacon.

Duffy, G. G. (1983). From turn taking to sense making. Broadening the concept of reading teacher effectiveness. *Journal of Educational Research, 76,* 134–139.

Dupuis, M. M., & Snyder, S. L. (1983). Develop concepts through vocabulary: A strategy for reading specialists to use with content teachers. *Journal of Reading, 26,* 297–305.

Eanet, M., & Manzo, A. V. (1976). REAP—a strategy for improving reading/writing/study skills. *Journal of Reading, 19,* 647–652.

Edwards, M. (1982). *Alef-bet: A Hebrew alphabet book.* New York Lothrop, Lee & Shepard.

Egan, K. (1989). Layers of historical understanding. *Theory and research in social education, 17,* 280–294.

Eisner, E. W. (1985). *The educational imagination: On the design and evaluation of school programs* (2nd ed.). New York: Macmillan.

Eisner, E. (1991). The celebration of thinking. *The Maine scholar, 4,* 39–52.

Eisner, E. (1969). Instructional and expressive educational objectives: Their formulation and use in curriculum *AERA monograph series on curriculum evaluation.* Chicago: Rand McNally and Co.

Elbow, P. (1973). *Writing without teachers.* New York: Oxford University Press.

Feelings, M. (1971). *Moja means one: swahili counting book.* IL J. Feelings. New York: Dial.

Fetterman, D. M. (1989). *Ethnography step by step.* Newbury Park, CA: Sage Publications, Inc.

Fitzgerald, E. A. (1987, December). Things worth keeping. *Pace Magazine,* p. 9.

Flavell, J. H. (1976). Metacognitive aspects of problem solving. In L. B. Resnick (ed.), *The nature of intelligence* (pp. 38–62). Hillsdale, NJ: Erlbaum.

Flavell, J. H (1981). Cognitive monitoring. In P. Dickson (ed.), *Communication skills*. New York: Academic Press.

Freedman, G., & Reynolds, E. G. (1980). Enriching basal reader lessons with semantic webbing. *The Reading Teacher, 33*, 677–684.

Fry, E. (1977). Fry's readability graph: Clarifications, validity and extension to level 17. *Journal of Reading, 21*, 242–252.

Fugard, A. (1984). *"Master Harold"...and the boys*. New York: Penguin.

Fulghum, R. (1989). *It was on fire when I lay down on it*. New York: Villard Books.

Gagne, E. D. (1985). *The cognitive psychology of school learning*. Boston: Little, Brown.

Gagne, R. (1970). *The conditions of learning* (2nd ed.). New York: Holt, Rinehart and Winston.

Gallant, R. A. (1980). *Memory: How it works and how to improve it*. New York: Four Winds.

Gallant, R. A. (1991). *Earth's vanishing forests*. New York: Macmillan.

Gambrell, L. B. (1980). Think-time: Implications for reading instruction. *The Reading Teacher, 33*, 143–146.

Gere, A. R. (ed.) (1985). *Roots in the sawdust: Writing to learn across the disciplines*. Urbana, IL: National Council of Teachers of English.

Gillet, J., & Kita, M. J. (1979). Words, kids and categories. *The Reading Teacher, 32*, 538–542.

Gillet, J., & Temple, C. (1982). *Understanding reading problems*. Boston: Little, Brown & Company.

Goble, P. (1991). *I sing for the animals*. New York: Bradbury.

Gold, P., & Yellin, D. (1982). Be the focus: A psycho-educational technique for use with unmotivated learners. *Journal of Reading 25*, 550–552.

Goodall, J. (1979). *The story of an English village*. New York: Atuneum.

Goodall, J. (1987). *The story of a main street*. New York: Macmillan.

Goodall, J. (1990). *The story of the seashore*. New York: Macmillan.

Goodlad, J. (1984). *A place called school*. New York: McGraw-Hill.

Goodman, K. (1976). The reading process: A psycholinguistic view. *Language and thinking in schools* (2nd ed.). New York: Holt, Rinehart and Winston.

Graves, D. (1978). *Balance to basics: Let them write*. New York: The Ford Foundation.

Graves, M. F., Prenn, M. C., & Cooke, C. L. (1985). The coming attraction: Previewing short stories. *Journal of Reading, 28*, 594–597.

Graves, M. F., Cooke, C. L., & LaBerge, M. J. (1983). Effects of previewing difficult short stories on low ability junior high school students' comprehension, recall, and attitudes, *Reading Research Quarterly, 18*, 262–276.

Green, J., & Harker, J. (1982). Reading to children: A communicative process. In J. Langer and M. T. Smith-Burke (eds.), *Reader meets author/bridging the gap*, pp. 196–221. Newark, DE: International Reading Association.

Grove, N. (1981, March). Wild cargo: The business of smuggling animals. *National Geographic, 159*, 287–315.

Haggard, M. R. (1986). The vocabulary self-collection strategy: Using student interest and world knowledge to enhance vocabulary growth. *Journal of Reading, 29*(7), 634–642.

Hahn, A. (1984). Assessing and extending comprehension: Monitoring strategies in the classroom. *Reading Horizons, 24,* 225–230.

Haines, G. K. (1988). *Micromysteries: Stories of scientific detection.* New York: G. P. Putnam's Sons.

Halliday, M., and Hasan, R. (1976). *Cohesion in English.* London: Longman.

Hamilton, V. (1985). *The people could fly: American Black folktales.* New York: Alfred A. Knopf.

Hamilton, V. (1988). *In the beginning: Creation stories from around the world.* San Diego, CA: Harcourt Brace Jovanovich.

Hansell, T. S. (1978). Stepping up to outlining. *Journal of Reading, 22,* 248–252.

Hansen, J. (1981a). The effects of inference training and practice on young children's comprehension. *Reading Research Quarterly, 16,* 391–417.

Hansen, J. (1981b). An inferential comprehension strategy for use with primary children. *The Reading Teacher, 34,* 665–669.

Hare, V. C., & Borchardt, K. M. (1984). Direct instruction of summarization skills. *Reading Research Quarterly, 20,* 62–78.

Hayes, D. A. (1989). Helping students grasp the knack of writing summaries. *Journal of Reading, 33,* 2, 96–101.

Hayes, D. A., & Tierney, R. T. (1982). Developing reader's knowledge through analogy. *Reading Research Quarterly, 17,* 256–280.

Healy, M. K. (1982). Using student response groups in the classroom. In G. Camp (ed.) *Teaching writing: Essays from the bay area writing project.* Montclair, NJ: Boynton/Cook.

Hearne, B., & Kaye, M. (eds.) (1981). *Celebrating children's books.* New York: Lothrop, Lee & Shepard.

Heathington, B. S. (1975). *The development of scales to measure attitudes toward reading.* Unpublished doctoral dissertation. The University of Tennessee, Knoxville.

Heathington, B., & Alexander, J. E. (1984). Do classroom teachers emphasize attitudes toward reading? *The Reading Teacher, 37,* 484–488.

Heinly, B. F., & Hilton, K. (1982). Using historical fiction to enrich social studies courses. *The Social Studies, 73,* 21–24.

Henry, G. (1974). *Teaching reading as concept development.* Newark, DE: International Reading Association.

Herber, H. L. (1978). *Teaching reading in content areas* (2nd ed.). Englewood Cliffs, NJ: Prentice-Hall.

Herber, H. L., & Nelson, J. (1975). Questioning is not the answer. *Journal of Reading, 18,* 512–517.

Herrmann, B. A. (1988). Two approaches for helping poor readers become more strategic. *The Reading Teacher, 42,* 24–28.

Highwater, J. (1986). *I wear the morning star.* New York: Harper & Row.

Hilke, E. (1990). *Cooperative learning.* Decatur, IL: Phi Delta Kappa.

Hindley, J. (1990). *The tree.* New York: Clarkson Potter.

Hittleman, D. (1973). Seeking a psycholinguistic definition of readability. *The Reading Teacher, 26,* 783–789.

Hobbs, W. (1989). *Bearstone.* New York: Atheneum.

Hoffman, J. V. (1979). The intra-act procedure for critical reading. *Journal of Reading, 22,* 605–608.

Hoffman, S. (1983). Using student journals to teach study skills. *Journal of Reading, 26,* 344–347.

Holland, N. N. (1975). *Five readers reading.* New Haven: Yale University Press.

Holly, M. L. (1984). *Keeping a personal-professional journal.* Deakin, Australia: Deakin University Press.

Homer, C. (1979). A direct reading-thinking activity for content areas. In R. T. Vacca and J. A. Meagher (eds.), *Reading through content.* Storrs, CT: University Publications and the University of Connecticut Reading-Language Arts Center.

Huck, C. S., Hepler, S. & Hickman, J. (1987). *Children's literature in the elementary school* (4th ed.). Fort Worth, TX; Holt, Rinehart & Winston.

Hudson, E. (ed.) (1988). *Poetry of the first world war.* East Sussex, UK: Wayland.

Huey, E. (1908). *The psychology and pedagogy of reading.* New York: Macmillan.

Innocenti, Roberto. (1991). *Rose Blanche.* New York: Stewart, Tiboria Chang.

Irwin, J. W., & Davis, C. A. (1980). Assessing readability: The checklist approach. *Journal of Reading, 24,* 124–130.

Iser, W. (1978). *The act of reading: A theory of aesthetic responses.* Baltimore: The Johns Hopkins University Press.

Johnson, D. W., Johnson, R. T., & Holubec, E. J. (1990). *Circles of learning: Cooperation in the classroom* (3rd ed.). Edina, MN: Interaction Book Company.

Johnson, D., & Pearson, P. D. (1978). *Teaching reading vocabulary.* New York: Holt, Rinehart and Winston.

Johnson, D., & Pearson, P. D. (1984). *Teaching reading vocabulary* (2nd ed.). New York: Holt, Rinehart and Winston.

Johnson-Weber, M. (1989). Picture books for junior high. *Journal of Reading, 32,* 219–220.

Johnston, N. (1991). *Louisa May: The world and works of Louisa May Alcott.* New York: Four Winds.

Johnston, P., & Winograd, P. (1985). Passive failure in reading. *Journal of Reading Behavior, 17,* 279–301.

Jones, B. F., Pierce, J., & Hunter, B. (1988–1989). Teaching students to construct graphic representations. *Educational Leadership, 46,* 4j, 20–25.

Judy, S., & Judy, S. (1980). *Gifts of writing: Creative projects with words and art.* New York: Scribner's Sons.

Kennedy, B. (1985). Writing letters to learn math. *Learning, 13,* 58–61.

Kindsvatter, R., Wilen, W., & Ishler, M. (1992). *Dynamics of effective teaching,* (2nd ed.). New York: Longman.

Kinneavy, J. L. (1971). *A theory of discourse.* Englewood Cliffs, NJ: Prentice-Hall.

Kintsch, W. (1977). On comprehending stories. In M. A. Just & P. A. Carpenter (eds.), *Cognitive processes in comprehension.* Hillsdale, NJ: Erlbaum.

Kintsch, W., & van Dijk, T. (1978). Toward a model of text comprehension and production, *Psychological Review, 85,* 363–394.

Kirby, D., & Liner, T. (1981). *Inside out: Development strategies for teaching writing.* Montclair, NJ: Boynton/Cook.

Klass, D. (1988). *A different season.* New York: E. P. Dutton.

Kletzien, S. B. (1991). Strategy use by good and poor comprehenders reading expository text of differing levels. *Reading Research Quarterly, 1,* 67–86.

Knight, J. (1986). *Journey to Egypt: A UNICEF pop-up book.* New York: Viking Kestrel.

Kuklin, A. (1989). *Fighting back: What some people are doing about AIDS.* New York: G. P. Putnam's Sons.

Langer, J. A. (1981). From theory to practice: A prereading plan. *Journal of Reading, 25,* November, 152–156.

Langer, J. A, & Applebee, A. N. (1987). *How writing shapes thinking.* Urbana, IL: National Council of Teachers of English.

Langstaff, J. (1991). *Climbing Jacob's ladder.* Macmillan.

Larson, C. O., & Dansereau, D. (1986). Cooperative learning in dyads. *Journal of Reading. 30,* 516–520.

Lawrence, L. (1985). *Children of the dust.* New York: Harper & Row.

Lehr, F. (1982). Identifying and assessing reading attitudes. *Journal of Reading. 26,* 80–83.

Leinhardt, G. (1990). Capturing craft knowledge in teaching. *Educational Researcher,* March 1990, 18–25.

Lester, J. D. (1984). *Writing research papers: a complete guide* (4th ed.). Glenview, IL: Scott, Foresman.

Levine, D. S. (1985). The biggest thing I learned but it really doesn't have to do with science. . . . *Language Arts, 62,* 43–47.

Levstik, L. S. (1990). Research directions: Mediating content through literary texts. *Language Arts, 67,* 848–853.

Lewis, J. P. (1992). *The moonbow of Mr. B. Bones.* New York: Knopf.

Lewis, R., & Teale, W. (1980). Another look at secondary school students' attitudes toward reading. *Journal of Reading Behavior, 12,* 187–201.

Lindemann, E. (1982). *A rhetoric for writing teachers.* New York: Oxford University Press.

Linek, W. M. (1991). Grading and evaluation techniques for whole language teachers, *Language Arts, 68*(2), 125–132.

Lobel, A. (1981). *On Market Street.* New York: Greenwillow.

Lowe, S. (1990). *Walden.* New York: Philomel.

Lukens, R. J. (1986). *A critical handbook of children's literature* (3rd ed.). Glenview, IL: Scott, Foresman.

Lundsteen, S. (1976). *Children learn to communicate.* Englewood Cliffs, NJ: Prentice-Hall.

Lyon, G. E. (1989). *A b cedar.* New York: Orchard Books.

Lyons, M. E. (1990). *Sorrow's kitchen: The life and folklore of Zora Neale Hurston.* New York: Scribner's.

McAndrew, D. A. (1983). Increasing the reality of audiences in the classroom. *Connecticut English Journal, 14,* 49–56.

Macaulay, D. (1978). *Castle.* New York: Houghton Mifflin.

—. (1973). *Cathedral.* New York: Houghton Mifflin.

—. (1982). *Pyramid.* Boston, MA: Houghton Mifflin.

—. (1988). *The way things work.* New York: Houghton Mifflin.

McGovern, A. (1968). *Stone soup.* New York: Scholastic.

McKenna, M., & Robinson, R. (1990). Content literacy: A definition and implications. *Journal of Reading, 34,* 3, 184–186.

McKinley, R. (1978). *Beauty: A retelling of the story of Beauty and the Beast.* New York: Harper & Row.

McNeil, J. D. (1987). *Reading comprehension: New directions for classroom practice* (2nd ed.). Glenview, IL: Scott, Foresman.

Macrorie, K. (1970). *Uptaught.* Rochelle Park, NJ: Hayden.

Malinowski, B. (1954). *Magic, science and religion and other essays.* New York: Doubleday, Anchor Books.

Mallan, J., & Hersh, R. (1972). *No g. o. d. s. in the classroom: Inquiry into inquiry.* Philadelphia: W. B. Saunders.

Mandler, J., & Johnson, N. (1977). Remembrance of things passed: Story structure and recall. *Cognitive Psychology, 9,* 111–151.

Manna, A. L., & Misheff, S. (1987). What teachers say about their own reading development. *Journal of Reading, 31,* 160–168.

Manzo, A. V. (1975). Guided reading procedure. *Journal of Reading, 18,* 287–291.

Manzo, A. V. (1969). The request procedure. *Journal of Reading, 11,* 123–126.

Marol, J. (1983). *Vagabul escapes.* Mankato, MN. Creative Education.

Maruki, T. (1982). *Hiroshima no pika.* New York: Lothrop, Lee & Shepard.

—. (1985). *The relatives came.* IL Stephen Gammell. New York: Bradbury.

Mathiason, C. (1989). Activating student interest in content area reading. *Journal of Reading, 33,* 170–176.

Meltzer, M. (1983). *The terrorists.* New York: Harper & Row.

Meyer, B. J. F. (1975). *The organization of prose and its effect in memory.* Amsterdam: North-Holland.

Meyer, B. J. F., Brandt, D., & Bluth, G. (1980). Use of top-level structure in text: Key for reading comprehension of ninth-grade students. *Reading Research Quarterly, 16,* 72–103.

Meyer, B. J. F., & Rice, E. (1984). The structure of text. In P. D. Pearson (ed.), *Handbook of reading research,* pp. 319–352. New York: Longman.

Mikulecky, L. (1990). Literacy for what purpose? In R. L. Venezky, D. A. Wagner, & B. S. Ciliberti (eds.), *Toward defining literacy* (pp. 24–34). Newark DE: International Reading Association.

Miletta, M. (1992). Picture books for older children: Reading and writing Connections. *The Reading Teacher, 45,* 555–556.

Milton, J. W. (1982). What the student-educator should have done before the grade: A questioning look at note-taking. In A. S. Algier and K. W. Algier (eds.), *Improving reading and study skills.* San Francisco: Jossey-Bass.

Monjo, F. N. (1991). *Letters to Horseface: Young Mozart's travels in Italy.* New York: Puffin.

Moore, D. W. (1983). A case for naturalistic assessment of reading comprehension. *Language Arts, 60,* 957–968.

Moore, D. W., & Cunningham, J. W. (1986). The confused world of main idea. In J. F. Baumann (ed.), *Teaching main idea comprehension*. Newark, DE: International Reading Association.

Moore, D. W., Readence, J., & Rickelman, R. (1983). An historical exploration of content area reading instruction. *Reading Research Quarterly, 18,* 419–438.

Moore, M. A. (1981). C2R: Concentrate, read, remember. *Journal of Reading, 24,* 337–339.

Moseley, K. (1985). *Flight: Great planes of the century.* New York: Viking Penguin.

Murray, D. (1980). Writing as process: How writing finds its own meaning. In T. R. Donovan and B. W. McClelland (eds.). *Eight approaches to teaching composition.* Urbana, IL: National Council of Teachers of English.

Murray, J. (1982). *Modern monologues for young people.* New York: Plays, Inc.

Myers, J. (1984). Writing to learn across the curriculum. Bloomington, IN, Phi Delta Kappa.

Myers, W. D. (1988). *Fallen angels.* New York: Scholastic.

Neal, J. C. & Morre, K. (1991). *The very hungry caterpillar* meets *Beowulf* in secondary classrooms. *Journal of Reading, 35,* 290–296.

Nelson, J. (1978). Readability: Some cautions for the content area teacher. *Journal of Reading, 21,* 620–625.

*New directions in reading instruction.* (1988). Newark, DE: International Reading Association.

Newell, G. (1984). Learning from writing in two content areas: A case study/protocol analysis. *Research in the Teaching of English, 18,* 205–287.

Niles, O. (1964). Developing basic comprehension skills. In J. Sherk (ed.), *Speaking of reading.* Syracuse, NY: Syracuse University Reading and Language Arts Center.

Niles, O. (1965). Organization perceived. In H. Herber (ed.), *Developing study skills in secondary schools.* Newark, DE: International Reading Association.

Nye, R. (1968). *Beowulf: A new telling.* New York: Hill.

O'Brien, D. G. (1988). Secondary preservice teachers' resistance to content reading instruction: A proposal for a broader analysis. In J. E. Readence, & R. S. Baldwin (eds.), *Dialogues in literacy research.* Thirty-seventh yearbook of the National Reading Conferences (pp. 237–243). Chicago: National Reading Conference.

O'Brien, D. G., & Stewart, R. A. (1992). Resistance to content area reading: Dimensions and solutions. In E. K. Dishner, T.W. Bean, J. E. Readence, & D. W. Moore (eds.), *Reading in the content areas: Improving classroom instruction* (3rd ed.) (pp. 30–40). Dubuque, IA: Kendall/Hunt.

O'Brien, R. C. (1975). *Z for Zachariah.* New York: Atheneum.

Ogle, D. M. (1992). KWL in action: Secondary teachers find applications that work. In E. K. Dishner, T. W. Bean, J. E. Readence, & D. W. Moore (eds.), *Reading in the content areas: Improving classroom instruction* (3rd ed.). Dubuque, IA: Kendall-Hunt.

Ortiz, R. (1983). Generating interest in reading. *Journal of Reading, 28,* 113–119.

Otto, J. H., & Towle, A. (1973). *Modern Biology*. New York: Holt, Rinehart and Winston, pp. 206–207.

Palinscar, A. S., & Brown, A. L. (1984). Reciprocal teaching of comprehension-fostering and comprehension-monitoring activities. *Cognition and instruction, 1*, 117–175.

Palmatier, R. (1973). A notetaking system for learning. *Journal of Reading, 17*, 36–39.

Paris, S. G., Lipson, M. Y., & Wixson, K. K. (1983). Becoming a strategic reader. *Contemporary Educational Psychology, 8*, 293–316.

Paris, S., & Meyers, M. (1981). Comprehension monitoring, memory, and study strategies of good and poor reader. *Journal of Reading Behavior, 13*, 5–22.

Parnall, P. (1984). *The daywatchers*. New York: Macmillan.

Parnall, P. (1991). *Marsh cat*. New York: Macmillan.

Paterson, K. (1980). *Jacob have I loved*. New York: Crowell.

Pauk, W. (1978). A notetaking format: Magical but not automatic. *Reading World, 16*, 96–97.

Paulsen, G. (1987). *Hatchet*. New York: Viking Penguin.

Paulsen, G. (1990). *Woodsong*. New York: Macmillan.

Pearce, D. L. (1983). Guidelines for the use and evaluation of writing in content classrooms. *Journal of Reading, 27*, 212–218.

Pearson, P. D. (1981). A retrospective reaction to prose comprehension. In C. M. Santa and B. L. Hayes (eds.), *Children's prose comprehension: Research and practice*. Newark, DE: International Reading Association.

Pearson, P. D. (1982a). *Asking question about stories*. Ginn Occasional Papers, No. 15. Columbus, OH: Ginn and Company.

Pearson, P. D. (1982b). *A context for instructional research and reading comprehension*. Urbana, IL: University of Illinois Center for the Study of Reading Technical Report No. 230.

Pearson, P. D. (1974–1975). The effects of grammatical complexity on children's comprehension, recall, and conception of certain semantic relations. *Reading Research Quarterly, 10*, 155–192.

Pearson, P. D., & Johnson, D. (1978). *Teaching reading comprehension*. New York: Holt, Rinehart and Winston.

Pearson, P. D., & Spiro, R. (1982). The new buzz word in reading as schema. *Instructor, 89*, 46–48.

Peet, B. (1985). *The kweeks of Kookatumdee*. New York: Houghton Mifflin.

Perry, W. G. (1959). Students' use and misuse of reading skills: A report to the faculty. *Harvard Educational Review, 29*, 193–200.

Peters, C. (1975). A comparative analysis of reading comprehension in four content areas. In G. H. McNinch and W. D. Miller (eds.), *Reading: Convention and inquiry*. Clemson, SC: National Reading Conference.

Pichert, J. W., & Anderson, R. C. (1977). Taking different perspectives on a story. *Journal of Educational Psychology, 69*, 309–315.

Plato (1966). Theatetus, 194c–195b. In E. Hamilton, & H. Cairns (eds.), *The collected dialogues of Plato*. New York: Pantheon.

Plotz, H. (ed.) (1982). *Saturday's children: Poems of work*. New York: Greenwillow.

Pradl, G. M. & Mayher, J. S. (1985). Reinvigorating learning through writing. *Educational Leadership, 42,* 4–6.

Pringle, L. (1982). *Water: The next great resource battle.* New York: Macmillan.

Purves, A. C. (1983). Teachers are real, too. *Connecticut English Journal, 14,* 43–44.

Quandt, I. (1977). *Teaching reading: A human process.* Chicago: Rand McNally College Publishing Company.

Raphael, T. (1986). Teaching question answer relationships. *The Reading Teacher, 39,* 516–520.

Raphael, T. E. (1982). Question-answering strategies for children. *The Reading Teacher, 36,* 186–191.

Raphael, T. E. (1984). Teaching learners about sources of information for answering comprehension questions. *Journal of Reading, 27,* 303–311.

Rapp-Haggard Rudell, M. (1992). Integrated content and long-term vocabulary learning with the vocabulary self-collection strategy. In E. K. Dishner, T. W. Bean, J. E. Readence, & D. W. Moore (eds.), *Reading in the content areas: Improving classroom instruction* (3rd ed.) (pp. 190–195). Dubuque, IA: Kendall-Hunt.

Readence, J., Baldwin, R. S., & Bean, T. (1981). *Content Area Reading: An integrated approach.* Dubuque IA: Kendall/Hunt.

Resnick, L. B., & Resnick, D. P. (1991). Assessing the thinking curriculum: New tools for educational reform. In Gifford, & O'Connor (eds.), *Changing assessments.* Boston: Kluwer.

*Responding to the Bradley Commission Report on teaching history in schools.* (1991). New York: Houghton Mifflin.

Rico, G. L. (1983). *Writing the natural way: Using right-brain techniques to release your expressive powers.* Los Angeles: J. P. Tarcher.

Riley, J., & Pachtman, A. (1978). Reading mathematical word problems: Telling them what to do is not telling them how to do it. *Journal of Reading, 21,* 531–533.

Robinson, F. (1961). *Effective study.* New York: Harper and Row.

Roby, T. (1987). Commonplaces, questions, and modes of discussion. In J. T. Dillon (ed.), *Classroom questions and discussion.* Norwood, NJ: ABLEX.

Roby, T. (1968). *Small group performance.* Chicago: Rand McNally.

Rodrigues, R. J. (1983). Tools for developing prewriting skills. *English Journal, 72,* 58–60.

Rosen, H. (1986). The importance of story *Language Arts, 63,* 226–237.

Rosenberg, M. B. (1991). *On the mend: Getting away from drugs.* New York: Bradbury.

Rosenblatt, L. M. (1982). The literary transaction: Evocation and response. *Theory Into Practice, 21,* 268–277.

Rumelhart, D. E. (1982). Schemata: The building blocks of cognition. In J. Guthrie (ed.), *Comprehension and teaching: Research reviews.* Newark, DE: International Reading Association.

Rycik, J. (1992). *An exploration of student library research projects in seventh grade English and social studies classes.* An unpublished doctoral dissertation. Kent, OH: Kent State University.

Rylant, C. (1984). *Waiting to waltz: A childhood*. IL Stephen Gammell. New York: Bradbury.

Rylant, C. (1982). *When I was young in the mountains*. New York: Dutton.

Salisbury, R. (1934). A study of the transfer effects of training in logical organization. *Journal of Educational Research, 28*, 241–254.

Samples, R. (1977). *The Wholeschool book*. Reading, MA: Addison Wesley.

San Jose, C. (1988). Story drama in the content areas. *Language Arts, 65*, 26–33.

Santa, C. M., & Havens, L. T. (1991). Learning through writing. In C. M. Santa, & D. E. Alvermann (eds.), *Science learning: Processes and applications*. Newark, DE: International Reading Association.

*School daze: From A to Z* (1982). Kansas City: Hallmark Cards.

Schluck, C. (1989). Using international children's literature in the content areas. *Early Child Development and Care, 48*, 9–17.

Schumm, J. S., & Mangrum II, C. T. (1991). Flip: A framework for content area reading. *Journal of Reading, 35*(2), 120–124.

Schwartz, R. M., & Raphael, T. E. (1985). Concept of definition: A key to improving students' vocabulary. *The Reading Teacher, 39*, 198–204.

Schwartz, R. M. (1988). Learning to learn: Vocabulary in content area textbooks. *Journal of Reading, 32*, 108–117.

Sender, R. M. (1986). *The cage*. New York: Macmillan.

Seuss, Dr. (1984). *The butter battle book*. New York: Random House.

Shanahan, T. (ed.) (1990). *Reading and writing together: New perspectives for the classroom*. Norwood, MA: Christopher-Gordon Publishers.

Shanks, A. Z. (1982). *Busted lives: Dialogues with kids in jail*. New York: Delacorte.

Shulman, L. (1987). Learning to teach. *AAHE Bulletin*, 5–6.

Siegal, A. (1983). *Upon the head of the goat: A childhood in Hungary, 1939–1944*. New York: Signet.

Silverstein, S. (1964). *The giving tree*. New York: Harper & Row.

Simon. (1990). *Oceans*. New York: Morrow Junior Books.

Singer, H. (1978). Active comprehension: From answering to asking questions. *The Reading Teacher, 31*, 901–908.

Sirotnik, K. (1983). What you see is what you get: consistency, persistency, and mediocrity in classrooms. *Harvard Educational Review, 53*(1), 16–31.

Sizer, T. R. (1984). *Horace's compromise: The dilemma of the American high school*. Boston: Houghton Mifflin.

Slavin, R. E. (1988). Cooperative learning and student achievement. In R. E. Slavin (ed.), *School and classroom organization*. Hillsdale, NJ: Erlbaum.

Slavin, R. (1980). Cooperative learning. *Review of Educational Research, 50*, 315–342.

Slavin, R. (1982). *Cooperative learning: student teams*. Washington, D. C.: National Education Association.

Smith, F. (1975). *Comprehension and learning: A conceptual framework for teachers*. New York: Holt, Rinehart and Winston.

Smith, F. (1978). *Understanding reading* (2nd ed.). New York: Holt, Rinehart and Winston.

Smith, F. (1979). *Reading without nonsense.* New York: Teachers College Press.

Smith, F. (1988). *Understanding reading* (4th ed.). Hillsdale, NJ: Erlbaum.

Smith, N. B. (1964). Patterns of writing in different subject areas. *Journal of Reading, 7,* 31–37.

Smith, N. B. (1959). Teaching study skills in reading. *Elementary School Journal, 60,* 158–162.

Smith, S. L. (1982). Learning strategies of mature college learners. *Journal of Reading, 26,* 5–13.

Spiegal, D. L. (1981). Six alternatives to the directed reading activity. *The Reading Teacher, 34,* 914–922.

Spiegelman, A. (1986). *Maus: A survivor's tale.* New York: Pantheon.

Spier, P. (1978). *Bored—Nothing to do!* New York: Doubleday.

Spivey, N. M. (1984). *Discourse synthesis: Constructing texts in reading and writing.* Newark, DE: International Reading Association.

Staples, S. F. (1989). *Shabanu: Daughter of the wind.* New York: Alfred A. Knopf.

Stauffer, R. (1969). *Directing reading maturity as a cognitive process.* New York: Harper and Row.

Stauffer, R. (1975). *Directing the reading-thinking process.* New York: Harper and Row.

Stein, N., & Glenn, C. (1979). An analysis of story comprehension in elementary school children. In R. Freedle (ed.), *New directions in discourse processing.* Norwood, NJ: ABLEX.

Stenmark, J. K. (1991). Math portfolios: A new form of assessment. *Teaching Pre K–8, 21*(1), 62–66.

Stewart, R. A. (1989). *A microenthography of a secondary earth science classroom: A focus upon textbooks and reading.* Unpublished doctoral dissertation. West Lafayette, IN: Purdue University.

Sutherland, Z., & Arbuthnot, M. H. (1986). *Children and books* (7th ed.). Glenview, IL: Scott, Foresman.

Taba, H. (1975). *Teacher's handbook for elementary social studies.* Reading, MA: Addison-Wesley.

Taylor, B. (1980). Children's memory of expository text after reading. *Reading Research Quarterly, 15,* 399–411.

Taylor, D. (1983). *Family literacy: Young children learning to read and write.* Portsmouth, NH: Heinemann.

Taylor, W. (1953). Close procedure: A new tool for measuring readability. *Journalism Quarterly, 30,* 415–433.

Tchudi, S., & Yates, J. (1983). *Teaching writing in content areas: High school.* Washington, D.C.: National Education Association.

Thelen, J. (1984). *Improving reading in science* (2nd ed.). Newark, DE: International Reading Association.

Thelen, J. (1982). Preparing students for content reading assignments. *Journal of Reading, 25,* 546–547.

Thelen, J. (1979). Reading textbooks—close encounters of the worst kind? In R. Vacca & J. Meagher (eds.), *Reading through content.* Storrs, CT: The University of Connecticut University Publications.

Thorndike, E. (1917). Reading and reasoning: A study of mistakes in paragraph reading. *Journal of Educational Psychology, 8,* 323–332.

Thorndyke, P. (1977). Cognitive structures in comprehension and memory of narrative discourse. *Cognitive Psychology, 9,* 77–110.

Tierney, R. J., Carter, M. A., & Desai, L. E. (1991). *Portfolio assessment in the reading-writing classroom.* Norwood, MA: Christopher Gordon.

Tierney, R. J. & Pearson, P. D. (1983). Toward a composing model of reading. *Language Arts, 60,* 5, 568–580.

Tierney, R. J. & Pearson, P. D. (1992). A revisionist perspective on "Learning to learn from texts: A framework for improving classroom practice." In E.K. Dishner, T. W. Bean, J. E. Readence, & D. W. Moore (eds.), *Reading in the content areas: Improving classroom instruction* (3rd ed.) (pp. 82–86). Dubuque, IA: Kendall-Hunt.

Tierney, R. J., Readence, J. E., & Dishner, E. K. (1990). *Reading strategies and practices: A compendium* (3rd ed.). Boston: Allyn and Bacon.

Tierney, R. J., & Shanahan, T. (1991). Research on reading-writing relationships: Interactions, transactions, and outcomes. In P. D. Pearson, R. Barr, M. Kamil, & P. Mosenthal (eds.), *Handbook of reading research* (2nd ed.) (pp. 246–280). New York: Longman.

Tullock-Rhody, R., & Alexander, J. E. (1980). A scale for assessing attitudes toward reading in secondary schools. *Journal of Reading, 26,* 609–610.

Udry, J. M. (1956). *A tree is nice.* New York: Harper & Row.

Vacca, J. L., Vacca, R. T., & Gove, M. K. (1991). *Reading and learning to read* (2nd ed.). New York: Harper Collins Publishers.

Vacca, J. L., & Vacca, R. T. (1983). Process strategies for effective staff development: In *Dissemination report: Systematic planning for school improvement.* Columbus, OH: Ohio Department of Education.

Vacca, R. T. (1977). An investigation of a functional reading strategy in seventh grade social studies. In H. L. Herber and R. R. Vacca (eds.). *Research in reading in the content areas: Third report.* Syracuse, NY: Syracuse University Reading and Language Arts Center.

Vacca, R. T. (1975). Development of a functional reading strategy: Implications for content area instruction. *Journal of Educational Research, 69,* 108–112.

Vacca, R. T., & Rasinski, T. R. (1992). *Case studies in whole language.* Fort Worth, TX: Harcourt, Brace, Jovanovich.

Valencia, S. (1990). A portfolio approach to classroom reading assessment: The whys, whats, and hows. *The Reading Teacher, 43*(4), 338–340.

Valencia, S., McGinley, W., & Pearson, P. D. (1990). *Assessing reading and writing: Building a more complete picture for middle school assessment.* Champaign, IL: University of Illinois, Center for the Study of Reading.

Van Allsburg, C. (1990). *Just a dream.* New York: Houghton Mifflin.

Van Allsburg, C. (1987). *The Z was zapped.* New York: Houghton Mifflin.

van Dijk, T. A. (1979). Relevance assignment in discourse comprehension. *Discourse Processes, 2,* 113–126.

Ventura, P. (1987). *Venice: Birth of a city.* New York: G. P. Putnam's Sons.

Volkmer, J. A. (1990). *Song of the Chirimia: A Guatemalan folktale.* Minneapolis, Minnesota: Carolrhoda.

Walker, B. J. (1991). Convention highlights reading assessment changes. *Reading Today,* February/March, p. 20.

Walker, J. (1979). Squeezing study skills (into, out of) content areas, In R. T. Vacca and J. A. Meagher (eds.), *Reading through content,* pp. 77–92. Storrs, CT: University Publications and the University of Connecticut Reading-Language Arts Center.

Watson, D. (1989). Defining and describing whole language. *The Elementary School Journal, 90,* 129–141.

Wildsmith, B. (1980). *Professor Noah's spaceship.* New York: Oxford University Press.

Winograd, P. N. (1984). Strategic difficulties in summarizing texts. *Reading Research Quarterly, 19,* 404–425.

Winograd, P. N., & Bridge, C. A. (1986). The comprehension of important information in written prose. In J. F. Baumann (ed.), *Teaching main idea comprehension.* Newark, DE: International Reading Association.

Wixson, K. (1983). Questions about a text: What you ask about is what children learn. *The Reading Teacher, 37,* 287–294.

Wixson, K., Bosky, A., Yochum, M. N. & Alvermann, D. (1984). An interview for assessing students' perceptions of classroom reading tasks. *The Reading Teacher, 37,* 346–353.

Wlodkowski, R. J. (1982). *Motivation* (revised ed.). Washington, D.C.: National Education Association.

Wood, K. D. (1988). A guide to subject matter material. *Middle School Journal, 19,* 24–26.

*Yesterday's authors of books for children.* (1977). Detroit, MI: Gale Research.

# CREDITS

## Chapter 3

Page 72. Box 3.1, Postreading Activity for Southeast Asia Lesson, developed by Kathleen Krispen, Geneva, IL.

Pages 73–74. Instructional framework for science lesson, developed by Judy Serra, Cleveland Heights, OH.

Pages 74–77. Instructional framework for French lesson, developed by Louis Porter, Canton, OH.

Page 80. Table 3.1, Texts and Activities for Art Unit, developed by Marietta Raneri, Castleton, NY

## Chapter 4

Page 97. Box 4.1, Vocabulary Demonstration: Words in Content Areas, adapted from a workshop exercise developed by Robert Baker, Illinois State University.

Page 106. Figure 4.4, Graphic Organizer for Darwin's Theory of Natural Selection, developed by Maureen Wynter, Frederiksted, St. Croix, VI.

Page 110. Figure 4.8, Graphic Organizer, developed by Henry Coe, Durham, CT.

Page 111. Figure 4.9, Graphic Organizer, developed by Ann Russo, Durham, CT.

Page 112. Figure 4.10, Graphic Organizer, developed by Nancy Fishell, Durham, CT

Page 115. Figure 4.12, Semantic Map for Manufacturing, developed by Matthew Messino, Springfield, OH.

Page 117. Open sort activity, developed by Nancy Fishell, Durham, CT.

## Chapter 5

Page 139, Box 5.1, Problematic Situation in an American History Class, developed by Virginia Sazama, Storrs, CT.

Page 140. Box 5.2, Creating a Perspective in an Auto Mechanics class, developed by Richard McManus, Durham, CT.

Page 143. Box 5.5, An Example of an Analogy: The Orange and the Earth, developed by Dora Bailey, Youngstown State University.

Page 146. Box 5.6, Preview for "In the Heat" by Robert Cormier, developed by Frank Booth, Kent, OH.

Page 147. Box 5.7, Preview for "Chemistry of Cosmetics," developed by Nancy Knauer, Bath, OH.

Page 150. Box 5.8, Anticipation Guide Demonstration: "Crash Was No Tragedy," developed by Robert Ranieri, Wheeling, IL.

Page 152. Box 5.9, Anticipation Guide for Civil War Lesson, developed by Mary Lou Getchman, DeKalb, IL.

Page 153. Box 5.10, Anticipation Guide for Clichés About Weather, developed by Bruce Metzger, New Philadelphia, OH.

Page 153. Box 5.10, Anticipation Guide for "It's Raining in Love," developed by Pat Wittaker, Hudson, OH.

Page 156. Figure 5.2, Stages in the Development of Money. Robert Carter and John Richards, *Of, By and For the People*. Westchester, IL; Benefic Press, 1972, p. 360.

## Chapter 6

Pages 174–175. Box 6.2, QARs in a Science Class, developed by Cynthia Sefcik.

Page 176. Box 6.3, QARs in an English Class, developed by Kerry Mihal.

Page 189. Figure 6.7, Story Map for "August Heat," developed by Carol Barron, Itasco, IL.

# NAME INDEX

# SUBJECT INDEX